THE LIMITS OF STATE AUTONOMY:

POST-REVOLUTIONARY MEXICO

Nora Hamilton **The Limits of State Autonomy: Post-Revolutionary Mexico**

PRINCETON UNIVERSITY PRESS ‖ PRINCETON, NEW JERSEY

To My Parents

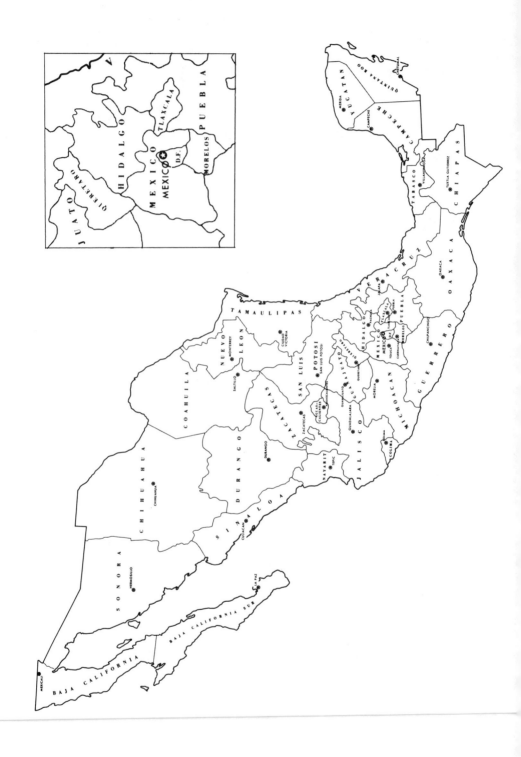

Preface

This study had its origins in a brief visit I made to Mexico in 1972. Like many other observers in Mexico I was struck by the disparity between the evidence of economic growth and prosperity, on the one hand, and the destitution of a large part of the population, on the other. The contrast is even more striking when Mexico's revolutionary past and the claim of the Mexican state to carry out the mandate of the revolution are taken into account. But if Mexico's dramatic economic growth can be attributed to the intervention of the state—and most would agree that the state has had a very important role—the state has been unable or unwilling to direct the Mexican economy so that growth benefits all of Mexico's population. The contradictions of Mexico's "revolutionary" state are central to those of Mexican society.

At the University of Wisconsin, where I was a graduate student, many of us were beginning to investigate questions relating to the state in late capitalist society. Did the state in fact operate in the interests of the dominant class, to maintain a given mode of production, and, if so, why? What were the role and functions of the state in capitalist society; how had these changed in late capitalist societies; and how could the differences among advanced capitalist states be explained? What class interests were represented by the state in post-colonial or "dependent" societies, and how did the conditions of economic subordination of these societies affect the role of the state? Central to many of these questions was the issue of state autonomy: to what extent, or under what circumstances, could the state in fact function independently of social classes or even against dominant class interests?

The issue of state autonomy provided an appropriate theoretical context for understanding the Mexican state. But as I read about contemporary Mexico I became increasingly convinced that, despite its evident economic power, the Mexican state was integrated with foreign capital and domestic private "economic groups," and structurally confined to a limited number of options. It was during the early post-revolutionary period, and particularly during the presidency of General Lázaro Cárdenas in the 1930's, that the state seemed to be sufficiently autonomous of dominant class interests, including foreign interests, to effect substantial changes in both internal structures and external relations. And the apparently sudden shift in the orientation of the state beginning in the late 1930's, from promotion of reform to protection of the status quo, suggested that this period was crucial for understanding the absence of autonomy of the contemporary Mexican state.

The problem of the Mexican state was thus rephrased as a historical question: what were the elements of continuity and change in the relations of the state with social classes in Mexico, as well as with foreign capital, from the pre-revolutionary period through the immediate post-revolutionary period, the Cárdenas years, to the present? Further reading and examination of the National Archives in Washington indicated that throughout this period U.S. business groups and government officials regarded Mexico as a market for exports, and there was also evidence of an early interest in investment in manufacture, although this did not become the predominant form of U.S. investment in Mexico until the 1950's and 1960's. When I subsequently began to do research in Mexican libraries and archives I was particularly interested in the historical origins of the dominant class in Mexico—notably the economic groups which dominate the private sector—and the relationship between these groups and the state. Did the economic groups emerge only in the post-World War II period, or did they have their origins in the earlier post-revolutionary era? To what extent did the reconstructed dominant class of post-revolutionary Mexico consist of groups from the pre-revolutionary period and to what extent was it a product of the revolution itself? With respect to the relationship between the state and the private sector, I suspected that financial ties constituted an important aspect of that relationship and focused on the formation of private and official banks during the early post-revolutionary 1920's and 1930's. As indicated in Chapter Six and the appendices, financial ties between the state and the private sector were indeed important in the development of class-state relations in post-revolutionary Mexico. This process as well as that of class formation were very complex, and while I do not claim to have reached definitive answers to the above questions I believe that I have gained some insight into these processes.

As is probably evident by now, my conceptual framework is Marxist, based on the belief that Marxist theory raises the most important questions and provides the most promising method for finding the answers. The methodological approach I use is that of historical analysis, attempting to trace the development of different social classes, the state, and the most relevant foreign interests in Mexico and the alliances and conflicts within and among these groups from the pre-revolutionary period, but with particular emphasis on the Cárdenas years. I found this approach very fruitful in identifying alliances and cleavages which were always complex and often obscured but emerged with increasing clarity during the confrontations of the 1930's.

The transformation of a few inchoate ideas into a dissertation and ultimately a book was a long process, and I was most fortunate in the advice and encouragement I received at every step along the way. First, I owe an immense debt to Maurice Zeitlin, who as my dissertation advisor provided invaluable guidance at all stages of the process—sharpening questions, clarifying theoretical issues, suggesting new directions, and consistently providing detailed and insightful criticism. His knowledge, experience, and support made the process of writing a dissertation an intellectually challenging and stimulating experience.

While at Wisconsin I benefited from comments and suggestions on initial ideas and research proposals by Robert Alford, Carolyn Baylies, Nancy DiTomaso, Al Gedicks, Roy Gesley, Joan McAuliffe, James O'Connor, and participants in the seminars on Research Design and Method (1972-1973) and Political Sociology (1974). Robert Aubey, Viviane Brachet de Marquez, John Coatsworth, Art Domike, Bob Halsted, Cassio Luiselli, Friedrich Katz, Enrique Krause, Julio Labastida, Tom McCormick, Bernardo Palomera, Luis Sandoval, and Peter Smith were helpful in suggesting research sources and providing introductions to contacts in the United States and Mexico.

During my two years in Mexico, I had the opportunity to discuss aspects of my study with Mexican scholars who generously shared their expertise in various fields, among them Alejandro Alvarez, José Ayala, Roberto Cabral, Ricardo Cinta, Luis González, Marcos Kaplan, José Luis Reyna, Roberto Salazar, and Francisco Soto Angli. Special thanks go to Alonso Aguilar, Juan Felipe Leal, and Lorenzo Meyer, who provided direction and feedback at critical junctures during my research in Mexico. I also benefited from discussion with several colleagues sharing research interests, among them Leif Adleson, Paul Ballard, Doug Bennett, Susan Kaufman Purcell, John Purcell, Ken Sharpe, and Don Wyman.

I was particularly fortunate in having the opportunity to interview several persons directly involved in the events of the period

I was concerned with, among them Valentín Campa, Renato Molina Enríquez, and the late Eduardo Suárez, who provided me with insights into post-revolutionary Mexico and the Cárdenas years which would not have been possible otherwise.

In the course of my research I have made extensive use of existing works, particularly on the Mexican state and the Cárdenas period, and my debt to their authors will be evident in the citations on the following pages. I am also grateful for the aid provided by the staff of the National Archives in Washington and of libraries and archives in Mexico, including the libraries of the Colegio de México and the Universidad Nacional Autónoma de México; the Biblioteca Nacional; the Hemeroteca Nacional; the Centro de Estudios de la Historia de México (CONDUMEX); the Biblioteca Miguel Lerdo de Tejada of the Secretaría de Hacienda y Crédito Público; the Biblioteca de México of the Secretaría de Educación Pública; the libraries of the Universidad Obrera, the Banco de México, the Asociación de Banqueros de México, and the Banco Nacional de México; the Archivo General de la Nación; the Registro Público de la Propiedad y del Comercio; and the Archivo General de Notorías. In particular, I wish to thank Juan Manuel Gómez Morín and Felipe García Beraza and the staff of the Centro Mexicano de Escritores who generously made available the private archives of Manuel Gómez Morín and Luis Montes de Oca.

I am also grateful for the criticisms and suggestions of those who read earlier drafts of chapters, including Sergio Alcántara, David Barkin, John Barchfield, Barry Carr, Jim Cockcroft, Cynthia Hewitt de Alcántara, Ignacio Marván, Ian Roxborough, and Irene Zea. Eugene Havens and Erik Wright made valuable comments on the dissertation and very helpful suggestions for revision, and I am grateful for their help and encouragement. I am also deeply indebted to Susan Eckstein and Ken Sharpe, whose thoughtful commentaries on the manuscript helped immeasurably in the final revision. As many others, I have benefited from the expertise, advice, and enthusiasm of Sandy Thatcher and the interest and competent editorial work of Miriam Brokaw at Princeton. I also want to thank Jean Devine, Patricia Johnson, and Rose Cruz for their patient and competent typing of all or part of the manuscript in its various stages.

Certain sections of this book appeared in articles published elsewhere and I thank the publishers for permission to reprint these sections. Portions of Chapter One were published in my article "State Autonomy and Dependent Capitalism in Latin America," in *The British Journal of Sociology*, XXXII, 3, September 1981, and are reprinted by permission of Routledge & Kegan Paul, Ltd. Portions of different chapters were published in my article "The State and Class Conflict: Mexico during the Cárdenas Period" in *Classes, Class Conflict and the State*, edited by Maurice Zeitlin, copyright 1980, and are reprinted by permission of Winthrop Publishers, Inc., Cambridge, Massachusetts. Also sections of Chapter Six and the appendices are from my article "The State and Capital Formation in Post-Revolutionary Mexico: 1920-1940," in *Latin American Perspectives*, forthcoming 1982, and are reprinted by permission of *Latin American Perspectives*.

Special thanks go to Shifra Goldman, Carol Wells, and Susan Sarnoff for their help with illustrative materials. I also want to thank Mariano Flores Castro of the Instituto Nacional de Belles Artes for permission to use photographs of the Diego Rivera murals "La Industria Azucarera," from the Palacio de Cortez in Cuernavaca; "La Maestra Rural," from the Secretaría de Educación Pública; and "La Guerra de la Independencia," from the Palacio Nacional. I am very grateful to artists of the Taller de Gráfico Popular (Workshop of Popular Graphics) Fernando Castro Pacheco, Mariana Yampolsky, Luis Arenal, and Elizabeth Catlett, for permission to use their work. The Taller was established in Mexico in 1937 and has been a valuable source of popular art commemorating events in Mexican history. The four graphics used in this book were taken from the collection "450 Anos de Lucha" (450 Years of Struggle). I wish to thank the Bureau of Business Research of the University of Texas for permission to use the map from Stanley A. Arbingast, *Atlas of Mexico*, copyright 1975.

Throughout this long process I have been fortunate in having colleagues whose friendship and critical support have been very important both to me and to my work. In the early stages of this project I benefited from long discussions with Carolyn Baylies, whose intellectual clarity and insights into theory and methodology helped to give direction to what I was doing. Mary K. Vaughan's understanding of Mexican history and thoughtful critiques and suggestions were very helpful at various phases of the study. Julia Wrigley, Carol Thompson, Mark Kann, Edna Bonacich, Johanna Brenner, Norma Chinchilla, and Barbara Laslett provided critical evaluation of several chapters and I benefited immensely from their comments and suggestions as well as their continued interest and encouragement.

While I am responsible for the shortcomings of this book, the individuals and institutions noted above deserve much of the credit for whatever merits it can claim.

Contents

List of Tables

List of Illustrations

Abbreviations

ABM	Asociación de Banqueros Mexicanos (Mexican Bankers' Association)
Banco Ejidal	Banco Nacional de Crédito Ejidal (National Ejidal Credit Bank)
BFM★	Boletín Financiera y Mineral
BNM★	Banco Nacional de México
CANACINTRA	Cámara Nacional de la Industria de Transformación (National Chamber of Manufacturing Industry)
CONCAMIN	Confederación de Cámeras Industriales (Confederation of Chambers of Industry)
CONCANACO	Confederación de Cámaras Nacionales de Comercio (Confederation of National Chambers of Commerce)
COPARMEX	Confederación Patronal de la República Mexicana (Employers' Confederation of the Mexican Republic)
CTM	Confederación de Trabajadores de México (Confederation of Mexican Workers)
CROM	Confederación Regional Obrera Mexicana (Regional Confederation of Mexican Workers)
CGT	Confederación General de Trabajadores (General Workers' Confederation)
CGOCM	Confederación General de Obreros y Campesinos de Mexico (General Confederation of Workers and Peasants of Mexico)
CSUM	Confederación Sindical Unitaria de Mexico (Central Union Confederation of Mexico)
CNC	Confederación Nacional de Campesinos (National Peasant Confederation)
CCM	Confederación de Campesinos Mexicanos (Confederation of Mexican Peasants)
CREMI	Crédito Minero y Mercantil
FIC	Fomento de Industria y Comercio
Nafinsa	Nacional Financiera, S.A.
PAN	Partido de Acción Nacional (National Action Party)
PNR	Partido Nacional Revolucionario (National Revolutionary Party)
PRM	Partido de la Revolución Mexicana (Party of the Mexican Revolution)
PRI	Partido Revolucionario Institucional (Institutional Revolutionary Party)

PEMEX	Petroleos Mexicanos (Mexican Petroleum)
SEN★	Secretaría de la Economia Nacional
SHCP★	Secretaría de Hacienda y de Crédito Público
SCOP★	Secretaría de Comunicaciones y Obras Públicas
SIC★	Secretaría de Industria y Comercio
SOMEX	Sociedad Mexicana de Crédito Industrial
Sofimex	Sociedad Financiera Mexicana
STPRM	Sindicato de Trabajadores Petroleros de la República Mexicana (Mexican Union of Petroleum Workers)
UNPASA	Unión Nacional de Productores de Azúcar (National Sugar Producers' Union)
VISA	Valores Industriales, S.A.
AN★	Archivo de las Notarías
Archivo MGM★	Manuel Gómez Morín Archives
Archivo LMO★	Luis Montes de Oca Archives
RPPC★	Registro Público de la Propiedad y de Comercio
NAW★	National Archives, Washington

★ These abbreviations are used in citations and references only.

THE LIMITS OF STATE AUTONOMY:

POST-REVOLUTIONARY MEXICO

The War for Mexican Independence. Detail from mural by Diego Rivera.

One ‖ **State Autonomy and Peripheral Capitalism in Mexico**

 THE PROBLEM OF THE MEXICAN STATE

The problem of the Mexican state derives from the apparent contradiction between its historical origins in the Mexican revolution and its contemporary function of maintaining conditions for peripheral capitalist development. The revolution of 1910 destroyed the pre-existing state apparatus and enabled the revolutionary leadership to form a new state within the context of structural options resulting from Mexico's prior development as well as new forces, alliances, and conflicts emerging from the revolution itself. The constitution of 1917 incorporated the ideal of a strong interventionist state which would eliminate privileges of foreign monopolies and national political elites, affirm national control over Mexican territory and resources, and defend the interests of subordinate groups and classes.

Moreover, during the administration of General Lázaro Cárdenas, President of Mexico from 1934 to 1940, this ideal of a progressive and implicitly autonomous state was to a large extent realized.

The Cárdenas administration carried out a far-reaching agrarian reform: distributing more land to more peasants than all of his predecessors combined, establishing collective farms on commercial agricultural estates—a move which was particularly controversial, given the importance of these estates for the Mexican economy—and effectively eliminating the power of the traditional landowning sector. The government also challenged the incipient capitalist industrial class by encouraging the mobilization and organization of urban and industrial workers, ultimately incorporating the major labor unions and confederations, as well as the major peasant confederation, into the government party structure. Probably the most dramatic example of apparent state autonomy during the Cárdenas administration was the expropriation of the British and U.S.-owned petroleum companies, eliminating foreign control of an important resource and export product. This move was particularly significant given the past success of the petroleum companies in resisting efforts by the Mexican state to regulate them (Weyl and Weyl, 1939; L. Meyer, 1972b; Raby, 1972).

But this orientation was reversed in subsequent years, during which the Mexican state cooperated with private domestic groups and foreign interests to promote rapid economic development, involving the relative neglect or open repression of subordinate groups. In the thirty years following the Cárdenas administration, Mexico was characterized by one of the highest sustained growth rates in the world, coexisting with increasingly high levels of unemployment and underemployment and the impoverishment of the majority of the population. Mexico's growth rate fluctuated in the past decade, and the situation of the majority has stagnated or deteriorated.

How can the relative autonomy of the Mexican state in relation to foreign capital and dominant Mexican groups under the Cárdenas administration be explained? And why was the progressive orientation of the government reversed under subsequent regimes? The transition from an apparently autonomous state to the contemporary Mexican state raises questions regarding the actual extent of relative state autonomy in post-revolutionary Mexico, which in turn is related to more general questions regarding the possibilities and limits of state autonomy. Since Marxist theory is particularly concerned with these questions, a review of Marxist literature on the state will help to provide a framework for analysis of the Mexican state.

MARXIST PERSPECTIVES ON THE CLASS NATURE OF THE STATE

Marx and Engels on the State. The question of state autonomy is a controversial one for Marxist theory because Marxists perceive the state in class societies as functioning to reproduce a mode of production in which a specific class is dominant.[1] Thus the state func-

[1] A mode of production consists of the forces of production (labor force, as well as skills, organization, technology, etc., which affect the level of productivity) and the relations of production, also relations of exploitation, whereby surplus produced by a given class of direct producers is appropriated by another class. In capitalist societies this involves control over the means of production by the capitalist class (largely through private property arrangements) and the sale of labor power by the working class, the direct producers, to the capitalists, who are thereby

tions to maintain a given system and, at least by implication, to promote the interests of the dominant class within that system. The works of Marx and Engels do recognize an early form of the state or "organizing authority" resulting from a division of labor in primitive, classless societies through which certain individuals or bodies are designated with authority to maintain order, look after common interests, and defend the community from outsiders (Moore, 1957: 17-21; Draper, 1977: 246). But while the modern state may continue to carry out these functions, the state as an institution common to all societies is of limited relevance. It is precisely those state functions which are not unique to the state nor common to all forms of the state which are of greatest interest in discussing the contemporary state.

And with the development of modes of production based on antagonistic social classes, the state takes on specifically class-related functions. As described by Engels, "the state is the product of society in a determined stage of its development; it is the confession that society is caught up in an insoluble contradiction with itself. . . . In order that the antagonists, the classes with economically opposed interests, not be consumed . . . the necessity of a power is imposed which, apparently situated above society, must soften the conflict, maintaining it in the limits of 'order': that power, coming from society but situated above it and increasingly foreign, is the state" (Engels, 1972: 229). The original functions remain, but become secondary to that of safeguarding the mode of production and existing class relations through the containment of class conflict and control of subordinate classes (Engels, 1959: 206). Thus the struggles of subordinate groups and classes also have implications for the form and nature of the state.

In capitalist societies, the function of the state is broadened, so to speak, to encompass the establishment and maintenance of conditions for private capital accumulation, which includes, but is not limited to, functions of social control (as well as earlier administrative functions).

Marx and Engels, as well as later Marxists, discuss the concept of a separate state interest and suggest certain circumstances in which limited state autonomy becomes possible. As described by

---

able to obtain surplus value through such mechanisms as extending the time worked by labor beyond the amount of labor needed to produce their own subsistence (absolute surplus value) or by increasing the productivity of labor (relative surplus value).

Engels, the state seeks to free itself and establish its own identity; it is "increasingly foreign" to the society from which it emerges (1972a: 229). In discussing the case of Germany in the middle of the nineteenth century, Marx and Engels note that, given the fragmentation of the bourgeoisie and its failure to organize itself with a class interest over and above the self-interest of individual members, the state itself becomes an apparently independent force (Marx and Engels, 1970: 80, 106). The specific historical instance of the emergence of the Bonapartist regime in mid-century France was described by Marx as resulting from the deliberate abdication of power by a bourgeoisie unwilling to exercise it (Marx 1963: 105-106). Thus, while the existence of a relation between the state and the dominant class is central to Marxist theory of the state, the nature of this relation is not obvious and is contingent upon historical and structural conditions. As these cases suggest, it is particularly in periods of transition, when no one mode of production is dominant or none of the contending classes is able to assert its hegemony, that the state, sometimes referred to as the Bonapartist or Caesarist state, may act with relative autonomy in determining the future structure of the social formation. Even in these circumstances the state is limited (by such factors as the level of development of the productive forces) to given historical and structural options, within which it may have a regressive role in reinforcing the old order, or a progressive role, supporting the class which represents a more advanced mode of production (Gramsci, 1971: 219-220), or in some cases elements of both.

The State Defined. Given the above noted conditions: the physical separation of the state and the dominant class under capitalism, the possibility of relative state autonomy under certain circumstances, and the necessity to demonstrate the class nature and functions of the state for any concrete social formation, the abstract conception of the state in terms of its functions within a class structure becomes problematic. For concrete historical analysis, the state must be defined as an entity analytically separable from class structure. Here we will draw upon the definitions of the modern state by Engels and Weber, who despite their different perspectives generally agree in their specifications of the attributes incorporated in the institutions of the state: "legitimate" monopoly of the means of coercion, or public force; administration over a given territory; and the establishment and maintenance of a system of support,

especially taxes and state loans. In summary, the state is constituted by the civil and military bureaucracy, or state apparatus, on
the one hand, and those having formal control of this apparatus,
the government (constituted in various branches, levels, etc.) on
the other (Engels, 1972: 228-233; Weber, 1958: 77-78; 1968 I, 194-
200). Formal control of the state apparatus is distinct from control
of the state; thus the question of the class nature of the state cannot
be determined on the basis of which class constitutes the government. Legitimacy, which for Weber is an essential attribute of the
state or, more specifically, of state authority (and of authority in
general) tends to be replaced in Marxist literature on the state by
the concept of legitimation, which involves not only a justification
of the state's own authority but also of the existing social order.
As indicated above, this involves a process of mystification whereby
government in the interests of a specific class becomes government
by a neutral authority in the interests of the whole (Offe, 1974: 5;
O'Connor, 1973: 6; Kaplan, 1969: 30).

According to Weber, the growth of the state bureaucracy makes
it a formidable apparatus of domination for those who control it
(Weber, 1968, III: 987). In particular, control of the means of coercion would appear to facilitate state autonomy. At the same time,
the different historical origins of state institutions and their interaction with different classes and class segments suggest that the
interests pursued by these institutions may be contradictory to each
other as well as to those of the government (which of course may
also be divided) (Poulantzas, 1976: 76; Oszlak and O'Donnell, 1976:
26; Kaplan, 1969: 33-34). This suggests that a certain level of cohesion among and within the various government factions and state
institutions (or the ability of certain factions or institutions to establish their hegemony over the rest) is a necessary condition for
state autonomy. Given the concentration of the coercive power of
the state in the military/police apparatus, its level of integration
and adherence or resistance to government authority is obviously
of crucial importance in state cohesion or in determining the outcome of divisions and conflicts within the state.

But if the possibility of state autonomy appears to be enhanced
by control of the means of coercion and by a high level of cohesion within the state, it is limited by the state's dependence upon
resources—chiefly taxes and loans—generated through the mode
of production and, in capitalist societies, the private sector. Control of the means of production thus constitutes control of the

sources of state revenues; the state is economically dependent upon the dominant class. Beyond this economic dependence, once a given mode of production becomes dominant, the state (or those who control it) is held responsible for the smooth functioning of the system, which both facilitates and requires action by the dominant class (Offe, 1974; Block, 1977). This dependence continues even when the state itself controls the means of production in certain economic sectors; as long as the social formation is predominantly capitalist the dominant class is in a position to weaken the state through economic measures (such as production cutbacks or capital export).

The Question of State Autonomy. Since under capitalism control of the means of production and the means of coercion have been concentrated in two separate entities—the capitalist class and the state, respectively—there is the appearance that the economic and the political constitute relatively autonomous spheres (Holloway and Picciotto, 1978: 24; Zeitlin, 1980: 16-17). This appearance is of course reinforced where the bourgeoisie do not have formal positions within government. Today, the separation of the economically dominant class from those who control the state apparatus appears less the exception than the rule and this separation obviously facilitates the appearance of state neutrality, or that the state is operating in the interests of society as a whole rather than those of a specific class. The problem for Marxist analysis becomes one of, first, demystifying the *appearance* of state autonomy and neutrality and, second, indicating the circumstances in which the state may indeed act with relative autonomy, as well as specifying the limits of such autonomy.

The problem of "demystifying" the appearance of state autonomy was addressed in the works of Domhoff (1967, 1970) and Miliband (1969), which challenged the prevailing pluralist thesis of state power, that of the state as an arena in which different groups, interests, and coalitions struggle over different issues within a general framework of agreement over norms and procedures. However, the strong "instrumentalist" perspective attributed to these authors in turn sparked a debate among Marxist theorists regarding the class nature of the state (Blackburn, 1973: 238-262).

The instrumentalist thesis suggests that the state is an instrument of the dominant class which intervenes directly or indirectly in its functioning, e.g., through direct recruitment into positions of state power or through such means as membership in advisory committees, campaign financing, lobbying, special relations with congressional and regulatory bodies—or more generally by the ability of the dominant class to control such agents as the media and/or the educational system through which state managers, as well as the rest of the population, are socialized (Domhoff, 1967, 1970; Miliband, 1969). The structuralist position, as stated by Poulantzas, is that the state is constrained by its position within a given social formation to preserve or reproduce that social formation; intervention by the dominant class is not necessary and may in fact be detrimental to this process. The autonomy of the state with respect to direct intervention by the dominant class enables it to operate more effectively in reproducing the dominant class structure and in organizing the hegemony of the dominant class (or the dominant fraction of that class) (Poulantzas, 1969: 239-240; 1976: 71).

For both the "instrumentalists" and the "structuralists" the state operates within the constraints of a given class structure or social formation; the debate is concerned less with the question of state autonomy than with how and why the state operates in the interests of the dominant class or to reproduce a given social formation. And on this issue the instrumentalist and structuralist positions are not very far apart.

Miliband and Poulantzas agree that a certain level of state autonomy may be necessary for the survival of an established class system—particularly when the requirements for system maintenance are contradictory to the actual or perceived interests of specific segments of the dominant class (Miliband, 1977: 87; Poulantzas, 1976: 75). An example would be concessions to subordinate groups that may have negative repercussions for the dominant class (and may even result in the elimination of a fraction of that class) but are necessary for the stability (or continuation) of the existing class system. In some cases, certain segments of the dominant class may be sufficiently cognizant of their long-term class interests to make necessary changes (or collaborate with the state to this end) against their immediate interests (Kolko, 1963; Weinstein, 1968). Otherwise, sufficient state autonomy is necessary to act directly against the resistance of these groups.

But the fact that such autonomy may be functional for the system of course does not mean that the state will necessarily be able to exercise this autonomy (Szymanski, 1978: 262). The state may

be prevented from acting autonomously—even if relative autonomy is necessary for the survival of the system—by resistance from
the dominant class. Even when this class is fragmented and incapable of cohesive action, individual members can exert negative
sanctions, such as—within capitalist societies—withdrawal of investments, capital export, etc., which if sufficiently widespread
will have the effect of destabilizing the economy.

And even when the state may exercise considerable "instrumental" autonomy (in terms of freedom from direct pressures by
dominant class fractions and interests) this generally rests upon the
willingness of those who control the state apparatus to confine
themselves to options within the existing class structure (Zeitlin,
Neumann, and Ratcliffe, 1976: 1008; Wright, 1978: 15-16). Structural state autonomy would consist of action against the real interests of the dominant class, which would ultimately result in a
basic structural change through which the existing mode of production, and with it the dominant class, would be superseded by
a new one. Within a capitalist mode of production, hypothetical
examples would be the socialization of the means of production
or state support of a revolution. But if in the absence of dominant
class cohesion the state attempts to go beyond structural boundaries, such action will in itself result in the rapid cohesion of previously antagonistic fractions of the dominant class. In short, the
effectiveness of structural constraints restricting the state to specific options within a given class structure rests ultimately upon
the ability and willingness of the dominant class to intervene if
these structural boundaries are transcended. Since those controlling the state apparatus are rarely willing to bring on such a reaction, dominant class intervention remains implicit, but it constitutes the ultimate sanction restraining the autonomy of the state
to options within the existing structure.[2]

Thus the possibility of relative structural state autonomy depends significantly on the extent to which a given mode of production and class structure are established. When the structure is

[2] Direct or conscious intervention constitutes deliberate attempts to force the
state to follow or to abandon certain policies. Indirect intervention refers to those
actions taken by individuals of the dominant class to protect their own interests
which have repercussions—not necessarily intended—on the state. It should be
noted that the *effects* of indirect intervention, if sufficiently widespread, may be the
same as those of conscious intervention, and the question of *intent* becomes problematic. Production cutbacks, withdrawal of investments, capital export, etc., will
ultimately affect the economic resources of the state, whether or not this is deliberately intended.

indeterminate, or the dominant class is considerably weakened due to internal or external crises, the possibility for state autonomy is enhanced.

Thus perhaps the strongest case for state autonomy may be found in recent analyses of social revolutions. In a brief discussion of the causes of revolution, Skocpol and Trimberger explicitly challenge several principles of the Marxist approach, arguing that political elites—as opposed to economically based social classes—have had a predominant role in "revolutions from above" and a significant, *autonomous* role in revolutions from below. In general, states are conditioned by economic structures but not shaped by them; "state structures and activities also have an underlying integrity and logic of their own, and these are keyed to the dynamics of international military rivalries and to the geo-political as well as world-economic circumstances in which given states find themselves" (1978: 127-128). Thus, in certain countries where the bourgeoisie was unable or unwilling to seize control of the state and use it to eliminate barriers to capitalist production in circumstances in which state centralization and economic modernization were essential to resist foreign pressures, the state (or groups controlling the state apparatus) has carried out a "revolution from above," establishing the necessary conditions for capitalist industrialization on the basis of a centralized state bureaucracy and a "fusion" of capitalist and pre-capitalist structures, as in Japan.[3]

Skocpol contends that conflicts may arise between the state and the dominant class over such issues as appropriation and use of resources and concessions to subordinate class demands at the expense of the dominant class. The international position of the state within the world system of states is also seen as a potential basis for autonomy. "International military pressures and opportunities can prompt state rulers to attempt policies that conflict with, and even in extreme instances contradict, the fundamental interests of a dominant class" (1979: 31).[4]

Differences regarding the possibility of autonomy depend to some

[3] Whether in fact it was an autonomous state or one controlled by a segment of the old dominant class has been debated. In any case, the state was autonomous in the sense that it was not controlled by the bourgeoisie and that it acted against the perceived interests, and to a considerable extent the actual interests, of the class ostensibly in power (Trimberger, 1977; Skocpol and Trimberger, 1978: 123-124; Moore, 1966: 229).

[4] The question of the international position of the state and its relevance for state autonomy will be taken up in the section on States in Peripheral Societies.

extent on how state autonomy is conceptualized. Trimberger suggests that bureaucratic autonomy exists when those groups that staff the state apparatus are not recruited from the dominant class, and do not form close ties with those classes after elevation to office (1978: 4). But bureaucratic autonomy may not be sufficient for state autonomy, which depends on the interests actually served by the state. There are several positions on this question. First, it has been argued that state autonomy exists if those who control the state apparatus are able to use it for ends *other* than those of the dominant class—e.g., to pursue specific state interests. Second, state autonomy may mean that the state acts independently of direct (or indirect) influence or intervention by the dominant class—what has been described above as instrumental autonomy. According to a third conception, state autonomy exists only if the state may act for ends *opposed* to the actual or perceived interests of the dominant class. The implication is that the dominant class is unable to constrain state actions which may threaten its interests or even its existence, i.e., the state is able to transcend structural boundaries, eliminating old structures and creating new ones, a situation which has been defined above as structural state autonomy.

Of these conceptualizations, only the last would be problematic from a Marxist perspective. The fact that state institutions may have "an underlying integrity and logic of their own," or that those who control the state apparatus are pursuing their own specific interests is not problematic for Marxist theory so long as state interests do not conflict with dominant class interests; it does not necessarily preclude state action on behalf of the dominant class or class system as well. And, as indicated above, instrumental autonomy may even be functional for the existing system since those who control the state apparatus may be more capable of perceiving and defending overall class interests than individuals or fractions from that class.

It is the third conceptualization—that of structural state autonomy—which challenges Marxist concepts of the class nature of the state and which Skocpol appears to be defending. Nevertheless, she notes certain restrictions on this autonomy. First, she suggests that state autonomy is likely to occur in periods of crisis (internal and/or external); these are often periods in which the dominant class is weakened and even the mode of production may be challenged or indeterminant. Second, and more important, she notes that revolutionary conflicts are limited by existing socio-economic and international conditions and points out that "ideologically oriented leaderships in revolutionary crises have been greatly limited by existing structural conditions and severely buffeted by the rapidly changing currents of revolution. Many conditions—especially socio-economic conditions—always 'carry over' from the old regime. These, too, create specific possibilities and impossibilities within which revolutionaries must operate as they try to consolidate the new regime" (1979: 171). These statements would appear to be in agreement with the propositions stated above—i.e., that the possibilities of state autonomy are limited to specific structural and historical options as a consequence of the previous development of the productive forces and the identity of the classes in conflict.

In general, the case for structural state autonomy—the ability of the state to act for ends antagonistic to dominant class interests—can be determined only through historical analyses of specific situations. And it is essential that such analyses seek out the underlying causes of state autonomy as well as its political manifestations, and attempt to identify the historical options available to an autonomous state in periods of crisis and transition.[5]

The State and Class Conflict. State autonomy is generally defined in terms of the relation of the state to the dominant class, since the presumption is that the state upholds the interests of that class.

---

[5] While Skocpol indicates that crises leading to revolutions result from political contradictions in old regime states (rather than strictly socio-economic causes), she in fact identifies underlying socio-economic conditions as the ultimate cause of political contradictions. Furthermore, what emerges from her analysis of pre-revolutionary states is precisely their lack of structural and even in some cases instrumental autonomy. As she puts it: "Caught in cross-pressures between domestic class structures and international exigencies, the autocracies and their centralized administrations and armies broke apart, opening the way for social revolutionary transformations spearheaded by revolts from below" (1979: 47). In fact, efforts by the states of pre-revolutionary France and China to initiate reforms in response to pressures from abroad were obstructed by dominant classes, especially landed upper classes, resulting in the disintegration of the state machineries which, ironically, made possible revolutions which destroyed the socio-economic order on which these classes were based. The fiscal crisis of the French crown—which precipitated the French Revolution—was due to the agrarian structure, on the one hand (which mitigated against commercial agricultural production and retarded the development of an industrial market—factors in the low level of per capita wealth which limited the crown's tax income) and resistance by privileged groups to efforts to abolish tax exemptions, on the other. Thus the fiscal crisis was directly and indirectly the result of the dominant structure of production.

However, the state is also constrained by the demands and pressures of subordinate groups and classes. At one level, state response to these pressures is in the interests of the survival of the system; it has been pointed out that capital would destroy the basis of its own existence if the state did not intervene, under pressure from the working class, to secure the minimum conditions for the reproduction of the work force. At least partial or occasional concessions to these groups are also necessary if the state is to retain a measure of legitimacy. But to the extent that the state acts in the interest of the dominant class—and may in fact constitute the class conscious and cohesive agent of that class—it will seek to destroy the cohesion and consciousness of subordinate groups, i.e., to "disorganize" them. Mechanisms include cooptive measures; preventive socialization; promotion of inertia, apathy, and submission; ethnic divisions and stratification schemes; and coercion.[6] Control of these classes is facilitated to the extent that the state successfully legitimizes its rule as based on the interests of society as a whole rather than on dominant class interests.

It follows that in contrast to the dominant class, whose interests may be integrated by the state, the subordinate classes must achieve unity and consciousness—a necessary condition for effective action on their own behalf—not only in opposition to the dominant class but also in opposition to the state. Also in contrast to the dominant class, whose control of economic resources enables individual members to take actions which (in sufficient number) may pressure the state even in the absence of class cohesion, members of subordinate classes can be effective only through unification and organization.

Despite the formidable mechanisms of control by the state, most of the historical advances of the working class and other subordinate groups have been the direct or indirect achievement of class struggle. Even where these struggles have not brought about structural change, they have resulted in modifications of their conditions of exploitation and their gradual incorporation into political and social institutions of the dominant society through the mediation of the state. The "success" of such struggles in fact raises

[6] In Vol. I of *Capital*, Marx discusses the necessity for state-imposed limitations to the extraction of surplus value (1977: 231-302. See also Holloway and Piccioto, 1978: 19-20). On efforts and mechanisms of the state to "disorganize" subordinate groups and classes, see O'Connor, 1973: 6; Poulantzas, 1969: 239-240; Miliband, 1969: 180; Draper, 1977: 264; Anderson, 1976-77: 27-28).

the problem of cooptation and a consequent loss of solidarity among workers, as well as the replacement of long-range objectives by more narrow economic goals. Class struggle also determines the form of the state: both democratic and authoritarian forms have resulted directly or indirectly from pressures on the state by subordinate groups and efforts of the state and dominant classes to control them.[7] Also, given the different historical origins of state institutions and their interaction with various classes and groups within a social formation, class struggle may to some extent be institutionalized *within* the state.

Class struggle may in fact enhance the possibility of state autonomy in certain circumstances if those who control the state apparatus can mobilize subordinate classes and groups for action against dominant class interests, or can form alliances with already mobilized classes in their conflicts with the dominant class. (Block, 1977: 22-23; Tardanico, 1978: 30.) But such an alliance is generally unstable; while it may strengthen the autonomy of the state with respect to dominant classes, the state must ultimately control its allies among subordinate groups and classes or risk an overthrow of the existing social order and with it the state's own basis of existence. And, as indicated above, such a threat to the existing structure would also result in increased cohesion of the dominant class, which would utilize the economic and political resources at its command to prevent such action.[8]

The State in Peripheral Societies. One of the major arguments on behalf of state autonomy is that the position and options of the state within the world system of states may be as important an

---

[7] See Anderson, Friedland and Wright, 1976: 191-192; Wolfe, 1974: 143; and Block, 1977: 537. For a discussion of the resistance of subordinate classes to the historical process of state formation and the significance of struggles by various segments of the population in securing specific political rights, see Tilly, 1975 (especially 21-23, 32-38, 71, 80).

[8] The fate of the Popular Unity government in Chile demonstrates the limits to the possibility of utilizing the state to effect a transition to socialism within the context of a capitalist society, although in this case the Popular Unity coalition controlled only the executive branch of government, with the legislative and judiciary branches and the military apparatus remaining under the control of or closely linked to the national bourgeoisie and foreign capital (Bossert, 1977: 14). It also demonstrates the rapidity with which previously fragmented interests and segments of the dominant class can achieve unity and cohesion when the class structure is threatened.

influence on state action as its position within a given internal social structure, and international pressures may in fact result in state
actions against the interests of the dominant class, even against its
existence as a class (Skocpol, 1979: 28-33). An examination of the
nation state must certainly take into account not only its relation
to internal classes and its function to reproduce a given social formation but also its relations to other capitals (or capitalist classes)
and states within a world system. The external relations of societies (particularly "peripheral" or "dependent" societies) have been
a primary focus of dependency theorists (Marxist and non-Marx-
ist) and more recently of world system theorists. In the late 1960's
and the 1970's the dependency perspective became a major contending paradigm for explaining underdevelopment in the third
world and especially in Latin America. It generally concentrates
upon the ways in which the advanced capitalist countries have
limited the development of less developed dependent countries; in
fact, the development of dominant (metropolitan or core) countries and the "underdevelopment" of dependent or peripheral
countries are seen as part of the same process. From this perspective internal classes and forces within the dependent country, including the state, have limited importance in shaping the development of these countries.[9] World system theory does focus upon
the state, but also emphasizes external or international relations to
the detriment of internal relations. According to this approach, the
world system is the basic unit of analysis, and state action is primarily oriented to improving or maintaining its position (or that
of its capital) within the world system of states and capitals (Wallerstein, 1974a: 16; 1976: 464; Chase Dunn and Rubinson, 1977:
469-470).

Critics of dependency and world system theorists accuse them
of removing the focus of analysis from the sphere of production
to the sphere of circulation, and from internal class struggle to
relations between (or among) dominant (core) and dependent (peripheral) societies or states. But, given the various origins of the
dependency perspective, there is considerable variation and disa-

---

[9] For statements of the dependency perspective and/or studies using this perspective, see Baran, 1957; Frank, 1967; Bodenheimer, 1970; Dos Santos, 1970;
Cockcroft, Frank, and Johnson, 1972; Chilcote and Edelstein, 1974; and Cardoso
and Faletto, 1978. For analyses and critiques of the dependency approach, see O'Brien,
1973; Warren, 1973; Harding, 1976; Brenner, 1977; Palma, 1978; and *Latin American Perspectives*, 1981.

greement within the dependency school itself. For example, the claim that dependency results in underdevelopment has been challenged on the basis of the experience of Brazil and Mexico; as noted by Cardoso, capitalism always results in distorted development and social and economic inequality, although the effects in dependent countries may be different from those in the advanced capitalist countries (Cardoso, 1975: 149, 63 f; 1975: 112 f). Certainly some works in the dependency school can be criticized for a mechanistic, ahistorical approach, a relative neglect of internal class structures and conflict, and a consequent inability to identify the possible sources and direction of change. At the same time, the dependency school has contributed significantly to an understanding of the effects of foreign capital in shaping the process of development and class structures within peripheral/dependent societies, and several Marxists have incorporated insights of the dependency and/or world system perspectives into their analysis of peripheral societies. The following discussion will focus on the implications of the peripheral or dependent status of a state, as defined in these perspectives, for the question of state autonomy.

The modern state has been immersed in relations with other states since its inception, which involved conflict with other incipient states as well as internal intra- and inter-class conflicts. Subsequently, with the development of a world capitalist system, the state has become the agent of integration of national capital for aggressive or defensive action on the world market (Braunmuhl, 1977: 173-174). Thus the state had a more aggressive role in capital accumulation in late industrializing countries such as Japan, Germany, and Turkey, partly in response to pressures from other capitalist states and the weakness of the national bourgeoisie. The prior development of capitalist industrialization in other countries also raised the capital requirements and increased the need for centralized planning for late industrializing countries; in some cases only the state had the necessary resources for a national industrialization project (Gerschenkron, 1972; Weaver, 1976).

The process of industrialization in the late nineteenth century under conditions of monopoly capitalism also had implications for the industrial structure, and more broadly the economic and political structures, of countries such as Germany (Moore, 1966: 434-440; Weaver, 1976: 34-35). Germany was able to borrow technology from industrialized nations, and since the state itself constituted an important market for industrial production (especially armaments), the need to expand the industrial labor force and internal markets was limited relative to conditions in countries which industrialized in the eighteenth century. This in turn meant that changes in the pre-capitalist agrarian structure to expand production for a growing urban-industrial population were also less important. As stated by Weaver, the German case indicated that "industrialization no longer had to come from below, transforming all dimensions of social life, but could come from above, preserving and strengthening pre-capitalist hierarchies and cultural forms" (Weaver, 1976: 35). At the same time, in the case of Germany, the process of capitalist industrialization and the scale of industrial production also accelerated the development of capitalist structures and the emergence of a highly conscious proletariat. In short, the existence of already industrialized capitalist societies had broad and sometimes contradictory effects on the process of industrialization, class structures, and the role of the state in late industrializing countries.

But those societies in which neither a bourgeoisie nor the state succeeded in industrializing in response to pressures from the capitalist states of the core were relegated to a peripheral or dependent position within the world economy. While the states of the more powerful capitalist or core countries are in a position to support capital accumulation by their dominant class in various parts of the world, the states of the periphery are or have been constrained due to economic and sometimes political domination by the more powerful capitals and states of the core.

Between the sixteenth and nineteenth centuries, through the world market as well as through more direct means of colonization and conquest, the core states succeeded in imposing on the rest of the world a division of labor in which the latter functioned to provide certain types of commodities to as well as markets needed by the core. The initial penetration of European states and merchant capital into other regions brought these regions into the world market as suppliers of bullion and precious metals; subsequently these "peripheral" regions provided raw materials and markets for the industrializing countries of northern Europe. The penetration of foreign capitals and states into the periphery was intensified with the immense technological advances of capitalist industrialization in the last third of the nineteenth century, which accelerated the processes of capital concentration and centralization and increased the need to secure industrial inputs and markets. The result was imperialism, involving the direct export of capital from the advanced core countries into the peripheral regions and the colonization of much of Africa and Asia. In Latin America, capital from Britain, the U.S., France, and Germany was invested in mines, plantations, and later petroleum resources, and financed the construction of railroads, urban transport, electric power systems, and communications, creating markets for European industrial goods. With this process, the integration of different formations into the world economy was intensified, and the respective position of these formations in the world division of labor was reinforced. At the same time, while foreign or core capital could not directly exercise political hegemony within non-colonial peripheral formations, it was often "integrated" into them and may to some extent be considered part of the dominant class or a class fraction within these formations.[10]

But while peripheral formations are, to a much greater extent than those of the core, shaped by external forces, it is their internal situation—the level of development of productive forces, the relative strength of contending classes, etc.—which generally determines the response of a given formation to external influences and in fact whether these influences will become dominant in shaping that social formation. Once a given region has become part of the world division of labor the reciprocal influence of external and internal structures continues to shape its development. Changes within peripheral formations result from internal conflicts as well as from changes in the needs of core capitals and states, and the interaction of external forces with internal structures produces the position of the peripheral formation within the world division of labor, as well as the mode of integration of foreign capital in its internal structure. Although the respective positions of core and periphery are relatively stable over time, the development of the forces of production within the peripheral formation may shift its position within the world division of labor and give it greater leverage in dealing with the core.[11] Relationships between core and

[10] Among the classic Marxist works on imperialism are Lenin (1964) and Bukharin (1973). The effects of capital penetration in Africa, Asia, and Latin America are discussed in Mandel (1940: 441 f), Wallerstein (1974a: 85 f) and Weaver (1976: 37-38). On the integration of foreign capital into non-colonial peripheral formations, see Petras (1978: 55).

[11] According to the world system approach, this "mobility" within the system results in the existence of a third category of states—the semi-periphery—which

peripheral formations are basically power relations; from the perspective of a given peripheral formation they may be described in terms of dependence.

Relations of dependence may take various forms: trade structures oriented to the export of one or a small number of primary products, or excessive trade dependence on a given core country; reliance on external capital and technology which shapes the development of the economy, or a significant sector of it, according to the needs of foreign capital rather than the needs and resources of the affected economy; severe foreign exchange bottlenecks resulting from capital export as a consequence of profit repatriation, interest payments, and loan amortization and imports of foreign technology. Dependence may involve direct or indirect foreign control of the most dynamic sector of the economy—whether it is the export enclave (the major export commodity and related infrastructure and services) or the most advanced industrial sectors.

Foreign capital includes not only the particular foreign interests involved (whether they are trading partners, owners of an export enclave, multinational corporations, banks, etc.) but also the state of the relevant core country as the "class conscious" agent of foreign capital. The core state in fact may have a central role in influencing the institutions and policies of the peripheral state in accord with the needs of core capital for accumulation in the periphery (Petras, 1978: 47-52). Thus the constraints imposed by imperialism are not limited to economic intervention by foreign capital but also include the military and political power the relevant core states are able and willing to bring to bear in a given situation (MacEwan, 1972: 47-48; Sunkel, 1972: 54; Murray, 1971: 91-92).

Above it was suggested that, given the different needs and resources of late industrializing countries such as Germany, the process of modernization may reinforce rather than eliminate certain traditional structures and cultural patterns while accelerating the development of new structures. To an even greater degree, certain of the apparent distortions produced in peripheral social formations may be due to the fact that foreign capital often affects pre-

---

may consist of states declining from a position within the core (as sixteenth- and seventeenth-century Spain) as well as the rise of certain states from the periphery (as contemporary Mexico and Brazil). The semi-periphery also has a "social control" function in introducing an intermediate strata into an otherwise polarized system (Wallerstein, 1974b).

capitalist formations selectively—accelerating the development of productive forces in one sector (as mining) which coexists with traditional pre-capitalist structures in other sectors. The latter may even be deliberately fostered by foreign capital in alliance with pre-capitalist groups within the social formation (Brenner, 1977: 90; Palma, 1978: 892-893; Kay, 1975: 103-105). The implications of this coexistence of different structures or modes of production within and among different sectors in a given social formation depend on the nature of alliances between foreign capital and internal classes (e.g., whether they are linked or not and, if so, which internal classes are affected) and the extent to which traditional modes of production constitute obstacles to the development of the peripheral formation as a whole. Another effect is mixed modes of production—the combination of different modes of production within a single system of production. In colonial and post-colonial Latin America, slave and quasi-feudal forms of exploitation were utilized on privately owned plantations and estates which were producing for export and in some cases reinvesting surplus to expand production, characteristic of capitalism. Moreover, once the core countries began to industrialize, advanced technology resulting from the rapid and constant development of the productive forces under conditions of competitive capitalism could be transferred to social formations at lower stages of development. The results of these mixed structures, in which the advanced sectors are articulated within the global rationality of specific core capitals rather than with the rest of the peripheral economy, are the accelerated development of certain sectors and the stagnation of others. This obviously affects the class structure and has implications for class conflict, with a class-conscious proletariat in such sectors as mining and the "internationalized" sectors of manufacturing industry coexisting with pre-capitalist or semi-proletarianized rural workers.

Imperialism and the relation of the peripheral formation with one or more core states and capitals, the "integration" of foreign capital into the internal class structure, the coexistence of different modes of production or the presence of mixed modes of production obviously affect the state in peripheral social formations and raise additional questions in an attempt to assess the possibilities and limits of state autonomy. For example, what is the position of a given society within the world division of labor and what is its relationship to core capitals and states? Is this relationship likely to be reinforced by political and military sanctions by core states? To what extent is foreign capital integrated as a segment of the dominant class or closely aligned with the dominant internal class fraction, and what are the implications of this for the class nature of the state? Has the penetration of foreign capital in certain sectors resulted in the coexistence of two or more modes of production, and, if so, has this led to divisions within the dominant class (or conflicts between two or more classes representing different modes of production) and what have been the implications of this situation for state autonomy? Does the coexistence of different modes of production accelerate or retard the development of class consciousness and solidarity within and among subordinate classes? Has the importance of foreign capital resulted in an increase in relative state autonomy vis-à-vis national classes?

While these questions should be addressed in examining specific peripheral formations, certain generalizations can be tentatively drawn from the historical experience of Latin American countries. First, that class or class fraction which controls the state is often the fraction most closely linked to foreign capital, and is generally interested in the maintenance of existing structural relations, internal and external. Throughout much of the latter part of the nineteenth century and the early twentieth century the hegemonic group consisted of the agro-export sector (which continues to be important in some countries). Today in the more advanced countries it consists of that fraction of the industrial bourgeoisie directly or indirectly linked to foreign corporations and the state.

Second, one result of the nineteenth-century alliances between a domestic export oligarchy and foreign interests in several Latin American countries was that the national industrial bourgeoisie was weak, and the process of industrialization has required the intervention of the state to promote the development of an industrial bourgeoisie and/or to expand its own economic control in confrontation with foreign capital (Amin, 1976-77; Cardoso and Faletto, 1978: 128-132, 205). In these countries, the state has also had a more direct role in capital accumulation, since the capital needs of industry at the more advanced (monopoly) stages of capitalism are beyond the means of individual entrepreneurs. This role, and the state's control of important economic sectors, may be expected to increase its autonomy with respect to national capital; but the process of industrialization also tends to strengthen the dominant segment of the national bourgeoisie, which may in turn limit state autonomy (particularly if this segment of the bourgeoisie is linked to foreign capital, as is often the case).

Third, given the influence of foreign capital, and the fact that it may constitute or be linked to the dominant segment of national capital within a given social formation, the relative autonomy of the state may be expected to increase to the extent that foreign capital is politically or economically weakened. The fact that the most decisive push toward industrialization in the more advanced Latin American countries occurred during the depression and the second world war has been attributed in part to the drastic reduction of trade and the consequent weakening of the agro-export sector as well as the reduced capacity of foreign states to directly intervene in the internal affairs of Latin American states during this period.

Possibilities and Limits of State Autonomy: Summary and Conclusions. The limits to state autonomy derive from the position of the state within class societies and the position of a given society within the world system. According to Marxist theory, in class societies the state functions to reproduce a mode of production in which a specific class is dominant. Since class societies are by definition characterized by exploitation and therefore class conflict, this involves neutralization of class conflict and control of the subordinate classes. In capitalist societies, the state establishes and maintains conditions for private accumulation; in peripheral societies this function may encompass accumulation by foreign as well as by national capital. In the latter, however, the class nature of the state may itself be in question, given the possible coexistence of two or more modes of production.

Therefore, for purposes of analysis, the state has been defined not in terms of its class nature and functions but as a set of institutions (the civil and military bureaucracy—the state apparatus) and those who formally control them (the government). Autonomy is defined as the ability of those who control the state apparatus to use it for ends other than, and particularly contrary to, those of the dominant class, since it is this class which benefits from the reproduction of the existing mode of production by the state. While control over the bureaucracy and especially of the means of coercion would seem to facilitate state autonomy, such autonomy is limited by divisions within the government and bureaucracy, and particularly by the dependence of the state upon resources generated through the process of production which is generally controlled by the dominant class. In peripheral societies, control over resources of the state may be directly or indirectly exercised by foreign capital backed by the relevant core state.

In general terms, then, state autonomy is limited by the position of the state within a given social formation in which a particular mode of production and class may be dominant, and by the position of that social formation within the world capitalist system. Within these structural constraints, state autonomy may be further limited by the direct or indirect intervention of the dominant class (including foreign class fractions, in some cases represented by foreign states) and by the necessity to legitimize itself through a response, however limited, to non-dominant groups. Since direct or indirect intervention, or the threat of such intervention, by the dominant class constitutes the ultimate sanction of structural constraints, the state may presumably exercise relative structural autonomy only in conditions when the possibility for such intervention is considerably weakened. It has been suggested above that this is most likely to occur in periods of crisis and transition, when the formerly dominant class is weakened, or when the mode of production is indeterminate, or when classes representing two or more modes of production are in conflict.

In peripheral social formations, the possibility of state autonomy would be positively related to a weakening of pressures from core capitals or states (due to international crisis and/or internal crises within the relevant core formations). In peripheral "late industrializing" societies the resources of the state may be increased by its role in industrialization, but this will not necessarily increase the relative autonomy of the state if the process of industrialization strengthens the national bourgeoisie (or certain fractions of the bourgeoisie) and/or the role of foreign capital in the economy. And the options of even a relatively autonomous state are limited to the historical possibilities resulting from the internal development of the productive forces and its position within the world system. This autonomy is also limited by the logic of development of the social formation, which may involve domination by a given class within the newly established mode of production. Thus, through its contribution to the formation of the new social order the "autonomous" state may "create" its own structural constraints. In the last analysis, state actions which threaten the structural basis of class dominance will generally result in increased cohesion of that class to control the action of the state.

Finally, pressures from subordinate classes and groups have several implications for state autonomy. In general, given its functions within a class society, the state will attempt to control these groups through various mechanisms ranging from cooptation to repression. In contrast to the dominant class, whose unity is organized within the state, subordinated groups and classes must organize outside of and against the state if they are to obtain and maintain class objectives. At the same time, at least to some extent state response to the needs of these groups is necessary for the survival of the system and for the legitimacy of the state itself. Thus class conflict not only effects change within the system but also affects the form and functions of the state. Also, class conflicts (as well as intra-class struggles) may be reproduced among different factions and institutions *within* the state. In exceptional circumstances, or for specific ends, the state (or factions within the state) may ally with subordinate groups and classes as a means of achieving relative autonomy with respect to the dominant class. But the state will seek to dominate this alliance, since control of the state by these classes would ultimately result in the elimination of the class system on which the existence of the state is based.

THE STATE IN CONTEMPORARY MEXICO

In Mexico, certain conditions facilitating relative state autonomy existed in the period following the Mexican revolution (1910-1917), which destroyed much of the existing state apparatus, weakened the Mexican bourgeoisie and instituted, through the constitution of 1917, the concept of a state "above classes" which would intervene directly in the socio-economic order for specific ends. Although the post-revolutionary state continued to be weak in relation to foreign capital, with the depression of the 1930's the capacity and inclination of the dominant core states representing foreign capital to intervene in Mexico was diminished. At the same time, the revolution had brought the peasant masses, and to a lesser extent the urban working class,[12] to the political foreground,

[12] Given the coexistence of various modes of production and of exploitation in the Mexican countryside during this period, there is no one term which adequately covers all those working in the rural sector. Here the term "peasant" will be used

where they continued to agitate for structural changes in the rural sector as well as for other reforms. The alliance of these groups with progressive factions within the state under the leadership of President Lázaro Cárdenas (1934-1940) further increased the possibility of state autonomy based on an assault by these groups against existing structures. Thus an analysis of the Cárdenas period can provide an insight into the question of state autonomy in Mexico and perhaps the more general question of state autonomy based on popular mobilization in a post-revolutionary society.

At the same time, we are concerned with explaining why the apparent autonomy of the state during the Cárdenas administration came to an end. And this raises a further question: given the economic power of the contemporary Mexican state—its control of resources, its regulation of the private sector, its apparent ability to bargain with foreign corporations—can the state in fact be considered less autonomous today than in the 1930's? Before we analyze the Mexican state in the post-revolutionary period it will be useful to briefly examine the contemporary state. First, since one of the assumptions of this study is the apparent contrast between the revolutionary origins of the state and its contemporary form and function, an understanding of this contrast requires some understanding of the contemporary Mexican state. Second, several authors have suggested that the Mexican state today exercises considerable autonomy in relation to dominant groups and classes, although it pursues its own interests rather than those of subordinate groups (Purcell and Purcell, 1977; Weinert, 1977; Kaufman, 1977). It is important to understand the bases of these perceptions of state autonomy in Mexico, since—in contrast to the position stated above—they assume that the state's capacity to act independently of dominant groups and classes has continued and perhaps increased in the contemporary period.

Several arguments have been advanced for the autonomy or independence of the contemporary Mexican state. First, those who control the state apparatus are recruited from different backgrounds and generally follow different career patterns than do members of the private sector. Second, the state's control of economic resources—and particularly its control of the means of pro-

---

as a direct translation of the Spanish word *campesino* to refer to those who work in agriculture whether as small farmers (individual or communal), migrant laborers, wage workers on estates or plantations, contract laborers, or debt peons. More specific terminology will be used for differentiating among various groups.

duction in basic sectors of the economy—enables it to act in its own interests, over and above those of the dominant class. Third, from a strictly empirical perspective, the contemporary state has demonstrated its ability to control capital, including foreign capital, and to pursue lines of development not directly in the interests of private groups.

The argument of separate origins of the state elite and dominant economic groups is supported by a thorough study of Mexican political elites, from the pre-revolutionary government through the Echeverría administration (1970-1976), which indicates that the economic backgrounds and career patterns of these groups differ substantially from those of economic elites (Smith, 1977, 1979). Government officials are only rarely recruited from the private sector, in keeping with the populist revolutionary ideology on which the state continues to base its legitimacy. This separate recruitment also challenges the simpler versions of the "instrumentalist" thesis regarding the class nature of the state—i.e., that the dominant class is also a ruling or governing class.

It is certainly true that the Mexican government bureaucracy is relatively free of some of the more obvious forms of dominant class influence which exist in the United States, such as direct recruitment of its members into the government, or campaign financing. But—as argued above—the absence of direct control by members of the dominant class is not a sufficient condition for state autonomy. In the case of Mexico, there are numerous and complex formal mechanisms for interaction between the state and the dominant class, including industrial and commercial chambers, sectoral organizations, advisory committees, and positions of private sector individuals on the boards of state banks and enterprises. Informal mechanisms are undoubtedly even more significant, as members of the most important national and international firms are able to bypass these organizations and negotiate with the government directly (Vernon, 1963: 18; Leal, 1975a: 60). Also reverse recruitment, whereby government officials "retire" into private business, has been a common practice and constitutes an important element in the class nature of the state (Labastida, 1972: 138-139; L. Meyer, 1977: 14).

At a more general level, it has been suggested in recent writings on the state that state control of or access to economic resources may be a factor in increased state autonomy—specifically, the ability of the state to pursue an independent "state" interest (Gold, Lo and Wright, 1975). State access to resources also enhances its power relative to other states within the world market. In the case of Mexico, the extensive and direct role of the state in accumulation has unquestionably expanded its control of economic resources. The Mexican public sector comprises over 500 firms which control the key sectors of petroleum, railroads, communications, and electric power, and has substantial investments in other sectors, including mining, steel, chemicals, sugar refining, paper, textiles, fertilizer, and transport equipment. In addition, government regulation of the private sector is extensive. Through the central bank (Banco de México), the official development bank (Nacional Financiera, Nafinsa), and a broad range of additional official credit institutions and special funds, the state is able to exercise considerable control over finance and investment. One mechanism is the central bank's flexible reserve requirements, which are utilized to direct private bank resources to productive investment; today a substantial proportion of private bank investments are in government securities.

But economic control has not necessarily resulted in increased economic independence. In fact, the expansion of state economic involvement has directly or indirectly aided private capital expansion, thereby strengthening the dominant factions of the bourgeoisie (Fitzgerald, 1979: 57). In many cases firms of the public sector provide services at reduced rates to private industries, or the state takes over industries which are confronting bankruptcy in order to keep them in operation, providing needed supplies or products and maintaining employment levels. Thus the government Federal Power Commission has over the years charged private companies 3 centavos per kwh, although its costs are 4 centavos per kwh. National industries pay PEMEX (Petroleos Mexicanos, the Mexican petroleum company) half the export price for petroleum. And the government has taken over many of the antiquated sugar mills of the country due to the inability of the private sector to profitably maintain them (LAER 22 June 1979; Bennett and Sharpe 1980). Nacional Financiera and other official credit institutions finance private industry directly and indirectly through the purchase of securities, facilitation of foreign credit, and other measures (Aguilar, 1972: 150). And Mexico has one of the lowest tax rates in Latin America; taxes are also regressive. In short, the expansion of the public sector and of state control of resources have served private accumulation, at the same time facilitating conditions for national capital accumulation—through such policies as Mexican-ization (the requirement that companies be 51 percent Mexican-owned)—in a context in which foreign capital tends to dominate.

A third set of arguments is based on empirical evidence—the fact that the Mexican state *has*, on occasion, operated against the interests of private groups and even of foreign enterprises. Two of the most powerful private economic groups in Mexico—those of SOMEX and the Banco Internacional—were nationalized by the government (see Appendix A). The ability of the state to use discretion in enforcing the numerous rules regulating private en-terprise constitutes a means of fragmenting and of controlling pri-vate interests. The state has also provided some protection to small and medium industrial firms, which are less capital-intensive and therefore constitute an important source of employment, although such protection may be contrary to the interests of dominant na-tional and foreign firms. The Mexican government has instituted policies to control foreign capital and to direct foreign investment to certain sectors, with some success, as indicated by the high proportion of foreign investment in manufacturing. Mexico's pe-troleum resources and the commitment of considerable foreign in-vestment have given the state leverage in negotiating with foreign companies and states (Purcell and Purcell, 1977: 196; Weinert, 1977: 113).

Nevertheless, there is also evidence to support the position that the state's ability to move against foreign interests and the national bourgeoisie is limited, in part by divisions within the state itself, which inhibits its ability to design and enforce consistent and co-herent policies. At the same time, certain state agencies may "in-ternalize" the interests and orientations of private capital—as ap-pears to be the case with the Finance Ministry in Mexico. Both the divisions within the state and the "internalization" of private interests were evident in the recent modification by the Finance Ministry of a tax reform proposed by officials within the Ministry of National Patrimony—in which several measures disagreeable to the interests of the private sector were eliminated *prior* to the sub-mission of the reform to private groups for suggestions and rec-ommendations. An earlier case was that of the initial negotiations between the Mexican government and various foreign auto com-panies in the late 1950's and early 1960's regarding the establish-ment of an auto industry in Mexico, in which the bargaining power of the state was considerably weakened by disagreements between the Secretary of Industry and Commerce, acting in close collaboration with the Ford Motor Company, and the Secretary of Finance (Bennett and Sharpe, 1979, 1980; Purcell and Purcell, 1976: 230-232).

Thus one factor limiting state autonomy in contemporary Mexico would appear to be the absence of cohesion among state factions and institutions. If any factions or institutions can be said to have disproportionate influence within the state, they are those most closely aligned with national or foreign capital.

Finally, dominant classes and foreign groups have obvious means at their disposal to prevent the state from substantially threatening their interests, as indicated during the Echeverría regime (1970-1976). In part due to the impetus of progressive, statist-oriented groups which controlled the Ministry of National Patrimony (which oversees the para-statal firms and decentralized agencies of the public sector), and in part due to investment cutbacks by the private sector (in turn a result of inflation and other economic problems) the government undertook substantial economic investments, thus expanding the state-controlled sector of the economy. But one of the results was an aggravation of Mexico's foreign debt, since needed fiscal reforms to increase government revenues were not implemented, and state expansion was financed largely by foreign loans. Between 1970 and 1976, direct foreign investments in Mexico fluctuated between $200.7 million (1970) and $362.2 million (1974), whereas *net* loans from abroad (disbursements minus amortizations) increased from $324.2 million to $2,930.0 million—$2,701.9 million to the public sector (Nafinsa 1977: 381-382). Furthermore, expansion of the state sector and other measures of the Echeverría regime viewed as antagonistic to private interests were factors in a loss of business confidence and increased political opposition by the private sector, manifested in capital export and further production cutbacks. Partly as a consequence of Echeverría's "independent" course, partly as a result of longer term economic conditions resulting from Mexico's economic structure (including the "import" of U.S. inflation due to the higher costs of imported technology), Echeverría's regime ended in an economic crisis, with the first devaluation of the peso in twenty-two years. The succeeding Lopez Portillo administration took a more openly pro-business stance and, as a condition for stabilization loans from the International Monetary Fund, instituted an austerity program which included cutbacks in state spending, removal of price controls, and wage ceilings, which have weighed most heavily on Mexico's low income population (Ayala, 1977: 35-45; Pellicer, 1977: 46, Reynolds, 1978: 1015-1016).

Thus the state may act against individual and even group interests within the private sector, but its ability to act against the dominant class as a whole, or even substantial segments of that class, is checked by the action of those segments and their representatives. In general, the independence of the state is limited by the socio-economic structure in which it functions to promote private capital accumulation, by the economic power of private capital (both national and foreign), and by divisions within the state and the identification of certain state factions with dominant class interests.

To argue that the autonomy of the Mexican state is limited is not to suggest that the state has not had an important role in Mexico's economic development. But the orientation of this development has been largely determined by foreign and national capital. The structural implications of this relationship between the state and private capital can be indicated through a comparison of Mexico with Brazil, another rapidly growing economy. Both countries can be considered part of the semi-periphery, which in this case designates countries that can no longer be considered peripheral although they are structurally distinct from core countries.[13] In both countries, efforts of the government to direct national and foreign capital have taken place within the broader context of a "dominant coalition" or "triple alliance" based on collaboration between dominant factions within the state, multinational corporations and other forms of foreign capital, and the dominant (or "internationalized") segment of the national bourgeoisie (Labastida, 1972: 103; Evans, 1979: 152 f). One effect of national legislation insisting on majority national ownership and other controls of foreign investment (where such legislation is not disregarded, as through exemptions, or the use of *prestanombres*—name-lenders—to "stand in" for foreign owners in stock listings, as in Mexico) has been closer integration of foreign capital with the state and/or national private capital through joint investments (in ad-

[13] For an attempt to develop objective criteria for distinguishing countries of the semi-periphery and an application of these to a comparison of Mexico and Brazil, see Evans, 1979: 290-308.

dition to loans, technology transfers, machinery imports, and marketing arrangements). In both countries foreign capital and technology have contributed importantly to their impressive growth rates. As of 1968, foreign investments in manufacturing constituted 65 to 70 percent of total foreign investment in Mexico and Brazil (compared with 34 percent for Latin America as a whole). Although foreign investors are more diversified in Brazil than in Mexico, where U.S. corporations predominate, in both countries approximately 60 percent of the top 100 firms are foreign-controlled; and multinationals are dominant in the most dynamic industrial sectors: chemicals, machinery, electrical machinery and equipment, and transport equipment. Even in those sectors and firms where national capital is dominant there is often dependence on foreign technology in the form of machinery imports as well as in the use of foreign brands, patents, and processes.

The economies of Brazil and Mexico have been characterized as examples of dependent capitalist development, a concept which assumes that development can occur in economies dependent upon foreign capital; that such development, as capitalist development elsewhere, results in certain distortions; but that these distortions will be different from those resulting in advanced capitalist countries (Cardoso and Faletto: 1969; Cardoso, 1975). One of the major distortions produced by dependent capitalist development in both Brazil and Mexico has been the extensive use of capital intensive technology in countries with a large labor surplus, with the effect that industrialization has had little impact on employment. A market orientation to a relatively small high income group which emulates consumption patterns of the advanced industrial countries results in an emphasis on the production of consumer durables, reinforcing the use of capital intensive technology and the exclusion of a significant proportion of the population from the labor market. The problem is aggravated in a country such as Mexico, where the encouragement of agribusiness has resulted in land concentration and rural mechanization, leading to massive unemployment and underemployment in the countryside and accelerating the exodus of workers into the cities, where few industrial jobs await them. It is no coincidence that Mexico and Brazil, the most advanced industrial economies in Latin America, have the most regressive income distribution; while Mexico, unlike Brazil, has experienced some income redistribution within the top 20 percent of the population, in both countries the lowest 20 percent of the population receives less than 4 percent of the total income.[14]

In both countries, rapid industrialization on the basis of foreign capital and technology has benefitted certain segments of the bourgeoisie to the detriment of others. In Mexico, the dominant class segment appears to be comprised by those individuals and families who control the so-called economic groups. These groups consist of industrial firms (often vertically integrated), commercial houses, financial institutions (in many cases integrated into powerful "financial groups"), and, sometimes, transportation firms, mines, or other economic firms, which are related through common ownership and interlocking directorates. Ownership of the firm in each economic group is generally concentrated in an "investment group" consisting of one or a few families or business associates, sometimes interrelated by marriage. While the existence of economic groups is universally recognized in Mexico, information regarding their number and composition is still imprecise.[15] If an economic group is defined in terms of its inter-sectoral linkages and of its control of a substantial proportion of assets in one or more sectors of subsectors of the economy, there are probably no more than 35 to 50 such groups in Mexico. Existing information also suggests that the majority of these groups are linked with the state and/or with foreign capital (through joint investments, loans, technology arrangements). As indicated above, many economic groups also include their own financial groups, which in turn concentrate the financial resources of Mexico. In the mid-1970's, twenty-six financial groups controlled 90 percent of the resources of the banking system; and the four principal groups controlled 68 percent (Casteñeda, 1976: 65n.).

[14] On the effects of foreign investment on the industrial structure, and more broadly the structure of production in Mexico, see Sepúlveda and Chumacero, 1973: 54-58; Cinta, 1972: 195-196; Fajnsylber and Martínez Tarrago, 1976: 367-368; and Weinert, 1977: 110. For Brazil, see Cardoso, 1973: 143 and Evans, 1976: 50 and 1979: 300. Both countries are discussed in Newfarmer and Mueller, 1975. Effects on income distribution are discussed in LAER, 3 August 1979, and Eckstein, 1982.

[15] A recent study identified over 100 economic groups, but many of these consisted of only a few firms and others constituted firms of only one sector (Cordero and Santín, 1977). Despite these problems, this is the most systematic study of the economic groups to date. An earlier study suggested that the Mexican oligarchy consisted of some 1,000 families of which perhaps 100 were of national importance; these were grouped in some 25 to 35 groups (Aguilar and Carmona, 1967).

In both Mexico and Brazil, the linkages among the dominant state factions, foreign interests, and the dominant segment of the national bourgeoisie are varied and complex, and each may seek to maximize its specific interests with varying degrees of success. But the state is limited to options available within the framework of a structure in which these groups are dominant; while it may attempt to redefine the relative position of various groups and interests—including foreign capital—within this structure, it is unable to change the structure itself.

Since subordinate groups and classes are forced to bear the costs of the dependent model of capitalist development, political control of these groups is a major function of the state. And here there are important distinctions between the Mexican and Brazilian states. The Brazilian state has been described as the most successful example of the bureaucratic-authoritarian state, a concept which was developed to explain a specific historical phenomenon: the emergence in the 1960's and early 1970's of repressive and relatively enduring military regimes in several South American countries which had been characterized by relatively high levels of economic development and/or a highly mobilized proletariat. The emergence of these regimes in "developed" Latin American countries contradicted a basic tenet of traditional development theory which posited a correlation between increasing levels of economic development and growing democratic participation (O'Donnell, 1973: 1-8). The explanation provided by the bureaucratic-authoritarian perspective is that the pattern of development followed by most Latin American countries—that of import substitution—led to bottlenecks once the relatively easy initial stage was passed; these bottlenecks as well as policies to overcome them tended to penalize the working class and the urban "middle" groups. But since these groups had achieved a high level of political mobilization (in part due to their incorporation into "populist" alliances during an earlier expansionist phase of import-substitution industrialization), they reacted to these policies with increased mobilization, eventually leading to political instability. Since civilian political regimes were unable to insure the level of political stability believed essential to attract the foreign capital and the technology needed to overcome economic bottlenecks they were suceeded by military regimes, generally led by development-oriented officers who projected a long-term tenure in order to firmly establish their specific models of development. These regimes were characterized by the economic "exclusion" of previously mobilized groups—indicated by decreases in wage and consumption levels—which was facilitated by their political exclusion through the repression of dissident groups and by the elimination of virtually all democratic processes and institutions. These states, under the direction of the military, have established alliances with foreign corporations and in some cases with dominant sectors of the national bourgeoisie to implement a model of industrial development increasingly oriented to the production of consumer durables for relatively high income groups and for export.[16]

The Mexican state has many similarities to the bureaucratic authoritarian state, but it has distinguished itself (to date) by its ability to maintain the desired social and political stability for private accumulation without recourse to a military dictatorship. The continuity of Mexico's civilian government has been attributed in part to its "prior exclusion" of the masses of workers and peasants through their "pre-emptive" incorporation into state-controlled structures—i.e., the government party and its sectoral organizations.

Ironically, this structure as well as the "legitimacy" of the Mexican state relative to other bureaucratic authoritarian states in Latin America is a legacy of the revolution and of the Cárdenas administration of the 1930's, the most progressive period of post-revolutionary Mexico.

The chief instrument of "exclusion" or "controlled inclusion" is the Institutional Revolutionary Party (PRI), composed of three sectors: labor (incorporating the major labor confederations and industrial unions), peasant (dominated by the National Peasant Confederation, the CNC), and the so-called popular sector (consisting of organizations of small landowners, teachers, state employees, etc., loosely joined in the National Confederation of Popular Organizations, CNOP). The party structure, which deliberately excludes the more powerful economic groups, reinforces the state's ideological use of the Mexican revolution to present itself as defender of the interests of the working class, peasants, and marginal sectors, and as an opponent of privileged groups and monopolies. The party structure does function to some extent as a mechanism

---

[16] See O'Donnell, 1975, and Oszlak and O'Donnell, 1976. Several studies elaborating and/or critiquing the bureaucratic authoritarian approach can be found in Collier, ed., 1979.

for representation of the interests of constituent organizations, but it is chiefly a means for state control of their membership.[17]

Incorporation is facilitated by the authoritarian structures of the basic member confederations, particularly the labor and peasant organizations, as well as by the use of such devices as the exclusion clause (prohibiting employers from hiring or retaining any worker who is not a member of the recognized union) and by *charrismo* (government imposition of union and peasant leaders in their respective organizations) as a means of discipline. The government and party structures permeate all levels of Mexican society; their monopoloy of economic and political resources limits the ability of local communities and groups to effectively resist their political control. Formal structures are reinforced through informal mechanisms of vertical clientele relations whereby government and party officials provide limited favors for specific groups, communities, etc. in return for support; these vertical relations also serve to obscure the more basic division in a society characterized by sharp contrasts in the living standards of the wealthy and the poor (Alvarez and Sandoval, 1976: 21-22; Reyna, 1974: 24-35; Eckstein, 1977: 78 f).

On the basis of its claim to be the party of the revolution, the PRI seeks to exclude powerful opposition from the left: left-wing movements which have attempted to challenge the hegemony of

[17] The concept of corporatism as a set of institutional arrangements for structuring interest group representation (Schmitter, 1972: 90-91) thus has limited relevance for the "corporate" party structure of Mexico, which constitutes a mechanism for state control of subordinate groups and classes. Certain elements of the concept, however, are relevant—e.g., the fact that the state attempts to limit horizontal linkages between groups, which is accomplished in Mexico through the separation of peasant and labor organizations as well as the inclusion of certain unions (such as those of bank employees, government workers, and teachers) in the popular rather than labor sector. Other quasi-corporate structures in Mexico consist of the peak business organizations and tripartite commissions. The former are of secondary importance to informal mechanisms relating business interests to the state. Tripartite commissions are a relatively recent phenomenon; they include representation from the government, the private sector, and coopted sectors of labor, and closely resemble the corporate bodies formed in the U.S. in the early decades of this century (see Weinstein, 1968). The discussion by O'Donnell (1977) of the different implications of corporatism (under the bureaucratic authoritarian state) for the popular sector, which is deprived of the possibility for independent organization, and the bourgeoisie, which retains its own organization, as well as informal relations with the state, seems to be particularly appropriate in the Mexican case. Further discussions of corporatism in Latin America and in Mexico can be found in Malloy, 1977, Reyna, 1977 and Stepan, 1978.

the PRI have been coopted or repressed; leaders of dissident movements have been drawn into the state or party apparatus; or leftwing parties are relegated to the status "loyal opposition." Thus the ability of the popular sectors—working class, peasants, local communities—to form independent organizations and to join forces to promote common interests, is effectively controlled. The state may respond to certain demands of dissident groups in the process of coopting them; at the same time, the party structure enables the state to mobilize large sectors of the population in support of specific policies—both further elements in its legitimacy.

The evident success of the control and cooptive mechanisms of the Mexican state has led to a tendency to regard the Mexican population as passive and acquiescent and to ignore the repressive mechanisms which underlie the authority of the state. But resistance to government domination has ranged from rank-and-file struggles against goverment-imposed leaders in various unions and peasant organizations to armed guerrilla uprisings which have at certain periods encompassed several states. And repressive mechanisms of the state—for those groups which cannot be coopted— have taken various forms: the jailing of dissident labor leaders; official tolerance of daily repression in the countryside and at the local level by landowners, political bosses, and government officials, including the assassination of independent leaders; and the use of the army to repress dissident groups that cannot be neutralized.[18]

In summary, the characteristics and functions of the contemporary Mexican state contrast sharply with those of the progressive "revolutionary" state projected in the constitution of 1917, which became a model for the Cárdenas administration in the 1930's.

---

[18] Mechanisms of cooptation and control are discussed in Anderson and Cockcroft, 1972: 230-240, Fagen and Tuohy, 1972: 214-215, Reyna, 1974, and Hellman, 1978. A recent effort of Mexican workers to liberate themselves from state-dominated union organizations was the "tendencia domocrática" within the electrical workers' organizations, which subsequently gained adherents among other groups of workers and became the vanguard of a movement for a democratic, independent labor movement. In part due to the nationalist initiatives and attempted reforms of the Echeverría regime, the electrical workers proposed a new pact between the labor movement and the "regenerated" national state. Their faith in state support proved unfounded, as the Echeverría regime proved unable or unwilling to confront the entrenched labor bureaucracy, and the "tendencia democrática" within the electrical workers' movement was forced to disband (Gilly, 1978: 107; Baird and McCaughan, 1979: 104-117).

Instead of an "autonomous" state, above classes, which would promote independent, national development, the contemporary Mexican state is intricately linked with the national bourgeoisie and with foreign capital in promoting a form of dependent capitalist development from which these groups benefit. While the "revolutionary" state was to exercise a protective if paternalistic role in promoting the rights and interests of the peasants and the working class, the Mexican state is primarily concerned with the political control of these groups, whether by cooptive or more repressive measures, which are all the more necessary, given the fact that these sectors have been made to bear the costs of Mexico's model of development.

This brief examination of the state in contemporary Mexico hardly does justice to the complexity of the subject, but is perhaps sufficient to demonstrate the lack of state autonomy and to provide a point of departure for an examination of its historical origins and development. The following chapters will seek to establish the conditions which led to *relative* state autonomy in the 1930's (relative in comparison to state autonomy before or since) and to explain the limits of this autonomy.

The next two chapters will discuss the historical forces resulting in the revolution and shaping the context within which the new post-revolutionary state emerged, focusing on two questions: to what extent and how did existing class forces and structures establish the parameters within which the state could act? And how did the action of the state within this context establish the parameters for subsequent state action? In Chapter Four, the processes resulting in the formation of a new alliance around the candidacy of Lázaro Cárdenas, who was elected president in 1934, will be discussed, and Chapter Five deals with the contradictions of this alliance, manifested in the collaboration of the government with mobilized groups of peasants and workers to bring about substantial reforms while at the same time it sought to control these groups.

Chapter Six shifts to a focus on the relation between the state and private capital, which prospered during most of this period, largely due to state intervention even though most of the powerful segments of capital opposed the Cárdenas government. This chapter is concerned with the apparent contradictions in the state's policy to support private capital accumulation at the same time that it sought to control capital, in keeping with its concept of an "autonomous" state above *all* classes.

Chapter Seven is concerned with the context and actual events of the nationalization of the foreign-owned petroleum companies as well as its effects in sharpening the contradictions of the "autonomous" state. Chapter Eight describes the process by which the progressive alliance is transformed and ultimately destroyed, first, by the incorporation of its constituent groups into the state-party structure, and then by the shift in control over this structure to conservative elements within the state, linked to private capital.

The final chapter re-examines the question raised above regarding the possibilities and limits of state autonomy within the context of the experience of the Cárdenas years in Mexico.

Two || **The Mexican State and the Revolution**

 The contemporary Mexican state can be understood only in the context of changes resulting from the Mexican revolution. There is considerable debate, however, regarding the effects of the revolution. It has customarily been regarded as a turning point in Mexican history through which the antiquated institutions of the previous order were destroyed and new directions established for Mexico's development. Even after it became evident that Mexico's post-revolutionary experience contradicted the alleged revolutionary goals of social justice and independent development, the belief remained that the revolution itself—however much deflected from its original purposes—had been a decisive event which changed the course of Mexican history.

But this view has recently been challenged by analysts who focus on the continuity between the pre-revolutionary regime of Porfirio Díaz (1876-1911) and the post-revolutionary period, in some cases suggesting that the revolution constitutes little more than an interruption of a process of modernization well under way during the Porfiriato (Carr, 1980: 7; Bailey, 1978). The Porfirian modernization process included the centralization of state power in the federal government; the conversion of traditional agricultural estates to commercial agriculture accompanied by widespread expropriation and even proletarianization of the peasantry; the emergence of a bourgeoisie based on land, commerce, and finance; and the rapid acceleration of production and productivity by opening the economy to foreign trade and investment (Córdova, 1973; Semo, 1975; Villa, 1972; L. Meyer, 1974a). In short, conditions for dependent capitalist development seem to have existed prior to the revolution. From this perspective, the effect of the revolution was initially to interrupt this process, ultimately to reinforce and rationalize it.

The issue of continuity and change between pre-revolutionary and post-revolutionary Mexico raises questions regarding the degree and significance of relative state autonomy in post-revolutionary Mexico, and more broadly in post-revolutionary contexts in general. In the case of Mexico, it is generally agreed that the revolution resulted in the destruction of the Porfirian state apparatus and the emergence of a new state, although there are divergent viewpoints regarding the class bases of this new state. At the same time, post-revolutionary states never operate in a structural vacuum; while revolutions may bring new groups to power who seek a transformation of the social order, elements of the old order remain, and to a greater or lesser extent influence the process of reconstruction.

One of the purposes of the next two chapters will be to identify the elements of continuity and change in Mexico following the revolution as these affected the state. In this chapter, we will be concerned with the formation and characteristics of the pre-revolutionary order in Mexico, the contradictions within it which resulted in the revolution, and the immediate effect of the revolution on the Mexican state and on state-class relations. In Chapter Three we will examine the efforts of the new state at social and economic reconstruction within the context of structural constraints resulting from the previous social order and from the revolution itself.

THE PRE-REVOLUTIONARY STATE AND CLASS DYNAMICS

Colonization and the Early Republic. The territory which is now Mexico was drawn into the Spanish empire, and thus into the world market, with the Spanish conquest of the Aztec empire in 1521. By the end of the century, the Viceroyalty of New Spain extended south from Mexico's central valley to include what is now Central America and north to encompass much of the present southwestern United States. With the Viceroyalty of Peru centered in Lima, it was one of the two major centers of the Spanish empire in America; in each case the political importance of the center derived from its economic significance as a source of minerals, particularly silver, for export to Spain.

Initially tracts of land and the resident indigenous communities were bestowed by the Spanish crown on the conquerors and their descendants as land grants or encomiendas—the latter constituting a type of trusteeship in which the colonizer received the right to collect tribute from the resident population. By the middle of the sixteenth century, systems of forced labor were imposed on the communities for work in the silver mines and on the agricultural and livestock estates which supplied the mining regions. But by the end of the century mining production had declined. At the same time, the Indian population had been decimated to a fraction of its original number (variously estimated at 7 million to 25 million at the time of the conquest) through disease, overwork, and famine. Through such measures as the takeover of lands of Indian communities within the encomiendas or the purchase of land from the crown, a large proportion of the land of the central valley was converted into relatively self-sufficient agricultural estates, or haciendas, and the Indians of the communities (and their descendants) were converted into peons, forced to work on the estates of the Spaniards or Creoles (descendants of the Spaniards born in Mexico) and of the Church. A special system was established for the remaining communities which were allotted land to be held by the village and worked, individually or collectively, by the village members. For the next three centuries of colonial rule and into the first decades following independence, these two societies—the estates worked by a stable resident labor force supplemented by seasonal labor, and the inalienable (non-transferable) communities of the Indian villages—coexisted in an uneasy symbiosis. During periods of economic expansion (generated by a new mining boom or by expansion of agricultural exports) the haciendas would expand their territories to incorporate the land (and labor) of outlying Indian villages; in periods of recession they would contract and previously incorporated villages might again become relatively autonomous. Revolts by Indian communities resisting the takeover of their villages were brutally repressed (Wolf, 1959: 189-232; Chevalier, 1963; Stein and Stein, 1970: 28-39).

The decade preceding independence was characterized by massive revolts by Indians and mestizos (of mixed Indian and European blood) in conjunction with Creoles seeking autonomy from Spanish domination. But the achievement of independence in 1821 brought no improvement in the conditions of the indigenous population. For the next forty years, political power was fragmented among relatively isolated regional centers controlled by local landowners and caciques (political strongmen), while a conservative coalition of landowners and the Church struggled with liberal anticlerical professionals and intellectuals of the urban middle class for national political supremacy.

The Central American states separated from Mexico shortly after independence, and by 1850 Mexico had lost over half of its territory to the United States as a consequence of the annexation of Texas and the Mexican-American war. In 1855, the liberals gained control of the government and promulgated new laws which threatened the lands and prerogatives of the Church, as well as a new constitution (the constitution of 1857) which established the basis for a liberal state and electoral democracy. A period of civil war followed, during which the landowners and clergy collaborated with the French government in imposing a puppet regime under Maximilian, brother of the Austrian emperor, who was designated emperor of Mexico. This government was ousted by the liberals in 1867 under the leadership of Benito Juárez, who became president of the succeeding reform government.

The reform brought two important changes. In the first place, Church properties were expropriated and sold (generally intact), and concessions to vast uncultivated tracts in northern Mexico were awarded by the government to generals who had fought successfully with Juárez against the French intervention. In the second place, village lands belonging to the Indian communities were divided among the inhabitants and declared transferable. While intended to create a class of small property holders, in effect these lands were often sold or mortgaged, many going to haciendas or to land companies and leaving the former Indian owners landless. Thus the process of land concentration was accelerated, and new landowners replaced the Church and Indian communities (Cumberland, 1968: 185, 262; Wolf, 1973: 15-16).

Mexico's brief experience of liberal democracy ended in 1876 when Porfirio Díaz, a former general in the Juárez army, overthrew the government of Lerdo de Tejada, who had succeeded Juárez. With the exception of a four-year period (1880-1884) when Manuel González was president, Díaz directly controlled the presidency, largely through fraudulent elections, for the next thirty-five years. During this period he established the basis for Mexico's subsequent development: eliminating obstacles to the creation of a national market, opening Mexico to investment by foreign capital, and consolidating the Mexican state through the centralization of power under the control of the national government. The cost of this process was an accentuated repression of the peasantry, which bore the brunt of new forms of exploitation added to existing ones, and the loss of control over vital sectors of the economy to foreign interests.

THE PORFIRIATO

The creation of the national market was facilitated by the suppression of sub-national state and municipal tariffs, which had inhibited the free circulation of commodities, and through the elimination of physical barriers to integration by the extension of the railroad system. Both processes had the effect of increasing the political power of the federal government, centralizing financial control, and facilitating the movement of administrative personnel and troops to various parts of the country. The extension of the railroads also helped to accelerate the conversion of traditional estates in affected regions of Mexico to commercial agriculture, particularly in tropical products for export but also in products destined for internal consumption (such as sugar) and industries (such as cotton for the textile industry). For similar reasons, it was a factor in the development of mining, chiefly for export, and manufacturing, oriented to internal markets. The expansion of industry was accompanied by the development of a banking and financial system, and the growth of mining centers (particularly in the northern and north central states) also stimulated commerce.

The elimination of barriers to the national market also opened Mexico to the world market, as was evident in the growth of foreign trade: between 1877 and 1911, Mexican exports increased 700 percent from 40.5 million pesos to 288 million, and imports by over 400 percent from 49 million to 214 million. It also resulted in a change in the structure of trade: precious metals which had accounted for 65 percent of Mexico's exports in 1877 accounted for only 50 percent in 1911, and copper, henequen, rubber, coffee, and petroleum had become increasingly important. Between 1877 and 1911, the proportion of consumer goods to total imports was reduced from 75 percent to 43 percent, reflecting the increased imports of primary materials, machinery and other capital goods for railroads, mining, and manufacturing.

Díaz also opened Mexico to foreign capital at a time when the capital of the industrial countries was seeking new investment outlets abroad. Given Mexico's scarce resources, Díaz was convinced that foreign capital was necessary for Mexico's development. United States companies, with British and U.S. capital, built the railroads, taking advantage of generous concessions provided by Díaz to Mexico's mining resources; the railroad lines (often extensions of U.S. lines) provided outlets from mining areas to U.S. markets and principal ports. By the end of the Porfiriato, mineral resources, the main source of export earnings, were largely foreign controlled. Electrical utilities and communications systems were also built and owned by foreign companies, and by the first decade of the twentieth century U.S. and British interests were competing for domination of Mexico's newly discovered petroleum reserves. Commercial agricultural production was in many cases foreign controlled, either through direct ownership of land or through control of finance and marketing, and large tracts of vacant public land fell into foreign hands through the government policy of giving land surveyed to surveying companies or selling it at low prices. Between 1883 and 1892 approximately one-fifth of Mexico's land was turned over to surveying companies, and beginning in 1894 public lands were awarded to political favorites. In the western state of Sinaloa, U.S. firms held 75 percent of the irrigable land used for sugar, cotton, and fresh vegetable production.

Apart from increased foreign control of important sectors of the economy, the Porfiriato was characterized by growing commercial dependence on the U.S., which absorbed much of Mexico's increase in trade. In 1872 the U.S. took 36 percent of Mexico's exports and provided 26 percent of its imports; during the last decade of the Porfiriato (1901-1911) imports from the U.S. fluctuated from 55 to 60 percent of the total, while exports to the U.S. ranged between 65 and 75 percent, over half of these mineral products.[1]

As indicated above, the abolition of regional tariffs eliminated the major source of economic and therefore political power of regional government authorities, and the extension of the railway system facilitated military control of the country. Foreign loans and investments further multiplied the resources of the national government in comparison with those of state and local governments, with the national government becoming the principal intermediary between foreign capital and local interests. The national government maintained close relations with the major landowners, merchants, and industrialists at the state level, gen-

[1] Sources on the Porfiriato include Coatsworth, 1975; Leal, 1974; Katz, 1974; Rosenzweig, 1965a, 1965b, and 1965c; Cockcroft, 1972; and Wolf, 1973. In addition to these, information on foreign trade and investment may be found in Coello Salazar, 1965; Thiessen, 1972, Wright, 1971; and the Council on Foreign Relations, 1931.

erally negotiating with these groups prior to designating candidates for local office (Scott, 1959: 103).

Manufacturing industry benefited from the establishment of a national market and was further promoted through specific government policies, such as tax concessions, at the local and national levels. Manufacturing developed from several origins: the refining and processing of primary materials, often on agricultural estates (flour mills, sugar refineries); capital from commerce (especially in Monterrey); and investments by European immigrants. The oldest manufacturing center was the city of Puebla, where textile manufacturing had been centered since the first half of the nineteenth century. Around 1890, many textile manufacturers sold their factories to French entrepreneurs, and by the end of the nineteenth century the textile industry was French controlled (Bazant, 1971: 288). Many of the new industrialists of the Porfiriato were French and Spanish businessmen who established light industries to stock their commercial firms, previously dependent on imports (D'Olwer, 1975: 1116). These immigrant groups established two different types of manufacturing enterprises: the first type, the family firm of the Spanish immigrants, was later to a large extent superseded by the second type, the economic group, consisting of a cluster of industrial, commercial, and financial enterprises with concentrated control and ownership, characteristic of the French industrial groups (Salazar, 1971: 46-49). Many Spanish industrialists subsequently became hacendados (owners of large agricultural estates), in some cases selling their industrial properties, and, with the exception of those who entered into alliances with other sectors, many subsequently experienced substantial losses due to the revolution. But some Spanish businessmen from this group succeeded in founding industries during the post-revolutionary years. The Cervecería Modelo (Modelo Brewery) was established in 1922 by a group of Spanish businessmen and by the 1930's had become one of the three major breweries of the country. The Cia. Manufacturera de Corcha Lata—later the Artículos Mundet para Embotelladeros—established by the Spaniard Arturo Mundet Carbo in 1918 is today one of the major Mexican soft drink bottling companies (Salazar, 1971: 34-35, 57-59, 62-64).

Among the French, of particular importance was the Barcelonnette group, settlers from the French province of Barcelonnette who came to Mexico in the late nineteenth and early twentieth centuries. In 1900, the French Banque de Paris et des Pays Bas and a consortium of Swiss banks, in collaboration with the Barcelonnette group, formed the Societé Financiere pour l'Industrie du Mexique, with the primary objective of making commercial, financial, and real estate operations in Mexico. Members of the Barcelonnette group, in some cases with financing from the Societé, established several of the major industrial firms of this period, including the Moctezuma brewery, the San Rafael Paper Company, and several textile firms.[2] Members of the Barcelonnette group also founded two of the major commercial houses still operating in Mexico—El Puerto de Liverpool and Palacio de Hierro (D'Olwer, 1965: 1123-1124).

Some of the most important Mexican-owned industries were concentrated in the northern city of Monterrey, which had benefited from its commercial links with the U.S. and with the seaport of Matamoras during much of the nineteenth century. Commercial capital was invested in cotton cultivation in La Laguna, import houses in Nuevo Laredo, mining properties in Nuevo León and neighboring states, and livestock in northern Nuevo León and the state of Coahuila—but most investment was in industry, especially after 1890 (Vizcaya Canales, 1969: 26, 30-31). Among the industrial firms established in the next several years, two were to have particular importance for the subsequent development of Monterrey: the Fundidora de Fierro y Acero de Monterrey (Iron and Steel Foundry of Monterrey, or Fundidora Monterrey), established in 1900 by an international group (Vicente Ferrara of Italy, Leon Signoret of France, Eugene Kelly of the United States, and Antonio Basagoiti of Spain), with capital from commerce and mining; and Cervecería Cuauhtémoc (Cuauhtémoc brewery), established in 1891 by members of the Sada and the Garza Sada families, which subsequently gave birth to a broad range of industries, establishing its

---

[2] In 1935, the holdings of the Societé Financiere included: Cervecería Moctezuma (Moctezuma brewery, established by a German group in 1896 but later becoming the property of the French Souberbie brothers); the Fábrica Nacional de Malta (an affiliate of Moctezuma); Cia. de Fábricas de Papel de San Rafael Anexas (established in 1894 by Juan Ebrard, José Spitalier, and Mexicans Tomás Braniff and Fernando Pimental y Fagoaga); and the CIDOSA complex, consisting of the Cia. Industrial de Orizaba, S.A. (CIDOSA), a textile firm in Rio Blanco, Veracruz, established in 1889 by Enrique Tron, Juan B. Ebrard, and Eugenio Roux; the Fábrica de Tejidos de Lana San Idelfonso established in 1895 by Ebrard, Honorato Reinaud, and Ernesto Pugibet; and the Cia. Industrial Veracruz, established by Reinuad, Eugenio Caire, and Joaquín Manuel in 1896, as well as other textile firms (Salazar, 1971: 38-39).

founders as a virtual dynasty in Mexican business (see Appendix B).

The accelerated pace of economic development during the Porfiriato resulted in the economic and political domination of a small clique which included major officials of the Díaz government (particularly the *cientificos*, who promoted development on the basis of foreign capital and foreign settlement), foreign interests, and national (and immigrant) groups, often linked to both. At this level, boundaries between the economic and political sphere, between national and foreign interests, and between various economic sectors (industry, agriculture, mining, commerce) tended to be muted. Government officials and political favorites were shareholders and directors of major banks and industries, or were given titles to large tracts of land. National businessmen were partners or representatives of foreign firms in Mexico (e.g., Olegario Molina, who controlled the Yucatán sisal market on behalf of International Harvester) or lawyers for foreign firms negotiating for government concessions; or they benefited from collaboration with U.S. investors, as was the case of mining, agricultural, and industrial interests in San Luis Potosí (Wolf, 1973: 13-14; Cockcroft, 1972b: 45-59). In many cases domination by a small clique of economic interests was replicated at the regional level. Perhaps the most outstanding case was the Terrazas-Creel family, which in alliance with foreign entrepreneurs dominated the economy and politics of the state of Chihuahua (Wasserman, 1980: 16-18). The dominant families of San Luis Potosí were also characterized by the breadth of their economic (and political) interests; many families had holdings in mining and agriculture and in some cases commerce and industry, and often had held top political offices within the state (Cockcroft, 1972: 59-60). Inter-sectoral links are also evident in the investment of commercial capital in industry by the Barcelonnette group and the Garza Sada family. Perhaps the best example of these linkages on the national level is José Limantour, Finance Minister under Díaz, who was shareholder and director of the two major private banks, the Banco de Londres and the Banco Nacional de México, both controlled by foreign capital; his brother, Julio Limantour, participated in various companies of the Barcelonnette group as well as the Societé Financiere (Lobato López, 1945: 218; Keremitsis, 1973: 131-132).

These relationships are also evident in the development of the banking system. The banks, controlled by foreign capital and serving the dominant interests in mining, commerce, and agriculture, flourished during the Porfiriato and became symbols of Porfirian privilege. As indicated above, Finance Minister Limantour had interests in two of the most important banks of this period (the only two to survive the revolution and become major banking institutions in post-revolutionary Mexico). The Banco Nacional de México (BNM) was formed in 1884 through the fusion of two existing banks created with French and Spanish capital; it held a privileged position as banker of the government and intermediary between the state and foreign financial resources. By 1911 it had a capital of 32 million pesos of which 22.5 million (70.3 percent) belonged to French shareholders, chiefly the Banque de Paris et des Pays Bas, and major decisions of the bank were referred to its junta in Paris. The remaining 29 percent was apparently held by Mexican, Spanish, German, and North American shareholders (D'Olwer, 1965: 1055-1077). A substantial proportion of the shares of the Banco de Londres, initially established with British and some Mexican capital in 1864, also came under French control. In 1905, the capital of the Banco de Londres was increased from 15 million to 21 million, with the Banque de Paris taking an important part, and at the end of the Porfiriato over 45 percent of the capital of the Banco de Londres was French (D'Olwer, 1965: 1057). The Banco de Londres also had ties with Mexican industrialists such as Tomás Braniff as well as the Barcelonnette group (linked to the Banque de Paris through the Societé Financiere) and with the new industrial groups in Monterrey.

The Banco Central Mexicano, established as a clearing house for regional banks, also linked members of the government intelligentsia and Mexican industrial groups with important regional interests: in 1904 its board included Joaquín D. Casasus, of the official financial sector, Enrique Creel, from the dominant Terrazas-Creel family of Chihuahua, and Francisco Madero, a representative of mining, financial, and landowning interests in Coahuila.[3] Its manager was Fernando Pimental y Fagoaga, who with

[3] Foreign capital was also dominant in the Banco Central Mexicano, with half its initial capital of 6 billion pesos provided by the Deutsche Bank and the Casa Blechroeder of Germany and by J. P. Morgan of New York. When the capital of the Banco Central was increased to 21 million, the Banque de L'Union Parisienne participated, and at the end of the Porfiriato, French groups held 60 percent of its total capital (18 million of 30 million); two million of the total was North American and one million German (D'Olwer, 1965: 1058).

Tomás Braniff had collaborated with members of the Barcelonnette group in the establishment of several industries and had served on various government commissions to study and draw up legislation on banking and monetary matters. The state banks were supported by regional, political, and economic interests—henequen planters in Yucatán; mining interests in Chihuahua, Zacatecas, and Durango; industrialists and commercial interests of Nuevo León—in some cases linked with financial and official circles of Mexico City and/or foreign investors or merchants, such as U.S. mining interests in Chihuahua (Espinoza Porset, 1954: 9-10; Rosenzweig, 1965b: 451).

Private banking interests collaborated with the government in the development of banking legislation. Banks were entitled to issue their own banknotes, though under certain restrictions, e.g., only the notes of the Banco Nacional and the Banco de Londres were acceptable at the national level, and only those of the Banco Nacional were acceptable for tax payments. Government regulation of banking was weak (as indicated by the fact that the government-appointed interventor for the Banco Refaccionario de Campeche was the brother of the bank's major shareholder), and government intervention in the banking system seems to have been oriented primarily to providing conditions for their general development and for negotiating conflicts among different banks.[4] Access to credit tended to be reserved to foreign interests and to members of the national and regional oligarchies; loans to smaller interests were limited on the grounds that their costs would make them unprofitable (Rosenzweig, 1965c: 847-848, 854).

In short, despite the importance of landowning and the growth of commercial agriculture, to the extent that a dominant class fraction was emerging in Porfirian Mexico it seems to have been based

---

[4] These tended to be quite frequent, due to the privileges enjoyed by the national banks relative to the regional banks and by the Banco Nacional relative to all the rest. When the Banco Nacional was first established, the government agreed not to authorize any new issue banks and to restrict those which already existed; protests by the latter, especially the Banco de Londres, resulted in a withdrawal of this privilege. But the Banco Nacional continued to enjoy certain prerogatives over other banks, resulting in protests when these privileges were allegedly abused. Regional banks were also disadvantaged by the fact that their banknotes could be accepted only in their respective states, a problem which was resolved with the establishment of the Banco Central Mexicano as a clearing house for banknotes from banks of different states (Rosenzweig, 1965c: 806-807; Lobato López, 1945: 216 f).

on groups and families whose interests spanned several sectors—manufacturing, commerce, finance, as well as, in some cases, landowning and mining. These groups were linked to the Porfirian state bureaucracy and in some cases to specific foreign interests.

Modernization of Mexican society on the basis of integration in the world market and foreign control of vital sectors of the economy introduced new contradictions and sharpened existing ones. While foreign capital multiplied the resources of the national government and facilitated the centralization of power, it limited the government's control over these resources and thus its ability to direct economic development. Díaz himself attempted to modify the dependent economic structure through such measures as partial nationalization of the railroads, and to offset the increasing preponderance of U.S. interests by encouraging European investment, e.g., concessions given to British petroleum interests to balance those of the U.S. (Coatsworth, 1975: 207, 226-277). But, aside from incurring a massive railroad debt and antagonizing affected U.S. interests, these measures seem to have been of limited effectiveness.

More important, the favoritism shown by Díaz to foreign interests antagonized Mexican commercial landowners, ranchowners, mineowners, and small farmers, especially in northern Mexico, whose expansion was blocked or who were in some cases displaced by American and other foreign interests supported by the government. In manufacturing, large firms, especially those linked to financial institutions, enjoyed a definite advantage over smaller, isolated companies lacking such connections, which were often unable to obtain credit. Problems also developed as a consequence of the limited growth of markets for industrial products, reflecting the low wage scales of urban workers and the exclusion of the peasantry (over 70 percent of the population) from the market economy; this was an added factor in the frustration of small and medium industrialists and in the replacement of some of their factories by larger concerns (Rosenzweig, 1965b: 451; Wolf, 1973: 22-23; García, 1901: 7-8; Leal, 1974: 113-114).

The extension of the railroads and the development of mining and manufacturing expanded the industrial proletariat—in railroads, mines, textile industry, petroleum—who were incorporated into a structure of production which was basically foreign-controlled (Leal, 1974: 105; Dunn, 1972: 66-67). But in 1910 the industrial working class was still small and dispersed. The non-rural labor force consisted of 906,000 workers in industry—most of them in artisan activities—and 762,000 in the service sector, particularly sales personnel and domestic servants. Although certain trades (such as building trades) benefited from economic expansion, industrialization had an adverse effect on artisans in other areas. For example, the number of artisan weavers declined from 41,000 in 1895 to 12,000 in 1910, while the number of textile workers increased from 19,000 to 32,000—a net loss of 16,000 occupations. In addition to dangerous and unhealthy working conditions, long working hours were the norm. In the 1870's workers in textile mills might work 12 to 14 hours a day (Anderson, 1976: 47-53).

Since the policy of the Díaz government was to maximize conditions for private capital accumulation, efforts at labor organization and mobilization often met with repression or efforts to coopt labor leadership, especially in the 1880's and 1890's. There were some 250 strikes during the Porfiriato, but although in isolated cases state government officials or local politicians supported workers on certain issues, in general the workers confronted the combined power of capital and the state (Rivera Marín, 1961: 225). A series of economic crises between 1900 and 1910 resulted in a revival of the labor movement and in important strikes, especially among the railroad, mine, and textile workers, for improved working conditions and against favoritism shown to U.S. workers. These were crushed by owners and/or government forces, but provided an indication of the level of dissatisfaction and mobilization among the certain groups of Mexican workers at that time (Gilly, 1975: 21, 25; Leal, 1974: 114-121).

The most significant changes were occurring in the countryside, which contained 75 percent of the Mexican population. The expanded production of commercial crops—henequen for sisal in Yucatán, sugar in the southern state of Morelos and the western states of Veracruz, Tamaulipas and Nuevo León, coffee in Veracruz and Chiapas, cotton in the Laguna area of the northwest (Coahuila and Durango) and the region of Mexicali, Baja California; beef, wheat, and export vegetables in the north—resulted in the introduction of new structures of production coexisting with the traditional patterns still dominant in the haciendas of the central mesa. The traditional hacienda production—chiefly of wheat and maize—was oriented to local markets and its work force generally consisted of *peones acasillados* (peons, a resident labor force

The Rio Blanco Strike: The Textile Workers Begin the Struggle. By Fernando Castro Pacheco.

tied to the estates through accumulated debts) and day laborers. Since there was a labor surplus, wages were low (and actually declined with the Porfiriato), further discouraging mechanization. During this period the haciendas continued to expand at the expense of peasant communities which had been divided under the reform (Katz, 1974: 24 f).

The rapid development of commercial production in the tropical lowlands of the southeast resulted in a plantation economy entailing heavy exploitation of the labor force, including local labor (e.g., an estimated one-third to one-half of the Mayan population who were recruited to work on the henequen estates of Yucatán) supplemented by contract labor, including Koreans and Chinese, Yaquis (Indians of northwest Mexico who had resisted conquest until finally defeated by Díaz in 1908, when they were sent to work on the plantations), political dissenters, unemployed workers, and expropriated peasants (Katz, 1974: 15-16). Because of this system of neo-slavery, supported by the government through the rural police force, labor was cheap and mechanization was limited to the transformation of raw materials; there was practically no effort to use machines for planting and harvesting. In southern Morelos, already characterized by intensive land use, the expansion of sugar cane production encroached upon remaining village communities, resulting in a drastic increase in the rate of expropriation of peasant owners. The process of hacienda encroachment on village lands and minifundia was accelerated in general in those regions affected by the expansion of the railway system and the access it provided to new markets (Leal and Huacuja, 1977: 22). In some cases, a three-tiered system of domination evolved, as in Yucatán, where the majority of estate owners were heavily in debt to International Harvester (or to its commercial intermediaries), which controlled the sale of sisal to U.S. markets, and in the cotton-growing regions of Laguna, where many of the plantations were owned by foreign companies but rented to Mexican landlords and worked by Mexican *peones acasillados* and migrants (Wolf, 1973: 41; Senior, 1958: 49, 56-61).

The north was also affected by a sharp increase in agricultural demand as a result of the opening of new mining centers, the development of the American southwest, and the establishment of railroad lines into Mexico, which opened this market to Mexican cotton and livestock as well as to industrial metals. But, in contrast to the central mesa, the northern states were sparsely populated;

labor shortages on the large agricultural and livestock estates resulted in high wages and relatively better working conditions; and a different type of labor force emerged—free and relatively mobile, which shifted between work on cattle ranches, in the mines, on the railroads, and as seasonal labor on the smaller farms (Katz, 1974: 31-34). But the relative advantages enjoyed by these groups ended with the droughts of 1907 and 1908 and the U.S. depression of 1907, which resulted in a drop in mineral prices and investment, closing of mines, and widespread unemployment (Wasserman, 1980: 15, 24-25).

The elimination of inefficient local producers no longer protected by high transport costs and regional tariffs, the takeover of former Indian community lands by haciendas and commercial estates, the grants or sale of large tracts of public land to surveying companies and to foreign contractors, accelerated the process of land concentration. At the end of the Porfiriato, the bulk of the land was concentrated in a small number of vast estates of various types, estimated to number approximately 8,245 (but landownership was in fact more concentrated since a given family might own more than one estate). In Morelos, over 25 percent of the land, and almost all of the irrigated land, was controlled by 34 estates owned by 17 planters (Womack, 1968: 391-392). In 1910, some 8 individuals held 22.5 million hectares—one-eighth of the total land area of Mexico (Eckstein, 1966: 24). There was also a rural middle class consisting of proprietors of some 48,000 ranches of various sizes, chiefly in the north. But an estimated 90 to 95 percent of the rural population was landless, consisting of peons and day laborers on the haciendas and commercial estates, contract labor in the southeast, sharecroppers and migrant workers in the north (Wolf, 1973: 18; Simpson, 1937: 31-32).

There were frequent revolts by Indian communities, peasant villagers, and even peons during the Porfiriato,[5] although where traditional forms of exploitation prevailed, as in the haciendas of the

[5] As indicated by Jean Meyer, these uprisings had different and complex causes, among them efforts to obtain land usurped by the government or by new landowners, revolts against various abuses committed against indigenous groups, and efforts to form confederations of Indians, notably of the Yaqui and Mayo Indians in Sonora, to recover lands. On at least one occasion, uprisings were directed against anti-clerical laws of the liberal government. In several cases, revolts against landowners, caciques, and government officials were led by village priests (J. Meyer, 1973: 18-25).

central valley, relatively untouched by capitalist expansion, and where the rural work force had been fragmented and isolated as in the Yucatán peninsula, peasant mobilization was limited even during the revolution itself (Goldfrank, 1978: 154–155; Joseph, 1980: 52–53). During the Porfiriato, individual rebellions were for the most part localized, and eventually repressed. But while the Mexican revolution had its beginnings in a political insurrection, launched in 1910 in the name of electoral democracy, it was through the revolt of the rural masses that it achieved its character as an agrarian revolution.

THE REVOLUTION

Forces in Conflict. Disregard by Díaz and his associates of the 1857 constitutional provisions regarding effective suffrage as well as other democratic principles became the issue which mobilized the divergent groups opposed to Díaz. This opposition coalesced around two groups. The first was led by Francisco Madero, Luis Cabrera, and other representatives of regional landowners, industrialists, and bankers who opposed the economic and political domination of certain individuals and families at the local level and the support of these groups by Díaz. The second consisted of liberal groups— intellectuals and journalists, including Ricardo Flores Magón and Antonio Díaz Soto y Gama, among others, who began to agitate for goals of nineteenth-century liberalism: democracy, anti-clericalism, and free enterprise. Although initially addressed to the upper and middle classes, the liberalism of the latter group gradually evolved to a more radical and anarchist position and its adherents broadened their orientation to include demands of peasants and workers. They established the Liberal party and in 1906 issued a program which constituted the most articulate statement to that time of what would become some of the major goals of the revolution—among them completely secular education, compulsory to age 14; the elimination of Church schools and the nationalization of its lands, confiscation of unproductive land, and minimum land grants to those who work it; and, for workers, an eight-hour day, minimum wage, hygienic and safe working conditions, indemnity for accidents on the job, and other benefits (Leal, 1974: 161-162; Cockcroft, 1968: 4-5, 239-243). The Liberal party was linked to the IWW and to anarchist groups in Mexico and directed the most important strike movements of the last decade of the Porfiriato, including a mineworkers strike at Cananea (1906), a strike of textile workers in Rio Blanco (1906-1907), and various railroad workers' strikes.

Apart from recognized groups, a probably crucial role in articulating opposition to the Díaz regime was played by intellectual leaders of the rural areas and small towns. These were often schoolteachers, lawyers, and even priests who were members of their communities and at the same time specifically endowed with the capabilities to organize and represent them and articulate their grievances. During the revolution itself, many of them helped to organize local revolts and to provide an ideological reconciliation of revolutionary goals and popular symbols (Knight, 1981).

A promise made by Díaz in 1908 to step down from office in 1910 resulted in the formation of the Anti-Reelectionist Party, which ran Francisco Madero as presidential candidate with the slogan: "Effective suffrage, no re-election." But Madero, a popular candidate, was jailed by Díaz before the elections could take place. He escaped, fled to the United States, and subsequently issued the Plan of San Luis Potosí, calling upon Mexican citizens to take up arms and to end the government of *cientificos* who were squandering the nation's wealth (Wilkie and Michaels, 1969: 37-39). A promise to return lands unjustly usurped from small property holders to their former owners attracted the support of peasant guerrillas in the state of Morelos under the leadership of Emiliano Zapata, who, after years of unsuccessful efforts to reclaim their usurped community lands by legal means, had finally resorted to arms (Womack, 1968: 70). Madero's revolt was the signal for a series of uprisings in key states, which defeated the federal troops, resulting in Díaz's resignation in May 1911 and thus ending the first phase of the revolution.

Elections were subsequently held which Madero easily won. But assuming that a democratic government in itself constituted the goal of his revolt, Madero left the existing state apparatus intact, including the military, and failed to fully address himself to Mexico's social and economic problems. Labor repression continued, with Madero tending to support business in conflicts with labor, although a Labor Department was established and its first director, Antonio Ramos Pedreza, made some effort to improve working conditions in order to control and channel the labor movement (Ruíz, 1976: 188, 193-194). Also, under the more open conditions of the Madero regime new labor organizations were formed, including the anarcho-syndicalist Casa del Obrero Mundial, established in 1912 by workers, artisans, and intellectuals of Mexico City under the influence of Spanish anarchists and the Flores Magón brothers.

But pressures from southern landowners and federal army officers convinced Madero to delay implementation of his promise to restore lands illegally usurped from peasant villagers. He rejected proposals by advisors such as Luis Cabrera for a limited agrarian reform which would provide communal lands for the peasants by purchasing part of the haciendas in order to eliminate causes of unrest. Failure to restore peasant lands turned Zapata and his followers against the Madero government, and the Zapata forces revolted in November 1911. Their program, the Plan de Ayala, called for the overthrow of Madero and went beyond the previous demands of the peasant armies, proposing not only the restoration of lands usurped from the communities but also expropriation of one-third of the large landholdings for distribution to landless rural workers. While the movement of Zapata, centered in Morelos, was the most cohesive, peasant revolts in other states—Chihuahua, Durango, Hidalgo, Jalisco, Guerrero—also resulted in takeovers of land previously expropriated by the haciendas (Womack, 1968: 402-403; Gilly, 1975: 47, 81-83).

But in February 1913 Madero was ousted in a counter-revolutionary attack led by Victoriano Huerta, a Porfirian general whom Madero had allowed to keep his military command and had in fact sent against the Zapata forces in Morelos. With the compliance of U.S. Ambassador Henry Lane Wilson (but apparently not that of the U.S. government), Huerta arrested Madero and his Vice-President Pino Suárez; he later had them assassinated, arrested the congress, and took over the government.[6] This action unified the diverse forces which had initially opposed Díaz and who now turned against the counter-revolutionary government of Huerta. In the north, the Constitutionalist army was formed under the leadership

[6] The U.S. Ambassador, Henry Lane Wilson, had opposed Madero from the beginning. Allegedly Madero turned down a request by Wilson to receive a subsidy from the Mexican government to supplement his allowance as U.S. ambassador. Wilson was deeply implicated in the plot by Huerta to remove Madero. He himself admits to having been forewarned, and made no effort to warn Madero of the plot. Following the overthrow Wilson was asked by various individuals and organizations—including the wife and sister of Madero—to intervene to save Madero's life, but to no avail.

of Venustiano Carranza, landowner from Coahuila, with three divisions: that of the northeast, under Pablo González; that of the northwest, under Alvaro Obregón, a small landowner from the state of Sonora; and the division of the north centered in the state of Chihuahua, under the command of Francisco (Pancho) Villa. The Constitutionalist army was formed chiefly of peasants and rural workers, but, with the exception of the northern division, most of its leadership was drawn from the provincial petty bourgeoisie—teachers, municipal employees, farmers, and ranchowners. Villa's division attracted members of the mobile proletariat of mineworkers, ranch and agricultural workers, and railroad workers, the last having a particularly important role in placing trains and railroads at the disposition of the revolutionary forces. In the south guerrilla forces formed by peasants of the southern states and estate workers of the haciendas of the central mesa united under the leadership of Zapata, and also fought against the Huerta government although they never became part of the Constitutionalist army.

Huerta was supported by British interests as well as by the dominant Porfirian groups of landowners, bankers and large industrialists, and the clergy. However, members of the regional bourgeoisie who had supported Madero in opposition to the Díaz government now supported Carranza, and the same was true of certain U.S. interests, especially Standard Oil, due to opposition to the British oil interests in Mexico (Grieb, 1971: 61).

The revolutionary armies and divisions maintained an uneasy alliance until the defeat of Huerta in 1914, but victory over a common enemy ended their unity, and the third and last phase of the revolution was in fact a civil war between the Constitutionalist army under Carranza and Obregón and the forces of Zapata and Villa who had broken with Carranza. In this struggle, the Constitutionalist generals sought to win popular support through extensive reforms in those areas which fell under their control and through the promulgation of an agrarian reform law (Córdova, 1973: 264; Gilly, 1975: 177). They also succeeded in obtaining working-class support through an agreement with the workers of the Casa del Obrero Mundial, who agreed to fight with the Constitutionalist army in return for concessions to labor.[7] This alliance was significant because it indicated the failure of the urban proletariat and

[7] This proposal was in fact rejected by a substantial proportion of the workers and agreement was reached only when the leadership met in secret (Gilly, 1975: 183-185). The working class recruits were designated the "Red Battalions."

the peasantry to achieve an alliance which might have been able to develop a cohesive national program and to effectively confront the problem of the state. The principles of Zapata's Plan de Ayala (which Villa also accepted) were limited to the goals of the expropriated peasantry and the landless rural workers. The armies of Villa and especially Zapata could, and did, transform the countryside, taking over haciendas and distributing land. Although in the case of Villa's armies the result was generally a reconstitution of the hacienda under the ownership of Villa's generals, the south, and especially Morelos, was characterized by an effective restructuring of the agricultural sector with the land turned over to peasant communities and experimentation with new forms of democratic government.

But the limitations of a peasant revolution had already become evident in 1914 when the armies of Villa and Zapata gained control of the capital as well as of two-thirds of Mexico's territory. Unable to follow up their military domination with a national program, they lost political control of the revolution long before their eventual military defeat by the Constitutionalist army.[8] The military struggle continued for several years (until the assassination of Zapata in 1919 and the surrender of Villa in 1920); when it ended, over ten percent of the Mexican population (an estimated 1.5 to 2 million of a total population of 15 million) had lost their lives.

The Constitution of 1917 and the Formal State. By April 1916 the Constitutionalist forces were in sufficient control for Carranza to return to Mexico City, where he took power as first chief of the Constitutionalist army and provisional president and called a convention to draw up a constitution, which would legitimate his position. However, long-term divisions within the Constitutionalist forces became evident at the constitutional convention, where delegates divided into a liberal faction, generally consisting of followers of Carranza, and a radical group more closely identified with Obregón—the "Jacobins," including officers of the Constitutionalist army such as Francisco Múgica, who as provisional

[8] On the achievements and limitation of the Zapata forces, see Gilly, 1975. Zapata himself did eventually perceive the importance of an alliance between the urban proletariat and the peasantry. In a letter of February 14, 1918 he compared the Mexican revolution with the Russian revolution and emphasized the connection between the emancipation of the workers and the freedom of the peasant (Gilly, 1975: 285-287). But by this time the constitutionalists were in political control.

governors in states controlled by the Constitutionalists had carried out substantial reforms (Cumberland, 1972: 357-359).[9]

On December 1, 1916 Carranza presented the assembled delegates with a draft constitution, modeled very closely on the constitution of 1857, which incorporated the liberal principle of a state not compromised with any sector of society. But it departed from the constitution of 1857, which provided for legislative supremacy, in calling for a strong executive, with limited powers to the legislature, an expanded executive role in proposing laws and legislating by decree, and direct presidential elections (Goodspeed, 1955: 47; Córdova, 1973: 26-28).

However, the final document also reflected the input of the Obregonistas under the leadership of Gen. Múgica, as well as certain principles of the Liberal party platform of 1906. While the Carranza draft had provided for a strong executive but a liberal state, the constitution of 1917 called for a strong interventionist state, expanding its functions to encompass measures to secure national sovereignty over natural resources, the access of peasant communities to land, and the rights of labor.

Its most important provisions included Article 3, prohibiting religious organizations from establishing or directing primary schools and giving the state responsibility for education; Article 27, which vested the nation with the inalienable ownership of natural resources, provided for the expropriation of private property in the public interest and, specifically, the division of landed properties and their distribution to population centers having no land or insufficient holdings, prohibited religious institutions from acquiring land, and provided that foreigners must bind themselves not to invoke the protection of their governments before being given concessions for the exploitation of resources and waters; Article 28, which prohibited the formation of monopolies; and Article 123, a bill of labor rights (called "the most enlightened state-

---

[9] Following the defeat of Huerta, the Obregonistas sought—unsuccessfully—to form an alliance with Villa and Zapata. For an analysis of this effort, see Gilly (1975: 126-137). The army of Villa suffered a decisive defeat at the end of 1915, although Villa and his followers continued to fight in northern Mexico for several years. Zapata's forces had in the meantime withdrawn to the state of Morelos where the former state apparatus had been destroyed, the hacienda lands expropriated and distributed to the peasants, and a democratic government instituted based on elections to representative municipal organizations. Following the defeat of Villa, the constitutionalist forces launched an attack against Morelos, resulting in the defeat of the Zapatistas and the assassination of Zapata in 1919.

ment of labor protective principles in the world to that date"), which provided for the eight-hour work day and a day of rest, minimum wage, and the right to organize and strike (Niemeyer, 1974: 62-165).

According to the constitution, the state was the representative of the revolutionary classes, and would implement their goals and shape the reconstruction of Mexican society. The state would have an explicitly revolutionary and anti-imperialist function—the elimination of previously dominant institutions and structures, including the prevailing land tenure structure and foreign control of natural resources. Anti-monopoly provisions, establishment of national sovereignty over subsoil rights, as well as Article 123, outlining labor rights, were in large part directed against foreign interests. The state also had an integrative role: to eradicate the influence of the Church, especially by taking over its function of education, i.e., the formation of a national consciousness.[10] But the constitution was not anti-capitalist; the elimination of previous institutions would establish the necessary conditions for capitalist production. At the same time the state was given basic responsibility for economic growth and retained sufficient autonomy to shape the new order, and specifically to intervene on behalf of the weaker classes and subordinate groups (Alejo, 1974: 58). In the case of labor and capital, it became the arbiter of class conflict, a conception explicit in the introduction to Article 123 presented to the constitutional convention, which emphasized the interventionist and protective role of the state in defense of the working class due to the relative weakness of labor in confronting capital (Córdova, 1973: 234).

The constitution of 1917 is of interest in that it brought together the distinct goals of different revolutionary groups and gave the state the function of implementing them. According to the constitution, the state was implicitly autonomous, not in the sense that classes were not recognized, but in that the state was conceived to be above classes and capable of exercising its authority

[10] The ideology of the Mexican revolution, incorporated in its constitution, had an impact on nationalist movements elsewhere in Latin America. It became an important element in the ideology of APRA, whose founder, Victor Haya de la Torre, was exiled in Mexico during the 1920's and was strongly influenced by the Mexican revolution (Jiménez Ricárdez, 1978: 96). See Hodges and Gandy (1979) for a discussion of the influence of the Mexican revolution on APRA and other revolutionary movements in Latin America.

independently of their influence. But conditions in post-revolutionary Mexico prevented the strong interventionist state formally legitimated in the constitution from being implemented in practice.

The Government of Carranza: Barriers to State Formation. Although the Constitutionalist army continued to struggle against the forces of Villa and Zapata until 1920, and the following decade was punctuated by military revolts against the central government, the promulgation of the constitution of 1917 and the subsequent election of Carranza as president may be regarded as the end of the revolution itself and the beginning of a long process of institutionalization and legitimation of the post-revolutionary Mexican state.

The revolution had eliminated the Porfirian state bureaucracy and enabled the Constitutionalist army, once it had established its hegemony over the armies of Villa and Zapata, to establish itself as the new state. But several constraints limited the options available to the state in the early post-revolutionary years. The first was the absence of an economic base. Railroads, mining infrastructure, and sugar mills had been destroyed by the revolution. The end of armed conflict also found Mexico financially bankrupt and heavily indebted to the creditor nations of Europe and the U.S. (including debts which the post-revolutionary governments inherited from the Porfiriato as well as those arising from the revolution itself). The Mexican state's need for foreign exchange in turn constituted an important lever of power for foreign capital, particularly the United States, in dealing with Mexico, the second constraint on the power of the Mexican state. While the revolution had weakened the national owning classes, foreign capital continued to control key enterprises, and the new government was confronted with the increased power of U.S. capital, which had emerged from the first world war stronger than ever and anxious to assert its hegemony with respect to foreign capital in Latin America.

A third constraint on the power of the state was the mobilized peasantry, and to a lesser extent the working class. While the pressures exercised by foreign capital dated from the Porfiriato, the strength of the peasantry and urban and rural workers derived from the revolution itself. Unable to exercise political power on their own behalf, they nonetheless had to be taken into account by those who attempted or claimed to exercise this control in the name of all sectors of the nation.

A final constraint was the fragmentation of the revolutionary leadership, which constituted itself as the new Mexican state. Various regions of the country were under the control of revolutionary generals who commanded their own personal armies, and the leaders who controlled the federal government could be said to be only the "first among equals." In certain respects post-revolutionary Mexico resembled the politically and economically fragmented Mexico of the pre-Díaz epoch, with generals establishing virtual fiefdoms in areas under their control—ever reinstating local taxes and tariff barriers which had been eliminated under the Porfirian regime (Bartra, 1975: 17).

Thus while the constitution of 1917 and the subsequent election of Carranza as president gave formal legitimacy to the authority of the federal government, this authority had to be consolidated in practice. The leadership of the new state-in-formation also had to establish the basis for the new economic order (and in the process its own economic base), and to construct alliances which would enable it to consolidate its control over the considerably weakened Porfirian bourgeoisie and to negotiate with foreign capital (Leal, 1975a: 50-53; Córdova, 1973: 35-37). This process, and the structures which eventually emerged, were shaped by the struggle of mobilized popular groups demanding that the promises of the revolution be met, and the attempts of the Porfirian groups to reassert their prerogatives—initially in opposition to the constitutionalist state, ultimately by penetrating it (Bartra, 1975; Labastida, 1972: 104-107).

The Carranza government moved decisively against the financial groups, which had been closely identified with the governments of Díaz and Huerta, placing the previous issue banks under the authority of the state. Carranza also sought to establish a base among private industry and commerce to counter the Porfirian interests and to incorporate these sectors into the work of national reconstruction. He established the Ministry of Industry and Commerce, and in 1917 its Secretary, Alberto Pani, organized congresses of commerce and industry which established the bases for commercial and industrial chambers and confederations and the articulation of these organizations with the state (Shafer, 1973: 22; Puga Espinosa, 1975: 101-102; Torres Mejía, 1975: 5). Carranza also attempted to force foreign companies to renegotiate their concessions with the state, but foreign interests resisted these efforts, in part through the formation of regional and national organizations to defend their interests, in part through pressures on their respective governments to support their resistance, and in part through their ability to negotiate separately with military commanders who controlled the regions in which they operated.[11] The relative autonomy of these officers constituted a major obstacle to an integrated national policy well into the next decade.

In contrast to Madero, Carranza had recognized the necessity of destroying the Porfirian state and particularly the Porfirian army. But he failed to establish a social base for the new revolutionary state. He alienated much of the revolutionary leadership as well as urban workers and peasantry due to his failure to institute reforms. He broke his promise to the Casa del Obrero Mundial to institute labor reforms, which resulted in a general strike in Mexico City in July 1916; the leaders were imprisoned and the Carranza government issued a decree threatening the death penalty for those involved in planning or implementing strike movements in firms providing public services (Córdova, 1973: 195-198, 212-213, 463-464). The defeat and assassination of Zapata in 1919 and attempts to reverse the land reform in the state of Morelos antagonized the Zapatistas. Workers, followers of Zapata, and military groups desiring social reform—or antagonized by Carranza's efforts to reduce military expenditures—began to look to Alvaro Obregón for leadership. And Obregón, recognizing that a mass base would be necessary to confront obstacles to the creation of a national state, deliberately cultivated the support of these groups.

When Obregón announced his candidacy for the 1920 presidential election, he became a rallying point for those dissatisfied with the Carranza regime. Carranza chose a virtually unknown civilian, Ing. Ignacio Bonillas, to oppose Obregón in the election. After an unsuccessful attempt by Carranza to capture and possibly assassinate him, Obregón issued the Plan of Agua Prieta on April 23,

[11] Among the most important organizations formed during this period to represent foreign interests in Mexico were the Association of Petroleum Producers in Mexico (APPM), established in 1918, which maintained close contact with the Department of State until the expropriation in 1938, and the American Chamber of Commerce in Mexico, founded in 1917, which maintained contact with the U.S. government through the U.S. Consul General in Mexico. For a discussion of these and other pressure groups in post-revolutionary Mexico, see L. Meyer (1973) and Delli Sante (1979).

1920 calling for the overthrow of Carranza. Obregón was supported by most of the revolutionary generals, and Carranza was
forced to flee the capital; he was subsequently assassinated on May
21. On May 24, General Adolfo de la Huerta was named provisional president by congress, and subsequently elections were held
which Obregón won. While rebellions by leaders and factions of
the military continued for over a decade, that of Obregón was the
last successful rebellion against the central government, which now
concentrated its efforts on the consolidation of the Mexican state
and economic reconstruction.

Three ‖ **The State and Class Formation in Post-Revolutionary Mexico: 1920-1934**

 One of the hypothetical conditions facilitating state autonomy suggested in Chapter One is a revolution in which the dominant class is destroyed or considerably weakened and the mode of production itself may be threatened. At the same time, it was noted, the options of the new revolutionary state are historically constrained by the previous development of the productive forces and remnants of pre-revolutionary structures. Several of the constraints affecting the post-revolutionary Mexican state were noted in the last chapter. Here we are concerned with the efforts of those who controlled the state apparatus to operate within these constraints and how these efforts in turn helped to establish the options of subsequent governments.

The consolidation of the new Mexican state took place under the auspices of regional groups which came to power with the defeat and assassination of Carranza. Sometimes referred to as the Sonoran dynasty, they consisted of revolutionary officers from the northern state of Sonora, two of whom dominated Mexican politics for the next fourteen years: General Obregón, president from 1920 to 1924, and General Plutarco Elías Calles, president from 1924 to 1928. Obregón was elected in 1928 (after passage of a constitutional amendment permitting re-election, following an intervening period, for one more term) but was assassinated before he could take office. In the following six years there were three presidents: Emilio Portes Gil, interim president from 1928 to 1930; Pascual Ortiz Rubio, who was elected in 1930 and resigned under pressure from Calles in 1932; and General Abelardo Rodríguez, who completed the term of Ortiz Rubio between 1932 and 1934. However, General Calles continued to govern the country behind the scenes, and this period is generally known as the Maximato in honor of Calles' designation as the Jefe Máximo.

The era of the Sonoran dynasty can be divided into two phases. The initial policy orientation of the Sonoran group was in large part determined by its petty bourgeois origins as small farmers, schoolteachers, and state employees and envisioned a program of economic development based on small and medium property holders, in opposition to the monopoly privileges enjoyed by foreign and certain national groups during the Porfiriato. At the same time, this petty bourgeois conception did envision a natural progression from small owner to capitalist, a progression which was in fact epitomized in the career of Obregón as owner of a small property of 1.5 hectares which was ultimately expanded to include holdings of 3,500 hectares (Bartra, 1975: 15-16). At the same time, the state was still divided and economically weak, and the structures of domination of the pre-revolutionary period continued to exist although the dominant Porfirian classes and groups—traditional and commercial landowners, the commercial, financial and industrial bourgeoisie—had been considerably weakened. Most important, foreign capital continued to control major sectors of the economy. In its efforts to counter pressures from these groups, the government relied on an alliance with the working class and the peasantry and had to respond to their demands for improved working conditions and for land distribution. The concept of development based on small property holdings coincided with the ideas of certain exponents of the agrarian reform movement; during the 1920's land distribution programs focused upon the small holding, with the communal holding or ejido seen as a preliminary stage to prepare peasant villagers to become small farmers (Córdova, 1973: 339).[1] At the same time, the federal government also sought to control the labor and peasant movements through the formation or cooptation of labor unions and confederations, peasant leagues, and labor and agrarian parties.

By the end of 1926 the central government was relatively secure economically and politically and had begun to seek rapprochement with dominant groups and to abandon its former allies. Although petty bourgeois principles continued to prevail in policy statements, government actions were characterized by efforts to establish conditions for large-scale capitalist development, including guarantees for national and foreign capital. Here the causes behind this apparent policy shift will be examined in terms of the rela-

[1] The ejido consists of a form of land tenure based on the traditional communal holdings of the pre-Hispanic Indian villages (although the term is Spanish, referring to communally owned pastures and woodlands of the Spanish municipalities). Ownership is vested in the community, but the land may be farmed individually or collectively; in the former case it is distributed as individual or family plots among members of the community (Chevalier, 1963: 159).

tionship of the state with foreign capital, the domestic bourgeoisie, and the working class and peasantry. This examination will take into account questions raised earlier regarding the continuity between pre- and post-revolutionary Mexico as well as the broader question of the constraints limiting state autonomy in a post-revolutionary society.

THE STATE AND FOREIGN CAPITAL

The period of state formation in Mexico coincided with the growing hegemony of U.S. interests in Latin America and efforts by the U.S. government to push U.S. industrial exports. "The industries of the nation have expanded to such a point," exclaimed President Wilson in 1912, "that they will burst their jackets if they can't find a free outlet to the world" (cited in Mayer, 1973: 66). The first world war had accelerated the transformation of the U.S. from a debtor to a creditor nation, and was followed by a new interest in the opportunities provided by Latin America and other "backward" areas of the world for U.S. trade and investment (Hammond, 1919: 155-156; Kies, 1920: 145-148). As asserted by one observer: "Our ideal foreign policy is one that would give America the greatest degree of commercial independence and would compel the greatest dependence from the rest of the world" (Hammond, 1919: 153). But while the world war had forced a partial withdrawal of European interests in Latin America, and thus facilitated the expansion of U.S. trade, U.S. government officials feared a resurgence of European penetration in Latin America following the war. In the case of Mexico, this was accompanied by concern regarding safeguards to U.S. property, threatened by the revolutionary armies and ultimately by Article 27 of the constitution. U.S. government intervention in Mexico during the revolution itself had been constant, if not particularly consistent, in part due to confusion regarding the scope and complexity of the forces in conflict.[2]

---

[2] See Gilly, 1975: 203-206. U.S. policy toward the revolutionary conflict was dictated by concern for the extensive U.S. property in Mexico, and was oriented to avoiding or terminating the conflict as soon as possible and insuring the protection of U.S. property under the post-revolutionary governments. In 1914, President Woodrow Wilson sent a naval force to the port of Veracruz to block arms shipments to the counter-revolutionary government of Victoriano Huerta—an in-

Following the revolution, the critical financial situation of the
Mexican government constituted a lever for U.S. officials negotiating with Mexican officials regarding existing claims of U.S.
property owners due to loss or damage during the conflict as well
as future security for U.S. property in Mexico (Smith, 1963: 576,
578-579). An important element of U.S. pressure on the Mexican
government in the post-revolutionary decade was recognition or
non-recognition of the government—a crucial factor in that unsettled period since it determined whether the U.S. would aid the
government or the insurgents (e.g., through manipulation of arms
shipments to assist one or another party) in the event of a military
revolt (Stuart, 1938: 25). Nor was U.S. intervention limited to
pressures on the Mexican government; dependence of local firms
on imports from the United States constituted a powerful mechanism in influencing or manipulating their policies.[3]

One of the most effective instruments for U.S. financial pressure on Mexico during this period was the International Bankers
Committee, which was formed in 1918 under the leadership of
Thomas A. Lamont of J. P. Morgan and Company to represent
holders of Mexican bonds in the U.S. and Europe in negotiations
with the Mexican government. For the U.S. State Department, it
had several advantages. As a vehicle for loan negotiations with the
Mexican government, it would be in a position to promote safe-

tervention which antagonized all factions within the revolution. After Huerta's
defeat, the U.S. government attempted to reconcile the Constitutionalists and the
forces of Zapata and Villa and, when that failed, offered support to the latter since
the nationalist orientation of Carranza and the Constitutionalists was seen as a
threat to U.S. interests in Mexico. But when it became evident that the agrarian
reform of the peasant armies would affect U.S. properties as well as those of Mexicans, the U.S. government shifted its support to Carranza, cutting off arms supplies to Villa and Zapata. A second military intervention occurred in 1916, when,
following an incursion of the Villa forces into the U.S., where they attacked the
town of Columbus, the U.S. government sent General Pershing at the head of a
force of 12,000 men into Mexico against Villa (Womack, 1968: 211, 185; Gilly,
1975: 216; Cockcroft, 1979: 62-66).

[3] An example of the type of pressures exerted by the U.S. is an incident in
Monterrey during the First World War, where several employees of the steel foundry,
Fundidora Monterrey, were accused of participating in an anti-allies demonstration. The managing director of the Fundidora was summoned to the U.S. consulate in Monterrey, where he was advised to take whatever action would be expedient so that "it might not be necessary to bring the matter to the attention of the
Embassy and the State Department, which might have unpleasant consequences to
his firm, through the possible action of the War Trade Board" (Gracey, 1918).

guards to foreign property in Mexico as well as claims of foreign debtors. At the same time, it would oblige leading investment bankers of Europe to deal with an American-dominated committee informally under instructions of the U.S. government—an obvious advantage for establishing U.S. hegemony among foreign interests in Mexico (Smith, 1963: 579-581).

Following the defeat and assassination of Carranza, the United States government had refused recognition to the government of Obregón in the absence of guarantees to U.S. petroleum and mining companies. Petroleum production had accelerated during the revolutionary period; by the early 1920's Mexico was the second most important producer in the world and petroleum accounted for three-fourths of Mexico's exports. In 1921, Obregón doubled the tax on oil exports, to which the companies responded by stopping production, leaving 20,000 workers unemployed. The U.S. State Department supported the oil companies, and Obregón was forced to reduce this tax. In the meantime, the oil companies began to cut back production in Mexico, shifting to Venezuela. In a series of meetings between U.S. and Mexican government officials in 1923, an agreement was reached, although apparently never formalized, whereby the Mexican government affirmed that Article 27 would not be retroactive and set up a claims commission to deal with U.S. losses before and during the revolution, in return for which Washington recognized the Obregón government (Córdova, 1973: 304-305). This arrangement was followed by renewed interest in Mexican markets by U.S. exporters and investors (Wyeth, 1925).

But U.S.-Mexican relations again became tense in the first years of the Calles government. In December 1925, the Calles government passed the Alien Land Law and the Petroleum Law, both of which were seen as a threat to foreign, and specifically U.S., interests in Mexico. The Alien Land Law provided that foreigners could not own land within 50 kilometers of any border, and that aliens or foreign companies could not have majority interest in land development companies. The Petroleum Law required foreign corporations to apply for "confirmatory concessions" on pre-1917 holdings within one year; fifty-year concessions would be given for properties on which positive acts had been performed; and claims could be filed for 30-year concessions on undeveloped holdings (Smith, 1973: 231). The oil companies, backed by U.S. Ambassador to Mexico James Sheffield and U.S. Secretary of State

Frank Kellogg, challenged the petroleum legislation in the Mexican Supreme Court and instituted a campaign designed to force a confrontation—military if necessary—between the U.S. government and Mexican authorities.[4] During the first half of 1927, when this conflict had reached a critical point, Lamont, head of the International Bankers Committee, and other officers of J. P. Morgan, met regularly with representatives from Mexico, including Alberto Pani (Secretary of Finance until February 1927), Luis Montes de Oca, his successor, and Agustín Legorreta of the Banco Nacional de México (the major private bank in Mexico) and also arranged for meetings of these officials with members of the U.S. State Department and oil company officials, including Palmer Pierce of Standard Oil (Smith, 1973: 250, 256).

Negotiations of the New York bankers and Mexican officials with the State Department may have been instrumental in the decision, indicated in a statement of the U.S. Secretary of State to the oil companies on August 9, 1927, not to break relations with Mexico nor to consider armed intervention because of the oil question (Smith, 1973: 254). In the long run, they were undoubtedly effective in structuring the cordial relations between U.S. and Mexican financial and government authorities which persisted through the critical phase of Mexican nationalism in the 1930's. The crisis ended in 1927 when the Mexican Supreme Court decided in favor of the oil companies, declaring the 1925 legislation unconstitutional, and new legislation was passed which considerably softened the requirements of the 1925 Petroleum Law.[5] Cordial relations were confirmed with the replacement of Sheffield by Morgan banker Dwight Morrow as U.S. Ambassador to Mexico. Morrow saw his role as establishing Mexico's finances on a "sound basis" and exercised a strong influence on Calles and consequently on government policy.

By the end of the decade, government policy had shifted to one which would provide guarantees for modern sectors of the

[4] See Smith, 1973: 233-237 and Stuart, 1938: 166-168. A detailed history of the petroleum conflict during this period can be found in Lorenzo Meyer, *México y los Estados Unidos en el Conflicto Petrolero (1917-1942)* and Meyer, *Los Grupos de Presión Extranjeros en el México Revolucionario*.

[5] The legislation of December 1927 provided that unlimited confirmatory concessions would be given for all holdings on which positive acts (e.g., exploration) had been performed prior to May 1, 1917; owners or lessors of properties which had not had such positive acts would be given preferential consideration for 30-year concessions (Smith, 1973: 256).

bourgeoisie, including groups from the Porfiriato and foreign interests (Bartra, 1975: 18). Foreign companies already in Mexico expanded their operations: the foreign-owned railroad network and mining installations were reconstructed in the 1920's and the value of mineral production increased 14 percent in relation to its 1910 value. The electrical industry, which had suffered little physical damage but heavy financial loss due to non-payment by paralyzed mining companies and financially bankrupt municipalities during the conflict, initiated major expansion programs in the 1920's (National Chamber Foundation, n.d.: 17-18).

U.S. capital became increasingly dominant. Between 1923 and 1926, the American Foreign Power Company bought all major generators and transmissions facilities in Mexico outside of Mexico City, although electrical facilities in Mexico City remained in the hands of the British Mexican Light and Power Company. American capital accounted for approximately 80 percent of mineral production and 95 percent of refinery production in 1929 (Lewis and Achlotterbeck, 1938: 206). During the 1920's, Mexican exports to the United States averaged 65 to 85 percent of its total, chiefly in minerals and agricultural products. In 1929, U.S. exports to Mexico constituted nearly 75 percent of Mexico's imports, and consisted largely of iron and steel products, machinery, tools, automobiles, and construction materials, especially wood (Council on Foreign Relations, 1931: 54-55).

Mexican government officials and businessmen also encouraged foreign investment in Mexico, although with the hope of channeling it according to the needs of Mexican capital (J. Meyer, 1977: 286-287). In 1925 the first steps were taken for the establishment of the Ford Motor assembly plant, which began operations in 1926 (Smith, 1973: 231). This move also realized an objective of certain groups within the U.S. State Department, which as early as 1918 had encouraged the Ford Motor Company and other firms to build factories in Mexico as a means of tying Mexico to the U.S. economically, thereby expanding opportunities for U.S. interests and restraining European penetration (Smith, 1963: 579). During the 1920's, Palmolive Peet, Simmons, Dupont, International Match, British American Tobacco, and United Shoe and Leather also began to invest in Mexico. In some cases foreign companies established links with national capital. One example is the B. F. Goodrich subsidiary in Mexico, which in 1930 entered into a marketing agreement with the Euzkadi rubber company, owned by Mexican and Spanish businessmen; subsequently the two companies merged.

By the end of the Calles administration, the Mexican state and that of the U.S. had established a new basis for cooperation, involving the free operation and protection of foreign capital in Mexico in return for formal recognition of Mexican sovereignty. The new era of cooperation between the Mexican state and U.S. interests was evident in an assessment of the Calles regime by Ambassador Morrow to the effect that foreign residents considered Calles "the best president the country has had since Díaz" (Smith, 1973: 259).

CONSOLIDATION OF THE STATE

As noted above, one of the immediate effects of the revolution had been a resurgence of the relative regional autonomy which had characterized Mexico through the early years of the Díaz regime. During the revolution, Carranza had authorized generals under his command to raise funds for the maintenance of their forces within the regions they controlled, which was accomplished through levying taxes, issuing paper money, and taking over property. While Carranza was president, military commanders continued to govern their zones like regional fiefs, reinstating regional taxes and in some cases negotiating directly with foreign interests in their regions. Carranza had no control over the generals and bribed officers to keep them loyal; governors of the distant western and northern states often ignored orders and requests of the central government (Greuning, 1938: 313; Lieuwen, 1968: 36-39). Carranza finally aroused the opposition of the military by reductions in military spending, as well as by his failure to carry out what many of the revolutionary officers saw as necessary reforms.

The subsequent Obregón administration was characterized by an uneasy truce with regional generals who had been his allies in the conflict with Carranza but who now sought to fortify their own political bases. Since many saw themselves as potential presidents, they represented a military threat to the central government as well as a political and economic barrier to national unification. In certain states, such as Veracruz, Yucatán, and Michoacán, where agrarian movements, supported by reform-oriented governors, were attempting to institute land reform programs, the regional generals often allied with traditional landowners in their efforts to suppress these movements, with the apparent acquiescence if not the direct support of the central government (Bartra, 1975: 17; Huizer, 1970: 43-50).

The truce between the central government and regional generals ended when General Adolfo de la Huerta, former interim president and subsequently Finance Secretary under Obregón, led over half of the generals in a revolt against the central government with the support of the Church and the landowners. As had occurred under Carranza, military opposition to Obregón was due in part to reductions in government military spending; Obregón had also reduced the number of military officers in government positions. In contrast to Carranza, however, Obregón had secured the support of organized labor and the peasantry; and the rebellion was defeated in April 1924 by the central government supported by the armed peasants.

The government sought to retain peasant support through limited land distribution programs, and at the same time to prevent the formation of independent peasant movements through the formation of centralized peasant organizations and parties. The government also rewarded CROM, the major labor confederation, which had been formed in 1918 and backed Obregón in the revolt against Carranza as well as in the de la Huerta revolt, by supporting CROM strike movements and its efforts to obtain control of organized labor (Tardanico, 1979: 22-23, 27-29). The ratification of the Mexican-United States agreements of 1923 may have been a further factor in Obregón's victory, since the U.S. sent arms to the government and placed an embargo on arms shipments to the de la Huerta forces (Stuart, 1938: 116-117).

The defeat of the de la Huerta rebellion constituted an important step in the government's efforts to control the military. Many of the dissident generals were eliminated in the process or subsequently purged, and the central government undertook a series of measures to control those remaining. Under the succeeding administration of Calles and with the assistance of his Secretary of War (General Joaquín Amaro), these measures were accelerated and included, among others, efforts to break down the loyalties of regional armies to their commanders by frequent re-assignment of commanders to new posts without their troops; measures to create a more professional orientation among army officers (e.g., by re-opening the Military College which had been closed from 1914);

and the use of material incentives to persuade restless generals to satisfy their ambitions in private enterprise (Córdova, 1973: 368 f).

These efforts were evidently successful in controlling military threats to the central government; subsequent revolts by dissident officers did occur but were relatively small and isolated and quickly put down by forces loyal to the government. The generals of the revolutionary armies—particularly those linked to the Sonoran groups—continued to dominate political positions; it has been estimated that half of the state governors between 1920 and 1935 as well as a substantial proportion of cabinet members, senators, and deputies were military officers (J. Meyer, 1977: 76). But perhaps the most important determinant of the subsequent role of this cohort of revolutionary officers consisted of the opportunities for self-enrichment provided by their military and political positions, and in many cases encouraged by the central government. The actual and potential enrichment of the revolutionary officers engendered an increasing interest by these groups in the maintenance of political stability, and a declining interest in reform.

Ambitious military generals constituted the most dangerous threat to the hegemony of the central government, but there were others. State governors and other regional leaders sought to build their own political bases, often through peasant and labor organizations within their regions. The central government sought to neutralize these leaders—as well as to control peasant and labor movements—through the formation or control of centralized labor and peasant organizations and the suppression of regional organizations or parties which threatened to become vehicles for state governors or other local powers. Functions previously performed by state governors were gradually taken over by the central government, a process which culminated in the 1930's and was reflected in legislation giving the federal government ultimate jurisdiction over agrarian reform and the implementation of labor legislation. At the same time, factional struggles among groups and cliques of the federal government itself—often organized in congressional blocs or cabinet cliques—continued throughout the decade.

The most important instrument for the control of regional groups and dissident factions was the National Revolutionary Party (PNR), formed at the instigation of Calles early in 1929, shortly after the death of Obregón. Initial announcements of the formation of the PNR stated that the autonomy of other existing parties would be recognized, and nearly all political groups, including such regional and local parties as those of Tamaulipas, Veracruz, and Yucatán, were invited to the first national convention in 1929. But while the party was projected as a loose confederation of existing state and national parties, in operation it was centralized and authoritarian: political careers became institutionalized within the PNR, and the organizational base was shifted to emphasize individual membership, reducing the influence of political groups and ultimately eliminating local and regional parties. Its dependence on the state was established through a system of financing based on withholding a portion of the salaries of federal government employees.

The ostensible purpose of the party was to institutionalize the transfer of political power; its latent purpose was to centralize political power, in the process becoming an instrument for political control by Calles. In 1929, at the same time that the party was formed, Calles succeeded, where Carranza had failed a decade earlier, in imposing a virtually unknown civilian candidate for the presidency, Pascual Ortiz Rubio. He was opposed by a relatively popular candidate, José Vasconcelos, who had been rector of the Universidad Nacional and later Minister of Education under Obregón. The victory of Ortiz Rubio demonstrated the capabilities of the PNR machinery; Calles' power was demonstrated two years later when Ortiz Rubio sought to challenge his supremacy and was forced to resign.[6]

If the major impediment to the centralization and consolidation of the state consisted of regional powers, the chief obstacle to ideological hegemony was the Church. From the period of the Spanish conquest, the role of the Church had been ambiguous. While village priests had led the early Indian and mestizo movements for independence and social justice, the Church hierarchy was basically conservative and identified with the landowning class, of which it was in fact part, having amassed immense landholdings during the colonial period. Much of its economic wealth was lost through

---

[6] Detailed information on the internal political conflicts of this period can be found in J. Meyer, 1977 and L. Meyer, 1978b. On the relationship between the government and the military, see J. Meyer, 1977: 60-76. On the formation of the party and the election of Ortiz Rubio, see Furtak, 1974: 26 f, and L. Meyer, 1978b: 22-24, 36-46, 85-104. On the conflict between Calles and Ortiz Rubio, see L. Meyer, 1978b: 146-156. Other sources on these themes include Leal, 1975a: 52-53; Córdova, 1973: 368; and Brandenberg, 1964: 63-67.

Attack on Guadalajara train directed by priest. By Mariana Yampolsky.

expropriations during the liberal reform, but it continued to have an important ideological role, in part through its control of education, but perhaps most importantly through the assimilation of Catholicism in the culture of the peasantry. If the liberal precursors of the revolution and the Jacobins within the Constitutionalist armies regarded the Church as a pernicious influence, this was not the case of the peasant armies (particularly in southern and central Mexico), which set priests free, reopened churches, and often included chaplains with their troops (J. Meyer, 1976: 11-12).

In the 1920's resistance to government efforts to take control of education resulted in the harassment and even assassination of schoolteachers sent to rural areas. During the Calles administration, following Church support of the de la Huerta rebellion, anticlerical provisions were introduced which seriously impeded the functioning of the Church as a religious institution. Efforts to enforce these provisions were resisted by local populations, particularly in the southwestern states of the Bajío region, where the influence of the clergy and traditional landowners remained strong.

Resistance leagues were formed, composed largely of the peasantry, and in 1926 the conflict led to a civil war in which the largely peasant armies of the Bajío region—the Cristeros—fought the troops of the federal government, assisted by peasants who had benefited, or hoped to benefit, from the agrarian reform. The Cristero rebellion finally ended with a truce in 1929, in which the government stated its intention to maintain the integrity of the Church and not to intervene in its spiritual functions. But the Cristero revolt failed in its attempt to challenge the efforts of the state to expand its ideological influence, specifically through control of education. At the same time, the strong antagonism engendered by the rebellion against the central government continued to have repercussions in this region.[7]

THE STATE AND PRIVATE DOMESTIC CAPITAL

The centralization of the state was of course an important factor in its ability to establish conditions for capital accumulation. Control of regional generals and politicians limited the possibility of instability resulting from revolts by these groups and/or from their ability to mobilize peasants and urban workers.

It was also during this period that much of the institutional machinery for government intervention in the economy was established. Several agencies were formed to complement existing private firms, especially foreign firms, in key sectors. A National Power Commission (Comisión Nacional de Fuerza Motriz) was established in 1922, and in 1926 a national electrical code was adopted, calling for government regulation of electricity rates and having the general purpose of expanding federal control over hydroelectric sources (Wionczek, 1964: 37 f). The government also

---

[7] Few episodes in Mexico's post-revolutionary history have aroused as much controversy as the Cristero rebellion. The official government view was that the Cristeros were led into a fracticidal war against pro-revolutionary peasants by the landlords and the priests of the traditional haciendas of central and southwestern Mexico. There is undoubtedly some truth to this version, but many have blamed the Calles government for a tragic war which could have been avoided, in some cases suggesting that Calles substituted a strong anti-clericalism for meaningful social and economic reform (Medín, 1971: 4). Jean Meyer's three-volume work *La Cristiada* (1973-74) challenges many of the existing assumptions regarding the Cristero rebellion and focuses upon the peasants who were its protagonists and victims. Meyer sees the Cristiada as the last spontaneous mass uprising of the revolution.

established the National Commission of Roads and began to issue road bonds (to be repaid through a gasoline tax) to finance the construction of roads and highways, and established the National Irrigation Commission to construct hydraulic works (García Díaz, 1953: 91).

The institutionalization of state intervention in the economy .required a strengthening of fiscal resources and control. This was to a large extent accomplished under Alberto Pani as Secretary of Finance from 1924 to 1927. Aside from the establishment of the central bank (to be discussed below), Pani broadened the tax base, establishing an income tax which complemented existing revenue sources (export taxes, taxes on mineral production, and sales taxes), and strenghtened the Finance Ministry relative to other government agencies by giving it jurisdiction over budgetary decisions (Haynes, 1981: 13). Thus the centralization of political power in the federal executive was accompanied by a centralization of financial control *within* the executive in the Ministry of Finance.

These initiatives were undertaken to complement private capital, to promote conditions for capital accumulation, and in some cases to channel the direction of capital, but not to replace it. In fact, the post-revolutionary economic reconstruction of Mexico involved considerable cooperation between the state and the private sector. Nowhere was this cooperation more evident than in the reconstruction of the banking system.

The Porfirian banks had been considered centers of reaction and became major targets of the Carranza government. As early as 1913 Carranza had spoken against the privileges enjoyed by private banks as a consequence of their right to issue banknotes, and stated that the right of note issue should be the exclusive privilege of the nation, a principle subsequently ratified in Article 28 of the constitution. But the critical shortage of government funds and the failure of efforts to obtain foreign financing delayed the implementation of its provision for the establishment of a single issue bank until 1925 (Moore, 1963: 35; Torres Mejía, 1975).[8] Also, while

[8] The International Finance Conference held in Brussels in 1920 under the auspices of the League of Nations had recommended the formation of central banks in each country—in part motivated by a concern of financial groups having loans and investments in Latin America and other areas to establish the necessary mechanisms for debt repayment and profit repatriation. During this period the Kemmerer mission, headed by Edwin W. Kemmerer, professor of Economics and Finance at Princeton, was directly instrumental in establishing central banks in Bolivia,

U.S. bankers, and apparently officials of the Mexican Finance Ministry, wanted the bank to be privately operated, Calles and other government officials wanted it to be controlled by the government (Jones, 1925).

It was therefore not until the consolidation of the state fiscal system, in part through the establishment of the income tax, that the government could secure funds for a government controlled central bank. In February 1924 Pani called a convention of bankers—chiefly Porfirian bankers—who in collaboration with government financial officials established the principles for the reconstitution of the banking system, which were incorporated in legislation by the end of the year. Pani also appointed a mixed commission of government and private financial officials (Fernando de la Fuente, Director of the Credit Department of the Finance Ministry; Elías S.A. de Lima, a private banker; and Manuel Gómez Morín, a young lawyer who had collaborated in Pani's fiscal and administrative reforms) to draw up legislation for a single issue bank, and the organic law and statutes of the new central bank, the Banco de México, were promulgated in August 1925.

Under the new system only the central bank could issue notes, and private banks would be regulated by the state through the central bank and the National Banking Commission, formed within the Finance Ministry to oversee their functioning. Although the central bank was technically independent of the state and had input by the private sector as well as by the government, the government held the majority of shares and controlled five of the nine board positions. It was also subject to policy direction by the state to insure that central bank policy was compatible with the public interest, and the Secretary of Finance had veto power over resolutions of the board having national importance or related to general government policy (Koch, 1941: 436–437; Córdova, 1973: 361). In short, through the central bank and the Secretary of Finance, the state would exercise control within the new financial system.

One of the major goals of the reconstructed banking system was

---

Chile, Ecuador, and Peru along the lines of the Federal Reserve System. Apparently the establishment of these banks through a U.S. commission was utilized by New York banks to push high-cost loans on these governments. In contrast, the Mexican central bank was established without direct foreign assistance, although on the basis of studies of the U.S. system, the Bank of France, and the Bank of England; it subsequently obtained loans from the House of Morgan (Tamagna, 1965: 39–40; Furtado, 1976: 96, Wood, 1961: 130; Krauze, 1976: 225).

to promote development by channeling bank funds to productive investment in agriculture and industry. At the time that the 1924 banking legislation was passed, Finance Secretary Pani made a distinction between "traditional capitalists" and "revolutionary capitalists," pointing out that funds obtained under the new banking system should be used to increase the national wealth and not to create monopolies for certain industries and individuals (Bennett, 1965: 40). This theme—that a major objective of the banks was to finance economic development—was reiterated by government officials and agencies, incorporated in banking legislation, and promoted by various measures (Moore, 1963: 78-79; Mexico, SHCP, 1957: 26; 1964: 11). Central bank loans were provided for banks established to finance specific commodities, particularly those destined for export (coffee), import substitution (sugar), or national industry (cotton). The banking legislation of 1932 required that foreign as well as national banks associate with the Banco de México and invest in businesses operating in Mexico. A by-product of this law was that most foreign banks, which had been accused of exporting funds to their home countries while refusing credit to Mexico, left the country, opening the field for the establishment of national private banks, which proliferated in the 1930's (see Appendix A). In 1928 the Mexican Bankers' Association (ABM) was formed; one of its purposes was to facilitate communication between private banking interests and the government.

Finally, the state created its own financial institutions to supplement the activities of private banks: the Agricultural Credit Bank (Banco Nacional de Crédito Agrícola), created in 1926 to provide loans to small farmers and ejiditarios who received land through the agrarian reform; the Public Works Bank (Banco Nacional Hipotecario Urbano y de Obras Públicas) to finance municipal infrastructure as well as road construction through the issue of road bonds; and Nacional Financiera, a development bank which would subsequently have a significant role in financing public and private investment.[9]

[9] The Public Works Bank was actually created to promote industrial development as well as to finance urban facilities, but in 1935 the function of industrial promotion was turned over to Nacional Financiera. The Asociación Hipoteceria Mexicana (Mexican Mortgage Association) was established at the instigation of the Public Works Bank to meet needs for credit for housing construction and debt payment; it was innovative in introducing mortgage certificates guaranteed by real estate, which were more successful in attracting public investment than non-tangible assets.

There was also extensive collaboration between the Mexican bankers, government and private, and financial circles in New York and Washington. Although the central bank was apparently established with national funds, it subsequently received loans from the House of Morgan, and when Morgan banker Dwight Morrow became U.S. Ambassador to Mexico in 1927 he took direct charge of Mexican government finances. The Mexican peso was tied to the dollar, and Mexican financial officials frequently asserted the importance of linking the Mexican financial system to that of the U.S. The Banco de México worked closely with the U.S. Federal Reserve Bank which on various occasions sent representatives to advise the Mexican central bank (Krauze, 1977: 59, 70; Lockett, 1934).

A special example of the collaboration between the state, foreign capital, and the national bourgeoisie is provided by the Banco Nacional de México, one of the two major private banks which survived the revolution. Under the direction of the Legorreta family, who were also important stockholders (although ownership was still predominantly French) the Banco Nacional succeeded in reestablishing its position as a special envoy between the Mexican government and foreign capital. As indicated above, Agustín Legorreta was involved in negotiations with the International Bankers Committee and with the U.S. government and Morgan bankers over the petroleum crisis; he had also attempted (unsuccessfully) to obtain foreign funds for the establishment of the new central bank. Subsequently, when the central bank gave up its commercial bank operations it turned over its branches to the Banco Nacional (BNM, 1900-1975; *Informe 1934*). The Banco Nacional also collaborated closely with representatives of foreign interests in Mexico, and apparently instructed its branches to provide confidential information to representatives of the U.S. government in Mexico regarding Mexican firms, trade conditions, feasibility of investments, and other matters (Hillyer, 1929).

Legorreta also appears to have cooperated with foreign groups in attempting to pressure Calles to abandon his more radical policies. In a letter to Thomas Lamont, E. R. Jones of the Wells Fargo Company of Mexico (and representative of the International Bankers Committee) described a meeting between President Calles, Finance Minister Pani, and Legorreta as reported to Jones by Legorreta. Allegedly, Legorreta had been persuaded by Calles to state his exact views on the situation in Mexico, and had responded that Mexico's problems were not economic but political, and specifically due to the government's policy; that this policy should be modified to protect both Mexican and foreign capital; and that land laws, oil laws, and mining laws should be changed to the extent necessary to encourage foreign capital to come to Mexico with a full sense of protection. According to Legorreta, Pani agreed with this assessment, noting that he had advised Calles along the same basic lines (Lamont, 1926).

In general, government policies toward the private sector reflected contrasting attitudes to different segments of capital as well as the shifts in the government orientation in the 1920's. Of the Porfirian groups, the traditional landowners were considered the most expendable, but while some landowners experienced considerable losses during the revolution itself or during the Cristero rebellion, comparatively few were directly affected by the expropriation policies of the government during the 1920's. With respect to other Porfirian groups, initial ambivalence toward commercial landowners, industrialists, and commercial and financial interests had been transformed to support as these groups reached an accommodation with the revolutionary state—an accommodation which at the same time involved a much more direct state role in the economy than had prevailed during the Porfiriato.

Both initiatives which increased state intervention in the economy (as the creation of specific government commissions and agencies) and state promotion of private capital accumulation were at least to some extent designed to offset and ultimately counter foreign domination of key sectors of the economy. At the same time, important sectors of the dominant class and to an increasing extent the government itself envisioned an important role for foreign capital in Mexico's future development.

THE CAPITALISTS OF THE REVOLUTION

Pressures by foreign capital and members of the Mexican capitalist class, and collaboration between the state and the bourgeoisie in economic reconstruction, are not the only explanations for the shift in government policy in the mid-1920's. A major factor was undoubtedly the transformation of Calles and many of his associates into capitalists. In fact, the most significant change in the owning class in the period between 1910 and 1934 was its expansion through the incorporation of new wealth. The revolutionary conflict itself had provided numerous opportunities for the rapid enrichment of victorious generals, in addition to easy access to land expropriated from previous landowners (Lieuwen, 1968: 39). Military chiefs in frontier zones secured fortunes through the operation of gambling casinos, as in the case of Abelardo Rodríguez, President of Mexico from 1932 to 1934, whose wealth, initially accumulated during his tenure as military chief of the northern zone of Baja California, was subsequently invested in vineyards, seafood packing houses, urban and rural properties, and various industries, smelters, and financial institutions (Naranjo, 1948: 31 July).

Not only revolutionary officers benefited economically from the revolution. Substantial profits could be made in the purchase and resale of real estate, even beginning with a very small base (Espinosa Porset, 1958: 41-42). One of the most successful examples of post-revolutionary self-aggrandizement was that of William Jenkins, a former U.S. consul in the city of Puebla. Following the revolution he provided loans to sugar plantation owners in the state of Puebla who were attempting to reconstruct sugar refineries and other equipment destroyed or damaged during the revolution. Many of these defaulted on their loans and Jenkins took over their properties, thus becoming owner of eleven haciendas containing the best crop lands of Matamoras valley (Ronfeldt, 1973: 9-10). Subsequently Jenkins expanded into other areas, including substantial control of one of the major banks of the country.

Government ministers, senators, generals, and state governors utilized politics for economic advancement through such means as control of construction firms which received government contracts for new roads, or mergers with existing national or foreign private interests (J. Meyer, 1977: 310).

Fortunes were also made in industries related to tourism, which the post-revolutionary governments sought to encourage as a means of drawing funds into Mexico. The brief government of Abelardo Rodríguez was characterized by the acceleration of construction of modern hotels and public buildings, as well as offices and apartment houses, especially in Mexico City (Naranjo, 1948: 10 Sept.). Local and national politicians were able to use their position to sell favors to members of the Porfirian elite threatened by reforms of the new government, particularly landowners, for whom local officials obligingly postponed or prolonged indefinitely land grant proceedings, or arranged for land reform "beneficiaries" to receive uncultivated areas and enabled previous owners to retain the best land of their estates (Mendieta y Nuñez, cited in Córdova, 1973: 378, n.). Other forms of corruption became institutionalized at the local level, where municipal authorities, military officials, and local bosses (caciques) utilized their positions to gain control of lucrative concessions (as the sale of alchohol), to tax and otherwise force payments from communities under their control, and to prevent the organization of peasants and to maintain order on behalf of dominant groups and classes (J. Meyer, 1977: 307; Greuning, 1929: 289-334). As stated by an official of the National Agrarian Commission in 1924, one of the hacendados in his region was "sufficiently rich to be able to 'buy' all the local authorities, civil as well as military, from the president of the municipality to the last policeman, and from the lieutenant in charge of the local garrison down to the last soldier—as indeed it has in times past and is doing now" (cited in Simpson, 1937: 467).

As noted above, revolutionary generals were actively encouraged by the central government to go into business as a means of channeling their political ambitions into less dangerous directions. This was particularly true during the government of Calles, when the process of self-enrichment became "peacefully regularized," and "revolutionary capitalists" became one of the most dynamic sectors of the dominant class (Córdova, 1973: 30, 379). The revolutionary leadership—generals, government officials and their associates—also entered the ranks of the landowning oligarchy, in many cases linked to the Porfirian landowners, a process facilitated through loans provided by the Agricultural Credit Bank, e.g., for the purchase of haciendas by General Joaquín Amaro (Secretary of War under Calles) and Luis León (Secretary of Agriculture) and the purchase of the Cia. Richardson, a producer of chickpeas, by General Obregón.[10]

[10] See Gómez Jara, 1970: 42 and Krauze, 1977: 120-122, 156-157. In its first two years of operation, the Agricultural Credit Bank provided loans of 19 million pesos, of which 17 million constituted individual loans to approximately 1,000 large landowners, while two million went to credit societies to benefit 10,000 small farmers. A detailed indictment of the functioning of the bank in its early years can be found in the letter of resignation of Eduardo Villaseñor, director of the bank's Departamento de Sociedades, to the bank manager, Elias S.A. de Lima (Villaseñor, 1974: 214-221). See also Krauze (1976: 232, 237), according to whom the corruption of the bank and disillusionment with the government in general were major factors in the decision of Manuel Gómez Morín, who had drawn up much of the banking legislation of that period, including that of the Agricultural Credit Bank, to leave government service and work for private enterprise.

In this sense, the state was an important source of the capitalist class in post-revolutionary Mexico. The "recruitment" from the state to the private sector is exemplified by the career of Aarón Sáenz, a post-revolutionary government official and close associate of Calles, whose official connections paved the way for his rapid ascent to a position of control within the sugar industry. During the revolution, Sáenz had served as a member of the General Staff in the army of Alvaro Obregón, with whom he continued to be closely associated until Obregón's assassination in 1928. In 1917 he was elected to the Chamber of Deputies as representative of the state of Nuevo León, and in 1919 and 1920 he served as Ambassador to Brazil. He held several posts in the cabinets of Obregón, Calles, and the three presidents of the Maximato: Under-Secretary of Foreign Affairs (1920-1924); Secretary of Foreign Affairs (1924-1927); Secretary of Public Education (1930); Secretary of Industry, Commerce, and Labor (1930-1931); and Head of the Department of the Federal District (1932-1935) (Hefley, 1970: 53, 60-70). He was elected governor of Neuvo León in 1927 and, with an interruption in 1928 to serve as manager of the presidential campaign of Obregón, held this position until 1930, during which time he apparently consolidated relations with conservative economic interests of Monterrey. It was, in fact, the open nature of his respect for Monterrey businessmen which was instrumental in eliminating him as a "revolutionary" presidential candidate in 1929, although he had been considered the logical successor to Obregón within Mexican political circles and had apparently assumed that he would be the candidate of the new National Revolutionary Party which he had helped to establish (Portes Gil, 1954: 150, 155-157).

As a member of Calles' cabinet, Sáenz took advantage of the encouragement provided to political and military officials to become entrepreneurs. He founded the construction company FYUSA, apparently the initial source of his wealth (and believed to have been an important source of wealth for Calles as well), which was multiplied in various other enterprises (Córdova, 1973: 376-377). Calles, to whom Sáenz was related by marriage (his sister having married Calles's eldest son), was also associated with Sáenz in the construction of a sugar refinery at El Mante in the state of Tamaulipas. The lands were taken over by officials of the Calles government (having previously been in the hands of a few Chinese owners) when negotiations were underway for the construction of a dam on the Rio Mante to provide an irrigation system. The dam and irrigation canals were constructed by the J. G. White Engineering Corporation at a cost of 4.5 million pesos, paid by the Federal Government. When the work was completed in 1929, the lands were sold, most of them coming under the control of three families—those of Calles, Sáenz, and Lamberto Hernández (another public official) (Treviño Sillar, 1944: 22-23). Subsequently, a modern sugar refinery was constructed on the Sáenz property at El Mante with the assistance of a substantial loan from the Banco de México (Hefley, 1970: 85, 93).

Sáenz was also able to take advantage of efforts by the governments of Obregón and Calles to promote sugar production—which had declined drastically as a result of the revolution and particularly the occupation of sugar plantations of the southern states by the peasant armies of Zapata, which had reconverted them to subsistence production.[11] President Obregón incorporated a provision in the Agrarian Code declaring that property devoted to the production and processing of sugar cane could not be affected by the agrarian reform, which was a factor in the resurgence of the sugar industry, but in highly disorganized conditions. In 1926, overproduction began to be a problem, resulting in a price decrease and in government efforts to force producers to associate. These efforts were successful temporarily, but by the early 1930's an accelerated increase in production combined with a decrease in demand due to the depression resulted in a sharp decline in price from 30 centavos per kilo in 1928 to 14 centavos in 1930 (Maturana and Restrepo, 1970: 38). At the instigation of the Secretary of Finance, Montes de Oca, and Sáenz, who was then Secretary of Commerce, Industry, and Labor, the Cia. Estabilizadora del Mercado del Azúcar was established at the beginning of 1931, associating the majority of producers with the purpose of regulating production and stabilizing the price. The concern of the government for the stabilization of the industry was indicated by 70 shares held by the government agricultural bank.

However, the Estabilizadora did not include all the refineries (notably, those of Jalisco), and lacked a mechanism for enforcing production quotas and prices. Although it engaged in such meas-

---

[11] See Ganem, 1967: 165. Zapata had in fact attempted to encourage peasants to utilize at least some of the land to grow sugar cane, pointing out that the region would continue to be poor if it relied exclusively on production for local consumption. But apparently he had little success, and the resumption of war in this region subsequently precluded commercial sugar cane production (Gilly, 1975: 242).

ures as burning surplus crops, sugar production continued to increase (Maturana and Restrepo, 1970: 38; Ganem, 1967: 168). By the end of 1931 several private growers, including Sáenz, were convinced of the necessity of forming a cartel of all sugar-mill owners with measures to control production and sale which would be binding (Redo, 1931). Sugar producers would be obliged to carry out contracts with the sales organization, to deliver their entire production to it, and to reduce their harvests to quotas established by the state. In January 1932 an independent company, Azúcar, S.A., began operations and soon included all sugar mills of the country. Its purpose was to stabilize sugar prices through the distribution and sale of all sugar produced in the country and, if necessary, to establish quotas to limit production. At the same time, the Banco Azucarero was established to take partial responsibility for financing sugar production; its shareholders included most of the sugar-mill owners of the country as well as the government Agricultural Credit Bank.

Azúcar, S.A., was apparently successful temporarily in stabilizing sugar production and sales. In May 1932, Aarón Sáenz, who was president of Azúcar, S.A., as well as the Banco Azucarero, stated that the new arrangement was perhaps without precedent in the history of the sugar industry—not only in Mexico but also in other parts of the world. He acknowledged the support and stimulus of the government and the Banco de México (which had an important function in orchestrating financing for the sugar industry through various private and official banks), and expressed confidence that the arrangement for sugar production could serve as a precedent for similar arrangements in other industries (Sáenz, 1932). Subsequently Sáenz expanded into other sugar plantations and refineries and also diversified his holdings into hotels, airlines, steel products, and food products. He obtained control of the Banco Azucarero (later renamed the Banco de Comercio y Industria). Today the Sáenz holdings constitute one of the major economic groups of the country (Cordero and Santín, 1977: 51).

The Sáenz career pattern is of interest in that he not only was able to utilize his political position to further his economic interests, but also benefited from government policies affecting the sugar industry, including its role in the formation of a cartel to rationalize sugar production (and guarantee profits). Sáenz was also a beneficiary of government promotion of the tourist industry and loans by government banks—initially the Banco de México, later

Nacional Financiera, the development bank—to specific firms and projects.

Thus the state not only fostered conditions for private accumulation but also had an important role in class formation in post-revolutionary Mexico: indirectly, through the promotion of specific industries (such as sugar and tourism) and directly, through opportunities (including direct subsidies) enabling military officers and government officials to become capitalists of the revolution. The career of Sáenz, who benefited from cartelization of the sugar industry under state auspices, government promotion of tourism, and direct state financing of the irrigation system and refinery of El Mante, constitutes an outstanding example of the complex relationship between the state and the private sector which would continue to characterize post-revolutionary Mexico.

THE STATE AND LABOR

The establishment of conditions for capital accumulation involved not only the consolidation and institutionalization of state power, and the accommodation (and expansion) of private interests, but also, under the guise of class collaboration, control of the labor movement and the peasantry. At the same time, Obregón's victory over Carranza and subsequently over the de la Huerta forces, as well as the defeat of the Cristero rebellion, were due at least in part to support by organized labor and the armed peasantry. Consequently the central government's policy toward both groups during this period was to attempt to maintain their support and at the same time tighten its control over them.

The government's strategy was to prevent a unified, independent organization of workers and peasants by coopting existing organizations and/or setting up government-directed and controlled institutions. These efforts were opposed by independent organizations of workers and peasants and to some extent by attempts of state governors to organize urban and rural workers within their particular regions under their own auspices. Thus the basic struggles of the labor force against the owners of factories, mines, petroleum fields, and of peasants against landowners, were complicated by conflicts between the central government and state governments as the former consolidated its control over the country, and between independent labor organizations and the government-controlled labor movement.

Throughout most of this period, the dominant labor confederation was CROM, the Confederación Regional de Obreros Mexicanos (Regional Confederation of Mexican Workers). CROM was established in 1918 as an independent organization, and its statement of principles reflects the influence of anarchist delegates to its constitutional congress. However, its secretary general, Luis Morones, and other leaders soon instituted a policy of "creative opportunism" (e.g., collaboration with the state), justified with the assumption that labor would be helpless without state protection (Carr, 1976, I: 127-135). While rejecting Carranza's efforts to control it, CROM supported Obregón's revolt in 1920 and collaborated closely with the administrations of Obregón and Calles. CROM's rapid shift from an independent, anarchist position to a reformist one was probably reinforced by CROM's early association with the American Federation of Labor, which hoped to use the Mexican labor movement to establish a Pan American Labor Federation to implement a "Monroe Doctrine" for labor, "safeguarding" Latin American labor against foreign intervention (Levenstein, 1971: 90). Within two years, anarchist members abandoned the new confederation in protest against the political maneuvers of its leadership.

During the administration of Calles, CROM reaped the benefits of full government support. Morones was designated Secretary of Industry, Commerce, and Labor, and various other CROM officials received minor cabinet posts or became senators or deputies. The federal government sanctioned efforts of CROM to bring Mexican labor under its centralized control, threatening firms with confiscation if the CROM unions were not given recognition (Basurto, 1975: 245-248; Ashby, 1965: 11-12; Levenstein, 1971: 137).

Initially, CROM was able to secure genuine advantages—recognition and economic benefits for weaker unions in return for their loyalty—particularly against the relatively small and dispersed national firms. Its strongest base was among textile workers in the states of Puebla and Veracruz. With the shift in the orientation of the Calles government to open support for the dominant class, the government began to permit lockouts, production cutbacks, and dismissal of workers by employers, and CROM utilized its control of the labor movement to discourage strikes and to promote class collaboration. CROM also attempted to take over independent unions and to destroy the independent labor movement, often through violence, in collaboration with employers and local government officials (Carr, 1976 II: 41-44, 16-17). The relationship which evolved between CROM and local union leaders facilitated top-down control of workers in CROM-affiliated unions. In CROM itself, decisions were taken in secret, generally by the small Grupo Acción, composed of Morones and trusted associates. Thus the development of CROM in post-revolutionary Mexico helped to reinforce two basic tendencies within the Mexican labor movement: the authoritarian control of the rank and file by the labor bureaucracy, and the dependence of organized labor on the government.

CROM domination of the labor movement in the 1920's did not go unchallenged. Certain local government officials responded to peasant and labor demands, either due to genuine commitment or as a means of building their own power base. In several states, labor movements were able to establish their independence of CROM, but only through increased dependence on the state governor or other local officials. One example was Emilio Portes Gil, governor of the state of Tamaulipas (1925-1928), who succeeded in maintaining the state free from CROM influence through the establishment of rival labor and peasant organizations (Huizer, 1970: 52-53).

The hegemony of CROM over the labor movement was also challenged by rival labor organizations, particularly the Mexican Communist party and the anarchists. As indicated above, anarchist influence in Mexico dates from the pre-revolutionary period through the influence of European immigrants and the IWW, which was active among miners in the northern states and among petroleum workers in the Tampico area on the east coast (both involving foreign-dominated industries). In 1921, Mexican anarchists and members of the Communist party joined forces to form the Confederación General de Trabajo (General Labor Confederation), the CGT. (Communist members were subsequently expelled.) The CGT played a militant role in the strike movements of the early 1920's and in defending the independent unions against intervention by CROM. By the end of the decade, however, it had lost its dynamism and much of its membership; by the 1930's its role had been considerably weakened, in part through struggles with

CROM (which had state support) and internal splits (Basurto, 1975: 196-198; Fuentes Díaz, 1959: 330; L. Meyer, 1978a: 125-126).

As in other Latin American countries, the Mexican Communist party was formed in the wake of the Russian revolution through the influence of the Third International. It initially concentrated its efforts among the peasantry and helped to establish several agrarian leagues in the early 1920's, which attempted to unite in a national confederation in 1926. In 1929, following the sixth congress of the Comintern, which had called for a revolutionary class struggle against imperialism and the national bourgeoisie, the Communist party formed the Confederación Sindical Unitaria de México (Central Union Confederation of Mexico), the CSUM. The Communist party and the CSUM attracted a following among rural and urban workers due to the militance of their leaders in defense of labor interests, but their ideological influence was limited (Anguiano et al., 1975: 77). Communist party support for a 1929 military rebellion resulted in the party's being declared illegal and in the imprisonment of several of its leaders (Fuentes Díaz, 1959: 329).

Aside from state governors and the Communist and anarchist organizations, CROM hegemony among the working class was challenged by independent industrial labor confederations, among them confederations of railroad workers, the Mexican Electricians' Union, and local unions of petroleum workers. But, despite the corruption and opportunism of Morones and the majority of CROM leaders, not to mention the tactics of gangsterism used against independent unions, CROM continued to dominate the Mexican labor movement as long as it had government support. The unskilled workers in traditional industries were in a more precarious position than skilled workers in the above-mentioned unions, and the CROM justification of its relations with the Mexican state as due to the weakness of the working class in these industries may have had some basis in reality. In any event, they were least able to withstand CROM intervention.

It was the loss of government support which resulted in the disintegration of CROM as a national organization by the early 1930's, although it still retained a following in certain locations, particularly among textile workers in Puebla and Orizaba (Veracruz) (Basurto, 1975: 273). The break between CROM and the government occurred as a result of the assassination of Obregón, president-elect, in 1928, in which Morones was indirectly implicated. Although CROM had enjoyed certain prerogatives under the first Obregón government, Obregón's campaign as a presidential candidate against corruption indicated that his election would end the privileges enjoyed by CROM leadership. The antipathy of Morones toward Obregón was well known, and when Obregón was assassinated by a religious fanatic, Morones was accused by the Obregonistas of being the intellectual author (Basurto, 1975: 263-265; Medín, 1971: 20). In withdrawing support from CROM, the government also weakened its own control of the labor movement, but by this time its alliance with capital had lessened the importance of support from labor.

It was during this period in which labor organization was fragmented and state control of labor was relatively weak that the Mexican congress passed the Federal Labor Law to implement the provisions of Article 123 of the constitution. This again constituted part of the process of centralization of state power in the federal government; previously labor legislation had been implemented only at the state level. Among the immediate factors in the passage of the law were complications resulting from differences among state laws, as well as pressures from both labor and business interests objecting to local political intervention in labor conflicts. Similar complaints by workers and employers regarding political intervention in the procedures of state and local labor boards had resulted in the efforts of the Federal Labor Board to unify procedures for arbitration of labor conflicts (Krauze, 1977: 205; Clark, 1934: 214-215, 257). At the same time, certain business sectors were wary of efforts to implement Article 123 of the constitution at the national level. In 1928, Monterrey business groups took the lead in forming the Confederación Patronal de la República Mexicana (COPARMEX), the Employers' Confederation of the Mexican Republic to insure employer input into the new labor legislation. In contrast to the other peak organizations formed in the early post-revolutionary years, COPARMEX is an explicitly class-conscious organization representing the interests of the owning class in its conflict with labor.

Although Aarón Sáenz, then Secretary of Industry, Commerce, and Labor, suggested that the Federal Labor Law would introduce an era of order and cooperation for capital and labor, the final legislation pleased neither employers nor workers. On the one hand, it restricted the ability of employers to dismiss workers, permitted strikes except when they involved violence or the suspension of government services during the war (although in practice many further limitations were introduced, e.g., that a strike could not be "contrary to the general interest"), and prohibited lock-outs by employers except when justified by overproduction and approved by the labor board. On the other hand, it institutionalized the power of the state over labor unions, requiring them to register with government authorities to be legally recognized, to hand over confidential information (list of members, amount and use of dues, etc.), to local government officials, and submit conflicts to arbitration by labor boards on which the government had controlling vote. Implicit in the Labor Law, as in Article 123 of the constitution, was a paternal relation between the state and labor in which the state would guarantee the protection of the rights of workers, and the concept of class conciliation, i.e., strikes should have the object of balancing the factors of production, harmonizing the rights of labor with those of capital (Middlebrook, 1977: 6-7; Iglesias, 1970: 103; L. Meyer, 1978a: 153-154).

Labor groups fought for the inclusion of the clausulas de exclusión (exclusion clauses) in contracts—i.e., that workers could not be hired unless they belonged to the union and that if separated from the union they must be dismissed from their jobs. In the law, this stipulation remained ambiguous, but it was subsequently defended by strikes, including a strike of petroleum workers against El Aguila (owned by British-controlled Royal Dutch Shell) in 1934, which resulted in a ruling by President Rodríguez in favor of the *clausulas de exclusión*, effectively settling the matter. As noted above, this clausula subsequently became a major device for the control and manipulation of workers by corrupt union leaders.[12]

In summary, the Federal Labor Law reflected the ambiguous effects of the post-revolutionary state-labor alliance for the Mexican labor movement. On the one hand, the Labor Law (as Article 123 of the constitution, which it in effect implemented) potentially provided substantial benefits for the working class through the

---

[12] Several observers foresaw the effects of the clausulas de exclusión. Rosendo Salazar noted: "The union will be a tyrant when the exclusion clause is used to its full extent, since the unionized worker will not be able to raise his voice against the leader . . . everything will be arranged bureaucratically, through orders, bribes, fear, servility" (Salazar, 1956b: 52). Lucio Mendieta y Nuñez also pointed out that while the clausula de exclusión constituted a powerful arm of the labor movement, it could become a device for the dictatorship of the union leadership over the workers (Mendieta y Nuñez, 1942: 189).

protection of a paternalistic state in facilitating labor organization and strikes and restricting arbitrary actions by employers (Carr, 1976 II: 178). On the other, it established the legal framework for control of workers by union leaders and government officials, and constituted a further stage in the process of centralization of government institutions and control of the working class.

THE STATE, PEASANT ORGANIZATION, AND AGRARIAN REFORM

Although the revolution brought some immediate benefits in terms of land distribution, vast sectors of the rural population remained unaffected by the conflict itself and the expropriation programs of the immediate post-revolutionary governments. During his campaign in Chihuahua and in neighboring states, Francisco Villa expropriated the vast holdings of dominant landowners, but most of these fell into the hands of Villa's generals, who constituted a new landowning group, often entering into alliances with U.S. enterprises. Peasant communities which regained land by force of arms, as in the state of Morelos, were able to retain them, and lands could be reclaimed by those having clear titles to them. But this did not affect the majority of the rural population, and only in Morelos was the previous land structure transformed (Wolf, 1973: 36, 44; L. Meyer, 1978a: 174-175).

During the 1920's, government agrarian policy was dictated by several considerations, in many respects contradictory. On the one hand, the mobilization of the peasants and their increased level of expectations meant that some reform was necessary as a safety valve. In addition, the revolutionary governments needed peasant support to repress various rebellions, including the de la Huerta revolt of 1923-1924 and the Cristero rebellion of 1927-1929, which involved giving arms to the peasants and obviously required government responsiveness to their demands. At the same time, inefficient landowners constituted the most "expendable" group of the Porfirian elite; the post-revolutionary governments consistently attacked them as socially and economically regressive (Labastida, 1972: 104-106; Córdova, 1973: 277, 333-334).

On the other hand, the low level of the country's economic and financial resources led the government leaders to give priority to raising levels of production, including agricultural production, and made them reluctant to break up agricultural estates, especially the relatively efficient holdings oriented to commercial production. The initial policy of the Sonoran presidents was oriented to the creation of a petty bourgeoisie of small farmers which would constitute an intermediate strata between the ejidos (which for the most part were considered a temporary expedient until the ejiditarios gained the experience and skills necessary to become small farmers) and the commercial landowners including traditional landowners expropriated through the agrarian reform, who would be forced to cultivate the land remaining to them more efficiently (Krauze, 1977: 120, 136). An alternative approach was suggested in a circular issued by the Agrarian Commission in 1922 which advocated the formation of cooperatives for collective production on expropriated estates since the small farm could not efficiently utilize machinery and other inputs. But the cooperative policy was not implemented (except to a very limited extent) during this period, and after three years it was decided that the policies recommended by Circular 51 "did not work" (Simpson, 1937: 322; Eckstein, 1966: 48-51). By the end of the decade, the early orientation to small holdings gave way to the assumption that in the agrarian sector social and economic goals were incompatible; neither the small holding nor the ejido was economically efficient.

Aside from the ambiguities and shifts in government policy, the agrarian reform suffered from bureaucratic inefficiency and corruption. As indicated above, state agrarian commissions were often more responsive to landowners than to peasants; the National Agrarian Commission was slow and inefficient; and its decisions could be overruled by the Supreme Court. Also, landowners were able to pit *peones acasillados* who could not receive land under the existing law against the day laborers and village peasants whose demands for expropriation could deprive the peons of the little security they had (L. Meyer, 1978a: 281-282). Lands distributed were often of poor quality, with the landowners having the option to retain the best land. In some cases, land reform affected the properties of the small peasants who, in contrast to the landowners, lacked the financial and political resources to defend themselves—a trend which inevitably resulted in confrontations between different groups of rural workers and was a factor in the Cristero rebellion (Krauze, 1977: 132).

Throughout most of this period final jurisdiction over agrarian reform rested with the state government, and the level of support for land distribution and peasant organization varied widely among different states and in some cases from one period to another in a given state. While the majority of state governors were conservative, several progressive governors (most of them in the southern or central states) became spokesmen for the rights of the peasants and workers and undertook land reform programs in collaboration with the organized peasants. However, their work was often frustrated by regional military commanders, generally acting in league with landowners (and often with the acquiescence of the federal government); the armed mercenaries (white guards) of the landowners; or succeeding, more conservative state governors.

Thus, as governor of Michoacán in the early 1920's General Francisco Mújica succeeded against strong opposition in distributing 23,000 hectares to ejidos, but he was removed by the military commander of the region, Enrique Estrada, allied with the landowners. Subsequently, General Lázaro Cárdenas, who became governor of Michoacán in 1926, distributed land to 15,373 peasants, arming women's leagues (*ligas femininas*) to guard the fields where their husbands worked against landowner attacks; the succeeding governor again tried to reverse the process of land distribution.

In the state of Yucatán, dominated by the production of henequen, the structure of production had been altered with the occupation of the state by the Constitutionalist army in 1915 under the leadership of Salvador Alvarado. Debt peonage was ended, peasant and worker leagues were established, and control of the sisal market passed from agents of foreign firms, especially International Harvester, to a commission serving the Constitutionalist army and subsequently to the state government, but no land distribution measures were enacted. Subsequently, as governor of Yucatán, Carrillo Puerto organized the rural workers on the plantations into the Popular Socialist Party (PPS) and distributed 210,000 hectares to 36 communities. However, with the de la Huerta uprising Carrillo Puerto was shot, the PPS disintegrated, and the land was returned to the landowners. In Nuevo León, urban and rural properties confiscated on grounds that the owners had been partisans or sympathizers of the Victoriano Huerta regime were later returned (Wolf, 1973: 41-42; Huizer, 1970: 43; Joseph, 1980: 55-60; Vizcaya Canales, 1969: 142-144).

The most important center of peasant mobilization and agrarian radicalism during the 1920's was the state of Veracruz, where labor and tenant unions and the Communist party organized agrarian leagues which were supported by Adalberto Tejeda, Governor of Veracruz from 1920 to 1924 and again between 1928 and 1932. The leagues were armed by Tejeda to defend themselves from the armed guards of the haciendas, which were supported by the state military commander Guadalupe Sánchez until his defeat in the de la Huerta uprising in 1923-1924. Under the leadership of Ursulo Galván, a member of the Mexican Communist party, the leagues became increasingly radicalized, calling for the ulitmate socialization of all means of production. Between 1915 and 1933 some 614,763 hectares were distributed to 88,548 beneficiaries, in some cases in the form of collective ejidos. Through the agrarian leagues and union movement, Tejeda established a new power base, with labor and agrarian leaders controlling the major political and administrative posts of the state (Huizer, 1970: 46-57; Salamini, 1976: 278-288; Gómez Jara, 1970: 46-47; Falcón, 1978: 347).

But the growing power and political ambitions of Tejeda were viewed as a threat to the faction which controlled the central government. Tejeda had proposed that the new National Revolutionary Party (PNR) be established on a peasant/working class base, and showed little inclination to support it when it took the form of an organization of political strata. The implementation of agrarian reform in Veracruz increasingly involved ignoring directives from the central government. Also, by the end of 1931 Tejeda had begun to spread his influence outside the state and to indicate presidential ambitions. The Calles faction began to move against the Veracruz government, intervening in the agrarian leagues and state organizations to promote splits and factionalization, ordering the end of the ejidal program, and, finally, at the beginning of 1933, disarming the agrarian militia. This weakened the most militant peasant movement of the 1920's and at the same time eliminated the most significant threat to central government hegemony.

The central government, through the PNR, also attempted to gain control of the National Peasant League, which had been formed in 1926 under the auspices of the Veracruz League of Agrarian Communities and had united peasant leagues in several states. This effort was only partially successful; the PNR attempt to take over the National Peasant League at its sixth convention (in February 1930) resulted in a three-way split, with two minority groups joining the PNR and the Communist party, while the majority followed the independent leader Ursulo Galván (subsequently taking the name Liga Nacional Ursulo Galván after his death later that year).

The net results of the various land reform programs of the 1920's were meager. In 1930, 70 percent of the non-ejidal rural population who owned land held less than 1 percent of the privately owned land, in holdings of less than 5 hectares, while 2.2 percent of the landowners held over 33 percent of the privately owned land in holdings of 500 hectares or more. An estimated 2.5 to 3 million peasants, consisting of *peones acasillados* and day laborers, were without land, while the ejiditarios, comprising 15 percent of the agrarian population, often had small holdings of less than one hectare. In June 1930 Calles declared the land reform program a failure and suggested that each governor establish a limited period within which to terminate land distribution in his state in order to provide guarantees to small and large landowners. Aside from pressures from commercial landowners, defense of the new "landowners of the revolution" was undoubtedly a consideration, particularly in the state of Sonora, which through the assistance of the state and loans from New York banks had become a modern and prosperous agricultural center.[13] Thus the government's agrarian policy constituted a particular case of its general shift in orientation in favor of large-scale capitalist production.

But while the government had succeeded in destroying independent centers of power based on the organized support of peasants and workers in various states, and in fragmenting peasant organizations, renewed peasant mobilization and organization remained a possibility. Furthermore, the needs of the peasants were being articulated by an increasingly vocal group of agrarians within the state itself, including members of the National Peasant League who had joined the PNR. The importance of these groups was reflected in legislation of the early 1930's, which threatened certain prerogatives of the landowners and deprived them of the assurances they had hoped to derive from the termination of the agrarian reform. The efforts of the Calles faction to bring an end to agrarian reform had simply postponed the resolution of the agrarian question.

[13] Sources on the land reform during this period include Reyes Osorio, 1974: 56; Shulgovski, 1968: 24; L. Meyer, 1978a: 197-200. On the reasons for government efforts to end the program, see L. Meyer, 1978a: 213, 215; Krauze, 1977: 162; Medín, 1972: 26, 33; Anguiano, 1975: 14.

CONCLUSIONS

The revolution of 1910-1917 destroyed the Porfirian state apparatus, weakened the national bourgeoisie, and brought the masses of Mexico's peasantry and working class into national political life. The leaders of the victorious Constitutionalist army—drawn chiefly from the provincial petty bourgeoisie—had the task of constructing the new Mexican state and restructuring the economic system. But their options were limited by the previous level of development of productive forces in Mexico and the remains of pre-revolutionary structures. Most important, while the national bourgeoisie had been weakened, the dominant economic structure of the Porfiriato, based on the control by foreign capital of key sectors of the economy, remained virtually intact.

The uneven development of productive forces in pre-revolutionary Mexico, and the importance of foreign capital in their development, severly restricted the national resources available to the new state-in-formation and increased the attraction of foreign capital. Efforts of post-revolutionary governments to control and channel foreign capital thus met with limited success: the sovereignty of the state over national territory and resources was initially opposed by foreign corporations and governments and subsequently subordinated by the Mexican state itself to an alliance with foreign capital.

Added to limitations resulting from pre-revolutionary structures were new constraints on state action resulting from the revolution. In a certain respect, the problems confronted by the post-revolutionary governments were similar to those initially faced by Díaz, in that the country had again been broken down into regional centers of political and economic power, this time controlled by revolutionary generals. In contrast to the Díaz government, the constitution of 1917 gave legitimacy to the concept of a centralized, interventionist state, but it was only through military struggle—in which those revolutionary leaders constituting the central government depended upon support by peasant militia and assistance from the U.S.—that successive threats to its dominance were overcome. The hegemony of the federal executive was subsequently reinforced through various tactics to control the military and the elimination of organized bases of power of state governors and regional officials, and the incorporation of these groups in the

National Revolutionary Party controlled by the dominant faction of the central government.

A second parallel between pre-revolutionary and post-revolutionary Mexico can be found in the shifting state orientation toward the nature of capitalist development in Mexico. The reform of 1857 and the revolution of 1910 had both constituted attacks against monopoly privileges enjoyed by a small elite—the Church and traditional landowners in the case of the Reform, the landowners, foreign interests, and Porfirian elites in the case of the revolution. The government of Juárez and (to a lesser extent) the Sonoran dynasty of the 1920's had initially envisioned Mexico as a nation of small proprietors. In the case of the Reform, this concept was reversed under the government of Díaz, convinced that Mexico could develop only through foreign assistance, including not only foreign capital but also foreign ideas and values. The dominant productive institutions became the large-scale capitalist enterprises—commercial farms and plantations, or foreign-controlled enterprises in mining or petroleum. In the post-revolutionary years, this transition took place in a relatively short period: the structural base of capitalist enterprise survived the revolution and again dominated the economy. In the process, many of the dominant groups of the Porfiriato—commercial landowners, industrialists, even bankers—were able to reinstate themselves within the economic system, although with increased regulation by the state, and these were joined by the "capitalists of the revolution"—military officers and government officials who took advantage of their position to become part of the bourgeoisie. The ideology of the government and the new National Revolutionary Party continued to be nationalist and anti-monopoly, but the economic position of many government leaders reinforced an increasing orientation to economic development based on large-scale enterprise, foreign as well as national.

But if dependence on foreign capital and the centralization of state power had precedents in the Porfiriato, the extent of mobilization of the peasantry and the industrial working class constituted a new constraint on state autonomy in post-revolutionary Mexico. At the same time, the fact that the central government sought to control rather than respond to these groups impeded its consideration of alternative economic models to dependent capitalism, the model which emerged. Even the paternalistic role assigned to the state by the constitution and by subsequent legislation, as the Federal Labor Law, was limited in implementation. Instead, the post-revolutionary state sought to utilize these groups to consolidate its own power and attempted to control and coopt them through limited reforms. The bases for working class and peasant organizations independent of the central government were eliminated or weakened, but the state failed in its efforts to incorporate these groups into state-dominated labor and agrarian organizations. The objectives of those who actually fought the revolution had not been met, but neither had they been effectively precluded.

The constraints within which the leadership of the new state operated limited its options although they did not determine the direction it actually took. But by the end of the 1920's, this direction had reinforced certain pre-existing structures and established new ones which to some extent shaped the parameters within which subsequent governments could act. The effectiveness of these structural constraints would be tested in the following decade when the government of Lázaro Cárdenas established a new basis for state action through an alliance with the mobilized peasantry and working class.

Four || Cardenas and the New Alliance

 When a new president was inaugurated in Mexico at the end of November, 1934, most business interests expected a continuation of the Maximato. General Lázaro Cárdenas was known to be a protégé of Calles; as described by U.S. Ambassador Daniels he was a "loyal soldier" who would be guided by orders from a "superior authority" (Daniels, 1934). When a representative of General Motors took an informal survey among Embassy personnel and U.S. businessmen in Mexico, the general consensus was that Mexico was a good place to do business, and the assumption was that Calles would remain in control (Norweb, 1935). Mexican businessmen as well believed that the policy orientation of recent years would be continued under the new president (BNM, 1934-41: Aug. 1934).

In fact, two decades after the outbreak of the Mexican revolution, and approximately a dozen years after the 1917 constitution had charted a new course for the Mexican nation, Mexico seemed to be embarked on a process of development having much in common with that of the Porfiriato. Foreign capital continued to control the basic sectors of the economy and foreign investment had increased in the last decade. Mexican trade was more closely than ever tied to that of the United States. Remnants of the Porfirian bourgeoisie had been accommodated into the post-revolutionary economy, although in a dependent relationship with the state, and had been joined by a new group of capitalists which had emerged from the revolution and from the state itself. And the limited nature of agrarian reform as well as efforts to control the peasant and labor movements suggested that the majority of the population would continue to be excluded from participation in the benefits of economic growth.

THE DOMINANT ALLIANCE

Parameters of Mexico's Dependence. Mexico's foreign trade was based on the export of minerals—particularly silver and, to a lesser extent, copper and other industrial minerals—and petroleum, which together constituted up to 80 percent of Mexico's exports. The petroleum industry was dominated by British and U.S. capital, the two most important companies being El Aguila, owned by Royal Dutch Shell (predominantly British) and Huasteca, owned by Standard Oil of New Jersey, with important holdings by Sinclair, Gulf, City Services, and others. The major mining companies were American-controlled. Foreign capital was also dominant in communications (American Telephone and Telegraph, and Ericcson, a Swedish firm), and electric power (the U.S.-owned Electric Bond and Share and a British company, Mexican Light and Power). The national railway had been partially nationalized under Díaz but was heavily indebted to foreign bondholders.[1] American companies also controlled substantial agricultural holdings, including the U.S. Sugar Company in the state of Sinaloa and the Hearst estates in the northern state of Chihuahua (Shulgovski, 1968: 27-31). With the loss of foreign exchange through the repatriation of profits by foreign companies in Mexico, a substantial surplus of exports over imports—estimated in 1937 at 40 percent—was required for a favorable balance of payments (Banco de México, 1939: 20-21; Balanza de Pagos, 1937). Foreign investors also constituted an important source of tax income for the Mexican government; in the 1930's the mining industry alone provided approximately 25 percent of government revenues through various taxes (Bernstein, 1965: 188).

Export earnings fluctuated considerably during the post-revolutionary period, partly due to fluctuations in prices for mineral products as well as a decline in petroleum production after 1921. Export earnings jumped from $198 million to $425 million between 1920 and 1921, when Mexico was the second major producer of petroleum in the world. After that year petroleum production declined steadily as U.S. and British companies shifted production to Venezuela, and export earnings did not reach their 1921 level again until 1947. Between 1922 and 1929 income from

---

[1] This pattern was fairly typical of Latin American countries at that time. The petroleum industry was for the most part controlled by U.S., British, Canadian, and Dutch companies, whereas other minerals were chiefly U.S. controlled. Telephone facilities were nationally owned only in Uruguay, Guatemala, Honduras, and Nicaragua, and only in Uruguay was there a policy of government ownership of electric power. During this period there was a trend toward state ownership of the railroads (formerly foreign controlled); in Mexico the remaining four foreign-controlled lines were nationalized under Cárdenas (Rippy, 1944: 239-243).

exports fluctuated between $275 million and $375 million, with a gradual decline discernible from 1926. The world depression had a significant effect on exports, and after 1929 export earnings dropped sharply to a low of $96.5 million in 1932. In the following years they began to recover, reaching approximately $240 million in 1937, by which time mineral products, especially silver and copper, accounted for approximately 60 percent (Nacional Financiera, 1977: 385).

As indicated in Chapter Three, Mexico's foreign trade was heavily dependent on the U.S., which between 1925 and 1939 accounted for over 50 percent—and in some cases as much as 85 percent—of its imports and exports. After 1934 an important element of Mexico's trade relations with the U.S. was the purchase of silver by the U.S. Treasury on the basis of the U.S. Silver Purchase Act, which provided a significant proportion of Mexico's earnings from exports and also benefited U.S. mining interests in Mexico. In addition, it gave the U.S. an important foreign policy weapon, since withdrawal of U.S. Treasury purchases could result in sudden sharp declines in Mexico's silver exports and export earnings (Bernstein, 1965: 178; Moore, 1963: 89-90).

As indicated above, efforts of the post-revolutionary governments to restructure Mexico's relations with foreign capital on the basis of Article 27 of the constitution had resulted in agreement whereby foreign companies would in effect recognize Mexican sovereignty provided the Mexican state did not threaten their interests. After Dwight Morrow became U.S. Ambassador to Mexico in 1927, he established close relations with Calles and Mexican government officials, which included extensive intervention in Mexican financial and economic affairs in the interests of restoring Mexico's international credit standing and debt repayment capacity. Morrow was at least in part responsible for the government's decision to halt the agrarian reform due to its costs to the federal treasury.

Cordial relations between the two governments were reinforced with the initiation of a "good neighbor" policy under the Roosevelt administration. One of the effects of the world depression beginning in 1929 was to focus the attention of governments in advanced countries on internal problems, to some extent distracting them from pursuit of imperialist interests abroad. The election of Roosevelt in 1932 also reinforced a shift in U.S. policy toward Latin America—from defense of existing investments in extractive industries to recognition that U.S. interests in Latin America would best be served by trade expansion which would be facilitated by good relations with Latin American governments and even a certain level of prosperity as a means of expanding markets in the relevant countries. U.S. hemispheric policy was also increasingly influenced by events in Europe and Asia, ultimately culminating in World War II. As early as 1933 Mexico and the U.S. signed an agreement to coordinate defense policies (L. Meyer, 1978b: 255).

In Mexico, the good neighbor policy was represented by Josephus Daniels, who succeeded Morrow as Ambassador to Mexico and held this position throughout the Cárdenas administration. Daniels seems to have been a sincere believer in the New Deal and the good neighbor policy, feeling that U.S. interests in Mexico could be reconciled with the interests of Mexico itself. In this respect he differed from the American consulate general and local consulates in Mexico, which tended to take a hard-line position in support of U.S. business interests, reminiscent of U.S. policy in the early and middle 1920's.

While the Mexican government continued to be wary of foreign interests in the export sector, government officials and private Mexican interests were in agreement that foreign capital, particularly in manufacturing, was essential for Mexico's development. However, they wished to direct it according to the needs of national capital and had a vested interest in the formation of a national capitalist class to confront the hegemony of foreign capital.

The State and the Bourgeoisie. Similarly, an accommodation had been reached between the revolutionary state and the Porfirian bourgeoisie, and a dominant class fraction was taking shape formed by groups of the old bourgeoisie and new "revolutionary" capitalists drawn from the military leaders of the revolutionary armies and the new revolutionary state. In the countryside, traditional landowners, considered inefficient and unproductive, constituted the major targets of agrarian reform (which had been limited). But commercial landowners were considered an asset to the economy; foreign and domestic owners on farms producing for export or domestic markets had been joined (or in some cases replaced) by new landowners emerging from the revolution or the upper levels of government, such as Obregón, Calles, and Sáenz, or opportunists able to take advantage of chaotic conditions following the revolution, such as Jenkins. Government officials had collaborated with Porfirian bankers to restore the financial system, although the level of financial resources remained below that of the Porfiriato for several decades, and industrial groups from the Porfiriato (including individuals from the Barcelonnette group and business groups in Monterrey) maintained and in some cases increased industrial production. For the most part, whatever their differences with government policies, the bourgeoisie were dependent on the state not only for maintaining conditions for private accumulation but even for direct capital input (J. Meyer, 1977: 284-287).

In short, following a decade of controversy and confrontation, an understanding had been reached between foreign interests (including U.S. and British business interests in Mexico, banking interests represented by the International Bankers Committee, and the U.S. government), the leading faction in the Mexican State (i.e., the Callistas), and dominant segments of Mexican businessmen—an understanding based on their common efforts in constructing the institutional base of the Mexican economy and a common interest in the direction of Mexico's economic development. This understanding was in turn the basis of a latent alliance among the most powerful economic and political groups in Mexico. It did not seem likely that a new election in Mexico—one which had gone smoothly and without incident—would disturb the status quo.

ELEMENTS OF A NEW ALLIANCE

Structure and Organization of the Popular Sectors. The reconstruction of Mexico on the basis of a capitalist economy dominated by a coalition of foreign capital, private Mexican capital, and the state left the major question posed by the revolution unanswered: the role of Mexico's millions of landless peasants in a reconstructed Mexico in which the agrarian reform they had fought for had allegedly been "completed." The mobilization of these groups during the revolution and through land invasions, agrarian leagues, and armed militia in the 1920's had transformed them into political actors which the state had to take into account. This period had also been characterized by the growth and militance of certain sectors of the industrial/urban working class, for most of whom the labor provisions contained in Article 123 of the constitution were still no more than promises. The methods utilized by the post-revolutionary state to control these groups—limited agrarian reform and the attempted incorporation of independent labor and peasant organizations into state-controlled institutions—had ultimately resulted in the fragmentation of these groups but not their demobilization.

The Mexican labor force was predominantly rural. In 1930, approximately 3.6 million of a total labor force of 5.1 million were peasants or rural workers; of these, approximately 70 percent were still landless. Except for the limited number who had received small plots of land or ejidos under federal or state land reforms, or through the restitution of village lands and the distribution of latifundia in areas occupied by the peasant armies during the revolution (chiefly under Zapata), modes of exploitation in the countryside had not changed much, even if some of their worst abuses had been eliminated. Approximately 90 percent of the land was in private holdings and, as indicated in Chapter Three, 70 percent of these holdings included less than one percent of the privately owned land area. It is estimated that in the early 1930's approximately 12,000 large landowners controlled four-fifths of the rural property (González, 1979: 28). In the central and western states of Mexico, where the traditional hacienda prevailed, peasant laborers continued to be tied to the estate through forms of debt peonage. During the 1920's these groups had mobilized in the Cristero rebellion not to demand land but to defend their religion, the foundation of their culture and way of life, which had been threatened by the anti-Church policies of the government. The commercial estates continued to be worked by laborers tied to the estates, wage workers, and migrants.

In some areas militant peasant movements had formed, often with the support of state governors (Veracruz, Hidalgo, Michoacán, Tamaulipas). But these movements, viewed as threats to the centralization of state power and to the hegemony of the Calles faction within the state, had been destroyed or considerably weakened through divisive or repressive tactics of the central government.

The urban/industrial work force was smaller than that of the Porfiriato and also divided. Approximately 773,000 workers were in the industrial sector, including manufacturing, mining, electric power and construction workers, and approximately 750,000 in services, including domestic services and petty trade as well as commerce, transportation, and government. With the exception

TABLE 4.1. Economically Active Population by Sector: 1910–1940 (thousands)

Year	Total Work Force	Primary Sector	%	Industry	%	Services	%
1910	5,264	3,596	68.3	906	17.2	762	14.5
1921	4,884	3,490	71	660	14	734	15
1930	5,151	3,626	70	773	15	752	15
1940	5,858	3,831	65	909	16	1,118	19

Source: Ministry of Industry and Commerce, General Bureau of Statistics (Nacional Financiera, 1977: 13). Percentages added

of workers in transportation—railroad workers (who will be discussed below), streetcar workers, and taxi drivers, probably the only sector among government and service workers which achieved an important degree of organization in this period was that of schoolteachers. During the 1920's several state federations and national confederations were formed, but the latter were largely paper organizations (Raby, 1974: 66–69). The most important contribution of teachers to mobilization was through their links to peasant movements in the countryside, a role which would be expanded in the following decade.

One of the explanations offered for the attraction of the urban industrial labor force to populist, state-controlled coalitions in several Latin American countries during the 1930's is the recent rural origins of the labor force, which allegedly made it susceptible to paternalism and manipulation by employers and/or the government (Ianni, 1975: 118–121). But statistics of this period do not indicate a strong rural-urban trend in Mexico.

The combined industrial/services labor force increased only 10.6 percent in the decade between 1921 and 1930; in neither sector had it reached its 1910 level. In the following decade it increased by approximately one-third, largely due to the increased number of workers in services (trade, transportation and communication, and "other," which would include government workers—approximately 150,000—and domestic servants—approximately 250,000—as well as private employees). But these figures should be interpreted in the context of shifts in the total labor force, which declined between 1910 and 1930 (from 5,264,000 in 1910 to 4,884,000 in 1920 to 5,151,000 in 1930), obviously a result of the revolution. And while the number of workers in the primary sector had passed its 1910 level by 1930, the number of industrial workers did not again reach its 1910 level until 1940. (The number of workers in manufacturing and construction in 1940 was still below the 1910 levels.) This trend suggests a reverse pattern of migration—i.e., from urban/industrial employment to rural employment, which would have been facilitated by close family and community ties to rural areas. Most of the industrial workers seem to have been part of this sector for several decades; it is logical to assume that increases in the urban labor force after 1921 consisted of workers forced out during the revolution who subsequently returned.

More important than its rural origins were the small size and heterogeneity of the urban/industrial working class, a consequence of the uneven development of capitalism in Mexico and resulting in strong divergences in experience and consciousness. The stronger and more independent sectors of the working class consisted of skilled workers in highly capitalized industries generally developed by foreign capital—the railroads (approximately 47,000 workers in 1930), mining (50,000), petroleum (15,000), and electric power (17,000)—a total of approximately 130,000. Because they were in a position to obtain better conditions than other workers, they tended to maintain their distance from the national confederations, and during the 1920's they had been more successful than workers in other sectors at resisting integration into CROM, the government-controlled confederation (L. Meyer, 1978a: 131).

The railroad workers had played a strategic role in the Mexican revolution and had been in the vanguard of the unionization movement prior to the revolution. During the 1920's efforts toward unification had been countered to some extent by inter-gremial conflicts, largely due to attempts by CROM to obtain control of the railroad workers' unions. In 1921, the Confederación de Sociedades Ferrocarriles (Confederation of Railroad Societies) was formed, grouping sixteen *gremios* or guilds of railroad workers. In 1925 CROM formed the rival Federación Nacional de Ferrocarriles, which attempted, with some success, to draw members from the Confederation. Subsequently a small group of railroad workers, members of the Communist party, attempted to restructure the earlier organization, forming in 1927 the Confederation of Transport and Communication, which tenaciously opposed CROM. The Confederation, which became the Sindicato de Trabajadores Ferrocarilleros de la República Mexicana (Union of Railroad Workers of the Mexican Republic) grouped approximately 40,000 of the 47,000 railroad workers in 1932 (Gill, 1971: 39; L. Meyer,

1978a: 131). In contrast, the streetcar workers of Mexico City had difficulty in achieving unity; in a ten-year period they joined, left, and rejoined CROM; twice declared themselves independent; joined the CGT; and finally split into three unions (Spalding, 1977: 110).

The electrical workers (with the exception of those in Yucatán) were joined in the Confederación Nacional de Electricistas y Similares (National Confederation of Electrical and Related Workers) of which the most important union was the Sindicato Mexicano de Electricistas (SME) which grouped the workers of Mexico City. The SME had been relatively successful in obtaining high wages and benefits for its workers through direct negotiation with foreign companies; although there had been numerous conflicts between the electrical workers' confederation and CROM during the 1920's the Confederation had maintained its economic and political independence of the state. It was oriented to economic goals and basically apolitical (L. Meyer, 1978a: 142-143; Clark, 1934: 167-170).

In contrast, the petroleum workers and mineworkers were not organized on an industry-wide level, although both sectors had been influenced by the IWW in the early 1900's and had a strong tradition of labor organization and militance on the local level. During the 1920's with the assistance of the CGT (Confederación General de Trabajo) and other local unions, the petroleum workers had resisted incorporation into CROM as well as government and employer efforts to break strikes and destroy the unions. Earlier efforts of the IWW to group them into an industry-wide confederation had been broken by the companies (Carr, 1976, II: 19-20; L. Meyer, 1978a: 140). The mineworkers were more fragmented, in part because they were dispersed throughout the country. Most of the workers lacked union protection; some local mineworkers' unions were linked to state federations, CROM, or other national confederations (L. Meyer, 1978a: 137).

In general, the independent industrial unions and confederations also differed with CROM-dominated unions in that their internal structure was basically democratic; at the same time, they were characterized by a strong sense of solidarity with workers of other labor organizations, as indicated by frequent sympathy strikes among petroleum, railroad, and electrical workers in different localities (Anguiano et al., 1975: 105).

Most of the industrial workers—approximately 600,000—were in manufacturing, but probably half of these were artisans or operatives in small workshops. Only about 215,000 were in industries valued at 10,000 pesos (L. Meyer, 1978a: 113). The largest number of factory workers were in the textile industry, which was concentrated in the states of Puebla, Tlaxcala, and Veracruz. The textile workers had been organized by CROM and the CGT, which fought for the allegiance of different locals throughout the 1920's. They were very militant, and the labor-intensive character of the industry was one of their achievements. However, the industry was characterized by unstable conditions during much of this period and consequent efforts of tripartite boards (with representatives of owners, workers, and the government) to stabilize conditions (Nafinsa, 1977: 13; L. Meyer, 1978a: 145; Talavera Aldana, 1976).

None of the national confederations were particularly strong in the early 1930's. As noted above, CROM had lost much of its membership when it lost government support, and the anarchist Confederación General de Trabajo (CGT), formed in 1921, was considerably weakened by a combination of external pressures and internal splits by 1933. The Communist party and its labor organization, the Confederación Sindical Unitaria de México (CSUM) had been weakened through the exile or imprisonment of party leaders following an insurrection in 1929 and the withdrawal of the peasant contingent under the direction of Ursulo Galván in 1930. In June 1932, the Cámara de Trabajo was formed at the instigation of the CGT to unite various labor confederations, but it was taken over by pro-government elements who attempted to convert it into an appendage of the new PNR; in 1933 it had only 15,700 members and never attained national significance (Salazar, 1956b: 62-63; Basurto 1975: 273; Shulgovski, 1968: 70; L. Meyer, 1978a: 126-128).

However, in March 1933, several unions which had broken away from CROM united to form the CROM "depurada" (the "purified" CROM), which in the following October became the Confederación General de Obreros y Campesinos de Mexico (CGOCM) under the leadership of Vicente Lombardo Toledano, a middle-class intellectual and former CROM leader who had broken with Morones in 1932 (Basurto, 1975: 272-273). Taking the position, "the road is to the left," Lombardo Toledano established the CGOCM on the principle of independence with respect to the state and an orientation toward revolutionary struggle against capitalism, as well as toward immediate economic goals.

Initially there were three groups within the Confederation. The group led by Lombardo Toledano included the confederations of graphic arts and cinema as well as smaller unions. As a leader within CROM during the 1920's, Lombardo Toledano had held various government posts, including a brief stint as Governor of Peubla, and had been instrumental in the organization of school-teachers. His ideological orientation shifted to an increasingly left-ist, and ultimately Marxist, position, and in the early 1930's he finally broke with Morones, for reasons of ideology, opportun-ism, or both.[2] Lombardo Toledano's working-class base was lim-ited, but partly as a consequence of his intellectual gifts and evi-dent charisma he became an important ideologue and leader of the Mexican labor movement in the 1930's. (Other factors included his links with the Cárdenas government, on the one hand, and with Moscow and the Comintern, on the other, but at this point, i.e., the early 1930's, his position was apparently that of an inde-pendent leftist.) Lombardo Toledano was responsible for state-ments of principles, statutes, program declarations, and other doc-uments, and in general for the political orientation of the confederation.

The second group, led by Fidel Velázquez and Fernando Amilpa, also from the CROM leadership, controlled unions of the Federal District and the state of Puebla, grouped in state federations. This group combined organizational skills with opportunistic practices developed within CROM—including alliances with local govern-ment and business leaders to control workers in the relevant areas. They had broken with CROM in the late 1920's, and when Portes Gil was president he had appointed several of them as labor rep-resentatives to the labor arbitration boards, canceling the elections of 1928 which had given these positions to CROM members (Hernández Chavez, 1979: 123). The third group, from the CGT, was weakened by various defections and lost all influence within the confederation. Since the Velázquez-Amilpa group was strictly interested in organizational control and lacked a political line, its position was complementary rather than antagonistic to that of Lombardo Toledano, whose political orientation thus prevailed (León, 1977: 63-72). This was the beginning of a collaboration

[2] Lombardo Toledano stated in an interview that he remained in CROM in an effort to reform it from within (Wilkie and Wilkie, 1969: 305-306). However, by 1930 CROM had lost much of its membership, and Lombardo Toledano's speeches even at this time indicate unqualified support for Morones (Salazar, 1956b: 15).

between the two groups which would shape the development of the labor movement in the 1930's. The CGOCM organized new or existing unions into state federations—Regional Federations of Workers and Peasants (FROC)—in several states, and helped to organize strike movements among sugar, petroleum, and textile workers (Fuentes Díaz, 1959: 335). The CGOCM was undoubtedly the most dynamic of the national confederations, but still limited in size and scope.

Effects of the Depression. In the meantime, the effects of the depression had increased the alienation of peasants who were dissatisfied with the slow pace and the threatened termination of agrarian reform, and workers fed up with ineffective and corrupt union leadership. As elsewhere in Latin America, the effects of the depression were first felt in Mexico's export industry. Export earnings dropped from $274 million (U.S.) in 1929 to $150.9 million in 1931 and $96.5 million in 1932. The problem of contraction of export markets was aggravated with the application of the Hawley Smoot law of 1930, which raised duties for imports to the U.S., the market for over half (58 percent) of Mexico's exports. A sharp contraction of exports of mineral products (especially silver), petroleum, and henequen resulted in production cutbacks in these areas and consequent dismissals of workers. Rising rates of unemployment led to a general contraction of purchasing power, in turn affecting the principal manufacturing industries of food processing and textiles. Between 1929 and 1932 half of the mineworkers lost their jobs, their numbers reduced from 90,000 to 45,000; the number of employed textile workers dropped from 44,000 to 38,000; and between 1930 and 1932, 10,432 railroad workers were dismissed (Anguiano, 1975: 17; Shulgovski, 1968: 34-35; L. Meyer, 1978a: 44, 48, 145; Hernández Chavez, 1979: 133).

Whether the effects of the depression resulted in an increase in the level of mobilization of popular sectors or, on the contrary, led to a process of demobilization, is debated in analyses of this period. The issue is whether peasant and labor mobilization contributed to a dramatic shift in the government party orientation beginning in approximately 1933, or whether this shift represents a change imposed from above. According to some authors, this was a period of frequent though fragmented mobilizations: hunger marches to state capitals, land seizures, and agrarian revolts, including an uprising of 15,000 peasants in Veracruz provoked by government attempts to liquidate the collective ejido (García Cantú, 1965: 932; Shulgovski, 1968: 73; Córdova, 1974: 20). There was also increased mobilization among middle-class groups, such as consumer movements against increased electric rates, which were also supported by government technicians (Wionczek, 1964: 49).

But others point out that the depression affected only a small proportion of Mexico's labor force, since the majority of peasants—small holders or workers on agricultural estates—were engaged in subsistence agriculture or producing for domestic markets and were therefore unaffected by the decline in exports. Also, while mine and textile workers were affected, workers in other strategic industrial sectors, such as electric power, were not; major reductions in the number of petroleum workers had occurred earlier as a consequence of production cutbacks of the 1920's which had reduced the work force from between 30,000 and 50,000 in the early 1920's to approximately 15,000 at the end of the decade. In addition, some workers in industry or commercial agricultural estates could be absorbed into traditional agriculture, and wage cutbacks were to some extent offset by decreases in prices. The number of strikes was extremely low during this period, and many workers withdrew from unions. The uprising in Veracruz was in fact a reaction to the federal government's effort to disarm the Veracruz peasant league, a move which was seen as a major threat to its hegemony. The government's success over the most powerful peasant league in the country in fact demonstrated its ability to control mobilized groups (L. Meyer, 1978a: 11-12, 87; Spalding, 1977: 112; Falcón, 1978: 370).

To some extent the apparent low level of labor mobilization during this period can be explained by the fact that strikes were not officially permitted and that strikes not recognized by the government were considered legally "non-existent." While the number of recorded strikes is low, the number of labor conflicts increased from 13,405 in 1929 to 20,702 in 1930; 29,087 in 1931; and 36,781 in 1932 (Fuentes Díaz, 1959: 332; Córdova, 1974: 20). But perhaps this question can be examined more fruitfully if one does not expect an immediate cause-effect relationship between peasant and labor mobilization, on the one hand, and changes within the state, on the other. Rather, the process seems to have been a gradual one in which class forces and conflicts impinged upon the state in various ways and were reproduced within the state with varying degrees of clarity or distortion.

Throughout the period from 1924 to the early 1930's, the faction controlled by Calles dominated the government, but gradually during this period a group of "agrarians" emerged who became spokesmen in official circles for peasant discontent. The agrarians included state governors such as Lázaro Cárdenas in Michoacán, Adalberto Tejeda in Veracruz, Emilio Portes Gil in Tamaulipas, and Saturnino Cedillo in San Luis Potosí, who for reasons of opportunism or conviction sought to create a new power base through peasant (and in some cases working-class) mobilization and to carry out land distribution programs. Also part of this group were members of Congress such as Gilberto Fabila and Graciano Sánchez, who saw the solution for the agrarian problem in the distribution of large estates and in the ejido and sought to block legislation intended to slow down agrarian reform; and certain officials within the state agrarian bureaucracy, such as Marte R. Gómez, who had collaborated in the land distribution programs of Portes Gil in the state of Tamaulipas and subsequently as Secretary of Agriculture during the interim presidency of Portes Gil.

Government efforts to terminate the agrarian reform in the early 1930's therefore resulted in conflicts between these groups and the "veterans" grouped around Calles and the Secretary of Agriculture, Manuel Pérez Treviño, who extolled the landowners as "a factor of Mexican production" and spoke of the need to defend the "honest hacendado." For the veterans, the solution to the agrarian problem was increased productivity on the basis of modernization, a policy which called for an end to uncertainties caused by the agrarian reform and promotion of commercial landowners. Their model was the commercial estates of the north, especially in the state of Sonora, which had received substantial government assistance benefiting, among others, members of the Sonoran dynasty. In October 1931, at the instigation of the landowners, a law was passed exempting certain properties where strategic crops were grown (e.g., sugar, henequen, and coffee) from expropriation (Simpson, 1937: 439-444; Falcón, 1978: 358; Shulgovski, 1968: 223).

Efforts of state governors to resist national policies to end the agrarian reform met with limited success. In 1931, several state governors, among them Cárdenas of Michoacán and Tejeda of Veracruz, constituted an informal bloc which attracted left-wing groups in the party and in Congress. The central government responded by imposing its own governors in these states and disarming and neutralizing state agrarian movements. Splits also developed among the agrarians themselves, indicated in a division of the Ursulo Galván Peasant League into a radical (Veracruz) group and a "moderate" group, and the fact that it was Cárdenas, as Secretary of War, who ordered the disarming of the peasant militia of Veracruz, the last stage in dismantling the peasant movement in that state (Falcón, 1978: 377).

Nevertheless, the agrarians had some victories during this period. In June 1931, Congress rejected a proposal that the agrarian problem be "resolved" within three months, and at the end of that year they succeeded in having the agrarian *amparo*—through which landowners could legally appeal expropriation decisions—repealed.

As early as March 1932 certain groups among the agrarians had begun to propose Lázaro Cárdenas as presidential candidate for 1934. Cárdenas had joined the revolution in 1913 when he was eighteen years of age; subsequently he served under General Calles in the Constitutionalist army. Cárdenas distinguished himself during the revolution and subsequently in the conflict with the de la Huerta forces, rising to the rank of division general. During the 1920's he held various military positions, including that of military zone commander of Tampico for three years, where he had occasion to observe the discrimination against Mexican workers by the foreign-owned petroleum companies. Subsequently he became Governor of Michoacán, where he carried out expropriations against almost all the latifundia of the state (excepting those legally exempt from expropriation, where rural unions were organized). In 1930 he became head of the PNR, and in 1932 he was appointed Secretary of Government in the cabinet of Ortiz Rubio, where he attempted, without success, to bring about a reconciliation between the President and Calles.

By the end of 1932 the proposed candidacy of Cárdenas had obtained the support of most groups within the agrarian bloc as well as a substantial number of military leaders, including conservatives such as General Juan Andreu Almazán, allegedly frustrated by his exclusion from the Calles clique, and General Cedillo, the "conservative agrarian," who opposed Calles' anti-clerical policies. But despite the increasing incompatibility of Cárdenas' policies with those of Calles, by April 1933 Cárdenas had also obtained the support of Calles and his sons, as well as Callistas such as Aarón Sáenz and President Abelardo Rodríguez. In the following month the Cárdenas campaign became open with publication of a manifesto of the Confederation of Mexican Peasants (CCM), a new confederation consisting of the peasant leagues of the moderate wing of the Ursulo Galván Peasant League, which proposed Cárdenas as a candidate and asked other peasant and labor organizations to support him.[3]

Given Cárdenas' own career and the nature of his support, the meaning of his candidacy was somewhat ambiguous. Was Cárdenas the progressive young governor of Michoacán who had reinforced the radical traditions within the state through land distribution, the creation of a peasant militia, and the formation of agrarian and labor organizations? Or was he the "loyal soldier" described by Daniels who under Calles' orders had overseen the disarmament—and thus the effective destruction—of the peasant militia in Veracruz? Calles' own support for Cárdenas (against a potential Callista candidate, Manuel Pérez Treviño) must have been partly dictated by recognition that Cárdenas had a strong support base within the party. But he probably also assumed that he could "neutralize" Cárdenas' agrarian tendencies and continue to govern behind the scenes. Cárdenas had scrupulously avoided antagonizing Calles, undoubtedly mindful of the ease with which Ortiz Rubio had been deposed when he tried to free himself from Calles' tutelege. But aside from his progressive agrarian orientation on the one hand and his apparent loyalty to Calles on the other, there is another element underlying Cárdenas' action during the Maximato which also explained certain of his subsequent actions in the presidency: his concern for the stability of the new institutions of the state. It was no doubt for this reason that he supported Ortiz Rubio when Callistas pressured for his resignation; this may also have been a factor in his action against the Tejeda movement in Veracruz, which was seen as a threat to the authority of the central government.[4]

The Party Convention of 1933. By this time, the conceptions of progressive groups within the government and the government party regarding the revolutionary role of the state had been rein-

[3] Analyses of Cárdenas' candidacy may be found in Shulgovski, 1968: 77 f; Medín, 1971: 13; Cornelius, 1973; and Falcón, 1978: 365-375, 380.

[4] The defeat of the Tejeda forces in Veracruz also eliminated Tejeda as a possible candidate of the government party in the 1934 presidential elections, which obviously benefited Cárdenas' candidacy. See interpretation by Falcón, 1978.

forced by the influence of world events and external models. The depression had demonstrated the contradictions in capitalism at a time when the results of the first Soviet five-year plan were being publicized. Both the Soviet model and Roosevelt's New Deal, as well as the generalized trend toward statism in Western Europe, evoked a response among reform-oriented groups in Mexico, reinforcing earlier conceptions of the revolutionary state's actively shaping the national economy and intervening in production relations to insure the rights of peasants and the working class.[5]

Internal struggles and external influences converged at the PNR nominating convention in Querétero held in December 1933. Differences between the Callistas and the agrarians did not center on the nomination of Cárdenas, already a foregone conclusion, but a proposed six-year plan which was to shape the *sexenio*, the six-year period of his administration. A moderate plan proposed by Calles was criticized and radically modified by the opposition. Representing this group was Graciano Sánchez, who introduced a series of agrarian measures, among them recognition of the rights of resident peons (*acasillados*) on the large estates to land within the agrarian reform (from which these groups had been formerly excluded), and the creation of an autonomous Agrarian Department with jurisdiction over all aspects of land distribution and communal organization. The latter provision in effect removed control over agrarian reform from the Secretary of Agriculture and from the conservative influence of state governors, whose support for land expropriation and distribution had generally been limited (with the exception of the "agrarian" governors, indicated above). The incorporation of these measures into the plan indicated a shift from recent government policy by giving top priority to agrarian reform.[6]

[5] On the influence of external events and models, see Wionczek, 1964: 52-54; and Shulgovski, 1968: 84. Wionzcek points out the favorable impact of Roosevelt's *Looking Forward* when translated (apparently somewhat radicalized in the process) and serialized in *El Economista*. In 1934, the first issue of *Trimestre Económica* appeared with translations of articles by Keynes on national self-sufficiency and by Harold J. Lasky on the Roosevelt experiment (which he characterized as an attempt to use the power of the state to subordinate the axioms of capitalist society to certain vital social purposes) as well as an article by the Mexican economist Roberto López noting the need for a permanent planning agency to plan and administer the programs of the Mexican government.

[6] The text of the six-year plan may be found in PNR, 1934, and an analysis of its contents in Bosques, 1937. See also Medín, 1972: 44-52; Calderón Rodríguez, 1976: 218-223; and Córdova, 1974: 46-49.

The plan is of interest since Cárdenas made it his campaign platform, included several of its promoters in his cabinet, and in fact
implemented much of it once in office. Aside from the priority
given to agrarian reform, it reaffirmed the constitutional concept
of the active interventionist state, controlling and directing the national economy. It called for economic integration at the national
level and reasserted the constitutional principle of national sovereignty over subsoil wealth, including encouragement of Mexican
miners and the development of a national petroleum industry, as
well as tariffs on mineral exports and other policies to insure that
benefits from mineral wealth accrued to Mexicans. It also called
upon the government to promote industrialization, particularly
through the import of agricultural and industrial machinery, and
to increase government control over the generation and distribution of electrical energy in order to provide it at lower prices and
to link its distribution to the promotion of new industrial centers.
The government was also given a mandate to rationalize industry
through intervention in prices and quality control, import substitution, and utlization of national resources, and to regulate commerce to eliminate speculation and reduce the number of intermediaries. Physical integration would be promoted through the
construction of roads and highways.

With respect to labor, the plan explicitly recognized the class
struggle inherent in the existing system of production and called
on the state to promote and strengthen union organization. At the
instigation of delegates from Tabasco and Veracruz, it emphasized
the anti-clerical orientation of education; the state would have
complete responsibility for primary education, which should be
standardized throughout the republic. It also called for particular
attention to rural schools, state direction of secondary school education and, at the higher level, replacement of liberal professions
by scientific and technical training. In addition to eliminating clerical influence, "socialist education" should be anti-individualist and
prepare students to live and work collectively.

In most respects the six-year plan reflected the principles of the
1917 constitution, reinforced by the intellectual currents favoring
state intervention resulting from the world situation as well as
specific effects of the economic crisis in Mexico. The central element was the role of the state in directing and restructuring society, exercised in the name of the masses, including the strengthening of union organizations and the training of the workers and
peasants.

1934: Year of Transition. The year between the nomination of Cárdenas at the Querétaro convention and his inauguration as president in many respects marked a transition in the bases of power and the mode of operation of the state. Several proposals of the six-year plan were put into effect by President Abelardo Rodríguez, some of them almost immediately. On December 29, 1933, the Comisión Federal de Electricidad (CFE) was created to give the state direct participation in the generation of electricity. In September 1934, after an unsuccessful attempt to form an association with foreign firms to develop Mexico's petroleum resources for the Mexican market, the government formed Petroleos de Mexico (Petromex) with shares held by the state and national private capital, to explore and develop petroleum deposits, and ultimately compete with private firms. Given the limited resources of the state and the low level of support by private capital, the development of Petromex was limited, but Petromex and CFE represented tentative efforts of the state toward control of vital resources now monopolized by foreign capital (L. Meyer, 1978a: 54, 81; 12: 165, 233).

In January 1934 a decree was passed which transformed the National Agrarian Commission into an autonomous Agrarian Department, directly responsible to the President—thus removing the implementation of agrarian reform from the jurisdiction of the Secretary of Agriculture. In March an Agrarian Code was formulated which brought together existing legislation on the agrarian question, simplified the machinery for land distribution, and introduced new legislation, including the right of *peones acasillados* to participate in the land reform (Simpson, 1937: 456-458). Thus the institutional machinery for much of the agrarian reform was already in existence when Cárdenas became president.

In the meantime, Cárdenas took advantage of his position as official presidential candidate to launch an energetic campaign tour which took him to every state and to some of the most remote areas of the country. Throughout the campaign he stressed issues raised by the six-year plan: the necessity for labor unification, the priority of agrarian reform, the extension of physical infrastructure (dams, irrigation works, roads, and railroads) and the expansion of education. A central theme underlying these issues was that of integration: physical integration through the construction of roads and railroads which would connect remote areas to national markets; economic and cultural integration through the development of the "socialist school" which would foster collective solidarity and the pursuit of independent economic development; and the formation of a common front of workers (rural and urban) which could struggle more effectively against their common enemies and collaborate with the government in achieving economic integration and the independent development of Mexico.[7]

The essential message of Cárdenas' campaign was that the state was prepared to respond positively to the mobilization of peasants and workers. On numerous occasions he exhorted workers to forget their own differences (referring to the often bitter inter-union conflicts, especially among the textile workers, between those affiliated with CROM and those of the new CGOCM) and to form a united front against those who would exploit them. While Cárdenas envisioned a paternalistic and interventionist role for the state in supporting the struggles of the working class and peasantry, he also felt that the process of transformation of the economic structure could be carried out only through the mobilization of the sectors directly affected—the workers and the peasants. This mobilization would not only provide peasant and working class support to the government in carrying out reforms but would also enable them to demand that the government itself fulfill its promises.

The six-year plan and the campaign of Cárdenas indicated a shift in the orientation of the government which in turn evoked a response among important sectors of the working class. During this period the CGOCM organized unions and state federations; the miners and metalworkers succeeded in forming an industrial union (Sindicato de Trabajadores Mineros, Metalúrgicos y Similares de la Républica Mexicana—hereinafter referred to as the Mine and Metal Workers' Union); and there was a general resurgence of strike movements. The year was one of mobilization for the formerly apolitical electrical workers, especially those of the Electric Bond and Share Company (which controlled much of the electrical power system outside Mexico City), who called for strikes in several states and by the end of the year were aligned with those seeking to restructure the labor movement (Meyer, 1978a: 143). Between June 1934 and the first months of 1935 petroleum work-

---

[7] On the Cárdenas campaign, see Cárdenas, 1972b, which is a collection of his notes, especially pp. 275, 280-281. Some of Cárdenas' campaign speeches may be found in Muñoz, 1976: 115-152, passim. See also Córdova, 1974: 37-38, 55, and Weyl and Weyl, 1939: 127.

ers in different companies called seven major strikes to improve working conditions. During 1934 strikes were called by textile workers, cane workers, and railroad workers. In contrast to previous years, strikes were recognized by the government and in some cases resulted in important working-class victories (e.g., in several petroleum workers' unions, where workers obtained a 20 percent wage increase and payment for the seventh day of the week (Meyer, 1978a: 142, 170-171; Chassen, 1977: 99). In contrast to the peasant leagues joined in the CCM, the labor movement did not support Cárdenas directly, but it provided indirect support through the formation of a National Committee for the Defense of the Educational Reform, which included the CGOCM, CROM, CGT, the railroad workers' union, and several other labor organizations (Meyer, 1978a: 123).

Thus by the time that Cárdenas became president, much of the institutional framework for the initiatives of his *sexenio* was in place, and a new coalition of forces was taking shape which would challenge the hegemony of the dominant alliance formed over the previous decade.

VICTORY OF THE NEW ALLIANCE

The Break with Calles. But the ambiguity surrounding Calles' role in the new administration was not yet resolved. Calles could not have been too pleased with the radical tenor of Cárdenas' campaign speeches nor the level of "labor agitation" in the year preceding Cárdenas' inauguration. But Cárdenas had been careful to avoid direct confrontation with Calles, and emphasized issues on which they were in agreement, such as socialist education and anti-clericalism.[8] The assumption that the Cárdenas government meant "business as usual" was not confined to those favoring the status quo; the Communist party condemned the progressive stance of

[8] It was Calles who formally proposed the reform of Article 3 of the constitution, which provided for state control of education, to the effect that such education be socialist. Cárdenas' anti-clericalism was less virulent than that of Calles, but there is little doubt that he felt an intense antipathy for the ideological influences of the Church and its role in promoting ignorance and fanaticism. On one occasion, when rural teachers were attacked by fanatics opposed to the government education policy, Cárdenas went to the scene of the attack (Ciudad González, Guanajuato) and ordered that the priests responsible for inciting the people to violence leave the town within 24 hours. (Mexico, Cámara de Diputados, V: 760-762).

Cárdenas as an attempt to deceive the people, and ran its own candidate, Hernán Laborde, for president. This assumption was reinforced by Cárdenas' first cabinet which contained several Callistas, among them Calles' son, Rodolfo Elías Calles, as Secretary of Communications and Public Works; Callistas also controlled the Senate and Chamber of Deputies and major posts in the federal, state, and municipal government bureaucracies, and included several high-ranking officers of the military (Brown, 1971: 25; Cornelius, 1973: 439).

But the significance of the Cárdenas presidency in terms of a shift in the alignment of forces became clear in the first months of 1935, with a resurgence of the strike movements which began the year before. Apart from pro-labor decisions by the Federal Labor Board, Cárdenas defended the workers in newspaper interviews, stating that the striking workers were only trying to obtain their legal rights, and that the large number of strikes was simply a manifestation of the injustices in their treatment by employers (Salazar, 1956b: 139-140; *Excelsior*, 13 April 1935).

The frequency of strikes (their number increased from 202 in 1934 to 642 in 1935) and their obvious support by the Cárdenas government elicited a series of complaints from business groups, members of the Calles clique, and finally Calles himself. In a statement published on June 12 Calles condemned the working class as traitors to the national interest, called upon the government to suppress strikes which were leading the country to economic chaos, and criticized divisions in the ranks of the "revolutionary family" resulting from the maneuvers of radicals. Although careful not to attack Cárdenas directly, the document not only constituted an obvious challenge to the government's labor policy but also contained a veiled reference to the resignation of Ortiz Rubio as president in 1932 following a similar disagreement with Calles. This statement was supported by business organizations, senators and deputies, generals and state governors, as well as by CROM and the CGT (Shulgovski, 1968: 98-100; Iglesias, 1970: 65).

The Calles statement accelerated the process of labor mobilization and unification. On the day it appeared, delegates of several labor organizations issued a statement reaffirming their decision to defend their rights to the point of a general strike if necessary. Following discussions among the CGOCM, the Mexican Communist party, the electricians' union, and other organizations, the National Committee for Proletarian Defense was formed, group-

ing the CGOCM, the CSUM, and independent unions of telephone workers, electricians, and miners, as well as peasant fronts
and organizations, including the CCM, and the Liga Ursulo Galván (Anguiano, 1975: 52-53; Gómez Jara, 1970: 101). Although
the Communist party was instrumental in the formation of the
committee, which it conceptualized as an independent organization to defend the working class from attack, it maintained its
aloofness from the Cárdenas regime and the political struggle with
the slogan "ni con Calles ni con Cárdenas" ("neither Calles nor
Cárdenas").

At the same time, Cárdenas acted quickly to fortify his position.
Immediately upon becoming president, Cárdenas had begun making transfers of military zone commanders, placing those he trusted
in key posts. With the Calles statement, Cárdenas sent agents to
all parts of the country to determine the sympathies of military
commanders and state governors, transferring or retiring generals
who hesitated to express their loyalty to him. Cárdenas' long military career had won him support among a substantial number of
military officers; others were unwilling to risk their new wealth,
acquired during the Calles administration or the Maximato, in a
confrontation between Calles and Cárdenas, which weakened Calles'
support from this group. Army contingents known to be loyal to
Cárdenas were concentrated near the capital (Hernández Chávez,
1979: 45, 91; Cornelius, 1973: 444-445).

A report from the U.S. Embassy suggested that Calles and Cárdenas had met earlier, on June 7, to discuss the "excessive demands of labor" and the fact that the labor movement was "out
of control." They had reached agreement on a statement, but the
reference in Calles' interview to the Ortiz Rubio resignation had
been completely unexpected by Cárdenas, who at that point was
warned by General Francisco Múgica (a close associate of Cárdenas and Secretary of the National Economy) and by Manjarrez
(editor of the government newspaper *El Nacional*) that to follow
Calles' views on labor would amount to political suicide (Daniels,
1935). This version, which suggests that the break with Calles and
the decision to base his regime on labor support represented a
sudden shift in orientation on the part of Cárdenas, is of interest
but seems quite unlikely given the apparent continuity of Cárdenas' labor policy, the fact that military transfers had begun some
months before, and the speed with which he acted following the
Calles statement.

On June 13, the press carried Cárdenas' response to Calles. In a strongly worded statement, he defended the right of the workers to obtain better conditions "within the economic possibilities of the capitalist system" and stated the resolve of the federal executive to "fulfill the program of the revolution and carry out the dictates of the six-year plan without regard for the alarm expressed by the capitalist class" (Ashby, 1963: 24-26). With respect to the unity of the revolutionary family, such unity did not exist; it had been destroyed by sabotage and betrayal from the beginning of his presidency (Shulgovski, 1968: 101). On June 15 the cabinet resigned at Cárdenas' request, and by June 17 a new cabinet had been appointed with key posts given to Cárdenas supporters, among them Silvano Barba González (identified with the Cárdenas labor policy) as Secretary of Government; Luis Rodríguez as Secretary to the President; Francisco Múgica as Secretary of Communications and Public Works (replacing Calles' son); and Gabino Vázquez (a former Senator from Oaxaca) as Director of the Agrarian Department. In a move calculated to win the support of the Catholics the anti-clerical Tomás Garrido Canabel was replaced as Secretary of Agriculture by the conservative, pro-Catholic Saturnino Cedillo, an early Cárdenas supporter (Weyl and Weyl, 1939: 163). Cárdenas also sought the support of less radical sectors within the state and party through the selection of Emilio Portes Gil as Chairman of the PNR.

The Cárdenas declaration brought him immediate support from a broad range of sectors; in addition to demonstrations by workers, peasants, and students, there were declarations by military officers and governors of their adhesion to Cárdenas, and the left-wing Cárdenas minority in Congress—led by a small but vocal group of delegates from Michoacán—was swiftly transformed into a majority (Cornelius, 1973: 445). The shift of allegiances by individuals at various levels of the state bureaucracy indicated the fragility of the support for Calles, but it also suggested that support for Cárdenas from these groups would not be very dependable, based as it clearly was on opportunism (North and Raby, 1977: 42). Nevertheless, the events of June 1934 were significant in placing Cárdenas and his followers firmly in control of the state apparatus, cementing the relationship between the Cárdenas government and the organized working class, and demonstrating the effectiveness of labor mobilization as an element of reform. At a broader level, the previously dominant alliance, formed by shifting coalitions, overt or latent, between the Calles faction within the state and dominant class factions, including foreign capital as well as the old and new national bourgeoisie, had been replaced, at least temporarily, by a new "progressive" coalition which included the Cárdenas faction within the state and the mobilized working class and peasantry, to some extent organized in the Committee for Proletarian Defense. On this basis, Mexico entered the most progressive phase of its post-revolutionary history, which was to last only a brief period—1935-1938—but was to have an enduring effect on Mexican society.[9]

Contradictions within the State. The reforms of the Sonoran presidents had eliminated certain obstacles to state cohesion by eliminating the power of regional generals and concentrating political power in the central government. The successful confrontation of Cárdenas and his followers with Calles and his followers carried the process of institutionalization of the post-revolutionary state one step further, replacing the hegemony previously exercised by a series of caudillos and subsequently the Jefe Máximo with the hegemony of the presidency, which has continued to characterize the Mexican political system (Medín, 1971: 15-17; Córdova, 1974: 44-45). Presidential control was obviously essential for the state to carry out the functions of national integration and economic development envisioned by Cárdenas. As he stated in his inaugural address: "It is essential to see the economic problem as an integral whole and to recognize the connections linking each of its parts.

[9] Although Calles issued a declaration published on June 17 which was a virtual retraction, declaring his intention to retire from politics, and subsequently left for the United States, his agitation against the Cárdenas government continued. In December 1935 he returned to Mexico, announcing his intention to defend his regime against the attacks to which it had been subjected during the previous six months, and forming with his followers the Partido Revolucionario Constitucional. In the meantime, Cárdenas had purged Callistas at the middle and lower echelons of the party, government, labor, and agrarian organizations. Several deputies were expelled (following a shootout in the Chamber of Deputies); most of the remaining Callista senators and deputies resigned (Shulgovski, 1968: 105; Cornelius, 1973: 450). On December 22 the National Committee for Proletarian Defense organized a demonstration in which 80,000 to 100,000 workers, peasants, and students took part, demanding that Calles be expelled from the country (Anguiano, 1975: 56-57). Cárdenas intensified the purge of Callistas: five senators were expelled, the Senate voted to remove four *callista* governors, and several army generals were transferred to new posts (Cornelius, 1973: 452-453). Finally, in April 1936 Calles and three of his closest associates were expelled from the country.

The state alone embodies the general interest, and for this reason only the state has a vision of the whole. The state must continually broaden, increase and deepen its intervention."[10]

But the state apparatus was not a neutral instrument of the president. As indicated above, it had been formed in conjunction with the reconstruction of Mexican society in which former Porfirian elements and new capitalists, often from the government itself, had established or re-established their preeminent economic position. Even after the Callistas had been purged from various levels of government and key cabinet posts had been filled with Cárdenas supporters, officials at all levels of government were more open to influence from dominant class elements than to direction from a reform-oriented government, although they might opportunistically give lip service to the latter. These problems were reinforced by the wealth and vested interests of high-level military and federal and local government officials, low pay and a lack of motivation among lower level officials, and temptations to opportunism and corruption at all levels (Anguiano et al., 1975: 90).

Even within the Cárdenas faction there were strong divergences in orientation, reflecting the importance of personal loyalties relative to ideology in the establishment of political alliances. One implication was that different classes and interests were represented not only within the state apparatus but also within the government itself. It has been suggested that Cárdenas was part of the "left wing" of his government. Other members of this wing included General Múgica, Luis Rodríguez, Silvano Barba González, and the agrarians, among them Graciano Sánchez and Gabino Vázquez. Of these, Múgica was the most important. A close personal friend of Cárdenas, he had headed the Obregón faction at the constitutional convention of 1917; subsequently he had initiated an agrarian reform and other progressive measures as governor of Michoacán. Within the Cárdenas government he took a consistently progressive position; he was largely responsible for the decision to offer Trotsky asylum in Mexico and was a major proponent of the petroleum expropriation.

Others within the Cárdenas government supported progressive

[10] "Es fundamental ver el problema económico en su integridad, y advertir las conexiones que ligan cada una de sus partes con las demás. Sólo el Estado tiene un interés general, y por esa, sólo el tiene una visión del conjunto. La intervención del Estado ha de ser cada vez mayor, cada vez más frequente, y cada vez más al fondo" (Mexico, Cámara de Diputados, IV: II).

policies for frankly pragmatic reasons. As stated by Emilio Portes
Gil, an agrarian and self-styled "centrist," unionization was a
powerful asset to capitalism; its efforts to improve economic conditions of the workers also served to broaden the market (Iglesias,
1970: 100-101). As interim president following the assassination of
Obregón, Portes Gil had set a record in the amount of land distributed to the peasants, recognizing the government's need for
peasant support to defeat military uprisings (as occurred with the
Escobar rebellion of 1929). Although Portes Gil had supported
Calles in the showdown with Ortiz Rubio in 1932 he subsequently
broke with him when Calles imposed his candidate as governor in
Portes Gil's state of Tamaulipas, and was among the first within
the party-state bureaucracy to organize support for Cárdenas.

Another important group within the Cárdenas government was
comprised by reform-oriented economists, influenced by the work
of Keynes and interested in the application of Keynesian principles
to Mexico (Suárez, 1976). Within the Cárdenas government this
group was led by Eduardo Suárez, Secretary of Finance, who was
appointed to this position at the suggestion of Portes Gil. Suárez
promoted state intervention in the name of reformed capitalism,
and was specifically concerned with the promotion of industrialization through the provision of investment incentives to national
capitalists and the attraction of foreign capital. Considerably to the
right of Suárez was Luis Montes de Oca, former Secretary of Finance, who was director of the Banco de México during the Cárdenas administration. Montes de Oca's position can perhaps best
be described as one of nineteenth-century liberalism; while he did
not question government economic policies as director of the central bank, in later articles and speeches he adamantly opposed government intervention in the economy and interference with the
free enterprise system (Díez Artículos, n.d.). Both Suárez and
Montes de Oca retired into private business following their official
careers. Suárez, who was also Secretary of Finance in the succeeding Avila Camacho government, subsequently collaborated with
the New York firm of Hardin and Hess, establishing the legal firm
Hardin, Hess and Suárez in Mexico City, which represented various
national and multinational corporations. He was also president of
one of the major banks in the country, the Banco Comercial Mexicano, for a number of years (and subsequently vice-president until
his death in 1976) and a board member of numerous other corporations (Suárez, 1976). Montes de Oca founded the Banco In-

ternacional in 1941, of which he was president until his death in 1958, and was also instrumental in the establishment of several industrial and real-estate firms.

Representing the right wing within the government was General Saturnino Cedillo, who during the post-revolutionary years had been transformed from "a peasant leader in the style of Zapata, to a feudal landowner and defender of the status quo" (Campbell, 1976: 61). Cedillo had also been an early supporter of the Cárdenas candidacy, and Cárdenas had appointed him Secretary of Agriculture following the break with Calles. Cedillo was perhaps an extreme but by no means unique example of a substantial proportion of government officials whose allegiance to Cárdenas was based on personal loyalty or opportunism rather than a commitment to reform or ideological conviction. Former revolutionary generals, such as Cedillo and Juan Andreu Almazán; state governors such as General Maximino Avila Camacho in Puebla; high-level federal government officials, and senators and deputies, had been transformed into businessmen or were closely linked with them. While verbally supporting progressive policies, their control over specific agencies or states often enabled them to dilute, neglect, or subvert these policies in practice.

If the "left-wing" within the government constituted part of the progressive alliance, members of the "right-wing" had more in common with the previously dominant "conservative" alliance in terms of interests and ideology. Needless to say, the constituent groups of this alliance did not disappear, and members of the dominant class continued to find allies within the state, although their relations with the new government were considerably more uncomfortable than in the past. Certain of the more "progressive" elements within the dominant class, notably the Legorretas of the Banco Nacional de México, appear to have been close to Suárez in their orientation. More conservative groups within the private sector, particularly among private bankers, found an ally in Montes de Oca.

Cárdenas recognized from the beginning that the state bureaucracy at all levels of government constituted a weak instrument for the social and economic reforms he envisioned for Mexico. His notes taken during his pre-election trip are full of allusions to the ineffectiveness of local officials in dealing with government issues, and as president he frequently referred with regret to the apathy of government officials and their elitist and unsympathetic attitudes in dealing with the problems of the poor; the conservative orientation of many who called themselves revolutionaries; the lack of understanding of the social goals of the revolution by military officers; the vested interests of national politicians (Cárdenas, 1972b: 282-308 passim, 368, 433).

Tactics of the Cárdenas government for dealing with the problems of bureaucratic apathy, corruption, and general opposition to its programs included the removal or neutralization of high-level officials who were directly opposed to government measures and who were in a position to sabotage them; attempts to upgrade and motivate the civil service bureaucracy as well as lower levels of the military through pay increases, job security, training programs, and other measures; and, to the extent possible, the centralization of control over the execution of policy in his own hands and those of trusted associates. Several of these tactics had been used in the conflict with Calles; they were subsequently extended to other individuals and groups who did not cooperate with the administration.

Within the military, Cárdenas followed the policy begun under the Calles government: the elimination of obstacles to its institutionalization, elevation of its professional level, improvement in living conditions, as well as encouragement to military officials to "retire" into private business. To counter the conservatism which characterized many in the upper ranks of the military, Cárdenas cultivated support from junior officers and enlisted men—upgrading military pay and stressing technical training.[11] Another tactic was to encourage a self-image of members of the army as defend-

---

[11] In addition to higher salaries, the material incentives of the Cárdenas government included improved housing accommodations for officers, a school building program for the children of enlisted men, the construction of military hospitals, and the implementation of a life insurance program for military families. Cárdenas was able to implement these reforms without increasing the military share of the budget by placing a 55,000-man ceiling on the army and reducing the normal career span from 35 to 25 years, thus providing for more rapid retirement. On April 16, 1936, the government decreed that promotions of officers below the level of division chief would be based on competitive examinations. Another innovation was the 1939 Law of Obligatory Military Service, which replaced the volunteer system—the root of regional militarism—with a lottery drawing candidates from all sectors and regions. Obligatory military service was also a measure to promote national integration, inasmuch as within the army distinctions of birth and position would be eliminated, with the hope that this would result in greater mutual understanding and an elimination of class differences (Lieuwen, 1968: 118-120, 122; Mexico, Cámara de Diputados, IV: 137).

ers of the goals of the revolution and the initiatives of the government. Cárdenas also attempted to establish a genuine collaboration between the military and the popular sectors, encouraging soldiers to collaborate with peasants and workers in public works programs and giving army officers responsibility for such tasks as the training of labor and peasant militias.[12]

Many of the problems of the civil bureaucracy stemmed from the precarious situation of middle- and lower-level government employees: low salaries which were sometimes subjected to delays of several months, due to budgetary problems, and a lack of job security, since changes of government often meant a complete renovation of administrative posts at all levels (Mendieta y Nuñez, 1942: 150). Given these circumstances, public servants were often apathetic in carrying out their responsibilities and were prey to the corruption of those whose interests lay in seeing that these responsibilities were indeed ignored.[13] In the 1930's, federal employees began to organize. Cárdenas' predecessor, President Abelardo Rodríguez, established the precedent of not changing administrative positions when he came to power, renouncing the privilege (conceded to the president in the constitution) of appointing new persons to administrative positions. Cárdenas promoted a constitutional reform which would generalize this concession for all civil servants of the three branches of the federal government (Córdova, 1974: 125-126). In 1937, he presented to congress a civil service law designed to protect federal employees from electoral contingencies and from the caprices of politicians and government officials, providing for regular promotions. But the proposed law aroused considerable controversy since it also enabled public employees (excluding members of the army, the police, and "confidential employees"—i.e., those holding positions of authority) to organize and to strike under certain circumstances, such as nonpayment of wages or incapacity or immorality of superiors (Córdova, 1974: 131; *Mexican Labor News*, 7 July 1937). Although vigorously protested by certain groups in congress, the law was finally passed.

---

[12] Some of Cárdenas' tactics for dealing with the civil bureaucracy and the military are indicated in his speeches, which can be found in Muñoz, 1976: 151, 157-158, and PRM, 1940: 19, 33, 70-71, 121. Also see Córdova, 1974: 135-136, 142-144, and Lieuwen, 1968: 120.

[13] It was estimated, for example, that, due to bribing of tax collectors, the government received only half of the revenue due from income taxes.

Efforts of Cárdenas to centralize control in the hands of trusted associates took several forms. In some cases certain departments were created or expanded, staffed with trusted personnel, and given specific responsibilities for important government reform programs. An example was the Agrarian Department, entrusted to Gabino Vázquez who had worked with Cárdenas in the state of Michoacán, which was given responsibility for land distribution rather than the Ministry of Agriculture headed by the conservative General Cedillo. Cárdenas replaced several judges and various state governors during his administration (Brandenburg, 1964: 78). In other cases specific bureaucracies were created to perform key functions: with the acceleration of land distribution to rural communities in the form of ejidos, the important role of providing credit to the new ejiditarios was entrusted to the newly created Ejidal Bank.

The most dramatic method used by Cárdenas to centralize his control was his personal style of government—the attempt to make himself immediately accessible to the people and to directly intervene in important programs and reforms. His unprecedented pre-election trip to the remote areas of the country was followed by frequent and extended trips throughout his administration for the purpose of direct contact with the various regions of the country and their populations, their problems and needs. In 1936 he spent forty days in the Laguna cotton region overseeing the expropriation and distribution of the Laguna cotton plantations; the following year he went to Mérida, Yucatán, for the distribution of the henequen estates. Frequently he traveled to different cities to be present at the formation of state-level agrarian leagues, to intervene in inter-union struggles, as in Puebla, or to state his views with respect to employer-labor conflicts, as was the case in Monterrey in February 1936. The telegraph office was kept open for one hour each day to receive complaints from peasants and workers free of charge. Direct contact with specific problems and direct accessibility to the people obviously served as a check on bureaucratic performance; at the same time it enhanced the role of the president and the legitimacy of the presidency in the eyes of the population (Cornelius, 1973: 455). But Cárdenas also encouraged other government officials—state governors, municipal presidents—to follow his example in seeking direct knowledge of the conditions of areas under their jurisdiction and personal contact with the people and their problems. To the extent that the trips

The Rural Schoolteacher. Detail from mural by Diego Rivera.

and other forms of direct contact with the people also had the purpose of enlisting their support for government reforms and programs, they constituted a further element of Cárdenas' mass mobilization policy (Muñoz, 1976: 146; Anguiano, 1975: 47-48).

In fact, perhaps the most effective strategy for dealing with problems of opposition, corruption, and apathy at various levels of the bureaucracy was the mobilization of the affected groups, chiefly the peasants and workers. Mobilized groups not only demanded reforms; they had to exert consistent pressure on government officials to insure their implementation (Weyl and Weyl, 1939: 127).

Within the government bureaucracy itself, the rural schoolteachers had had an important role in mobilization since the revolution. Often from rural areas themselves, closely associated with the problems of the peasants, and aware of the contradictions of their own tasks (such as teaching methods of improved land cultivation to peasants who had no land), rural teachers had a tradition of militance, and their participation in local politics during the 1920's brought them into confrontation with landowners, members of the clergy, and conservative elements of the federal government, including members of the Ministry of Public Education.[14] In the early 1930's many joined the Communist party, where they constituted an important bloc between 1936 and 1939; one of eight teachers was a Communist and approximately half were believed to be Communist party sympathizers (Raby, 1974: 91-94).

Cárdenas envisioned the school as a key socializing agent for future generations of Mexicans; "socialist education"—oriented to collective work and achievement—would replace the fanaticism and superstition generated by clerical influence. The vague conceptualization of "socialist" education contained in the 1934 reform to Article 3 of the constitution, as well as opposition to the

---

[14] It should be pointed out that from the foundation of the Ministry of Public Education in 1921 its personnel had included several highly motivated officials responsible for a number of innovative educational and community development programs specifically adapted to the problems and needs of the rural population. The radical tendencies of the rural teachers had received support when Narciso Bassols was Secretary of Education (October 1931 to March 1934). At a congress of directors of education and other functionaries held in December 1932, a Bases for Rural Education was established according to which education would be basically oriented to the economic needs of the rural classes, and to transition to a collective system of production and distribution (Vaughan, 1981: 10; Raby, 1974: 35-39).

reform by many teachers, led to serious problems in implementation, but teachers were often successful in introducing practical skills and improvements and had a significant role in mobilization for agrarian reform.[15]

Under Cárdenas the number of schools and teachers multiplied, existing programs were expanded, and new initiatives introduced (Raby, 1974: 42 f). At the same time, the program of land distribution of the Cárdenas government structured an economic context within which other aspects of the educational program could be meaningfully implemented. The importance of the role of the teachers is indicated by the fact that they constituted a major target of violence by landlords and religious fanatics, many losing their lives as a consequence.

THE NATURE OF THE MEXICAN STATE
UNDER CARDENAS

In the 1930's the effects of the world crisis interacted with revolutionary forces emerging from Mexico's recent history to produce a period of substantial change and reform. However, the apparent uniqueness of the Cárdenas regime has been questioned— both by those who stress its resemblance to other "populist" regimes in Latin America during the 1930's and 1940's and by those who suggest its continuity with previous and subsequent regimes in Mexico. These questions will be briefly considered here as a context for the discussion of the Cárdenas period in the chapters which follow.

At first glance, the "progressive alliance," linking factions within the Cárdenas government and the mobilized peasants and workers appears to resemble the "populism" which allegedly characterized several Latin American countries during this period. According to

[15] Raby notes than in many communities their work included construction of wells, housing improvements, introduction of elementary hygiene, introduction or improvement of simple artisan skills (e.g., carpentry, weaving), road construction, improvement of agricultural techniques. But most important was their function in promoting agrarian reform, assisting with the difficult legal processes involved, and actively encouraging the peasants to sue for land (Raby, 1974: 100-101). A discussion of the controversy surrounding socialist education in the 1930's may be found in Lerner, 1979. For an interesting account of the content of socialist education during the 1930's, including an analysis of textbooks used during this period, see Vaughan, 1981.

the literature on populism, the export crisis resulting from the depression (in some cases followed by an "import" crisis during the Second World War) prompted a restructuring of the affected economies from dependence on imports generated by export earnings to industrialization, which was usually based on import substitution. This was carried out through the construction of a vertical alliance between the state and national industrialists and new urban sectors—including the urban working class. Given the weakness of the incipient industrial bourgeoisie, which has been unable to obtain control of the state, and the agro-export oligarchy, as a consequence of the export crisis, it is the state—and especially the executive power of the state—which forges this alliance, sometimes referred to as a "Bonapartist interlude" in the transition between oligarchic and industrial/urban bourgeois hegemony (Pompermayer and Smith, 1973: 105; Ianni, 1975: 53-54). The new industrial working class is drawn into this alliance through material and symbolic benefits (increased wages, official recognition of the right to organize and strike, nationalism). The industrial classes are brought together through an ideological mystification of class conflict with an emphasis on class conciliation, social peace, and the national interest (Malloy, 1977: 14; Ianni, 1975: 53-54, 121).

As other countries of the area, Mexico was affected by an export crisis as a consequence of the depression (although this was relatively short-lived) and the 1930's was a period of popular mobilization, supported by the state, as well as state-directed efforts at industrialization. But (as recognized by certain writings on the subject) Mexico does not entirely fit into the populist mold. In the first place, most discussions of populism apply more directly to countries (Argentina and Brazil) in which the export sector is nationally owned; the agro-export bourgeoisie is weakened but not threatened and may become part of the new coalition, and the rural popular classes continue to be marginalized (Cardoso and Faletto, 1978: 132). In Mexico, in contrast, the peasants have already been mobilized, and at least part of the landowning class marginalized, as a consequence of the revolution; the fact that most of the latter were not part of the agro-export sector made them more easily expendable. Commercial landowners were subsequently also weakened by the reduction in agricultural exports as a result of the depression, and the power of traditional landowners in the middle western regions had been diminished through the effects of the Cristero rebellion (Montes de Oca, 1977: 49). Thus it is the peasants, and not the agrarian owning classes, who become part of the "populist" coalition in Mexico, and the landowners are an explicit target of reform. Mexican nationalism also goes beyond that of other countries in that the government challenges a particularly powerful fraction of foreign capital in the export sector. Finally, although industrialists benefit from the policies of the state they are not formally part of the coalition, and important groups of industrialists come into conflict with it on various occasions. Related to this is the fact that class conflict is explicitly recognized: the paternalistic role of the state in taking the part of labor as the "weaker" party in the conflict with capital was part of the revolutionary ideology, evident in the constitution and other documents (including the Federal Labor Law) and reiterated in the speeches of Cárdenas, who constantly urged factions of organized labor to organize against their "common enemy."

In short, within the constraints of a capitalist system, the progressive coalition was not a vertical coalition but a horizontal one, and confronted a politically weakened but economically resourceful coalition of foreign capital, segments of the domestic bourgeoisie, and their allies within the state. This confrontation *was* limited by the fact that the state was at the same time establishing and maintaining conditions for capital accumulation. And the alliances were obscured by various elements—conflicts within classes, vertical links between employers, local officials, and coopted sectors of the working class; divisions among factions within the state on the basis of personal loyalty rather than of ideological orientation and class identification; and the fact that members of the government—including Cárdenas himself—were to some extent participants in both sets of alliances.

The role of the Cárdenas government in establishing conditions for private capitalist accumulation has in turn raised questions among analysts of Mexican history, who have questioned the extent to which this period represents a departure from previous regimes. Some suggest that even the more radical policies of the Cárdenas administration were oriented to the interest of capitalism, and that Cárdenas was simply continuing the orientation of his predecessors toward private capitalist development with considerably more foresight and vision. The agrarian reform brought social peace to the countryside. Wage increases as well as the agrarian reform increased the purchasing power of workers and peasants and thus expanded the market for industrial goods. Government support for the demands of workers and peasants, and state encouragement of labor and peasant organization, facilitated state control of these classes in the interests of capitalist production (Córdova, 1972, 1974; Anguiano, 1975). From this perspective, frequent allusions by Cárdenas and other members of his cabinet to the negative elements of capitalism—its "selfish individualism" in contrast to the "collective solidarity" of socialism—and to an eventual transition to socialism or to a workers' democracy could be dismissed as rhetoric. Since the revolution, leaders within the Mexican state had made references to a "socialist transition" in a relatively distant future. During the 1930's this "revolutionary" rhetoric was reinforced by ideological influences of the period and by a certain confusion regarding the meaning of socialism, which was often evoked to describe a form of welfare state or mixed economy.[16]

While many of the policies of the Cárdenas government have had the long-term effect of facilitating conditions of capitalist development, here it will be argued that the goals pursued by the Cárdenas administration were more complex.[17] First, the mobilization of popular sectors—workers and peasants—constituted a necessary element in the ability of the state to confront capital in certain sectors; while Cárdenas may have felt that he could control labor and peasant organizations, the ultimate effects of this conflict were far from assured (North and Raby, 1977). Second, Cárdenas' policies indicated a willingness to go beyond rhetoric and to experiment with non-capitalist, quasi-socialist forms of ownership and control of the means of production. Most of these experiments failed, given various problems of implementation and the hostile environment of capitalism. (These will be discussed in

[16] For example, an editorial published in *Rivista de Economía y Estadística*, a publication of the Ministry of the National Economy, defines a directed economy as socialization of the means of production through the organization of rural and urban workers in a manner that replaces capitalist firms with cooperativization, then goes on to note that businessmen will find in this procedure a solution to all their conflicts, and will imitate their colleagues in Sweden, England, Denmark, and other countries where capitalism has been controlled for the benefit of the population without destroying existing sources of wealth (21 January 1935: 3).

[17] The debate in earlier works by U.S. scholars between the "thesis of historical continuity" and that of "historical discontinuity" is discussed in Raby, 1972: 32-38. Raby also notes briefly the distinctions between the Cárdenas regime and that of Vargas of Brazil.

Chapters Five and Eight.) But they indicate an eclectic approach on the part of the Cárdenas administration and a willingness to encourage non-capitalist forms of control even while conditions for capitalist production were being promoted.

Finally, the policies of the Cárdenas government were based on an assumption that while capitalism was a necessary state of Mexico's development, it could be controlled and regulated by the state. Cárdenas' speeches frequently alluded to a state which was above classes and had to control capital as well as labor to insure economic development in the national interest (Mexico, Cámara de Diputados, 1966, IV: 11; PRM, 1940: 209). This assumption had an ideological justification in the constitution's recognition of the state as representative of national sovereignty. It was given further credibility with the international crisis of capitalism and the consequent "projection" of statist solutions in the most advanced capitalist countries, as well as by the continued weakness of the domestic bourgeoisie in post-revolutionary Mexico. This assumption was of course false, as Mexico's subsequent history demonstrates, but it was not illogical, given the uncertainties of that period.

In short, as will be demonstrated in the following chapters, the Cárdenas government envisioned, and in conjunction with mobilized workers and peasants implemented, a much more radical restructuring of society than its predecessors or populist regimes in other Latin American countries. The failure of Cárdenas' policies to have the effects intended can be explained by the failure of the government to fully understand the limits of state autonomy in the context of a capitalist society, even one which the state has had an important role in shaping.

Five ‖ The Contradictions of the Progressive Alliance

 The victory over the Calles faction and the subsequent achievements of the Cárdenas government in alliance with mobilized workers and peasants tended to obscure the contradictions of such an alliance. Not only the government, but also the peasants, workers, and their leaders acted with the assumption that the goals of these groups were identical with those of the state.

For the Cárdenas government, the mobilization of these groups had two purposes. On the one hand, the mobilization of urban/industrial workers would take place within the institutions of the capitalist system. Strikes of individual firms and industries had the purpose of achieving a "balance" between the forces of production: they were constrained by the limits of the law and by the resources of the relevant enterprise. Reflecting the paternalistic orientation implicit in the constitution and reinforced by the Federal Labor Law, Cárdenas reiterated that the state would take the side of labor, as the "weaker party . . . to strengthen their weakness in confrontation with the power of the owning class," but its purpose was to achieve "effective justice" within the capitalist system, not to change that system (Mexico, Cámara de Diputados, V: 753-756; PRM, 1940: 53; Cárdenas, 1972b: 317). In this respect, the alliance of the Cárdenas government with the working class resembles the populism of other Latin American countries.

On the other hand, for Cárdenas and the agrarians within the government, the 70 percent of Mexico's active population in agriculture still worked in feudal conditions. The purpose of peasant mobilization was structural change—the elimination of the economic and political domination of the landed classes and of "feudal" relations of production, including the exploitation of labor through debt peonage and other forms of coerced labor. The projected restructuring of the countryside went beyond the goals of populist governments elsewhere (Medín, 1972: 225-229).

For the Cárdenas government, the mobilized urban and rural working class and peasantry constituted necessary allies, both in obtaining and maintaining control of the state apparatus and in carrying out reforms and structural changes, but it assumed that the state would control this alliance. At the same time, few within the labor and peasant movements were prepared to challenge this assumption. Important groups within the urban and rural working class believed that they needed government support. The revolution itself had demonstrated that peasants could make a revolution, but could not bring it to fruition unaided. These factors, combined with the small size of the urban/industrial working class and its ambiguous role in the revolution itself had apparently precluded control of the state by an alliance of the proletariat and peasantry.

Subsequent developments had tended to reinforce the dependence of these sectors on the state as well as the development of authoritarian and paternalistic relations within their organizations. During the 1920's a substantial proportion of the urban labor force had been organized from outside or from above by CROM, which for most of this period was closely linked with the state. The unions organized by CROM were rarely characterized by democratic participation of their membership, and CROM itself was dominated by a small inner circle. State control of the union movement, and leadership control of members within the union, had been reinforced by the Federal Labor Law of 1931: the legal existence of unions depended on their recognition by local government authorities, and the clausula de exclusion enabled union authorities to have workers dismissed from their jobs by excluding them from union membership.

Also, from the perspective of most of the working class, their dependence on the state (and even corrupt labor unions) had to some extent been justified by historical experience. If, on the one hand, they had suffered from repression by local and national authorities, on the other hand they had also benefited from the support and intervention of the government and government-sponsored organizations. Also, the efficacy of labor organizations often depended on their ability to form alliances with representatives of the government; the loss of government support was the major factor in the rapid decline in the importance of CROM in the late 1920's.

If the experience of the majority of urban workers tended to reinforce authoritarian tendencies within the labor movement, the experience of the peasants made them even more directly dependent upon the state. The most powerful peasant movements of the

1920's had been based on their links to government power at the state level—Múgica and later Cárdenas in Michoacán, Portes Gil in Tamaulipas, Carrillo Puerto in Yucatán, and especially Adalberto Tejeda in Veracruz. And their experience also demonstrated the ease with which these movements could be destroyed or weakened if they were opposed by the central government.

Past experience of authoritarian leadership and dependence on government figures had weakened the bases for independent organization and made certain sectors of the working class and peasantry susceptible to authoritarian control by their leadership and/or the state. Nevertheless, the ultimate control of the labor and peasant movements by the state was not a foregone conclusion. In the first place, tendencies toward dependence upon the state were countered by independent and anarchist traditions among certain sectors of labor. Anarchist groups which had influenced the Mexican labor movement from the pre-revolutionary period had stressed direct action and independence of the state. Although both the CROM and the CGT, initially established on anarchist principles, had subsequently aligned themselves with the government, other unions influenced by anarchists (such as the petroleum unions) had maintained their independence of both the government and the dominant labor confederations. At the same time, these unions (and other independent organizations, such as the railroad workers and electricians) were apparently characterized by democratic internal structures, with substantial rank-and-file participation in decision-making. Thus they challenged both the authoritarian tendencies within the labor movement and those implicit in its dependence on the Mexican state. Also, in the 1920's several independent agrarian leagues (notably that of Veracruz) were characterized by an orientation to socialism and, while these movements had been effectively crushed by the central government, the legacy of struggle against the authoritarian tendencies of the state was part of their history.

In the second place, the process of mobilization involves its own dynamic and can result in a rapid increase in the level of consciousness of the sectors involved. As pointed out by North and Raby (1977) the struggles of the next several years would lead to an increasing polarization of Mexican society, and none of the leaders of the Cárdenas faction could have predicted the outcome. Thus in choosing to base itself on the urban and rural working class, and not on a passive, inert working class but one mobilized to *demand* its rights from the state, the Cárdenas government was charting a course with an unknown destination.

LABOR MOBILIZATION AND ORGANIZATION

In February 1936 two events took place which were of major significance in shaping the subsequent development of the Mexican labor movement and its relations with the state. The first was a dramatic confrontation between President Cárdenas and business groups in the northern industrial city of Monterrey, in which the president reaffirmed his support for the labor movement and outlined his labor policy. The second was the establishment of the Confederación de Trabajadores de México (the Confederation of Mexican Workers—CTM), which has continued to be the dominant labor confederation in Mexico to the present.

The occasion of the Monterrey confrontation was a lockout called by Monterrey industrialists following a strike by workers of Vidriera Monterrey, the major factory of the Garza Sada glass complex, which had refused to recognize the union affiliated with the CGOCM and had attempted to impose its own union. Monterrey was the birthplace of COPARMEX, the employer association formed to combat the Federal Labor Law, and company unions (*sindicatos blancos*) had constituted an important mechanism to undermine independent unions or those organized by the state. Monterrey business blamed the mobilization of workers of the glass factory on agitation by elements "external" to Monterrey, especially the Communists, and declared a lockout of all industries on February 6 (Salazar, 1956b: 181-183, 195).

Cárdenas traveled to Monterrey and addressed the Employers' Center of Monterrey, denouncing the refusal of businessmen to comply with labor laws and concluding with the suggestion that businessmen tired of the labor struggle turn their firms over to their workers or to the state. He also took advantage of the occasion to outline a fourteen-point labor program in which he emphasized the preeminence of the government, called for the unification of labor in a single labor confederation, gave assurances that labor demands would be consistent with the economic possibilities of the relevant firms, and pointed out that labor agitation was not the result of "Communist" pressures but the unmet needs of the workers and the failure of owners to comply with labor laws (Cárdenas, 1972a: 190-191).

The labor policy outlined by Cárdenas in Monterrey established the parameters within which the state would support the mobilization of industrial workers. It also coincided with the objectives of the Mexican labor leadership. While Cárdenas was calling for labor unification, existing confederations and unions were establishing the basis for a new national labor confederation, the Confederation of Mexican Workers (CTM), which responded to the unification goals of certain sectors of the labor movement as well as to those of the government. The formation of the CGOCM in 1933 had constituted an effort to establish a national labor confederation in the wake of the disintegration of CROM. Also during this period workers in several industries finally succeeded in forming industry-wide unions, among them the railroad workers (1932), the mine and metal workers (1934), and the petroleum workers (1935). One of the major objectives of the National Committee for Proletarian Defense, formed by labor organizations in June, 1935, in response to Calles' attacks on the labor movement, had been the establishment of a new national labor confederation which would incorporate existing unions and organize those workers not yet unionized.

The CTM, reflecting the heterogeneous character of the labor movement, incorporated craft guilds and unions of individual firms, regional federations, and industry-wide unions. It quickly became the dominant labor confederation in Mexico, taking part in all the major strike movements of the period. The CTM undertook the promotion and formation of national industrial unions where these did not exist and the creation of state federations which would group distinct and sometimes antagonistic local unions and organizations as well as local sections of national industrial unions within a given state. The Department of Labor within the government also intervened in the process of labor organization and unification. The direct and indirect intervention by the state and the CTM accelerated the process of labor organization in Mexico, but the fact that this process was "from above" undoubtedly reinforced authoritarian tendencies within the labor movement.

Apart from the importance given to labor organization and unification, the Cárdenas government and labor leadership were basically in agreement regarding the existing historical conditions of Mexico and the role of the working class within this context. The dominant ideological orientation of the new confederation was provided by Lombardo Toledano and, to a lesser extent, by the Mexican Communist party, both claiming a Marxist orientation. By this time, both were directly or indirectly under the influence of the Third International (Comintern) and the Popular Front strategy elaborated at its seventh congress in July 1935, which called for collaboration with progressive sectors of the national bourgeoisie in the conflict against internal and international fascism, its basic purpose being the defense of the Soviet Union.

The policy with respect to Mexico was based on the assumption that the long-term goal of socialism was not yet possible in view of the "weakness" of the working class and the "petit-bourgeois" nature of the leadership. The essential task at present was to eliminate the remains of "feudalism" and to free the country from imperialism, establishing conditions for capitalist development and, within this context, to struggle for the greatest possible benefits for the working class. There was no basic contradiction between this program and that of the Cárdenas government.[1]

The shift in Comintern policy as elaborated at the 1935 congress came as a complete surprise to the Mexican Communist party and resulted in an abrupt shift in its own policy. Following the dictates of the previous sixth congress (of 1928), the Mexican Communist party had opposed the six-year plan, the candidacy of Cárdenas (running its own candidate, Hernán Laborde), and the subsequent Cárdenas government. While it had joined other labor organizations forming the National Committee for Proletarian Defense as a means of defending the labor movement against the accusations

[1] The strategy developed at the seventh congress of the Third International and its influence on the Mexican Communist party as well as Lombardo Toledano are discussed in Márquez and Rodríguez, 1973; 182 f; Anguiano, 1975: 107–109; and Velasco, n.d. Lombardo Toledano's view may be found in Wilkie and Wilkie, especially p. 291. The Mexican Trotskyists in fact considered Cárdenas more progressive than either the Communist party or the CTM leadership. Thus the Trotskyist organ *Clave* stated that the right wing of the petit-bourgeoisie (the Communist party) constituted an obstacle not only to the development of socialism but also to the democratic bourgeois revolution being carried out by its left wing, *cardenismo* (*Clave*, 7 April 1939: 38). This opinion was of course not unbiased; Mexico had been the only country to offer Trotsky a permanent asylum following his flight from the Soviet Union. Cárdenas took this measure against the wishes of Lombardo Toledano and the Communist party, both of whom consistently criticized Trotsky and his activities while in Mexico. Trotsky's associates in turn lost no occasion to criticize or ridicule the "Stalinists" of the Communist party and the CTM bureaucracy.

of Calles, it had remained aloof from the political struggle. But after the seventh congress, the Cárdenas government was recognized as a progressive nationalist government—the most progressive that Mexico had had—and the Communist party encouraged active collaboration with it. Lombardo Toledano had little to do with the Communist party (at least openly); however he too had traveled to the Soviet Union in 1935 and his ideological orientation was similar.

Given the pragmatic orientation of the Amilpa-Velázquez forces (which, with those of Lombardo Toledano, had constituted the strongest group within the CGOCM), there was little opposition to a Marxist ideology within the new confederation. But at the same time there was no Marxist base from which to question the particular orientation of this ideology. The statement of principles, statutes, and early declarations of the CTM were compatible with the Popular Front strategy—i.e., based on the assumption that economic conditions and working-class consciousness were not sufficiently developed for the working class to carry out its final objective, the abolition of the capitalist system. The efforts of the CTM would therefore be directed to improving the economic and moral conditions of the proletariat and to defending Mexican autonomy against imperialism (Salazar, 1956b: 28). Thus the labor leadership was in basic agreement with Cárdenas that the purpose of the industrial labor struggle was to achieve a "balance" between capital and labor within the context of a capitalist system of production. In short, the possibility of ideological conflict with the government was eliminated: the Cárdenas government gave legitimacy to the state as representative of the Mexican revolution, while the Popular Front strategy had made the goals of the Mexican revolution and those of the Marxist leadership of the CTM virtually identical.

Labor Mobilization and the Labor Pact. Within the context of its objectives to improve conditions of labor within a capitalist system, the Cárdenas government supported most of the major strike movements of this period. Early in 1936, in response to several conflicts by individual unions demanding wage payment for the seventh day of the week as projected in the constitution, Article 78 of the Labor Code was reformed, making such payment mandatory. This measure, which increased wages automatically by approximately 17 percent, also had the purpose and immediate effect of raising the purchasing power of a significant proportion of the population—an effect which was not lost on more progressive business sectors (Mexico, Departmento de Trabajo, 1936; BNM, 1934–1941, Aug. 1935: 436). Government support for labor was not automatic. The government opposed the proposed railway strike in May 1936, on the grounds that since the railroad was 50 percent government-owned it was capitalist in name only, and since it was heavily in debt the criterion of "ability to pay" did not apply (Salazar, 1956b: 263).

In most cases, however, the government supported the workers, including a strike by 2,500 electrical workers against the British-owned Mexican Light and Power Company in Mexico City and surrounding states, which paralyzed nearly all industrial activity in the Federal District for ten days; a two-year strike by cotton textile workers for higher wages and other benefits; the strike of farm workers in the Laguna cotton region, which culminated in the expropriation and distribution of the cotton estates (see below); a conflict initiated by the British-owned transit company, which was defeated in its efforts to dismiss workers and reduce wages due to alleged financial problems; a strike by petroleum workers for a collective contract which led to the expropriation and nationalization of the oil industry (see Chapter Seven); and a series of strikes by the Mine and Metal Workers' Union to increase wages, improve working conditions, and obtain a standard contract which would provide uniform wages and benefits throughout the industry. These strikes also had the support of the CTM, which worked closely with the leaders and workers of the relevant unions.

The issues of the electrical workers' strike included promotion after a given period of time, occupation of technical posts by members of the union, and adequate provision for workers displaced by machinery, as well as increased wages. The company refused to discuss the proposed contract with the workers, hoping that the government would declare the strike illegal as it had in the projected railroad workers' strike two months before (Shulgovski, 1968: 383). Owners of companies forced to shut down operations due to the strike pressured the government for compulsory arbitration. But the workers apparently made every effort to provide essential health services, maintained the water supply, and continued to provide electricity to charitable institutions, hospitals, and government institutions, and the government refused to intervene, stating that the workers were acting responsibly and that their demands were well within the economic possibilities of the company. Allegedly only half of the gross revenues of the company went to operating expenses, permitting a profit-sales ratio of 50 percent, the bulk of which presumably went to the Canadian, British, and Belgian shareholders who controlled the company. The strike ended after ten days with a victory for the workers (*Mexican Labor News*, 20 July to 1 Aug., 1936).

The textile workers' strike, which lasted from February 1938 through April 1940, was considerably complicated by inter-union rivalries between the new CTM and CROM, which was still strong in the textile districts of Puebla and Orizaba, Veracruz, but divided between two factions—a pro-Morones wing and a dissident wing. The intransigence of the companies, particularly the Cia. Industrial de Orizaba (CIDOSA) was also a factor in the length of the conflict, which was finally concluded with a supreme court ruling supporting the Federal Labor Board decision in favor of the workers (Ashby, 1963: 112-116).

The transit conflict began when the British-owned transit company, which operated the streetcar system of Mexico City, entered a suit before the Federal Labor Board asking permission to dismiss workers and lower wages due to financial inability to maintain operations at existing wages. The workers claimed that the suit was an attempt to prevent revision of a collective contract which was under negotiation. The conflict was mediated by the government Labor Department, which appointed a commission to study the financial condition of the company. It concluded that the company could afford to meet the demands of the workers and even increase its profits by making economies elsewhere, and suggested that these profits be used for needed equipment repairs (Ashby, 1963: 119-120).

As a result of strike efforts by the Mine and Metal Workers' Union, wages in mining were increased about 40 percent in 1935 (bringing the average wage to about 4.15 pesos daily, or 25 pesos—$7 U.S.—per week), and 35 percent in 1936 (partly due to the legislation requiring wage payment for the seventh day of the week). By 1939 the daily wage was 8 pesos, but much of the increase in later years had been in response to the increase in the cost of living (Bernstein, 1965: 197). (The peso was devalued in 1938, from 3.5 to approximately 5 to the dollar.) Attempts were also made to enforce stipulations on health care and accidents, but these were apparently insufficient. In 1936, over half of the industrial accidents—and 80 percent of the fatal accidents—were in mining. In general, the number affected by industrial accidents increased during this period, from 19,994 in 1933 to 30,824 in 1939; mining accidents also increased, but declined relative to the total, with comparable figures of 10,584 for 1933 and 13,043 for 1939. The number of victims of fatal accidents declined between 1933 and 1937, but increased from 1938 to 1939 (from 59 to 159), with victims of fatal mining accidents up from 32 to 122 (Mexico, Depto. de Trabajo, 1939-1940: 283).

Major efforts of the mineworkers' union were directed to obtaining a standard contract. Although several foreign mining companies finally agreed to pay equal wages to their workers performing similar tasks, the intransigence of American Smelting and Refining officials, who rejected efforts of the Labor Department to set up a worker-employer convention and refused to open its books to government inspection, led to a series of one-hour strikes during each work shift. Ultimately the attempt to obtain a collective contract was abandoned as a consequence of government efforts to maintain favorable relations with the mineowners following the petroleum expropriation (Bernstein, 1965: 195-196).

In general, the objectives of strike movements were union recognition and the elimination of company unions, collective contracts (or revision of contracts) for specific firms, and, in some cases, standard contracts for an entire industry. These goals corresponded closely to those of the six-year plan and the Cárdenas government: the organization and unification of workers; the standardization of wages and benefits in a given industry where possible; and, basically, the increase in the standard of living of the workers—both as an end in itself and as a means to provide a market for industry. Implicit in the objectives of the government labor policy and of the labor movement was a "pact" between capital and labor, enforced by the state, which limited strike efforts of the working class to gains within the existing system. This "pact" obviously had much in common with the populist coalitions which allegedly characterized other Latin American countries during this period, although government support to the labor movement was vehemently opposed by most of the dominant Mexican (and foreign) business sectors.

There were cases in which the objectives of the workers and the government appeared to go beyond this pact. In several mines and industrial firms experiments in worker ownership and control were introduced, and forms of labor management were implemented in national industries. These initiatives seem to have reflected a preference of Cárdenas and certain groups within the government for non-capitalist, quasi-socialist forms of production, and further antagonized the business sector, nervous at the "instability" accompanying "labor agitation" which made them uncertain regarding the real intentions of the Cárdenas government. But for reasons which will be discussed later, these initiatives met with little success, and did not affect the limited objectives of the government and labor leadership.

The Organization of Labor. More important than the limited goals of labor mobilization during the Cárdenas government were the implications of developments within the confederation—the CTM—itself. While the leadership of the new labor confederation and the government were in basic agreement regarding the importance of labor organization and the objectives of the labor movement, a sharp conflict arose regarding the inclusion of rural workers in the new confederation. As indicated above, cooperation between the peasantry and the small urban industrial labor force had been limited in the past. During the revolution, collaboration between the two was effectively precluded when Carranza and Obregón succeeded in obtaining working-class support in their war against the armies of Zapata and Villa. During the 1920's the working class had become identified with CROM, the major labor confederation; its activities had aroused the distrust and antipathy of many of the agrarians. Conversely, the agrarian, Portes Gil, who as interim president had broken the power of CROM, was looked upon as anti-labor by important sectors of the labor leadership. During the Cárdenas *sexenio* this latent antagonism between the leadership of the two sectors was epitomized in the relationship of hostility between Vicente Lombardo Toledano as leader of the CTM and Emilio Portes Gil as head of the PNR.

This opposition between national leaders did not necessarily reflect the relationship among workers and peasants at the local level. In the first place, although the majority of the urban/industrial workers do not seem to have been of recent rural origin, many of them may have retained their ties with rural communities. In the second place, urban workers had had an important if not crucial role in the organization and/or support of agricultural workers in

such areas as Veracruz, the Laguna, and Yucatán. Previous confederations—CROM, the CSUM, the CGOCM—had included rural
unions, and when the CTM was formed it planned to incorporate
rural workers and peasant organizations as well as urban labor
organizations. One of the seven members of the Executive Committee was given responsibility for the agrarian question.

But Cárdenas had already (in July 1935) decreed the organization of agrarian communities in each state under the auspices of
the PNR as a first step in the formation of a separate peasant confederation, and government and party officials immediately objected to the CTM's projected inclusion of rural workers, stating
that any attempt by the CTM to organize rural workers in competition with the government would lead to divisions and conflicts
among the peasantry. Cárdenas claimed that the existence of competing organizations at the national and state levels would impede
the implementation of agrarian reform. The CTM responded with
a resolution stating that the Mexican proletariat should be organized in a single organization independent of the government, and
protested that the conduct of the PNR was dividing the working
class. The Communist party, however, following the new Comintern line, supported the PNR from the beginning, and eventually the CTM also decided to cooperate with the government,
relinquishing its rural unions (Shulgovski, 1968: 265; Gómez Jara,
1970: 117-119, 124-125).

The separate organization of the peasants and rural workers was
officially justified by the government's concern for coordinating
and directly controlling problems connected with the agrarian reform. It was also in keeping with its separate strategies for labor
and the agrarian problem (Medín, 1972: 95). Another factor may
have been a political debt to groups within the party who were
among the first to support the candidacy of Cárdenas. The CCM,
the peasant confederation which initially backed Cárdenas' nomination, had been established by Emilio Portes Gil and Graciano
Sánchez, among others; it was Portes Gil, as president of the PNR,
who was given responsibility for organizing the peasant confederation, and Graciano Sánchez became its first president (Anguiano
et al., 1975: 92-93). At the same time, the government's insistence
on controlling the organization of the peasant confederation was
undoubtedly also based on pragmatic considerations: Cárdenas'
desire to maintain this sector, which unlike the labor movement
had openly supported him from the beginning, as his own per-

sonal power base; and anxiety that too much power would accrue to Lombardo Toledano if the new labor confederation incorporated the peasants as well as the urban/industrial working class (Ashby, 1963: 80; Brandenberg, 1964: 82; Weyl and Weyl, 1939: 188-190). Another factor may have been fear of the possibility of a powerful alliance of these sectors against the state—which had been an important factor in state efforts to separate peasant and urban labor organizations in the past (Córdova, 1974: 163-164).[2] The possibility of such an alliance was further limited when the federations of state workers and teachers were subsequently discouraged from joining the CTM.

In the meantime, strains developed almost immediately within the new confederation on the question of control of key positions. The paramount organization was the national congress of representatives of all member organizations, which met every two years. In the interim, the major decision-making body was the national council of representatives from state federations and industry unions which would meet every three months. But decisive authority resided in the national executive committee, which was responsible for overall direction, convoking conventions for the formation of national industrial unions and state, regional and local federations; decisions regarding inclusion or exclusion of new members; and general strikes (CTM, 1941: 71-78).

The executive committee was composed of seven secretaries, three of which were crucial—the Secretary General, the Secretary of Labor and Conflicts, and the Secretary of Organization and Propaganda. The first two posts were filled quickly with the election of Lombardo Toledano and Juan Gutiérrez (head of the railroad workers' union) respectively, but a major struggle developed over the position of Secretary of Organization, which controlled procedures for the formation of state federations and national industrial unions and their admission to the CTM. Initially there were four candidates for this post, two of whom withdrew, leaving only Fidel Velázquez, of the former CGOCM, and Miguel Velasco, of the Mexican Communist party. In the first vote, Velasco received the support of the major industrial unions—including those of electricians, mine and metal workers, railroad work-

---

[2] This was also the opinion of a U.S. Embassy official at the time, who suggested that the separate organization of urban and rural workers was perhaps due to fear of a "union of discontents" if agricultural labor were controlled by leaders of industrial labor (Boal, 1938).

ers, petroleum workers, tramway workers and employees, teachers, and graphic arts workers, as well as the vote of the National Labor Chamber, a minor confederation, whereas Velázquez received the vote of only the CGOCM member organizations (CTM, 1941: 58-59; Velasco, n.d.: 21-22). The support for Velasco by independent unions was indicative of the respect for members of the Communist party by significant groups among the working class who did not necessarily share their ideology, as well as the distrust with which the former CROM members were regarded by many of the independent unions.

The decision in favor of Velasco was opposed by the CGOCM (although delegates of its two major national unions—the Sugar Workers' Union and the National Filmmakers' Union—supported it) and after a heated debate, including the threat of the CGOCM delegates to withdraw and divide the congress, the candidacy of Velasco was withdrawn by the Communists, over the protest of other delegates, in the name of syndical unity. The post was given to Velázquez, and Velasco was elected to the position of Secretary of Education and Cultural Affairs (León, n.d.: 10; CTM, 1941: 60).

Although it was apparently not evident at the time, the acquiescence of Communist party members in giving up the key post of Secretary of Organizations to Fidel Velázquez turned out to be a costly mistake.[3] Most subsequent conflicts within the confederation revolved around the manipulative tactics of Fidel Velázquez in the formation and recognition of state and industry federations. As Secretary of Organization, Velázquez was in a position to establish a network of unions directed by local leaders uncondition-

---

[3] In interviews, Velasco himself and Valentín Campa suggested that in the National Committee for Proletarian Defense, the Communist party had played a significant if not dominant role, and expected this to continue within the CTM. Within the CGOCM, Lombardo Toledano had been the dominant figure; Communist party members had relatively little contact with the Velázquez-Amilpa group (Anguiano et al., 1975: 108-109). Given the previous role of the Communist party, as well as the support of the relatively powerful independent unions for Velasco, members of the Communist party undoubtedly presumed that they would be able to hold their own within the confederation and control of the position of Secretary of Organization by the Velázquez faction probably seemed a relatively small concession. The Communist party in fact controlled two positions within the Executive Committee; in addition to Velasco, Pedro Morales was Secretary of Agrarian Reform; and Juan Gutiérrez of the railroad workers' union, who was Secretary of Labor and Conflicts, often sympathized with the Communist party position.

ally dependent upon him throughout the country. Alliances with local labor leaders and government officials had undoubtedly been facilitated by the past experiences of Velázquez, Amilpa, and others of this group in CROM and the CGOCM (León, 1975: 124). Thus in a given firm, a minority union linked to Velázquez was able to prevail over a large independent union because the former was registered and accepted by local officials and employers, who in turn benefited from a manipulated union organization. In some cases, corrupt labor leaders were bought by state governors seeking to increase their own power base who became linked to Velázquez (Anguiano et al., 1974: 102, 104).

Most conflicts took the form of confrontations between the independent unions and the Communist party delegates, on the one hand, and Lombardo Toledano and Velázquez, on the other. The fact that Lombardo Toledano, whose position as Secretary General gave him considerable weight within the confederation, consistently took the side of Velázquez has been explained by the widespread support for Velázquez among state governors and local officials (which would obviously facilitate union organization in their regions), and Lombardo Toledano's concern with maintaining the unity of the labor movement as support for Cárdenas (Fuentes Díaz, 1959: 338; Anguiano et al., 1975: 102). Another possible factor was that Lombardo Toledano wished to maintain control over the labor movement, and believed that the Velázquez faction could be more easily manipulated than the Communist party.

At the second session of the national council the large Mine and Metal Workers' Union left the CTM, accusing Fidel Velázquez of discriminating against the mine union sections in state federations (Anguiano et al., 1974: 144). In the next months, Lombardo Toledano complained of intervention by members of the Communist party in the organization of state and national federations, while the Communist party accused the Velázquez group of imposing its own unions and federations and refusing to recognize those which had been legally constituted. In some cases the Communist party position was backed by statements of the electricians' and railroad workers' unions.

The fourth session of the national council, held in April 1937, was the scene of a major confrontation of the Communist party and independent unions against Velázquez and Lombardo Toledano. Among the issues were the formation of two rival federations in the state of Oaxaca, suspension of relations with the Nuevo

León federation, and recognition of the new teachers' federation, formed of two pre-existing organizations in which the Communist party was dominant.

The constitutional congress for the Oaxaca federation, initially set for March 22, 1937 was subsequently postponed to April 15 at the request of two peasant organizations of the state. However, several federations had held the congress on the earlier date and formed the Workers' Federation of the State of Oaxaca, refusing to recognize the federation formed at the subsequent congress of April 15. The delegates of the first federation pointed out that Velázquez' order to postpone the original congress had come only two days before the congress was to begin: many of the delegates were already assembled, and delegates from all CTM-affiliated organizations were present. The assembled delegates therefore voted unanimously to continue the congress, which was also attended by representatives of the president and the state governor. But the national committee of the CTM rejected the delegates from this federation and gave them one month to join the second federation or be expelled from the CTM.

Leaders of the Nuevo León state federation were accused of attacks against the Secretary General and the Secretary of Organization. The former claimed that the federation had operated irregularly from its inception (often due to outside political interference); that initial members of its secretariat had been replaced by others, selected only by the delegates of Monterrey, the capital city; and that these had refused to submit to the discipline of the CTM executive committee. He asked that the national council approve suspension of relations with the Nuevo León federation. The electricians' union countered with a statement that almost all of the state organizations supported the executive committee of the Nuevo León federation, and that the vote to refuse it recognition had been taken by only three of the seven national executive committee members (an open violation of the statutes, which called for a majority of four votes on all decisions). It demanded that executive committee decisions be taken by the full committee, and that the autonomy of member organizations be respected.

The formation of the schoolteachers' federation was a complicated question involving rivalries among a number of national and state federations—among them the Confederación Mexicana de Maestros (CMM) formed in 1932 and closely identified with the Secretary of Public Education of the federal government; the more radical Confederación Nacional de Trabajadores de Enseñanza (CNTE), formed of various groups in 1935; and the Federación de Trabajadores de Enseñanza del D.F., a vehicle of David Vilchis, who was an associate of Lombardo Toledano. A congress of unification was scheduled for February 1937, instigated by the CMM and the CNTE. Since the Communist party had a strong following among members of both organizations (particularly the CNTE), the D.F. federation and other unions, at the instigation of Vilchis, tried to form a rival congress which would adhere more closely to CTM leadership. The attempt failed, and the majority of the teacher unions joined the Federación Mexicana de Trabajadores de la Enseñanza (FMTE) formed at the CMM–CNTE congress (Raby, 1974: 70-75). Although the new federation attempted to join the CTM, it too was refused admission by the CTM leadership.[4]

At the fourth session of the CTM national council, 23 delegations, including the electricians, the Mexican Federation of Teachers, the railroad workers, and the Federation of State (government) Workers, presented a document accusing specific members of the executive committee (Lombardo Toledano and Fidel Velázquez) of having violated CTM statutes. Although the dissident delegations included organizations which were completely independent of the Communist party, the report of the Secretary General to the Council attempted to blame differences exclusively on the divisionist tactics of Communist party members. After a heated debate, the 23 dissident delegations walked out of the meeting; they were joined by three of the seven members of the Executive Committee—Miguel Velasco and Pedro Morales of the Communist party and Juan Gutiérrez of the railroad workers' union. Lombardo Toledano claimed that the delegates who left the meeting represented only one-fourth of the membership; the Communists claimed that they represented more than half. In any case, it constituted a serious split within the CTM, since the dissident delegations included some of the major industrial unions. Their de-

---

[4] Other accusations made by the Communist party and the electricians' union against the Secretary General and the Secretary of Organization included the imposition of a delegate sent by Velázquez as Secretary General of the state federation of Coahuila; collaboration with reactionary elements in Oaxaca, Coahuila, Nuevo León, Aguascalientes, and the Federal District; failure to include important organizations of the state of Mexico in the organizing committees to form the state federation; and refusal to recognize the right of the railroad workers' union of Yucatán to dispose of a corrupt secretary general (*El Machete*, 17 and 24 April; 9, 16 and 22 May, 1937; Velasco, n.d.: 24-25).

parture led the Lombardo Toledano-Velázquez faction to accuse the Communist party of trying to destroy the CTM.

There was undoubtedly some truth to these accusations against the Communist party, which was subsequently guilty of strong-arm tactics in efforts to maintain control of the teachers' federation, and to this extent the struggle over the organization and inclusion of federations was a conflict between two factions for control of CTM delegates. But neither the electricians' union nor the railroad workers' union was controlled by the Communists (although there were Communist party members in the latter); nevertheless both defended the Communist party members, pointing out that the real issue lay in the anti-democratic methods of CTM leadership in crushing independent initiatives by worker representatives and ignoring the opinion of the rank and file. As stated by the electricians' union, the opposition of the CTM leadership to the Communists was due to their "unfortunate habit" of unmasking leaders who deceived and exploited the workers.

The CTM appealed to the twenty-three dissident delegations to return, but insisted that the Communist party accept full responsibility for the division within the CTM. Although the Communist party and the other delegations initially resisted these conditions, it was finally the Communists who conceded, largely as a result of pressures from the Comintern in the person of Earl Browder, head of the Communist party of the United States and representative of the Communist International, who persuaded the Communist party to collaborate with Lombardo Toledano and place CTM unity above all other considerations.[5] In a plenum of the Mexican Communist party in June 1937, the position of Browder was upheld (although not without opposition from certain groups, including local leaders and teachers) and the slogan "unity at all costs" adopted, justified by consideration of international and national conditions, including the pending European war and the petroleum conflict within Mexico.

The importance given to working-class unity was undoubtedly reinforced by past experience of splits and dissension in the labor movement, and the emphasis given to it by Cárdenas, both as candidate and as president. But, given the circumstances of the

---

[5] Comintern support for Lombardo Toledano rather than the Mexican Communist party has been attributed to his position within the CTM and his relationship with Cárdenas, which constituted a guarantee that his policy would be carried out in Mexico (Anguiano, 1975: 122).

CTM split, the costs of unity were high. The Communist delegates returned to the CTM on the conditions of the executive committee, which called for unconditional submission, giving up its two positions on that committee; Communist party members were also eliminated from the executive committees of state federations. The railroad workers also rejoined the CTM (and Gutiérrez was again given the position of Secretary of Conflicts within the executive committee, later resigning to become manager of the nationalized railroads), but the electricians' union refused to return, alleging that none of the grievances which had led to its withdrawal had been corrected.[6]

The abdication of the Communist party to the CTM leadership, the incorporation of its members and those of the other federations into the CTM on the terms of the Secretary General, and the refusal of the militant and independent electricians' union to rejoin the confederation were all factors which weakened resistance to the growing hegemony of the Velázquez-Amilpa faction. On several occasions, certain local and national federations attempted to oppose the CTM leadership, but this resistance was uncoordinated and was ineffective in confronting the authoritarian structure of the CTM through which the hegemony of the Velázquez faction became institutionalized.

In addition to the conflicts generated over the organization of federations and their representation and the principle of union democracy, the first years of the CTM were characterized by a less controversial, but equally important, process of linking the confederation to the government. The statutes of the CTM had established the principle of ideological and organizational independence of the government along lines similar to those of earlier confederations, including the CGOCM, reflecting the anarchist tradition within the Mexican labor movement. As stated, the organization would depend upon direct action—meaning the suspension of any intermediary between the worker and employer—in labor struggles. At the constitutional congress, however, Lombardo Toledano stated that while the organization was independent and autonomous, it would continue to support the revolutionary acts of the Cárdenas government, and would abstain from political strikes

[6] Sources on the conflict within the CTM and its resolution include CTM, 1941: 323-358 passim; *Mexican Labor News*, 5 May and 28 July 1937; *El Machete*, 5, 17, 19 and 24 April, 16 May and 26 June, 1937; Velasco, n.d.: 24; Shulgovski, 1968: 298-303; Márquez and Rodríguez, 1973: 202-205; and Anguiano, 1975: 113.

which could embarrass the government (CTM, 1941: 63, 69). At the second session of the national council (October 1936) there was a heated discussion regarding the invitation of the National Revolutionary Party (PNR) to members of labor unions to participate, as party candidates, in the forthcoming elections to the Senate and the Chamber of Deputies. Although the statutes had opposed any collaboration with the government, Lombardo Toledano convinced the delegates that since the government party was being reorganized it would be appropriate for the CTM to participate in the elections to defend its program (Salazar, 1956a: 100; CTM, 1941: 282). The CTM apparently regarded its association with the Cárdenas government as transitory, contingent upon the progressive orientation of the Mexican government at that time (Fernández del Campo, 1937: 17, 19). Nevertheless, the electoral process quickly became a means of cooptation, and since many of the candidates were chosen by the leadership, it also became an additional factor in the institutionalization of authoritarianism within the CTM (Fuentes Díaz, 1959: 339-340). In addition to its political participation in the PNR almost from the beginning, it is probable that the CTM was subsidized at least in part by the government.[7]

Cárdenas and the Labor Movement: A Summary. For most of the urban-industrial working class, the Cárdenas *sexenio* meant a real improvement in wages, benefits, and working conditions (although wage gains were to some extent eroded by price increases in the last years of the administration) as well as in increase in its organizational strength. Furthermore, a substantial proportion of the industrial labor force was unified in the new Confederation of Mexican Workers. However, as indicated above, this unity had its cost for the labor movement, given the rapid emergence of authoritarian tendencies within the confederation and its increasing ties to the state.

Historical trends to authoritarianism and the dependence of im-

[7] The constitutional congress of the CTM had established the requirement of a token payment by each member toward the expenses of the confederation, but the failure of the majority of constituent organizations to enforce this regulation and the confederation's growing debt constituted the central complaint of the Secretary of Finance at every meeting of the national council. At the same time, the balance sheets submitted by the Secretary of Finance appeared to include only part of CTM expenses, excluding such items as travel by the Secretary General and the Secretaries of Conflict and of Organization (Anguiano, 1975: 134; Ashby, 1963: 74; CTM, 1941: 209-993 passim).

portant sectors of the working class on labor leadership or the state were reinforced during the Cárdenas period by the manipulation of labor leaders, the rapid unionization of previously unorganized groups from outside or from above by the state or the CTM, and—at least to some extent—the influence of the Comintern. The large industrial unions had been characterized by different experiences of democratic organization and independence, but precisely for this reason they tended to be less dependent on the confederation and, in the case of the electrical and mineworkers' unions, opted to leave it when confronted with the opportunistic and corrupt practices of its leadership. The marginalization or fragmentation of most of the remaining groups enabled the leadership to isolate and deflect resistance where it occurred.

The control exercised by the leadership within the CTM enabled it to link the confederation with the Cárdenas government. The tendency to depend upon the state was also reinforced due to government support to the labor movement as well as its substantial reforms in other areas. The Cárdenas government in effect had given legitimacy to the state as representative of the revolution; this legitimacy in turn appeared to justify the linkage of the labor movement with the state.

THE STATE AND THE PEASANTRY

Peasant Mobilization and the Agrarian Reform. In August 1936 workers on the cotton plantations of the Camarca Laguna staged a general strike—the culmination of a period of intense organizing which had begun the year before and had antecedents in several decades of peasant-landowner conflict in the region. The Camarca Laguna was an irrigated region in the states of Coahuila and Durango which produced much of the cotton used in the nation's textile industry. At this time, approximately 70 percent of the land was foreign-owned, 40 percent by two British companies, but much of it was rented to a sub-elite of "dependent hacendados" whose insecure situation (due to the unpredictability of the water supply for irrigation as well as their dependence upon foreign creditors) had resulted in the extensive use of land, eventually incorporating land formerly allotted to peasants.[8] Similar arrangements existed

[8] Control by foreign companies often resulted from foreclosures on loans made to private owners of cotton plantations when the latter were unable to pay (Senior, 1940: 12). Prior to the absorption of haciendas by financial companies, peasants

elsewhere, as in the state of Yucatán, where the henequen haciendas were locally owned but often indebted to foreign companies responsible for financing and marketing. The estates in Laguna, again similar to other commercial estates, were administered as capitalist enterprises and used advanced technology, but relations between the landowners and rural workers were semi-feudal in character, and the rural police and other public officials supported the owners in crushing efforts at labor mobilization. The land was worked by approximately 15,000 to 16,000 *peones acasillados* (housed on the estates), 10,000 day laborers who lived in the nearby villages and worked on several estates, and migrants who traveled to the area to work during the harvest; in 1936 there were approximately 5,000 migrants in the region from other parts of the country.

Prior to 1915, conflicts between the workers and hacendados took the form of sporadic land invasions, which were severely repressed. Following the passage of the Agrarian Law of January 1915, and especially the 1917 constitution, several attempts were made by peasants within the Camarca Laguna and other groups within the two states to organize unions and agrarian committees to legally petition the government for land or to secure better working conditions in accord with Article 123 of the constitution. A militant peasant league was formed in Durango under the auspices of the state government in 1923, but this had been neutralized by 1930; the landowners (often with the compliance of local authorities) continued to repress efforts of the workers to organize and apply for land grants; and the federal and state government officials utilized various delaying tactics or cooptive measures which benefited some workers but left the basic system intact.[9] Never-

---

had been permitted to plant corn and beans on every tenth row of cotton fields, or to sharecrop—sometimes ending the year with a profit—but these privileges had been withdrawn by 1910 (Landsberger and Hewitt, 1970: 3-4).

[9] Some of the tactics of the landowners included flooding land and villages of peasants who attempted to organize or petition for land and tearing down the houses of those peasants who dared to join unions, as well as denying them work. The landowners also had a permanent organization in Mexico City (Cámara Agrícola de la Región Lagunera), with significant funds at its disposal with which to counter the petitions of peasant emissaries to the federal government. Under Calles, the latter generally supported the landowners. Secretary of Agriculture Luis León consistently put the workers off when they petitioned for land; his reward was the hacienda "Terrenates" in the state of Chihuahua. (See Landsberger and Hewitt, 1970: 8-12, and especially 126-134, which is a translation of a brief summary of the history of the agrarian movement in parts of the Camarca Laguna between 1917 and 1934 by one of its leaders, J. Cruz Chacón Sifuentes.)

theless, the experience of the 1920's and early 1930's had left an organizational infrastructure which could be quickly mobilized by rural labor leadership, working in conjunction with urban labor organizations of the area, when the candidacy and election of Cárdenas indicated that their demands would at last receive a response at the federal government level.

In the organization of the general strike of August 1936, the labor organizations of the Communist party and the rural school-teachers seem to have had a dominant role. Several unions of rural workers united in a single union which demanded a collective labor contract to equalize benefits throughout the region, and decreed a general strike to begin in May 1936. The strike was delayed several times in response to requests by federal labor authorities but finally began on 104 plantations on August 18. The hacendados attempted to break it, importing strikebreakers from other areas, with the support of local authorities who provided armed guards. The state labor boards decided in favor of the landowners, and the union attempted to have jurisdiction transferred to the Federal Labor Board.

In the meantime, in September 1936 the government passed a law permitting the expropriation of any property in the public interest, which made it possible to expropriate properties devoted to commercial agriculture and export, previously legally exempt. Thus, when a delegation from the Laguna union, accompanied by members of the CTM national council, went to interview President Cárdenas regarding the labor conflict, the government decided to implement the new law with the expropriation of the cotton plantations of La Laguna.[10]

The exemption of commercial estates from the agrarian reform by previous administrations meant that the region had been considered completely safe, and the Expropriation Law, followed by the expropriations in the Camarca Laguna, aroused considerable consternation among landowners and the owning class in general (Silva Herzog, 1964: 409). Since landowners and their supporters contended that expropriation would have disastrous effects on production levels, Cárdenas was determined to demonstrate that commercial production would not decline as a consequence of the transition in ownership. He proposed that the new ejidos be owned

[10] Sources on the Laguna expropriation include Senior, 1940; Landsberger and Hewitt, 1970; Restrepo and Eckstein, 1975; Shulgovski, 1968: 193-270 passim; and Ashby, 1963: 142-178 passim.

Lázaro Cárdenas and the Agrarian Reform, 1934-1940. By Luis Arenal.

and operated collectively; through collective operation the ejido could constitute not only a means of achieving social justice for peasants and rural workers but also a model of economic efficiency. This concern was evident in his speech on delivering the land to the new ejiditarios on October 6, 1936: ". . . the ejidal institution today has a double responsibility: as a social system which liberates the rural worker from the exploitation from which he previously suffered . . . and as a system of agricultural production, with a large part of the responsibility for providing the food supplies of the country."[11]

The Laguna expropriation became the model for subsequent expropriations of commercial estates, which included the majority

[11] "La institución ejidal tiene hoy doble responsabilidad sobre sí: como régimen social, y por cuanto que libra al trabajador del campo de la explotación de que fué objeto lo mismo en el régimen que en el individual; y como sistema de producción agrícola, por cuanto por que pesa sobre el ejido, en grado eminente, la responsabilidad de proveer a la alimentación del país" (Cámara de Diputados, V: 765).

of the henequen estates of Yucatán, rice and wheat estates of the Yaqui valley in Sonora (which included foreign-owned as well as Mexican properties), the rice and livestock haciendas of Neuva Italia and Lombardia in the southwestern state of Michoacán, and several of the major sugar estates.[12] In most cases, the expropriation was preceded by the mobilization and organization of the workers involved, often initially oriented to obtaining labor contracts, and frequently with the assistance of urban or industrial labor organizations or the Communist party (Restrepo and Eckstein, 1975: 10-27, 131). In each case, cooperatives or collective ejidos were formed to work the new properties.

The mobilization of the peasants and rural workers not only provided a political support base for the government agrarian reform, but also a political rationale for its challenge to vested interests, involving expropriation to a large extent without effective compensation due to the limited resources of the federal treasury. Cárdenas and other members of his government claimed that the administration could not stop the process of land distribution even if it wanted to without precipitating either a revolution or spontaneous uprisings throughout the country. This suggests a mutually causal relationship between the mobilization of the peasants and the Cárdenas agrarian reform: the extension of peasant agitation made the reform necessary for political stability; at the same time the Cárdenas government encouraged peasant mobilization (which it also sought to control) as a justification for agrarian reform.[13] Peasant mobilization, in part spontaneous but at the same

---

[12] Sources on Yucatán include Mesa Andraca, 1955 and Benítez, 1956; on Sonora, see Hewitt de Alcántara, 1978: 163 f. The expropriation of sugar estates, generally following peasant mobilizations and land invasions, included the sugar cane hacienda of Atencingo in Puebla, belonging to the former North American consul William Jenkins (who retained the sugar refinery); the lands and sugar refinery of El Mante in the state of Tamaulipas, belonging to Aarón Sáenz; and the U.S.-owned company of Las Mochis (United Sugar Companies) in the state of Sinaloa. These (as well as other expropriated estates) were operated by cooperatives, in some cases, as in Zacatepec, Morelos, where the government constructed a 13-million-peso sugar refinery at the request of the ejiditarios, by mixed cooperatives of peasants and refinery workers (Cárdenas, 1972b: 366-376; Shulgovski, 1968: 312).

[13] On Cárdenas' claim that peasant mobilization made agrarian reform necessary for political stability, see letter of Frank Tannenbaum to Josephus Daniels regarding his interview with Cárdenas and other members of the Mexican government (Daniels, 1938c, enclosure). On Cárdenas' conscious promotion of peasant mobilization to justify agrarian reform, see Córdova, 1974.

time responding to government encouragement, thus constituted a necessary condition for the implementation of structural reform in the face of opposition from Mexican and foreign landowners. The strategy of promoting peasant mobilization as a justification for reform departed radically from the programs of previous administrations, which had been largely motivated by the desire to contain this mobilization.

While innovative in terms of its implementation at the national level, the concept of the collective ejido did have certain precedents in Mexican government statements as well as collective experiments carried out at the state and local level during the 1920's. In 1922 the National Agrarian Commission had issued a circular (Circular 51) proposing that, for purposes of mechanization and technical efficiency, large estates which were expropriated should be passed on to the ejido intact and farmed in a communal form. The intellectual sources of Circular 51 ranged from concern with Mexican traditions of communal farming in certain pre-conquest Aztec villages to influences of socialist writers and experiments in the Soviet Union although, according to one of its authors, its inspiration was pragmatic rather than ideological (Simpson, 1937: 333, 402 f; Wilkie and Wilkie, 1969: 100-103). Circular 51 apparently had little effect on the government reform program, which continued to be based on the creation of small holdings with the ejido viewed as an intermediate stage. But independent peasant movements formed during this period stressed the ejido, and in some cases collective experiments were undertaken, particularly in the state of Veracruz, where the peasant league was supported by Governor Tejeda and influenced by the Mexican Communist party. During the 1920's several members of the league traveled to the Soviet Union, and the conceptualization of the collective ejido was influenced by the Soviet kolkhoz. When the National Peasant League was established, largely at the instigation of the Veracruz league, in November 1926, it stated that the cooperative ejido constituted an important factor in the progressive development of Mexico and that the socialization of land and of other means of production was its ultimate goal (Shulgovski, 1968: 216, 218-219; Eckstein, 1966: 61). An important group within the agrarians supported the conceptualization of the ejido as the fundamental basis of the agrarian sector and in some cases called for the elimination of private property in agriculture (Reyes Osorio, 1974: 32).

The decision of the Cárdenas government to establish collective ejidos apparently resulted from a combination of these ideological influences and practical considerations following from the decision to include commercial estates as well as traditional haciendas in the land distribution program. The collective ejido—actually a cooperative form of production—was seen as necessary to maintain levels of technical efficiency and productivity; at the same time it responded to the ideological orientation of those within the Cárdenas government favoring communal forms of production. Through the collective ejido, Cárdenas was able to combine the social goal of distributing land to those who worked it with the economic objective of maintaining economies of scale (Restrepo and Eckstein, 1975: 30-31; Barchfield, n.d.; Gutelman, 1974: 105-106).

The transformation of the commercial estates into collective ejidos encountered serious problems. In Laguna, the fact that the land distribution had to be carried out rapidly in order to irrigate land for the following season's crop resulted in several mistakes. Land which had previously supported 25,000 workers was distributed to 40,208 rural workers, including not only resident peons and day laborers but also migrant workers and even strikebreakers who were in the area at the time, causing an immediate problem of overpopulation. An overestimation of the amount of water available for irrigation (calculating that there would be sufficient water for 300,000 hectares instead of approximately 100,000) led to water shortages and disputes among land-reform beneficiaries. Also since existing legislation permitted the landowners to retain the equivalent of 150 irrigated hectares, the best lands as well as technical and administrative infrastructure remained under their control, leaving the workers with marginal lands often badly connected (Landsberger and Hewitt, 1970: 16-18; Whetten, 1948: 222).

Some of these problems were corrected in subsequent expropriations. In distributing the Yucatán henequen estates a detailed plan was developed in advance which among other things provided that peasants would receive the industrial machinery for processing the henequen as well as the land—a crucial provision since retention of processing equipment by hacendados would have enabled them to exert considerable control over the ejiditarios (Mesa Andraca, 1955: 292-293). In the case of Nueva Italia and Lombardia, the previous owners agreed to sell the acreage they were entitled to as well as livestock, machinery, and equipment.

The scope and nature of the Cárdenas agrarian reform aroused considerable antagonism among landowners and other owning groups. The elimination of the use of the amparo to appeal expropriations and the fact that Cárdenas, taking advantage of the Agrarian Code promulgated before he came to office, adhered strictly to existing legislation in carrying out the agrarian reform, left the landowners with little legal basis for complaint. As in the past, they resorted to violence. The most cohesive opposition developed in the traditional central region—the locus of the Cristero rebellions of the 1920's—which in the 1930's became the nucleus of the Sinarquista movement. A militant, religious, quasi-political movement, the Unión Nacional Sinarquista mobilized the most backward and deprived groups of the peasantry in a fanatical and bloody campaign against peasant petitioners and recipients of land grants and their allies—notably the rural schoolteachers. The Sinarquista movement seems to have been the only significant movement of this nature, but localized violence against ejiditarios, village peasants or resident laborers pressuring for land, and village teachers, was widespread. Attacks by mercenaries of the landowners (white guards) were an important factor in a decision by Cárdenas to arm the peasants. In January 1936, the creation of a rural reserve was decreed; by the end of the Cárdenas' sexenio it consisted of 60,000 peasants in 70 battalions and 75 calvary regiments (Cárdenas, 1972a: 114; Huizer, 1970: 71-72).

Apart from physical attacks on the ejiditarios or village peasants and their supporters, the landowners utilized their connections for attacks in the press, taking advantage of alleged or actual production declines and technical problems to publicize the "incompetence" of the ejiditarios and the lack of viability of the new tenure systems (Wilson, 1938; *El Universal*, 2 April 1938; *Excelsior*, 20 April 1938). The collective ejido was a prime target, condemned as "communistic" even by intellectuals with revolutionary credentials such as Luis Cabrera (Shulgovski, 1968: 254-256).

Landowners also used various tactics to divide the resident peons and the peasants of the villages who were staging land invasions by telling the former that there would be no work for them if village peasants received land. This tactic succeeded to some extent, although the plan by which the federal government applied the agrarian reform to Yucatán stipulated that resident peons as well as villagers would receive land. A similar tactic was successful in the case of the sugar estates of Atencingo owned by former U.S. consul William Jenkins. For years the villagers of this region had sought to have the agrarian reform applied to the Jenkins properties; finally, in 1937, the Cárdenas government decreed their expropriation. However, with the help of the Governor of Puebla, General Maximino Avila Camacho, Jenkins maneuvered to have the lands transferred to the relatively docile resident labor force rather than to the militant villagers (Ronfeldt, 1973: 18-19). But the most frequent form of conflict between different groups of peasants was between small landowners and village peasants or ejiditarios who were accused of invading their land. In some cases illegal land invasions undoubtedly did occur; at the same time "small landowners" were often stand-ins for powerful landowners who had divided their land to avoid expropriation (Whiting, 1977: 14).

The landowners were frequently supported by government officials at the state and local levels, as the case of Jenkins illustrates. While state governors might give ostensible support to the agrarian reform for political reasons, a large proportion—possibly a majority—opposed its application, although this opposition was countered by the agrarians who controlled the Agrarian Department and had jurisdiction in agrarian matters at the state level. Officials at other levels also supported the landowners on occasion—the decision of the state labor board in favor of the Laguna hacendados and the protection of strike breakers in that region by local officials constituting one example. There were also cases when the National Irrigation Commission refused to provide water for ejiditarios (Weyl and Weyl, 1939: 179). In short, at the level of the state, agrarian conflicts often took the form of confrontations between officials of the Agrarian Department, representing ejiditarios or peasants petitioning for land, against local government officials representing small or large landowners.

Finally, in addition to the fact that they retained considerable acreage and much of the infrastructure of their estates, landowners often controlled private financial and commercial firms, including those selling articles needed by ejiditarios. Control over processing equipment (e.g., the sugar mills) also gave them a certain degree of leverage over the ejiditarios and small peasants of the region (Landsberger and Hewitt, 1970: 65). In short, exploitation of the rural population came to be based less on ownership of land and increasingly on ownership and control of credit, marketing, and agricultural inputs. While landowners felt themselves to be on the defensive during the Cárdenas administration, with the help of official contacts at various levels they were often in a position to make the best of the situation.

The State and Peasant Organization. Given the hostile environment in which the new ejiditarios found themselves, external support was virtually essential for their maintenance and development. Political support could come from the working class and/or the federal government. As indicated above, the recruitment of the "Red Battalions" to serve in Carranza's army against the peasant armies of Zapata and Villa, and the maneuvers of CROM during the 1920's, as well as the largely successful efforts of Portes Gil to destroy CROM at the end of the decade, had left a residue of antagonism and distrust between the leaders of the peasantry and the working class. But in certain areas, such as Veracruz and the Laguna region, support from progressive sectors of the working class had played an important role in the post-revolutionary struggles of the peasants, as well as in the preparation of potential ejiditarios for collective ownership. What role the working class might have played in supporting the development of the collective ejidos had it retained its independence is unknown. In any event, subsequent developments within the major labor confederation and the segregation of labor and peasant organizations eliminated the possibility of an effective peasant-labor alliance which might have supported the continued development of "alien" structures within the Mexican agrarian sector.

But the ejido, and especially the collective ejido, did receive extensive state support during the Cárdenas period. Aside from the role of the rural schoolteachers and the agrarians within the Agrarian Department, the central institution for the implementation of the agrarian reform under Cárdenas, and especially for the administration of the collective ejidos, was the Ejidal Bank, created in 1937 for that purpose. In addition to providing credit through the organization of local ejidal credit societies it was responsible for organizing production and the sale of harvests; buying and reselling seeds, fertilizer and agricultural implements and other inputs; overseeing and supervising the functioning of the ejidos; and representing the members of the ejido before federal and local authorities. A basic assumption behind the organization of the Ejidal Bank was that the ejiditarios, particularly the former resident peons, were poorer, less educated, and less productive than the peasants from the villages who were given individual holdings; as a result they would have special credit problems and require close supervision and extensive training (Moore, 1963: 148-149; González Aparicio, 1934: 38, 54). The inexperience of the peasants in working collectively was another factor which allegedly necessitated close supervision of the cooperatives by the bank.

By August 1936, the Cárdenas administration had already surpassed the goal of 30 million pesos for ejidal credit proposed for the entire period of the six-year plan. Government disbursements to the Ejidal Bank during its six-year term totaled over 140 million pesos. In comparison, government support to the Banco Agrícola totaled 40 million pesos, indicating the preference given to the ejido over the small holding (Cámara de Diputados, IV: 126).[14] At the same time, within the ejidal system, preference was given to the large collective ejidos as part of the government's efforts to demonstrate the efficiency of the collective system in maintaining high productive levels.

The administrative structure established in the ejidos combined the paternalistic orientation inherent in the conceptualization of the Ejidal Bank with democratic elements. Ejidal representatives were elected democratically in a general assembly of ejiditarios under the supervision of Ejidal Bank officials. But bank officials were also responsible for the overall supervision of the ejidos: officers elected by the ejidos had to be approved by them; field inspectors from the bank met weekly with the ejidal committees and the work chief to prepare the work plan for the week; bank officials made final decisions on the overall program of the ejido. Refusal to abide by the bank's decisions would risk a loss of credit (Landsberger and Hewitt, 1970: 19-20; Hewitt de Alcántara, 1974: 165).

The Ejidal Bank officials did cooperate with the members of the new collective ejidos in confronting a broad range of internal

[14] The preference given the ejido is also indicated by comparative figures for credit disbursement by the Agricultural and Ejidal Banks in the period 1936-1940:

Year	Banco Agrícola	Banco Ejidal
1936	11,450,000	23,278,000
1937	19,440,000	82,880,000
1938	11,500,000	63,442,000
1939	6,281,000	61,177,000
1940	6,303,000	59,149,000

Source: Reyes Osorio, 1974: 836.

problems in addition to those resulting from external hostility: overpopulation, resulting in unemployment and/or work rotation; inequalities resulting from higher pay for specialized work or the tendency of some ejiditarios to shirk their responsibilities; and a host of technical and financial problems: water shortages in La Laguna, susceptibility of wheat crops to disease in the Yaqui valley, and extensive debts due to the necessity of purchasing equipment and machinery. The ejiditarios coped with these and other problems,[15] succeeded in maintaining and in some cases increasing the level of production,[16] brought new land into cultivation, and channeled part of their profits to a social fund to finance machinery purchases, school construction, installation of wells, and land clearing.

But in some cases the Ejidal Bank officials themselves constituted part of the problem. In the Laguna region, local bank officials included former administrators of the landowners' estates who were in sympathy with their former employer and/or skeptical regarding the possibility of collective enterprises (Whetten, 1948: 225). Bureaucratization reinforced the authoritarian structures, a consequence of the belief that the ejiditarios were incapable of managing their own affairs; in some cases, every step taken by the ejiditarios had to be approved by the bank, resulting in excessive

[15] For example, several experiments were undertaken to equalize pay and to enforce work discipline. In La Laguna, in each cooperative, the ejiditarios elected a three- or four-man administrative committee (as well as a vigilance council of the same number to supervise the administrative committee), which was responsible for the day-to-day operation of the ejido. The ejiditarios also elected a work chief, who assigned work to ejido members, and other officials for specific responsibilities as needed (e.g., warehouseman, storekeeper for the cooperative store, etc.). Since the land was worked collectively at first, and each cooperative ejido constituted a single credit society, the ejiditarios also elected representatives to the Ejidal Bank, which often served on the same government board as the administrative committee (Landsberger and Hewitt, 1970: 19-20, 49-50). Comparable systems were initially established in other collective ejidos, including those of Michoacán and the Yaqui valley in Sonora (Barbosa and Maturana, 1972: 19-20; Hewitt de Alcántara, 1974: 165).

[16] According to Shulgovski, between 1935 and 1940, cotton production in cooperatives increased by 64.7 percent, rice by 34.5 percent, henequen by 19.4 percent, and coffee by 14.2 percent (1968: 258). An exception was the Yaqui valley, where, due to climatic conditions, crop yields were low for private farms as well as ejidos during the first year, but these improved after 1942 (Hewitt de Alcántara, 1974: 167).

delays and considerable frustration. Finally, there were examples of corruption in the bank even in the early years.[17]

During the Cárdenas years, the government was responsive to complaints brought against bank officials. Regional and national meetings were held in which delegates from collective ejidos freely criticized the irregularities, incompetence, or rigidity of bank employees. On at least one occasion a commission of government officials and members of Congress visited La Laguna to investigate alleged irregularities in that area (Mexico, SHCP, 1963, III: 518-588). The relationship between the federal government, the Ejidal Bank, and the ejiditarios exemplifies Cárdenas' dual policy of state constraints on popular sectors, on the one hand, and popular checks on the state bureaucracy, on the other. If the Ejidal Bank, under the auspices of the federal government, became a mechanism for the control and direction of the ejiditarios, the ejiditarios, with federal government support, could demand an accounting from Ejidal Bank officials. The success of this system obviously depended upon the willingness of the federal government to support the ejiditarios, and, as noted above, this condition was generally met during the Cárdenas administration.

The paternal role of the Ejidal Bank was apparently meant to be temporary. In certain areas, notably La Laguna, the administrative functions of the Ejidal Bank were increasingly turned over to parallel organizations of ejiditarios.[18] But in some cases new forms

[17] In the second year of the Nueva Italia collective, those responsible for presenting lists of the time worked by members (which constituted the basis of payment) began to siphon off funds owed to members and to submit alternate lists, with the complicity of bank field inspectors and other authorities who shared in the distribution of these funds. Bank officials were also accused of keeping profits from the sale of harvests, and of selling inputs to the ejiditarios at prices well above their cost. These and similar complaints were widely publicized by the landowners and their allies to demonstrate the problems of the collective ejidal system (Landsberger and Hewitt 1970: 23; Barbosa and Maturana, 1970: 21; Shulgovski, 1968: 259; López Zamora, 1946: 143 f; Albornoz, 1966: 300-301).

[18] By mid-1937, leaders of the Laguna cooperatives were asking for greater responsibility in administration, and at the beginning of 1939 a central advisory committee was formed of seven members to cooperate with the bank in matters relating to education, agriculture, health, administration, complaints, credit, and marketing. The success of this committee led to the proposed formation of fifteen regional Unions of Credit Societies (to be united in a Central Union of Credit Societies) which would gradually take over administrative responsibilities from the Ejidal Bank, and this project was tentatively extended to the national level through

of domination emerged, as in Yucatán, where the state governor, Humberto Canto Echeverría, restructured the initial cooperatives into a single Gran Ejido under his control, administered by an association (Henequeneros de Yucatán) which would take over the functions of the Ejidal Bank and would have equal representation from the ejiditarios, the hacendados (who retained 150 hectares on the expropriated property), and medium and small landowners. In effect, the Gran Ejido was managed as a large hacienda in which the ejiditarios became wage workers and the governor constituted the new owner.[19] In certain respects, the Yucatán experience provides a negative example of the importance of a continued role of the federal government with the collective ejido, since the Cárdenas government had agreed to the creation of the Henequeneros de Yucatán due to its inability to meet the financial costs of organizing henequen production (Mesa Andraca, 1955: 295; Benítez, 1956: 169-170).

The new ejiditarios were linked to the state not only through the Ejidal Bank but also through the National Peasant Confederation (CNC). As indicated above, Cárdenas had insisted that rural workers be organized separately from the major labor confederation, and officials of the government party had been given responsibility for organizing the peasant confederation. When the organizing committee, composed of Portes Gil and officials from government ministries and departments concerned with agrarian matters, began its task, the largest agrarian organization was the Mexican Peasant Confederation (CCM), which had been formed to support the candidacy of Cárdenas and which grouped most of the existing peasant leagues. Many of the radical agrarian or peasant leagues formed in the 1920's had been destroyed or weakened as a result of government persecution or cooptation; there were a

---

incorporation in the Agricultural Credit Law of December 1939 (Landsberger and Hewitt, 1970: 28-32).

[19] The negative effects of the control of the ejidal economy by the state governor soon became evident. The subsequent governor, Ernesto Novelo Torres, transferred five of the six warehouses owned by the ejiditarios to an institution owned by the governor which was subsequently sold to private interests; the ejiditarios were then forced to pay for storage in warehouses rightfully belonging to them. In 1941, a Supreme Court decision favored the return of equipment for processing henequen to the hacendados; subsequently an agreement was signed whereby 52 percent of the income from henequen sold would go to the machinery owners (i.e., the hacendados) and 48 percent to the ejiditarios (Benítez, 1956: 172-179).

number of conflicting organizations in some states as well as fictitious organizations created by local politicians (González Navarro, 1963: 137-139).

Following a series of conferences in which agrarian leagues were formed in each state, the constitutional convention of the CNC was held in August 1938, attended by 300 delegates from the state leagues—the constituent organizations of the confederation—which included representatives of the ejidos, rural unions, peasant organizations, small landowners, and rural youth. Nearly 3 million peasants and rural workers were represented.

It is not clear to what extent peasants and rural workers attempted to resist government efforts to control the peasant organization. While years of neglect or persecution by local or national government officials and of being utilized opportunistically by politicians pursuing their own interests had made these groups deeply suspicious of government officials, the encouragement of peasant mobilization and extensive land distribution program of the Cárdenas government undoubtedly weakened their resistance to government intervention. Nevertheless there was some resistance. Rural organizations previously affiliated with the CTM often joined the new peasant confederation reluctantly, in some cases maintaining their affiliation with the CTM as well. The nature of control exercised by the CNC leadership and its constituent organizations was also resented by many members. At the constitutional congress, several delegates complained to President Cárdenas regarding the treatment they had received at the hands of politicians and state officials, and asked that only rural workers be given posts in the direction of the new confederation. They pointed out that certain state governors—mentioning those of Aguascalientes and Coahuila—were obvious enemies of the peasants, and that even PNR officials had attempted to usurp their rights. But Cárdenas attributed their complaints to a lack of solidarity, stating that groups which had participated in their struggles should be accepted in the leadership (González Navarro, 1963: 141, 154; Gómez Jara, 1970: 120n.). Complaints against certain leaders—that they were conservative, or too bureaucratic, or constituted an obstacle to agrarian reform—continued after the convention, and there was even discussion of forming a separate, independent organization. However, several groups, including the Communist party, recommended that efforts to change the organization be made from within, and again unity was preserved at the ultimate cost of internal democracy.

THE STATE, AGRARIAN TRANSFORMATION, AND THE PEASANTRY UNDER CARDENAS

The effects of the Cárdenas agrarian reform are still debated, but its scope is generally conceded. During the Cárdenas administration more peasants received land than under all previous administrations since the revolution (810,000 under Cárdenas compared to 778,000 previously), and more than twice as much land was distributed (17.9 million hectares compared to 8.7 million) (Chevalier, 1967: 167-168).[20] But the Cárdenas agrarian reform differed from those of his predecessors qualitatively as well as quantitatively. Land expropriations under previous administrations, when they touched the large agrarian estates at all, had generally been concentrated on traditional haciendas and unused and inferior lands; the Cárdenas government expropriated not only traditional holdings but also highly developed commercial estates. And, while previous administrations had emphasized the small productive unit, with the ejido seen as an intermediate stage to the small farm, Cárdenas stressed the ejido, and its collective operation, particularly for commercial crops, as necessary to maintain and increase production (Cárdenas, 1972a: 130-131; Chevalier, 1967: 163 f).

The agrarian reform carried out by the Cárdenas government resulted in a substantial restructuring of the rural sector. In 1930, less than 15 percent of the cultivated land was in ejidos; and the remaining privately owned cultivated land was highly concentrated. By 1940, the ejidos incorporated 47.4 percent of the total cultivated land and 57.3 percent of the irrigated land. The number of ejiditarios had more than doubled—from 668,000 in 1930 to 1,606,000 by the end of the decade, and the number of landless workers had declined, although less significantly, from 2,479,000

---

[20] Chevalier suggests that many of the subsequent distributions were probably based on an additional 9,861,000 hectares tentatively distributed by Cárdenas, subject to confirmation. Forty percent of all presidential resolutions on land distribution between 1915 and 1966 were taken during the Cárdenas administration, and 30 percent of the peasants benefited by agrarian reform received land during that period. (Reyes Osorio, 1974: 37).

to 1,912,600 (Reynolds, 1970: 139; Weyl and Weyl, 1939: 175-179).

The agrarian reform of the 1930's did not eliminate the large properties, as Cárdenas himself recognized; although the number of private holdings of 10,000 hectares or more had been reduced to 1,500, most of them in the arid and semi-arid northern states, these still controlled a substantial proportion of the privately owned land (Reyes Osorio, 1974: 18). And, as indicated above, even on expropriated estates landowners were able to retain the equivalent of 150 irrigated hectares and much of the infrastructure, permitting a continuation of capitalist agriculture (or necessitating more productive use of remaining lands where more traditional forms of cultivation had prevailed). In some cases landowners also gained (or retained) control of credit, marketing, and the sale of agricultural implements and machinery, which constituted a source of new relations of exploitation.

Nevertheless, the agrarian reform destroyed the power of the large landowners and succeeded in its goal of eliminating or at least significantly reducing "feudal" relations of production. In the process, it eliminated an important obstacle to increased agricultural production. In contrast to Latin American countries in which traditional forms of agriculture have persisted into the 1960's and 1970's, Mexico was self-sufficient in agricultural production until recently, and agricultural exports supported the growth of industry by providing income for the import of industrial machinery and other industrial inputs (Hansen, 1974: 58-59).

Debate regarding the agrarian reform under Cárdenas concerns the extent to which it promoted or impeded conditions for capitalist accumulation and resulted in a "re-peasantization" of a partially proletarianized rural population. On the one hand, private property was not eliminated, and capitalist agricultural production was not discouraged. On the other, the large proportion of land turned over to ejidos—which could not be sold, rented, or otherwise alienated—constituted an obstacle to capitalist accumulation in agriculture in that half of the agricultural land and a substantial proportion of the labor force were excluded from the capitalist land and labor markets. Politically, this process had a stabilizing function—ultimately to the benefit of capitalist agriculture—in controlling the destabilizing effects of too rapid a process of capitalist accumulation in agriculture. The rapid concentration of land

and the expropriation of the peasantry under the impetus of commercial agricultural development during the Porfiriato had been an important factor in the revolution, particularly in the formation of peasant militia under Zapata. It was in the interests of the postrevolutionary governments and the agrarian bourgeoisie to delay this process through a "de-proletarianization" or "re-peasantization" of part of the rural proletariat (Bartra, 1974: 129-131; Paré, 1977: 70-74; see also Reynolds, 1970: 136-137, 141-142). Thus through the expropriation of the large estates and their transformation into ejidos, Cárdenas delayed or reversed the process of land and capital concentration and proletarianization in the countryside.[21] In effect, the agrarian reform established conditions for capitalist agricultural production (by eliminating pre-capitalist relations of production and traditional forms of cultivation) but at the same time established checks on this process by limiting the size of private estates and removing substantial proportions of land and rural labor from the capitalist market.

According to one critique, which notes that the prior mobilization of estate workers (e.g., in Laguna and Nueva Italia) often took the form of requests for better working conditions, collective contracts, and other labor benefits, Cárdenas was in effect giving a peasant solution to proletarian demands. The effect was to transform an important segment of the "rural proletariat" into ejiditarios, which weakened the proletariat in its conflict with agrarian capital (Montes de Oca, 1977: 52; Rello and Montes de Oca, 1974: 72).

However, given the context of Mexico in the 1930's, rural unions and proletarian demands do not necessarily imply a rural proletariat. Not only were relations of production non-capitalist, but there were pragmatic reasons for expressing grievances in the form of labor demands. Prior to the Agrarian Code of 1934, the *peones acasillados* were not legally entitled to receive land under the agrarian reform, and in 1931 legislation had been passed exempting the commercial estates from expropriation. It was not until the passage of the Expropriation Law of 1936 that the possibility of expropriating the commercial estates became realistic. This was undoubtedly a factor in the organization of the *acasillados* on the Laguna

---

[21] For an analysis of the concept of rural proletarianization, see Harris, 1978, especially pp. 8-12.

estates into trade unions rather than peasant leagues by the CTM and the Communist party.

Also, while the communally owned but individually cultivated ejidos—which became, in effect, subsistence plots—do constitute peasant holdings, it is somewhat misleading to assert the same of the collective ejido, which was envisioned as a technically efficient and highly productive economic unit managed by workers (Guerrero, 1975: 51). Cárdenas and other agrarians seemed to view the collective ejidos as a collectivist alternative to capitalist agricultural production rather than a form of re-peasantization (De Janvry and Ground, 1978: 107).

In short, the motivations behind the agrarian reform and the establishment of collective ejidos were varied. A first objective was to eliminate remnants of "feudal" production in the countryside. Second, capitalist production was limited and controlled, but not eliminated. The expropriation of traditional estates and the creation of a class of small farmers facilitated conditions for capitalist development in the long run; the establishment of ejidos constituted a limit on the process of capitalist accumulation but stabilized conditions in the countryside—a result which was in the long-term interests of capitalist production. Third, the collective ejido was both a pragmatic solution to the problem of maintaining economies of scale on the expropriated commercial estates and a reflection of the preferences of Cárdenas and other agrarians within the government for collective forms of ownership and control.

But since the credit, technical assistance, and moral support required by the ejidos, especially collective ejidos, could come only from the state, the agrarian reform was accompanied by the emergence of new forms of domination and control. The Ejidal Bank, created to provide this support, became an instrument for the control and manipulation of the ejiditarios in many instances. Similarly, the CNC, ostensibly established to promote the political participation of peasants and rural workers, instead became a mechanism for their domination by the state.

To some extent such an outcome was projected by Cárdenas himself in his efforts to maintain state control over all aspects of the agrarian reform. And, as he stated in a speech to the new ejiditarios of La Laguna: "The intervention of the state in the overall direction of the national economy is . . . a function of the public order; socially, it guarantees economic autonomy to the recipients; economically, it insures that the global volume of agricultural production is not reduced to the detriment of consumption and foreign trade."[22] But the policy of Cárdenas encompassed the mobilization of these groups as well as their control—a mobilization through which the affected groups confronted not only the landowners and their allies but also the bureaucratic inefficiency and corruption of state officials themselves, particularly those of the Ejidal Bank. The effectiveness of this mobilization in countering state officials, however, still depended to a large extent on the sympathy of those who controlled the federal government, which became the ultimate arbiter of such confrontations. In short, implicit in the agrarian policy of the Cárdenas government was an assumption of state autonomy and neutrality which failed to take into account the class nature and functions of the state within a capitalist society.

THE CONTRADICTIONS OF THE PROGRESSIVE ALLIANCE

The contradictions of the alliance between the state (or what was now the dominant faction within the state) and the mobilized sectors of the working class and peasantry were not immediately apparent. For the Cárdenas faction, this alliance constituted an effective means of challenging the previously dominant faction and obtaining and maintaining control of the state apparatus. This in turn facilitated state action to bring about substantial reforms within the capitalist industrial sector and to restructure the pre-capitalist agricultural sector. For the urban-industrial working class, it meant a significant improvement in their material conditions within the framework of capitalist production relations and an increase in their organizational strength which would presumably enable them to maintain and increase these benefits. For the peasantry and the rural working class, it meant the elimination of traditional forms of exploitation and, for many, the fulfillment of the revolutionary goal of agrarian reform. The progressive alliance demonstrated the viability of a coalition between a dominant faction within the state and popular sectors as a means of enhancing the autonomy of the

[22] "La ingerencia del Estado en la dirección superior de la economía nacional es . . . una funcion de orden público: en la social, al garantizar autonomía económica a los pueblos dotados; y en lo económico, al cuida que no se reduzca el volumen global de la producción agrícola, en detrimento del consuma y del comercio exterior" (México: Cámara de Diputados, 1966, V: 764).

state and its ability to act against the perceived interests of the dominant class and indeed the actual interests of certain segments of that class. This relative state autonomy would again be demonstrated in the conflict with foreign interests which controlled the Mexican petroleum industry.

But from the perspective of the state, such an alliance is contradictory not only in terms of the function of the state within a class society but also in terms of the dynamics within the coalition itself. The dynamics of such a relationship involves a question of primacy: to what extent was the state acting on the basis of an alliance with these classes, and to what extent were the classes pursuing their interests through the state? In other words, the state had to control these groups, or their continued mobilization would enable them to control the state or even undermine its basis of existence.

It was assumed by the Cárdenas government that within the alliance the state would be dominant. In the first place, historical trends and structural conditions within the peasantry and working class had resulted in tendencies to depend upon the state. These conditions included the small size of the urban/industrial working class, the isolation and fragmentation of the peasantry and rural workers, and the failure of these two sectors to unite—in part due to the deliberate machinations of the state—except in isolated instances. As indicated above, these conditions had resulted in the development of authoritarian and paternalistic tendencies within both urban/industrial and rural labor movements as these groups were organized by the state and/or state-controlled labor confederations, and depended upon alliances with particular state officials for any benefits they obtained. In the second place, these conditions were consciously or unconsciously reinforced during the Cárdenas administration through the rapid organization of unorganized groups among urban and rural workers; the deliberate segregation of rural workers and peasants, as well as certain elements of the urban working class, from the major labor confederation; the erosion of the principle of union democracy and the reinforcement of authoritarian practices within that confederation and within the major rural organizations, the Ejidal Bank and the National Peasant Confederation; and the reforms of the Cárdenas government itself, which provided a rationale for continued dependence upon the state.

But Cárdenas' concern that the state should control the popular sectors (as well as the dominant class) was to some extent countered by a concern that these sectors be able to defend themselves against the dominant classes and even the state bureaucracy itself. Examples of this concern included the arming of the peasants, the encouragement of ejiditarios to criticize Ejidal Bank officials, and the promotion of democratic processes and ultimate self-sufficiency within the collective ejidos. At the same time, the effectiveness of these groups in confronting the hostility of the dominant classes and the inefficiency and corruption of state bureaucrats depended upon continued support at the highest level of government.

What is significant in explaining eventual state control of the popular sectors is not simply the intent or actions of the Cárdenas government but the apparent failure of the affected sectors to recognize the implicit contradiction in their alliance with the state and the importance of maintaining their independence. The development or reinforcement of authoritarian structures within the peasant and labor movements meant a loss of control of these movements by their membership. At the same time, the leadership of these organizations failed to develop an alternative ideology to that of the revolution, which had been appropriated by the state and given considerable credibility by the actions of the Cárdenas government. The failure of the labor leadership to envision goals beyond those of the revolution, and the assumption that the state could continue to implement these goals, weakened or eliminated the rationale for an independent labor and peasant movement. Thus not only the Cárdenas government but also most sectors of the rural and urban workers and their leaders assumed the continuation of an "autonomous" state, above classes, which could act as final arbiter in class conflict and in conflicts between these sectors and officials of the state bureaucracy.

Six ‖ The State and Private Capital

 In October 1936 Manuel Gómez Morín, a Mexican lawyer and banker, wrote enthusiastically to a friend in France about the resurgence of private enterprise in Mexico. The emergence of new "systems of cooperation and collaboration" among Mexican business groups was "making it possible to achieve things which would have seemed impossible" five years before—the formation of new insurance companies to replace the foreign ones which left the country, the establishment of banks and financial societies which were multiplying credit opportunities, and the placement of long-term securities in the market, and "many other activities of this nature" (Gómez Morín, 21 Oct. 1936).

One of the apparent contradictions of the Cárdenas administration is that a period of major confrontation between the government and owning groups was a period of growth and prosperity for the private sector. Between 1934 and 1940, gross national product increased by over 30 percent, from 15.9 billion to 20.7 billion pesos (Nafinsa, 1977: 23). Manufacturing output, which increased at a rate of 17 percent annually in the early 1930's (in part due to recovery from the depression) continued to grow at a respectable rate of 8 percent per year in the last years of the decade (Nafinsa/CEPAL, 1971). Manufacturing output increased 42 percent between 1935 and 1940 (compared to 35 percent in the previous decade) and increased as a percentage of GDP from 14.8 percent in 1935 to 16.7 percent in 1940 (see Table 6.1). Also, it is generally recognized that the Cárdenas government established conditions for the subsequent growth of manufacturing, including the creation of a market for manufactured goods. According to one source, sufficient industrial stock existed by 1940 to permit a 75 percent expansion in manufacturing between 1939 and 1946 without major new investment (Reynolds, 1970: 167).

According to informal surveys taken by the Banco Nacional de México, industry profits were high at least in the first years of the Cárdenas sexenio; although profits were subsequently reduced in certain industries due to problems related to the petroleum conflict and expropriation, they recovered by 1939 and 1940. In banking and insurance profits remained high—up to 20 percent—through-

The Sugar Industry. Detail from mural by Diego Rivera.

TABLE 6.1. Manufacturing Output as Percentage of GDP: 1910-1940

Year	GDP (million pesos)	Manufacturing Output (million pesos)	Manufacturing Output (percent of GDP)
1900	8,540	1,232	14.4
1910	11,825	1,663	14
1925	17,081	1,889	11
1935	17,820	2,555	14.3
1940	21,658	3,629	16.7

Source: King, 1970: 12. Percentages added

out this period (BNM, 1934-1941: Sept. 1934, Sept. 1935, Aug. 1937, Sept. 1938, June 1939, Aug. 1940).

For most members of the Cárdenas government there was no inconsistency in promoting conditions for private capital accumulation, on the one hand, and encouraging the mobilization of workers and peasants, on the other. To a certain extent, given capitalism as the dominant mode of production, efforts of the state to promote economic development—for example, in expanding infrastructure—automatically benefited private interests. Also, the continued dominance of foreign capital in the most important sectors of the economy meant that state intervention was necessary to insure *national* capitalist development. Finally, certain conditions favoring relative "structural" autonomy did permit progressive factions within the state to take a more aggressive stance with respect to private capital than would normally be the case. As indicated above, these conditions included the alliance of these factions with the mobilized popular sectors, the weakness of the national bourgeoisie in the aftermath of the Mexican revolution, and the shift in U.S. interests and policies, partly as a consequence of the depression. Approximately half of the total gross investment in the last years of the Cárdenas sexenio consisted of investment by the government or government enterprises (Reynolds, 1970: 284-285). These conditions seemed to indicate that the government could steer a "third" course for Mexican development which was neither capitalist in the traditional sense nor socialist in terms of worker or state control of the means of production. Given the incipient nature of industrial capitalism in Mexico, it was felt that through state intervention, Mexico could avoid certain contradictions of capitalist development. As stated by Ramón Beteta, Undersecretary of Foreign Affairs and a close associate of Cárdenas:

"We think that we should attempt to industrialize Mexico consciously, intelligently avoiding the avoidable evils of industrialism, such as urbanism, exploitation of man by man, production for sale instead of production for the satisfaction of human needs, economic insecurity, waste, shabby goods, and the mechanization of the workman. . . . We are convinced that the evils of capitalism are not to be found in the application of machinery to the productive process, but rather are due to a merely legal question: who is owner of the machinery. . . . We have dreamt of a Mexico of 'ejidos' and small industrial communities, with electricity, and sanitation, in which goods will be produced for the purpose of satisfying the needs of the people; in which machinery will be employed to relieve man from heavy toil, and not for so-called over-production" (Beteta, 1935: 44).

But the ability of the Cárdenas government to control and direct private capital continued to be limited by structural conditions. As will be seen, these included constraints resulting from Mexico's relations with foreign capital, particularly its economic relations with the United States, and the dependence of the state on resources generated in the private sector. At the same time, the process of private capital accumulation, to which the government contributed in the interests of promoting economic development, limited and conditioned state policies even in a situation of relative state autonomy. Given these structural constraints and the dynamics of capitalist development, government policies to promote and at the same time control private capital were inherently contradictory.

THE STATE AND PRIVATE CAPITAL: STRUCTURAL LIMITS TO STATE AUTONOMY

Certain of the major goals and strategies of the Cárdenas government which directly or indirectly affected private capital have been discussed above: encouragement of labor mobilization and the use of the strike to obtain increased benefits for workers within the context of industrial capitalism; legislation enabling the state to expropriate private property in the public interest; and an agrarian reform which gave peasants access to land, eliminated "feudal" relations in the countryside, limited the size of capitalist agricultural holdings, and introduced new structures of agricultural production. Here we are concerned with policies specifically oriented to regulation of relations between the state and the private sector, restrictions on foreign capital, and the encouragement of small producers, generally Mexican nationalists, as a means of countering foreign economic control and trends to capital concentration.

State Expenses and Fiscal Constraints. Among the manifestations of the government's statist orientation were a general increase in the federal budget and a shift in the character of federal government expenditures and investment policy. Between 1934 and 1940, federal government expenditures doubled from 265 million pesos to 610 million pesos, and per capital expenditures from 15.9 to 31 pesos (Nafinsa, 1977: 361-362).[1] Prior to the Cárdenas administration, over half of the federal government budget had been allotted to administrative expenses, much of this consisting of expenditure on the military, which had fluctuated between 30 and 40 percent of the budget in the 1920's. These figures presumably reflected the power of regional military commanders and the unsettled conditions resulting from frequent military uprisings against the central government as well as the Cristero rebellion. After 1929, the year of the last military revolt, when military expenditures constituted over 37 percent of the budget, this proportion declined to 23 percent in 1934 and 15.7 percent in 1939; although there was a slight increase in the actual amount after 1935, they did not reach their 1929 level again until 1941, when they reflected collaboration with the U.S. military in defense measures during the war years. At the same time, there was a dramatic shift in the importance of economic expenditures, which increased from 23.2 percent of the budget in 1934 to 42.6 percent in 1936. This increase was chiefly in the categories of communications and public works, and agricultural credit, which constituted 7.2 percent of the budget in 1935 and 9.5 percent in 1936—twice as high as any succeeding year (Wilkie 1970: 77-79, 102, 128-130, 139).[2]

Public sector investments, which are categorized separately from

---

[1] Unless otherwise noted, figures are given in current pesos. Given the inflation which characterized the Mexican economy in the late 1930's and the devaluation in 1938, the real increase is less dramatic, but still substantial.

[2] The distinction between administrative and economic expenditures is based on the classification of James Wilkie (1970), which breaks down the federal budget according to economic, social, and administrative expenditures, including both those budgeted and actual expenditures. This classification does not include government investments, which are budgeted separately.

the federal government budget, also reflected the changing policy orientation of the Cárdenas government. In the previous decade (1925-1934), authorized public sector investments had fluctuated between 85 million and 100 million pesos; during the Cárdenas sexenio they climbed from 137 million pesos in 1935 to 290 million pesos in 1940 (Nafinsa, 1977: 367-368). A listing of principal government investments in the three-year period between 1935 and 1938 indicates that the bulk of these investments were in agricultural programs connected with the agrarian reform (the Ejidal and Agricultural banks, the Emiliano Zapata sugar refinery in Morelos, and irrigation), and physical infrastructure (especially road construction):

Banco Nacional de Crédito Ejidal	126,361,696.54
Banco Nacional de Crédito Agrícola	37,300,000.00
Ing. "Emiliano Zapata"	14,429,803.44
Railroad construction	69,675,610.02
Road-building: total	151,800,704.54
(Road construction)	(68,700,704.54)
(Road bonds)	(83,100,000.00)
Irrigation systems	93,210,712.52
Hydraulic works	15,453,200.74
Port conditioning and dredging	18,904,431.69

Source: Mexico, SHCP: 1951: 624-626.

The emphasis upon expenditures connected with the agrarian reform represented a departure from the concerns of the previous governments. In contrast, the expansion of infrastructure, obviously a necessary condition for economic development, at the same time continued the policies of Cárdenas' predecessors in supporting private capital accumulation.

Since the state-owned sector was quite small and there was little concept of making profits through state enterprises, state expenditures were dependent upon resources generated in the private sector. The major tax sources of federal government revenues were the income tax; the tax on the development of natural resources; taxes on industry, imports, and exports; and the stamp tax. The foreign-owned mining and petroleum companies in Mexico provided much of this income, not only in the form of taxes on natural resources and exports but also a portion of the industry tax. In 1937, fiscal receipts from the above-mentioned sources ac-

TABLE 6.2. Major Tax Sources of Federal Government Revenues: 1937

Source	Amount (million pesos)	Percentage
Income tax	41	9
Development of natural resources	32	7
Industry	89	19.7
Imports	104	23
Exports	30	6.6
Stamp tax	30	6.6

Source: SHCP, General Bureau of Financial Studies (Nacional Financiera, 1977: 353)

counted for approximately 72 percent of federal government receipts (Table 6.2).

During the first years of the Cárdenas government, favorable economic conditions resulted in an automatic expansion of government revenue through an expansion of the existing tax base. By the time that Cárdenas became president in late 1934, the economy had begun to recover from the depression. The favorable price of silver in the world market and the increase in demand, as well as higher prices for lead, zinc, and copper, stimulated the mining industry, resulting in increased export earnings and government revenues (BFM, 1935-1941; 31 Dec. 1936: 3). The government also benefited indirectly from the growth in manufacturing output: in 1935 new products began to appear in the market and manufactured articles were exported to Central America; during 1936, in spite of strikes and concern regarding the Expropriation Law (passed in September of that year), industrial activity was increasing and industries were producing at full capacity at the end of the year (BFM, 1935-1941: 31 Dec. 1936; BNM, 1934-1941: Jan. 1937).

But by 1937 several factors (among them a recession in the United States which resulted in a decline in Mexico's exports, and pressures generated by the petroleum conflict) cut into the government's revenue as government expenditures continued to increase. The government was also constrained by its reluctance to increase taxes, since this might discourage investment (Suárez, 1976). It was left with two alternatives: loans from the private sector, and deficit financing through loans from the central bank. Private bankers readily invested in government road bonds but were hesitant to lend to the government for other purposes (due to financial conservatism, opposition to the Cárdenas government, or a combination of the two). The government also obtained loans and tax advances from foreign-owned companies in Mexico, particularly the mining and petroleum companies, to finance imports of machinery and equipment for its construction and irrigation programs, and sought credit on various occasions from the U.S. government and banks. But loans from these sources began to dry up at precisely the time that government need for them was growing, in part because of the increased opposition on the part of private capital (national and foreign) to government policies, an opposition now considerably aggravated by the petroleum conflict.

Unable to obtain sufficient credit from private sources, Finance Secretary Suárez, who supported the Keynesian notion of deficit financing as a means of stimulating the economy, began to depend increasingly on central bank loans. The government had already begun to exercise its drawing rights with the central bank within certain prescribed limits in 1936, but by the middle of 1937 government borrowing had surpassed the amount permitted by law, and the amount of the overdraft was growing rapidly.[3] Officials within the central bank became increasingly concerned, blaming deficit government spending for the inflation which was beginning to affect prices, and Suárez was forced to seek other expedients (Casas Alatriste, 1937: Banco de México, 1937).

The repercussions of the petroleum expropriation in March of 1938 further aggravated the financial problems of the government and led to a devaluation of the peso (Chapter Seven). In the following months the government passed a series of tax measures to redress certain imbalances resulting from the devaluation, including a special tax of twelve percent on exports—chiefly affecting the mining industry—which would eliminate part of the benefits exporters derived from devaluation. Half of its proceeds would cover the deficit of the federal government with the Banco de México; the other half would constitute a subsidy for imports, particularly of necessary articles (Banco de México, 1940; Mexico, Cámara de Diputados, 1966, IV: 87). Although protested by the mining companies as well as by other private groups, the tax was successful, having an immediate effect of raising government in-

---

[3] On July 3, the account of the Federal Government with the Banco de México was 96,513,410.20 pesos, which involved an overdraft of 63,161,599.48 beyond the legal limit. This surplus had increased by 16,238,932.08 pesos from 46,922,677 since May 29 (Casas Alatriste, 1937).

come from exports from an average of 29 million pesos in 1937 and 1938 to 75 million in 1939. The relative importance of export taxes among government revenue sources doubled from six percent in 1938 to 13 percent in 1939 (Nafinsa, 1977: 354).

In December the government presented a law project for a special tax on excess bank profits. Although its chief objective was to control speculation in foreign currency which had increased with the devaluation of the peso, the original bill went beyond the problem of speculation, providing for a tax on all profits derived from acts alleged to be illegal or alien to the purpose of banking institutions (ABM, 1937-1941: 21 Dec. 1938, enclosure). The banking community objected strongly to the bill and succeeded in obtaining a substantial modification, with the result that the final legislation called only for taxation of profits resulting from operations with foreign exchange and gold (ABM, 1937-1941: Circular 149).

In the following year, at the instigation of the private sector (backed by Luis Montes de Oca, director of the Banco de México), Cárdenas abolished a four percent tax on capital exports which had been in effect since the early 1930's. According to its opponents, the tax had not achieved its purpose of curtailing capital exports, and at the same time its contribution to the federal treasury was negligible (Mexico, SHCP, 1963, V: 49-51). (The difficulties of monitoring capital exports were undoubtedly a factor in the low level of tax revenues from this source.) It was also argued that the tax acutally encouraged capital export and discouraged capital repatriation, due to a generalized fear that the existing tax could be increased (Novoa, 1937a: 66-68; Montes de Oca, 1938; A. Rodríguez, 1935).

The most controversial tax project introduced by the Cárdenas government was an excess profits tax, sent to the Chamber of Deputies at the end of 1939. The proposed tax does not seem to have been very stringent: excess profits were those over 15 percent, and profits of 15-21 percent would be taxed only 20 percent, with a graduated tax rate for higher rates of profit; profits of over 33 percent would be taxed at 45 percent (BNM, 1934-1941: Nov. 1939). But the tax was violently opposed by the private sector; on December 14 the major business organizations sent a letter to the President, characterizing the project as an attempt to create a "fascist" tax regime and an example of "Hitlerist totalitarianism" (ABM, 1937-1941: Circular 179, enclosure). Undoubtedly reflecting the fact that profits were, indeed, excessive, the private sector and its representatives argued against the measure on technical grounds, claiming that it was retroactive, that it did not take into account long periods of unproductive investment, that it would tax the person who worked with his own capital more than the capitalist who hired labor (ABM, 1937-1941: Circular 179, enclosure; Mexico, SHCP, 1963, V: 55-82). The measure was passed in December with some concessions to business groups, including the reduction of the maximum tax rate from 45 to 35 percent. Even this rather cautious government attempt to reduce excessive profits evoked continued protest from affected groups.

The insufficiency of government resources to finance its expenditures was particularly acute in efforts to meet the credit needs of peasants who received land through the agrarian reform. Despite the level of government contributions to the Ejidal Bank, its resources were inadequate to provide credit to more than a small proportion of ejiditarios—less than 15 percent in 1940. The Agricultural Credit Bank also failed to meet the needs of more than a small percentage of small and medium farmers. Unable to obtain funds from private or government banks, many ejiditarios and small farmers were dependent on local merchants and moneylenders who frequently charged usurious interest rates (Moore, 1963: 151-152; Reyes Osorio, 1974: 812-813; Albornoz, 1966: 142).

The government's anxiety to prove the viability of collective production made the collective ejidos a particular target of concern. It also placed the administration in the somewhat untenable position of seeking loans from the private sector for programs which that sector opposed. On several occasions, government loan requests were turned down by private banks in Mexico or U.S. banks (Lockett, 1937d, 1938a). Nevertheless, the government succeeded in obtaining financing for the collective ejidos by providing guarantees through its own banks. After unsuccessful attempts to obtain loans from U.S. banks, in 1937 a loan contract was signed between the Ejidal Bank, the Banco de México (central bank) and three private banks (Banco Nacional de México, the Banco de Comercio, and the Banco Mexicano) providing that the Banco de México would serve as agent for a loan of 5 million pesos from the three private banks to the Ejidal Bank for the cultivation and harvesting of the Laguna cotton crop (Montes de Oca, 1937c). Finance Secretary Suárez persuaded the subsidiary of Anderson Clayton, a cotton firm in Texas, which had formerly operated

with the landowners of the Laguna region, to maintain its assistance, financing the new collective ejidos through loans to the Ejidal and Agricultural Credit Banks (Suárez, 1976). A similar arrangement was made in Baja California, where the Cia. Industrial
Jabonera del Pacífico, S.A. (two-thirds owned by Anderson Clayton, one-third by the Colorado River Land Company) would lend
2.5 million pesos—via the Secretary of Finance and the Ejidal Bank—
to the cotton and wheat ejiditarios of the Mexicali district (Myers,
1938). By 1938, an estimated 39 percent of all Ejidal Bank operations were made through private banks. In 1939, there was a 100
percent increase in private capital investment in ejidal societies via
the Banco Ejidal (50,928,065.44 pesos compared with 24,162,734.89
pesos in 1939), oriented chiefly to the commercial, collectively operated ejidos (Senior, 1958: 104; Banco Ejidal, 1936-1943, 1940:
17).[4]

Given the constraints on fiscal resources, failure to obtain private financing would have undoubtedly restricted the ejidal program. But success tied the ejidal system, and particularly the collective ejidos, to dependence upon private financial sources. This
had the unintended effect of reinforcing the existing structural im-
balance in the countryside between large-scale commercial estates
and small subsistence holdings. Prior to the Cárdenas administration the former had been almost entirely privately owned, whereas
most of the agrarian reform sector was in small holdings—ejidal
or private. With the expropriation of commercial estates and their
transformation into collective ejidos, this dichotomy between large
estates and small holdings had come to characterize the agrarian
reform sector as well as the private sector. The limited resources
of the Ejidal and Agricultural Credit Banks resulted in a debate
between proponents of social goals of helping the small peasant,
regardless of financial risk, and those favoring the utilization of
strict banking criteria in order to make the banks solvent. With
the preference given the ejiditarios during the Cárdenas years, the
Agricultural Bank found it necessary to confine credit to low-risk
borrowers. One of the effects of growing dependence on private
credit sources was to reinforce the use of private banking criteria

[4] Senior states that, in 1945, 77 percent of the national operations of the Ejidal
Bank were carried out through funds from private credit sources; this proportion
dropped to 19 percent in 1950 but increased to 87 percent in 1953 (Senior, 1958:
104). These have continued to be concentrated in the wealthier ejidal zones (Albornoz, 1966: 279).

(of guaranteed risk and profitability) in the disbursement of government loans, leading to a concentration on commercial ejidos at the cost of the small, less productive ejidos of western and southern Mexico. As of 1941, only 11.9 percent of the funds loaned by the Ejidal Bank had gone to the states of Guanajuato, Jalisco, Michoacán, and Guerrero, although these contained 21.6 percent of the ejiditarios in the country (González Navarro, 1963: 158). Thus a majority of ejiditarios and small farmers, including a large number who constituted reasonable credit risks, were not reached by government or private credit organizations.[5]

In short, the government's programs were restricted by its limited financial resources and its direct or indirect dependence on the private sector for revenues. To the extent that this dependence was direct rather than indirect (i.e., on loans, rather than—or in addition to—taxes), the private sector could withhold resources if government policies were perceived as a threat to its interests. Private groups who provided loans to the government in such circumstances were in a position to establish conditions which would shape the relevant government program, in some cases resulting in a subtle (or direct) distortion of the initial aims of the program.

Regulation of Private Industry. The major formal mechanisms for structuring the relationship between the state and the private sector were the so-called "peak" organizations. Most of these were sectoral; during the Carranza administration the Confederation of

[5] The 1945 annual report of the Banco Ejidal explicitly stated that in order to receive semi-official and private financing, the bank must utilize "banking criteria" and operate without losses; as a result it had concentrated on those ejidal societies which were not only solvent but also contributed to the maintenance of ejidal zone headquarters and agencies (Moore, 1963: 220-222). In 1944, the collective ejidos of La Laguna, the Yaqui valley, Las Mochis, Lombardia, Neuva Italia, and Soconusco (coffee and banana ejido in Chiapas) contained 14.7 percent of all ejiditarios cooperating with the Ejidal Bank, but received 57 percent of the credit. Approximately one-third of the credit of the Ejidal Bank went to La Laguna (Whetten, 1948: 215-216). By the late 1960's, approximately 50 percent of Ejidal Bank credit was concentrated in Yucatán, La Laguna, and the Yaqui valley, in many cases going to relatively prosperous ejidos which could attract credit from other sources (Reyes Osorio, 1974: 775-776). It has been argued that the conflict within agrarian credit agencies has led to a false dichotomy between destitute peasants who are unable to repay loans and should be served by other forms of government aid, and large-scale ejidal complexes capable of obtaining funds from private sources; more efficient lending policies would be targeted at a middle range group needing credit from government sources but having the capacity to repay loans.

National Chambers of Commerce (CONCANACO) and the Confederation of Chambers of Industry (CONCAMIN) were formed, and in 1928 the Mexican Bankers' Association (ABM) was established. In addition, at the instigation of Monterrey business groups an employers' association, the Employers' Confederation of the Mexican Republic (COPARMEX) was formed in 1929, having a definite class orientation and a specific goal of influencing the pending labor law from the perspective of owning class interests.

The Cárdenas government wished to formalize the organization of chambers of commerce and industry, and in 1936 legislation was passed requiring all industries and commercial establishments beyond a certain size (500 pesos, approximately $143) to join industrial, commercial, or mixed chambers at the local level which would be united in a single confederation at the national level under the jurisdiction of the Secretary of the National Economy. Its stated purpose was to regulate relations between sectoral interests and the state, with the confederations and chambers serving as advisory groups to the government. Previously membership in commercial and industrial chambers had been voluntary, and the new legislation was opposed by certain groups: industrialists would constitute a minority in such a confederation and desired their own organization; Monterrey interests argued that association in chambers should be voluntary and not government-regulated; and the bankers, already joined in the Mexican Bankers' Association (ABM) and regulated through the Finance Ministry, decided against forming a new organization that would be under the jurisdiction of the Secretary of the Economy (Shafer, 1973: 43-46; Mexico SEN, 1937; 165-166: ABM, 1937-1941: Dec. 1938). But this legislation does not appear to have aroused the controversy of other measures of the Cárdenas administration. While it affected the mode of association of private firms it did not affect their mode of economic operation; in contrast to the workers, it is primarily in their control of the means of production rather than in their organizational strength that the power of the dominant class resides. And, as will be seen, private groups had their own modes of association which fell outside state jurisdiction. Also, the most powerful business groups often had direct access to high-level government officials, and in many cases their interests were inter-sectoral rather than sectoral. Finally, government regulation did not stifle the activities of the chambers which sharply criticized government policies on various occasions. For example, the Confederación de Cámaras Nacionales de Comercio e Industria (which united the Chambers of Commerce and Industry in a single confederation following the 1936 legislation) published two documents during the Cárdenas sexenio—one a critique of labor administration of the railroads, the second a highly critical analysis of the economy during the six years of the Cárdenas administration.

Another form of regulating private interests was the formation of state enterprises in a position to compete with private firms, but these were not considered a source of profits for state revenues. In most cases the relevant private firms were foreign or the state enterprises were too small to be considered a threat. But in 1935 two major state enterprises were formed—a state insurance company, Seguros de México, and a paper company, Productora e Importadora de Papel, S.A. (PIPSA). Seguros de México was formed at the time that legislation was passed regulating the insurance industry and stipulating that insurance reserves be invested in Mexican enterprises. As a result, most foreign-owned insurance companies left the country; Seguros de México was established by taking over the assets of one of them, El Sol de Canada. Some private groups grumbled at state intervention in this area, but private insurance companies, taking advantage of the vacuum left by the departure of foreign companies, also thrived during this period. The fact that Seguros de México was oriented to social goals— e.g., encouragement of types of insurance which would meet the need of workers—limited competition with private insurance companies (Mexico: SHCP, 1951: 616).

The formation of PIPSA was justified on the basis of the virtual monopoly enjoyed by the major paper firm (Cia. San Rafael); its major function was to import paper to sell to newspapers at the purchase price and Cárdenas explicitly stated that it would not be oriented to profits (PRM, 1940: 26; Silva Herzog, 1975: 106). Although these two firms demonstrated the possibility of utilizing state enterprises to regulate private activity, their scope and resources were limited during the Cárdenas administration.

In general the orientation of the Cárdenas government toward the encouragement of private industry undoubtedly restrained its use of formal mechanisms of government regulation. Private groups complained about increasing "statism," but limited state regulation did not affect their ability to function.

Restrictions on Foreign Capital. As indicated above, the conditions of export enclave dependence had changed little between the Porfiriato and 1934, the year that Cárdenas became president. Foreign control of the export sector, the predominant role of the U.S. in Mexico's trade, and the dependence on exports to balance international payments (and for a substantial proportion of government income) meant that the Mexican economy was extremely vulnerable to external pressures, whether these were deliberate or the consequences of international prices and market conditions. Efforts of previous governments to enforce Article 27 of the constitution had evoked strong opposition on the part of affected interests and met with little success, and by the late 1920's links had been reinforced between government officials and private interests of the U.S. and Mexico which limited government efforts to restrict foreign interests in Mexico. The continued prominence of foreign capital in key sectors of the Mexican economy and Mexico's dependence on trade with the U.S. undoubtedly constituted the major constraints limiting the autonomy of the Mexican state during this period.

The six-year plan, passed at the time that the nomination of Cárdenas to the presidency became official, had returned to the nationalist orientation of the constitution, proposing effective nationalization of the subsoil (Article 98), increased government participation in the profits of firms dedicated to the development of natural resources (Article 98), and participation of national firms— public or private—in petroleum operations. In 1935 the Cárdenas government suspended certain tax exemptions enjoyed by the petroleum companies and other foreign interests, and passed the bill eliminating foreign control in the insurance industry. In September 1936 the Law of Expropriation was passed, and in that same month a new mining law was drafted providing that all mining concessions must be worked regularly, that 20 percent of mining profits must be invested in Mexico, and that the Secretary of the National Economy had the power to Mexicanize mining if the public interest so demanded (Bernstein, 1965: 183-184).

The Rodríguez administration had established government control over rates charged by the foreign-owned electrical companies, and the Cárdenas government created the Comisión Federal de Electricidad, which built hydroelectric and hydraulic works and purchased several small local electric companies as a first step in the eventual unification of the electric power industry under state control. Other initiatives included the creation of the Administración de Petróleo Nacional in March 1937 to explore petroleum reserves; the formation of the Comisión de Fomento Minero to assist small miners (who, in contrast to the major mining companies, were predominantly Mexican); the establishment of the Banco Nacional de Comercio Exterior (Foreign Trade Bank) to promote agricultural exports, which would benefit Mexican farmers and ejiditarios rather than foreign mining and petroleum companies (and also relieve Mexico's balance of payments situation); and the nationalization of the minority share of the National Railroads (already majority state-owned). Efforts to "control" foreign capital culminated with the expropriation of the foreign-owned petroleum companies, which had refused to respect Mexican laws and institutions. State control of the Mexican petroleum industry reinforced its ability to direct private capital, placing it in a strategic position to guide and subsidize national development.

But despite the efforts and achievements of the Cárdenas government in restricting foreign capital in the export sector, Cárdenas apparently shared to some extent the conviction of his predecessors that the "right kind" of foreign capital was necessary for Mexico's development. On several occasions he asserted to U.S. Ambassador Josephus Daniels and others that foreign investment in manufacturing would be assured of protection (U.S. Department of State, 1952-1969, 1936: 718; Duggan, 1937). Foreign companies, among them General Motors and Chrysler, opened plants and subsidiaries in Mexico during this period.

Given the continued decline in trade and financial relations with Europe as a consequence of the depression and subsequently the Second World War, dependence on foreign capital and technology was increasingly oriented to the U.S. This was reinforced by an orientation to a "hemispheric policy," with increased economic ties between the U.S. and Latin America, on the part of both Mexico and the U.S. (Wood, 1961: 129; Lockett, 1935b). The expansion of the role of the state in the economy, especially in the construction of infrastructure, also reinforced Mexico's commercial ties with the U.S. As the Cárdenas government expanded railroads, highways, municipal facilities, and other public works projects, it purchased increasing amounts of road-building machinery, construction material, and railroad cars and equipment from foreign, especially U.S., manufacturers.[6] Agricultural machinery was

[6] U.S. officials in Mexico were concerned with foreign trade competition during this period, particularly from Germany.

also purchased to provide for the new collective ejidos. The Fulton Iron Works of St. Louis, for example, contracted with the Mexican Finance Secretary to provide all steel, machinery and supervisory engineering for construction of the sugar mill at Zacatepec, Morelos (the Emiliano Zapata refinery), which would be administered by a workers' cooperative. In March 1937, Finance Minister Suárez presented a list of government purchases made in the U.S. to the U.S. commercial attaché in Mexico, most of them between December 1934 and January 1936—over 91 million pesos (approximately $28.8 million) of purchases, including 50 million pesos for rolling stock and other materials for the National Railways; 8 million for machinery for the Zacatepec sugar mill; 11 million for machinery, electrical products, vehicles and other products for the Ministry of Communications; and 5.8 million for irrigation machinery and equipment. As mentioned above, frequently foreign interests in Mexico, especially the petroleum and mining companies, provided financing for these imports in the form of loans or advances in tax payments (Lockett: 1935a, 1936a, c, and e, 1937b). The Federal Reserve Bank of New York continued its collaboration with the Banco de México, and both Mexican and U.S. officials indicated an interest in strengthening economic ties between the two countries (Snyder: 1937a and b).

Thus there is a strong element of continuity in Mexico's dependence on foreign capital even during a period when Mexican nationalism achieved its strongest expression. The belief among Mexican government officials and members of the private sector that foreign capital and technology were necessary for Mexico's industrialization was complemented by the desire of certain U.S. financial groups, manufacturers, and government officials to increase their control of Mexican markets. World conditions and the consequent hemispheric policy meant that increased dependence on foreign technology involved increased trade ties with the U.S., as indicated in the shift in the geographic distribution of Mexico's imports between 1935 and 1940.

Promotion of Small Producers. One element of government efforts to direct private capital was the emphasis given to small producers and to workers' cooperatives, with the establishment of several agencies to promote the development of small business in mining, transportation, and manufacturing. In February 1935 a law was passed creating a popular credit system composed of credit unions

TABLE 6.3. Geographic Distribution of Mexican Imports (million pesos)

Year	Total	U.S.	U.S. as % of Total	Europe	Europe as % of Total
1935	406.1	265.3	65	127.1	31
1940	669.0	527.3	79	91.4	14

Source: Ministry of Programming and of the Budget, General Bureau of Statistics (Nacional Financiera, 1977: 387)

of artisans, small businessmen and producers, with capital provided by the government and members of the unions (Mexico, Cámara de Diputados, 1966, IV: 18). Subsequently this system was incorporated into the Banco Nacional Obrero de Fomento Industrial (Labor Industrial Bank), created in 1937. The activities of the bank were restricted, due to insufficient funds, but it did represent an attempt to meet the credit needs of these groups. One of the objectives of the Ministry of the National Economy was the protection and promotion of small producers and of workers' cooperatives (particularly in mining); assistance to small miners and mining cooperatives took the form of tax exemptions, subsidies, and investment in metallurgical plants (*Seis Años*, 1940: 197-215). The Ministry also sought to promote small and medium industries, and to regulate distribution and prices of basic necessities (Mexico, SEN, 1937: 105, 145-147). The Ministry of Communications and Public Works also carried out reforms favoring small-scale business, which received favorable rates for rail transport of their cargo, and attempted to replace monopolistic control of transportation by large-scale firms through government concessions to individual drivers (Mexico, SCOP 1936b: 6, 183; 1937: 63 f).

The thrust of the government's programs and expenditures was in the agrarian sector. Apart from the expenditures associated with the agrarian reform, one of the first measures of the Foreign Trade Bank was to create an export-import company, CEIMSA (Cia. Exportadora e Importadora Mexicana, S.A.), which would eliminate intermediaries in the sale and resale of harvests—often obtained from small producers at minimal prices (Moore, 1963: 153-157).

In general the impact of programs designed to assist small producers and cooperatives is difficult to assess. Census data from the period indicate a substantial growth in the number of manufacturing firms (excluding artisan workshops), which nearly doubled between 1935 and 1940, from 6,916 to 13,510. The number of workers in manufacturing plants worth 10,000 pesos or more increased only from 318,041 to 389,953, indicating that the new firms were for the most part small, averaging slightly over ten workers each (Mosk, 1954: 316). (To the extent that existing firms expanded their work force this average would be less, but this could be offset by the practice of forming new plants from the departments of existing ones in view of tax incentives given new industries.) In any event, the expansion of small manufacturers was probably due less to specific government programs than to the general climate favorable to industry, including low taxes on industry and the growth of the industrial market. In the early 1940's small and medium manufacturers formed the Cámara Nacional de Industrias de Transformacion (The National Chamber of Manufacturing Industry), or CANACINTRA, which often confronted the large confederations, CONCAMIN and CONCANACO, on issues relating to foreign investment (which it opposed) and government intervention in the economy (which it supported).[7]

Government efforts to promote small producers and industries, which were often labor-intensive and oriented to the domestic market, constituted a departure from the orientation of previous governments (Reynolds, 1970: 36). As the agrarian reform reversed the process of capital and land concentration in the rural sector, the promotion of small producers to some extent countered the tendency to capital concentration inherent in the process of capitalist industrialization. But the dynamics of capitalist development, which the government promoted through various measures, ultimately contradicted government efforts to assist small producers as well as its aspirations to direct industrial production to the satisfaction of human needs.

PRIVATE CAPITAL ACCUMULATION AND THE STATE

The ability of the state to "control" capital was limited not only by its dependence on foreign capital, especially its relation with

---

[7] Several analysts of Mexican industrialization have suggested that CANACINTRA represented an important "new group" of manufacturers (Mosk, 1948; Reynolds, 1970). Shafer disagrees with this assessment, suggesting that rather it was an instrument of the government and the government party in terms of the perspectives it endorsed (Shafer, 1973: 56).

the United States, and its dependence on resources generated in the private sector, in some cases direct loans, for its own revenues, but also by the process of private capital accumulation, a process which the state itself promoted in the interests of encouraging economic development.

The Financial Sector. One example indicated above was the development of Mexico's financial infrastructure, which began in the 1920's and received further impetus with the banking legislation of 1932, involving close collaboration between financial officials of the Mexican government and private bankers. This development continued throughout the 1930's, with the growth of existing banks and the creation of new financial institutions. Total banking resources increased from 922 million pesos in 1933 to 2.2 billion in 1940. Following the departure of foreign banks after the 1932 banking legislation, the proportion of banking resources controlled by private institutions dropped from 61 percent in 1932 to 42.3 percent in 1934. Banking resources continued to be predominantly controlled by government banks throughout the decade, with the Banco de México controlling approximately 50 percent, other government banks holding an additional 10 to 20 percent, and the proportion controlled by private banks fluctuating around 35 percent (Cardero, 1979: 753).

But private bank resources also grew during this period. Several of the commercial banks founded in the early 1930's doubled and tripled their capital in their first decade. The Banco Mexicano and the Banco de Comercio both opened in 1932 with a social capital of 500,000 pesos (not quite $150,000): by 1940 (following a devaluation of the peso from 3.5 to 5 pesos to the dollar) the Banco Mexicano had issued shares for a total amount of 3 million pesos ($600,000) and the social capital of the Banco de Comercio had been increased several times during this period to 10 million pesos ($2 million). The Banco de Comercio initiated its policy of forming or buying into affiliate banks outside Mexico City, which were 49 percent owned by local capital and 51 percent by the Banco de Comercio, a policy which has increased its control of regional financial resources. Bank profits were high, especially for original investors; the Banco de Comercio issued dividends of 18 to 20 pesos (per 100 peso share) during the last years of the decade (see Appendix A).

Despite the aggressive growth of new banks, however, the Banco

Nacional de México continued to dominate the private financial sector of Mexico (see Appendix A). The mutually beneficial relationship between the Banco Nacional and the government continued. The government provided support for the Banco Nacional, which found itself in a weak financial position in the mid-1930's, due to its low level of capital in relation to deposits (Lockett, 1936b). And through its publications, the Banco Nacional supported the government, including (with certain reservations) the progressive wage policies of the Cárdenas government and the agrarian reform (BNM, *Examen*: 1934-1941, passim). The Legorretas who directed the bank continued to collaborate with Mexican government officials in their negotiations with foreign governments and banks, and in contrast to other private banks the Banco Nacional assisted in financing specific projects of the Cárdenas administration (Suárez, 1976; BNM, 1900-1975: *Informe* 1940).

Apart from the expansion of existing commercial banks, new financial institutions were established. The banking law of 1932 had called for the segregation of financial activities in different institutions, restricting commercial banks to short-term loans to insure their liquidity, and had called for the establishment of investment banks (financieras) oriented to the development of a capital market and long-term financing for agriculture and industry. By 1940, a total of 29 investment banks had been established, including several—Crédito Minero y Mercantil (CREMI) (1934), Crédito Bursatil (1936), Cia. General de Aceptaciones (1936), Financiera del Norte (1937), Cia. Central Financiera (1940)—which are among the most important financial institutions in Mexico today. In keeping with government policy to promote the formation of a capital market, public financial institutions contributed to the initial equity of these banks. Another form of government financial support to private institutions was introduced in the last years of the Cárdenas government; several private provincial banks were established under the auspices of the Banco de México, which subscribed up to 15 percent of their capital, in an effort to supplement government agricultural credit. Thus during the Cárdenas administration the policy of providing official financial support to private banks to promote productive activities was continued.

A second potential source of investment funds was the insurance companies. Prior to 1935, much of the insurance business in Mexico was tied up by foreign firms, which tended to invest their reserves in their home countries. Also, existing legislation restricted the investment of insurance reserves to securities in companies which had paid dividends or interest over at least five consecutive years, obviously foreclosing the possibility of investing in new firms. Mexican businessmen urged the government to change the law, freeing capital and reserves for investment in Mexican securities, and in 1935 a new insurance law was passed which provided for control of insurance companies by the Ministry of Finance and regulated the investment of reserves and capital, restricting such investment to Mexican goods and securities (Rodríguez, 1935; Gómez Arreola, 1967: 12-14). After a frustrated attempt to have the legislation changed, most foreign companies left the country, leaving the field open for the establishment of Mexican companies. These proliferated in the next few years, in many cases with technical personnel who remained in Mexico after the foreign companies left (Gómez Arreola, 1967: 14; Lavin Isla, 1939). Like other financial institutions, insurance companies proved to be an immensely profitable form of investment. The general insurance company Seguros América Latina (established in 1933 and associated with the Banco Nacional/Legorreta group) paid dividends of 12 percent every year between 1939 and 1943; La Provincial (established in 1936 by groups associated with the Banco de Londres) paid dividends of 12 percent between 1939 and 1942 and 18 percent in 1943; La Nacional (the oldest Mexican life insurance company, founded in 1901), paid dividends of 30 percent in 1939 and 40 percent from 1940 to 1943. Founding members of insurance companies also benefited from the increased value of stock: shares of La Nacional, which had been purchased for 50 pesos when the company was founded in 1901, were valued at 500 pesos in 1943; the cost of shares of La Provincial increased from 100 to 300 pesos between 1936 and 1943 (ABM, 1940-1975: 1944).

Apart from financial support to investment and provincial banks, the government introduced legislation regulating the relations between banks and their employees which favored the bankers. Bank officials, concerned regarding labor militance in general, became alarmed when bank employees began to organize unions in certain banks and a national committee was formed to organize bank employees. In July 1937, the Banco Nacional closed its branches in San Luis Potosí and Tampico when employees attempted to strike after their petitions for collective contracts were rejected (*El Universal*, 31 July 1937). It is not clear how widespread the unionization movement was or whether it originated among bank employees or the CTM, which certainly supported it. While the salaries of bank employees were low and their hours long, the fact that they were drawn from the middle class and were to some extent upwardly mobile may have mitigated against strong organized pressures for better working conditions ("Los bancos y el sindicalismo," 1937; see also Espinosa Porset, 1958, whose experience provides a case study of this situation). But, in any event organizational efforts by bank employees were sufficient to cause alarm among banking circles, which blamed "outside agitators" and enthusiastically responded to proposed legislation to strictly limit the ability of bank employees to organize and strike.

Within the government, the bank employees' legislation was engineered by Luis Montes de Oca, director of the central bank (Banco de México), who consistently supported the interests of the banking sector and in this case worked closely with the Mexican Bankers' Association. They were able to draw upon government fears of the disastrous effects which a withdrawal of confidence in the credit system (resulting from a strike by bank employees) would have on banking institutions and on the economy as a whole— particularly in view of the still fragile conditions of credit operations and banking institutions following the Mexican revolution (ABM, 1938; Montes de Oca, 1937a and b). Cárdenas met with the employees of the San Luis Potosí branch of the Banco Nacional and both Cárdenas and Suárez held meetings with the Organizing Committee of Bank Employees promising to study their petitions and in the meantime urging them to refrain from any activity that would disturb public confidence (BFM, 1935-1941: 22 July 1937; Torres, 1937).

The bank employee regulation, which was passed on November 29, 1937, did provide substantial benefits for bank employees (in some cases exceeding those obtained by strikes in other sectors). But its overall effect was to isolate bank employees and make them dependent upon appeals to the state (i.e., the Secretary of Finance or the Federal Labor Board) for redress of grievances. The regulation explicitly prohibited strikes by bank employees, provided that employee contracts should be individual rather than collective, and stipulated that any problem between the institution and its personnel should be resolved by the Secretary of Finance via the National Banking Committee, or appealed to the Federal Labor Board—in effect nullifying any benefits that bank employees could expect to gain from unionization. The regulation was clearly considered a victory in banking circles, and the ABM urged its member institutions to comply with the regulation and to avoid any legal controversy which would test its provisions (Suárez, 1976; Novoa, 1937b; ABM, 1937-1941: Circulars of 25 Nov., 1 Dec. 1937).

Montes de Oca's defense of banking interests constitutes a particular instance of what may be called the "internalization" of dominant class interests within the state. Montes de Oca carried out this function consistently during the Cárdenas administration. When the Ministry of Finance attempted to collect unpaid absentee taxes and fines from several banks, Montes de Oca interceded with Finance Secretary Suárez on their behalf, and he urged the elimination of the tax on capital exports (which was finally ended in 1939) (Lockett, 1936b, Montes de Oca, 1938). On at least one occasion he contradicted Suárez, who was attempting to obtain a substantial loan from several bankers for the Banco Ejidal, protesting that such a loan would be "political" and not a sound banking loan (Lockett, 1938a). He also continued Banco de México orchestration of the financing of the sugar industry in the interests of the sugar cartel. Montes de Oca was of course not alone in internalizing capitalist class interests, but he was one of the few members of the Cárdenas government who had the confidence of the private sector.

Private accumulation was also assisted through the expansion of the state financial structure during this period. The government development bank, Nacional Financiera, began to buy and place bonds and other securities of private banks and industries as well as government securities; in 1939 its securities included those of the Banco Nacional de México, Banco de Londres y México, the Banco de Comercio, and several industrial firms established during the Porfiriato: Fundidora Monterrey (a steel foundry), Cia. Industrial de Orizaba (a textile company), Cervecería Cuauhtémoc (a brewery owned by the Garza Sada family) and Buen Tono (a tobacco company). It also carried out loan operations, issued its own securities, and intervened in stock issues for the establishment of new enterprises. It was the agent for the purchase of several electrical firms by the government in its effort to bring the electrical industry under national control. As indicated by one observer, while Nacional Financiera's operations were on a very modest scale during this period, they established its future character as industrial promoter (Nafinsa, 1949: 6-9; Blair, 1963: 210).

The Public Works Bank also expanded its activities; aside from providing funding for municipal services, its most important activity was the placement of road bonds, chiefly with the Banco de México and private banks, which constituted the major source of financing for road construction. During the Cárdenas administration the stretches of the Pan American highway between Nuevo Laredo and Mexico City, and between Mexico City and Acapulco, were completed, benefiting the tourist industry which the government sought to encourage as a means of obtaining needed foreign exchange. Private interests in real estate and tourism also benefited from the establishment of Crédito Hotelero, S.A. de C.V., in 1937, at the instigation of Montes de Oca and Alfonso Cerrillo, manager of the Asociación Mexicana Hipoteceria (Mexican Mortgage Association), to finance hotel construction by private firms.

As indicated above, several new government banks were established during this period: the Banco Ejidal, the Foreign Trade Bank, and the Labor Industrial Bank, largely with funds from the Banco de México or other official banks. With the exception of the Ejidal Bank, however, the resources available to these banks were limited; the Labor Bank was liquidated after a few years, and the Foreign Trade Bank was unable to carry out its functions fully for several decades. Nevertheless, by 1940 the basic financial infrastructure of the Mexican economy had been created, including many of the dominant private and government financial institutions in Mexico today.

But the role of these institutions in expanding the capital market for industry and agriculture continued to be limited. On at least one occasion, Suárez urged private bankers to undertake a more aggressive loan policy in order to stimulate the economy. In part, conservative lending practices could be explained by the continued concern for liquidity and a general belief among leading bankers that commercial banks should focus on commercial operations (Suárez, 1977: 113-114, 161-162). But the banks were also accused of speculative activities, especially during the foreign exchange crisis following the petroleum expropriation in 1938, which led to the legislation taxing "excess" bank profits derived from speculation. The higher rate of return from speculation, real-estate investment, commerce, and other non-productive investments undoubtedly constituted a factor in restricting the amount of credit available for productive activities.

The Private Sector and Group Formation. Within the constraints of limited financial resources, certain groups were able to benefit disproportionately from government efforts to expand a capital market. A dual process seems to have been occurring within the dominant segment of the private sector. On the one hand, a "group consciousness" was developing as groups of investors, often linked through family ties and friendship, became concerned with maintaining and expanding their control over specific holdings, in some cases coming into conflict with other groups in the process. On the other hand, the systems of cooperation and collaboration mentioned by Gómez Morín enabled businessmen among different groups to establish informal capital markets which benefited all groups within the network. Both processes tended to reinforce capital concentration within the private sector.

The most obvious example of the development of groups was what has become known as the Monterrey Group, centered in the Garza Sada family. (For more information on this group, see Appendix B.) As mentioned in Chapter Two, the family initiated its industrial investments with the establishment of the Cuauhtémoc brewery in 1890; in the following years it expanded its activities through the creation of new departments or firms to manufacture inputs for the brewery industry, including a glass factory, Vidriera Monterrey, to manufacture bottles. Subsequently the family also diversified its activities in the latter sphere to produce different types of glass. By the mid-1930's its holdings had been divided into two groups: the Cuauhtémoc (brewery) group and the Vidriera (glass) group, with the major firm in each group also constituting a holding company for the others.

By this time the Garza Sada family was involved in several controversies which made it advisable to separate its various activities and to minimize evidence of their connections with each other and with the family. Throughout the post-revolutionary period Monterrey businessmen, and the Garza Sada family in particular, had led efforts to combat labor mobilization and union organization. They were instrumental in the formation of COPARMEX, which had the purpose of representing owner/employer interests in the labor struggle, formed company unions, and allegedly helped to finance the "gold shirts"—a fascist organization which emerged in the 1930's and frequently attacked leaders and members of independent unions. The employer lockout following a union dispute in their glass factory, Vidriera Monterrey, had been the occasion of the confrontation between Cárdenas and the Monterrey businessmen in February 1936 (Chapter Five). At the same time, the brewery industry was confronting problems due to intense price competition, which the Cuauhtémoc brewery unsuccessfully sought to contain through the formation of a cartel and subsequently by efforts to buy out the Moctezuma brewery (which would have given Cuauhtémoc a virtual monopoly of the Mexican brewery industry). (See Appendix C.)

Partly as a consequence of these controversies, the Garza Sada family reorganized the two groups, creating two holding companies, Valores Industriales, S.A. (VISA) and Fomento de Industria y Comercio (FIC) to control the firms of the brewery and glass groups, respectively. Controlling interest in the holding companies was held in turn by members of the family and close associates, enabling them to maintain control while minimizing visible links.

The Garza Sada group also sought to attract further investment to its firms by issuing preferred shares (which would have preference with respect to dividends but no voting power) and by expanding its financial network. Institutions of the Cuauhtémoc group were part of a majority block of shareholders which had been formed with the reorganization of the Banco de Londres in 1934, and within this majority block (hereinafter referred to as the Banco de Londres group) the Cia. General de Aceptaciones held the largest block of shares. The Garza Sada family cooperated with other members of the Banco de Londres group in the establishment of La Provincial Insurance Company in 1936 (following the new legislation regulating insurance in 1935) and the Sociedad Financiera Mexicana (Sofimex), an investment bank, in 1937. At the instigation of the Garza Sada family and other groups in Monterrey—among them the Santos Brothers (flour milling and finance), the Chapa Brothers (commerce), the Llaguno group (textiles), and Salinas y Rocha (commerce)—a financial holding company, Unión Financiera, was established in 1939 in Monterrey, again with the cooperation of individuals and institutions associated with the Banco de Londres group. Within the next few years Unión Financiera formed several financial institutions designed to increase the financial resources available to Monterrey firms, including an insurance company and a capitalization bank, and obtained controlling interest in a commercial bank, the Banco de Nuevo León.

The Cuauhtémoc and Vidriera groups constitute relatively early examples of the economic groups which have come to dominate the Mexican private sector. As indicated in Chapter One, these contemporary groups consist of firms, often from different sectors (industry, commerce, finance, etc.) and sometimes vertically integrated, controlled by a small number of shareholders and investors (investment groups). Through their links with foreign corporations and/or the state, these firms generally have preferential access to foreign capital and technology as well as to state financing (in addition to their own sources of funding through control of their own financial institutions). Many such groups are vertically integrated, and in some cases one group or a small number of groups virtually monopolizes a given sector of industry.

Already by the mid-1930's the two groups of the Garza Sada family displayed characteristics of contemporary economic groups, including the establishment of a financial network, the vertical integration of firms of the Cuauhtémoc group, efforts to control the brewery industry, and the issue of preferred shares and the establishment of holding companies (VISA, FIC, Unión Financiera) as mechanisms for maintaining group control over its firms. There seems to have been little if any foreign capital in the firms of the two groups, a situation which changed in succeeding decades as new firms were established with substantial foreign assistance in the form of loans, technology agreements, and joint investments.

There are further examples of incipient group formation during this period. The BUDA group took its name from four bankers—Raúl Bailleres, Salvador Ugarte, Mario Domínguez, and Ernesto Amescua—who were linked as stockholders and directors of various financial institutions established at this time, including the Banco de Comercio and the Crédito Minero y Mercantil. In 1938, members of the Banco de Londres/Sofimex group became involved in an extended controversy with members of the BUDA group over control of La Nacional, the oldest life insurance company in Mexico (see Appendix C). There were other cases of inter-group conflict for the control of specific institutions—again indicating the "group" mentality which characterized important segments of the private sector by this time.

But at the same time—perhaps in part because the "groups" were still in formation—different groups cooperated for certain ends. The Banco de Londres/Sofimex group was in fact a relatively stable coalition of different groups and interests. Aside from the Cuauhtémoc group, it included Maximino Michel of the Puerto de Liverpool, a major commercial house established by the Barcelonnette group in the nineteenth century; Angel Urraza of Hulera Euzkadi, a tire firm with important holdings by B. F. Goodrich; British interests represented by Federico Williams and Arturo Woodward; and Ignacio Hornik, a Swiss insurance agent. These individuals and groups had additional links with French, Spanish, American, and other European business groups with interests in Mexico. The Banco de Londres/Sofimex group had been largely engineered through Manuel Gómez Morín and undoubtedly constituted the major example of the systems of cooperation and collaboration to which he referred. By associating a broad range of groups it permitted the formation of a capital market to finance specific projects and initiatives of interest to these groups (see Appendix C).

In addition, different groups came together on an ad hoc basis for more limited purposes. One of these was the purchase and placement of securities by pools and syndicates formed by institutions from different groups. During this period several firms in the Cuauhtémoc and Vidriera groups issued securities to expand operations, among them Cervecería Cuauhtémoc (1937), Cervecería Central (1937), and Malta (1940). While the Banco de Londres cooperated in these ventures, and Sofimex as well as Monterrey financial institutions also operated as intermediaries, the placement of securities depended on the cooperation of institutions outside the Garza Sada and Banco de Londres groups—among them the Banco Nacional de México and institutions of the BUDA group (including the Banco de Comercio). Nacional Financiera and the semi-official Asociación Hipotecaria Mexicana also participated, indicating continued official support for private capital accumulation at a time when the government was confronting private business groups over labor policy (Archivo MGM: Malta, Inc.; Cerv. Central, 1937; Garza Sada, 1937b).

Thus the Banco de Londres group and ad hoc formation of pools and syndicates to finance and place securities of Monterrey (and other) firms enabled certain groups of businessmen to overcome the limits of the national capital market by forming an informal capital market among networks of institutions controlled by friends and business acquaintances. While these and similar arrangements were functional in providing financing to firms within these networks their indirect result was a further concentration of limited financial resources which were generally unavailable to firms outside these networks.[8]

SUMMARY AND CONCLUSIONS

Cárdenas and his associates believed that the state could guide and direct the process of capitalist development to avoid the contradictions normally resulting from this process. The shift in U.S. policy resulting from the depression and the pending war in Europe, as well as the relative weakness of the national bourgeoisie following the revolution, had in fact increased the possibility of a limited state autonomy in relation to foreign and national capital. But existing structural constraints and the process of capital accumulation (which the state of necessity helped to promote) restricted the scope and effectiveness of state policy.

Although state intervention in the economy reached new levels under Cárdenas (as indicated in the increase and shift in federal government expenditures), the government was indirectly or directly dependent upon resources generated in the private sector, which in turn depended upon national economic conditions or on the willingness of relevant private groups to provide loans to a government which it perceived as acting against their interests. When loans were provided by the private sector, they tended to shift the focus or dilute the effectiveness of the relevant government programs. While the government sought to regulate foreign capital in the export sector, it reinforced dependence on foreign capital and technology as well as trade ties with the U.S. through imports of machinery and materials for the expansion of infrastructure and its agrarian program and through its encouragement of foreign investment in manufacturing. Legislation regulating the relations between the state and industrial and commercial chambers did not affect the economic operations of private firms. The growth in the number of manufacturing firms during the period

[8] The process of group formation appears to be a relatively common one among private interests in "developing" countries. As in the case of Mexico, one purpose is to compensate for capital shortages by mobilizing resources beyond those of a given family (or even investment group). One of the effects—in Mexico as elsewhere—has been the creation of monopolies, with control over capital resources and certain products concentrated in the hands of a limited number of groups (see Leff, 1978).

suggests that the government was successful in encouraging small producers—as much through general incentives provided to industry as through specific programs aimed at these groups. But the formation of small, labor-intensive manufacturing firms oriented to production for the domestic market was countered by the continued trend to capital concentration resulting from the emergence of a dominant block within the capitalist class.

In general, there was a strong element of continuity in state efforts on behalf of private accumulation during the Cárdenas administration which tended, directly and indirectly, to benefit a small, relatively powerful segment of the dominant class. The contribution of official financial institutions to private investment and provincial banks continued the policy of state aid to private banks, and the insurance law was similar to the banking legislation of 1932 in paving the way for the formation of Mexican financial institutions. These and other efforts were directed primarily at the formation of a capital market to expand investment in productive activities, but, given higher returns for commercial loans, real estate investment, and speculation, as well as the limited availability of financial resources, bank financing of industry and agriculture continued to be limited. Activities of government banks also favored the private sector—notably through investment in securities by Nacional Financiera, the issue of road bonds by the Public Works Bank, and the establishment of Crédito Hotelero to finance private hotel construction. Continued collaboration between the private and government financial sectors was evident in the cooperation between Montes de Oca and the ABM with respect to the bank employees' regulation.

The tendency to group formation—an important element in the concentration of resources in contemporary Mexico—was already evident. The formation of informal capital markets among a small network of different groups was an additional element in capital concentration to the extent that these networks exhausted the limited resources available. Tendencies to capital concentration were of course reinforced in subsequent decades, when foreign capital became increasingly available to certain business groups in the form of investments, loans, and technology. But the emergence of informal, restricted capital markets suggests that there were already certain groups in a position to take disproportionate advantage of such opportunities and of state efforts to promote productive activities.

Efforts of the government to promote private accumulation and at the same time to control this process were thus inherently contradictory, since the process of private accumulation strengthened a small group of capitalists in relation to the dominant class as a whole and ultimately in relation to the state. However the most significant efforts of the state to "control" capital were not in the "statist" policies discussed here, but in programs implemented in alliance with mobilized popular sectors in confrontation with specific groups and segments of the dominant class. At the same time, these confrontations resulted in an increasing polarization and reaction by the affected sectors and by the capitalist class as a whole. The events surrounding the petroleum expropriation demonstrate the level of conflict generated by these confrontations and the possibilities and limits of state autonomy based on alliance with subordinate groups and classes.

Seven ‖ External Limits to State Autonomy: The Petroleum Conflict

 In July 1936 the newly formed Union of Mexican Petroleum Workers opened negotiations with the foreign-owned petroleum companies for a collective contract. This was the first stage of a conflict which would culminate nearly two years later, on March 18, 1938, with the expropriation of the petroleum companies, an action which challenged the hegemony of foreign capital in the Mexican export sector.

Petroleum was of course not the only industry controlled by foreign capital in Mexico, nor was it the most important in terms of export earnings and state revenues. Petroleum exports accounted for approximately 18 percent of Mexico's export earnings, while those of the mining industry were approximately 60 percent. Not only the mining and petroleum industries, but also communications and electrical utilities, were predominantly foreign-controlled, and there were important foreign investments in agriculture and livestock.

But the petroleum expropriation was significant for several reasons. In the first place, the petroleum expropriation involved a dramatic confrontation between the state as representative of Mexican sovereignty and a particularly abrasive group of foreign corporations. The relations of the petroleum companies with the Mexican state had been characterized by a consistent disregard for—and at times flagrant violation of—Mexican legislation regulating foreign investment, as well as dependence on their respective governments (particularly the U.S. government) to intervene on behalf of their interests, even to the point of military intervention. They had obstructed efforts of petroleum workers to form independent unions through the formation of company unions and dismissals of workers, not hesitating to employ mercenaries (white guards) to harass workers and even to assassinate independent labor leaders. Their profits had been high and occasionally exorbitant—reaching 40 to 60 percent in the early 1920's. They had reduced production in Mexico, shifting investment and production to Venezuela during the petroleum controversies of the 1920's, dismissing half of the petroleum workers and utilizing these shifts to pressure the Mexican government into granting concessions (although it has been suggested that these shifts were due to the inability of the companies to uncover new petroleum reserves in Mexico) (L. Meyer, 1968: 19, 27-28, 150, 230; Furtado, 1976: 189). In short, it is doubtful that the expropriation of any other foreign holdings could have evoked the same level of enthusiasm among all sectors of the Mexican population as the nationalization of the petroleum companies.

Beyond this symbolic level, the petroleum expropriation marked a structural change in Mexico's relations with advanced industrial countries, especially the United States. It constituted a first but important step in the elimination of a specific form of economic dependence based on foreign control of the export sector and infrastructure. Despite pressures by the companies, the expropriation was not reversed, i.e., nationalization was not succeeded by denationalization of either ownership or control. Nor was it an isolated phenomenon: in subsequent years the government or national private capital gained control of the remaining railroad systems, communications, and eventually the electrical industry. In the sense that the petroleum expropriation constituted an important structural change it was the most significant evidence of relative structural autonomy during the Cárdenas period.

Finally, petroleum was not only a source of export earnings but also an increasingly important resource for Mexican industry. As indicated in Chapter Four, by the early 1930's state officials had become alarmed that Mexico's petroleum resources would be insufficient to supply her industrial needs in the near future. The proportion of Mexico's petroleum production going to internal consumption increased from 10.5 percent of the total produced in 1926 to 37.5 percent in 1932. The government of Abelardo Rodríguez had formed Petroleos de México in 1934 for the purpose of developing a "genuinely national" industry, although the absence of sufficient government resources and private financial assistance had limited its activities. The nationalization of the petroleum industry gave the state control of this essential resource and to this extent increased its ability to guide and direct the process of industrialization in Mexico.

Why was the Cárdenas government able to expropriate the foreign-owned petroleum companies when previous governments had had difficulty in enforcing even the most minimal controls on foreign investment? Two of the hypothetical conditions suggested in Chapter One as favoring structural autonomy seem to be pertinent. First, the structural constraints limiting state autonomy—in this case, those resulting from Mexico's relations with core states, especially the United States—were to some extent weakened as a consequence of the world depression. This did not necessarily mean a decrease in foreign economic control, although the total amount of foreign investment in Mexico and other Latin American countries did decline during the 1930's. But, as indicated in Chapter Four, it meant that the states of the dominant capitalist countries were engrossed with internal problems and—in the case of the United States—less likely to intervene directly on behalf of specific investment interests in Latin America. At the same time, a shift was occurring in the nature of U.S. interests in Latin America, from an emphasis on extractive investments to the promotion of U.S. exports of manufactured goods. Combined with the effects of the depression, this shift in orientation had led to the declaration of a "good neighbor" policy with respect to Latin America and a promise of nonintervention in the internal and external affairs of Latin American nations at the Pan American conference in Montevideo in 1933. At the subsequent Buenos Aires conference in 1936 the Mexican delegation took the lead in pressing for a stronger policy which declared direct or indirect intervention inadmissible (L. Meyer, 1927a: 125; Wood, 1961: 118-121). These conditions had given the Mexican state (and other Latin American states) a certain space for maneuver which had not existed before; as Cárdenas and his associates agreed, conditions were more propitious for a move against the petroleum companies than at any other time in the post-revolutionary period (Cárdenas, 1972b: 387-388).

The second factor was the alliance of the state with important sectors of the working class and the peasantry—i.e., the progressive coalition, an alliance which had its roots in the revolution but which had been fragmented during the 1920's and had achieved national prominence only with the election of Cárdenas and his break with the Calles faction. That this alliance had strengthened the action of the state against dominant class interests was evident to some extent in the labor reforms and especially in the agrarian reform. The expropriation of the petroleum companies represented a continuation and culmination of state action—in alliance with labor—against these groups, as well as of state efforts to control capital.

More directly, the petroleum conflict and expropriation in-

volved a specific part of this coalition—the alliance between the
state and the petroleum workers. Previous relations between the
government and the petroleum workers had often been antagonistic, a situation the petroleum companies had been able to take
advantage of to promote their own interests with respect to each.
Efforts by the petroleum workers' unions to form an industry-
wide federation had been sabotaged by the companies and the
government in 1913, enabling the companies to deal with a number of small and divided unions (L. Meyer, 1968: 204). During the
1920's, the government had supported CROM efforts to bring the
petroleum unions under its control; in general, the companies also
preferred CROM over independent unions since it often accepted
conditions much more favorable to their interests. The government on occasion sent troops to break strikes or to end protests
by the petroleum workers against the companies.[1] The petroleum
unions—expecially in the Tampico area, where IWW influence had
been important—were characterized by internal democracy and also
by their solidarity with other workers in the region. Thus they
had the support of independent unions and in some cases the CGT
in their confrontations with CROM and government officials and
the companies. On the whole, the petroleum workers' unions were
relatively successful in resisting CROM efforts at incorporation
and in obtaining wage increases (Carr, 1976 II: 21-23).

Conversely, the workers often failed to support government efforts to implement constitutional provisions affecting state control
of foreign concessions. The companies were able to portray these
efforts to the workers as contrary to worker interests (i.e., resulting in production cutbacks and dismissals). The failure of the government and the petroleum workers to unite in opposition to the
petroleum companies undoubtedly diminished the effectiveness of
each in pursuing their respective interests.

In contrast, the Cárdenas administration encouraged the formation of an industry-wide union and on December 27, 1935 the
twenty-one local petroleum unions united in the Sindicato de Trabajadores Petroleros de la República Mexicana (the Union of Petroleum Workers of the Mexican Republic), STPRM. The coop-

---

[1] In June 1924 the petroleum workers of El Aguila rejected a contract negotiated
by CROM on the grounds that it contained unacceptable concessions and was
unconstitutional. La Corona closed its refinery in Tampico in February 1925 to rid
itself of a militant work force organized independently of CROM, with the intention of reopening it in three months with workers which CROM had approved
(Carr, 1976, II: 21, 23).

eration between the government and the petroleum workers continued throughout the two-year conflict and in the difficult months following the expropriation contributed significantly to its success.

The Cárdenas administration was not the only Latin American government to take advantage of the international conjuncture to implement nationalist policies, including in some cases the expropriation of foreign industries. But it was only in Mexico that nationalist policies involved a major confrontation with foreign capitals and states.[2] The alliance of the state with the militant working class and peasantry and the increase in the level of mobilization resulting from this alliance were important factors in sustaining this confrontation.

But while the petroleum expropriation constituted the most important act in the progressive offensive against capital, it also marked the beginning of a retreat by the progressive forces. The repercussions of the petroleum expropriation can be understood only in the context of the process of conflict and polarization occurring within Mexican society at this time. The period of the petroleum conflict—May 1937 to March 1938—coincided with other major offensives of the progressive alliance, and by the end of this period the reaction to these policies had resulted in various forms of direct and indirect intervention by dominant class interests. The petroleum conflict was a particular instance of these offensives and this reaction.

THE PETROLEUM CONFLICT

When Cárdenas became president, approximately 98 percent of the petroleum industry was controlled by 16 foreign companies,

[2] In other countries (such as Bolivia), where petroleum production and/or distribution were nationalized, foreign investment in petroleum was less important. Only in Venezuela was it comparable to Mexico, and the Venezuelan government did not nationalize its petroleum industry at this time, although following the Mexican petroleum expropriation it obtained an agreement with the companies to share profits on a fifty-fifty basis. In fact, it has been suggested that the petroleum expropriation in Mexico constituted an example to the rest of the continent, as other Latin American governments attempted to increase their control over petroleum resources, including nationalistic petroleum legislation in Colombia, Cuba, and Ecuador as well as in Venezuela. In 1938, Costa Rica attempted to nationalize services in the capital city, and in 1939, Chile made the distribution and sale of oil a government monopoly (L. Meyer, 1968: 230, 269; Rippy, 1972: 229).

among which Royal Dutch Shell (largely British controlled), owner of the Cia. "El Aguila," and Standard Oil of New Jersey, owner of the "Huasteca" company, were the most important. Beginning in 1934, individual unions had won increases in wages and other benefits through strikes against specific companies which the government supported. In July 1936, the newly formed Union of Petroleum Workers (STPRM) opened negotiations with the petroleum companies to obtain a collective contract in which wage and benefit payments would be based on the economic capacity of the companies. Their requests included union control of positions within the company (with the exception of 114 confidence posts as well as an unlimited number of lawyers) and a 40-hour week, as well as wage increases totalling 28,149,560 pesos annually and a total increase in wages and other benefits amounting to 65.5 million pesos (González, 1972: 154-155). The companies rejected the demand for a collective contract; the government intervened to prevent a work stoppage and established a worker-employer convention. The convention negotiated until May 1937 without reaching agreement and the workers declared a strike on May 28 (L. Meyer, 1968: 206).

The strike and the consequent decline in the fuel supply threatened a suspension of production in certain industries and difficulties in transportation and distribution, as well as a decline in exports. To avoid an economic crisis, in June 1937 the STPRM and the CTM—which had an important role in orchestrating the negotiations in collaboration with the STPRM—requested that the Federal Labor Board declare the litigation an economic conflict; the workers returned to work and the companies were requested to submit their accounting to the authorities to find if they could satisfy the union demands. A panel of experts was appointed by the Labor Board, consisting of Jesús Silva Herzog, government economist and professor of the Universidad Nacional; Efraín Buenrostro, Assistant Secretary of Finance; and Mariano Moctezuma, Assistant Secretary of the Economy, to determine the companies' ability to pay. Assisted by a team of 100 persons, the panel carried out a thorough investigation of the petroleum companies and their activities in Mexico, and within a month presented a 2,700-page report. The report listed forty areas in which the policies of the petroleum companies had contradicted the needs and interests of Mexico, including fiscal and political irregularities, the sale of refined products to internal consumers at prices above the world level while oil was sold abroad below the world price; failure to repair and replace rundown equipment; and a decrease in the real wages of the workers by 20 percent since 1934. One example of sales manipulation was that the Shell subsidiary, El Aguila, sold its production in the Mexican market at prices ranging from 134 percent to 350 percent higher than it sold the product abroad, while all exports to its Canadian subsidiary were sold at prices averaging 40 percent less than the Tampico market price—a clear device to transfer profits and evade Mexican export taxes. As stated by the report, the companies had left nothing in the country but the wages of the workers and taxes; the waste of resources and the lack of new explorations—perhaps a deliberate policy of the petroleum companies—had resulted in production declines, threatening to leave Mexico with insufficient resources and the need to import oil in the very near future (Cronon, 1960: 166-167). One result of the study was a decision by President Cárdenas to establish future wage and tax assessments on the basis of studies by Mexican government agencies (L. Meyer, 1968: 207-208).

The report concluded that the company could pay up to 26 million pesos annually—8.7 million in wages and the rest in additional benefits. While the workers accepted these findings, the companies objected to the principle of payment according to their economic capacity and, at the same time, claimed that they could not pay more than 20 million. The case was again in the hands of the Federal Labor Board until December 1937. On December 18, 1937, the board gave its decision, which closely followed the recommendation of the panel of experts, providing for a 40-hour week, wage increases amounting to 8,657,647.50 pesos, and a total increase in wages and benefits of 26,332,756 pesos (González, 1972: 161-162). The companies refused to accept this judgment, and appealed to the Mexican Supreme Court.

EXTERNAL CONSTRAINTS AND PRESSURES

During this period the companies, and to a lesser extent the U.S. State Department (despite an official stance of non-intervention up to the end of 1937), had begun to exert pressure on the Mexican government. The petroleum companies considered the Mexican policy a threat to all North American petroleum investments, since a successful challenge to the companies could establish a precedent for other Latin American governments. In the middle of the year, they began withdrawing their deposits from the Mexican banks, precipitating a loss of confidence and further bank withdrawals and capital exports by other foreign and some Mexican interests. In September, Salvador Ugarte of the Banco de Comercio and other Mexican bankers complained that several major U.S. companies had withdrawn nearly all their deposits through dollar purchases. Subsequently they stated that the U.S. companies would have difficulties obtaining loans from Mexican banks in the future (Lockett, 1937d and e).[3] By the end of October, the petroleum companies had sent all of their surplus funds out of Mexico, retaining only enough capital to meet current operating expenses, and by the end of the year all available funds not needed by business were exported.

The petroleum companies also utilized their influence with the U.S. press and Congress to launch a publicity campaign and to arouse American public opinion and members of Congress against Mexico's position—in turn an important means of pressure on the U.S. State Department. By the end of 1937, the State Department attempted to end the special arrangement for purchase of Mexican silver which had been an important element in Mexico's favorable trade balance. This move was opposed by Ambassador Daniels (who throughout the conflict was basically sympathetic to the Mexican position and sought to soften that of the State Department) and by U.S. Secretary of the Treasury Henry Morgenthau, partly because such a move would be detrimental to the interests of U.S. mining companies which controlled silver production in Mexico, partly due to fear that economic difficulties could force Mexico to turn to the Axis countries, especially Germany, for help, and probably also because Morgenthau felt that long-term U.S. interests would be better served by friendly ties with Mexico than by a hard-line victory on the petroleum question. In short, it was evident that U.S. interests had much to lose by taking a hard line on the petroleum question, a fact that Mexican government officials were able to take advantage of. At this time, a compromise was reached whereby the silver purchase agreement would have to be renewed monthly, thus becoming an instrument of pressure. At the same time, the mining companies took advantage of the petroleum conflict to force the Mexican government to withdraw

[3] This promise was apparently kept; in the last months of 1938 requests for loans by Ford and General Motors were turned down by several Mexican banks with the suggestion that they bring back the funds they had exported (Lockett, 1938b).

TABLE 7.1. Balance of Trade, 1934-1940 (million dollars)

	1934	1935	1936	1937	1938	1939	1940
Exports	178.9	208.3	215.2	247.9	185.4	176.1	177.8
Imports	92.8	112.8	128.9	170.6	109.3	121.4	123.9
Balance	86.1	95.5	86.3	77.3	76.1	54.7	53.9

Source: Ministry of Industry and Commerce, General Bureau of Statistics (Nacional Financiera, 1977: 385)

a proposed mining law which they opposed (L. Meyer, 1968: 215-216; 1973: 50; Cronon, 1960: 175-176).

In the meantime, events external to the petroleum conflict had further aggravated Mexico's international economic situation, among them the 1937 recession in the United States and the consequent decline in U.S. prices. Since prices in Mexico continued to rise, this resulted in a cutback in U.S. imports from Mexico, particularly affecting Mexico's mineral exports, which also cut into government tax revenues. Imports had been increasing, due to the need to import food to compensate for reductions in agricultural production and the purchase of agricultural and road building machinery by the government for its expanded programs in these areas. (See Table 7.1.) Although the trade balance remained positive, it ceased to be sufficient to cover outflows of funds resulting from capital repatriation and capital export, placing a strain on gold and foreign exchange reserves of the central bank. Also, as indicated above, the government had begun to depend increasingly on central bank loans to supplement its tax revenue, and government financial officials were concerned with the inflationary implications of deficit financing (Banco de México, 1937a).

In the last months of 1937, Mexican government officials met with officials of the U.S. Treasury Department in an effort to negotiate a loan of $10 million, part of it to be applied to the Mexican government debt to the Banco de México. In the course of the negotiations, in which Mexican financial officials supplied detailed information on various aspects of the Mexican economy, U.S. officials proposed a much more substantial program of economic assistance. As Treasury Secretary Morgenthau explained to Mexican Finance Secretary Suárez, President Roosevelt not only agreed to the loan but also wished to be Mexico's "doctor." Mexico was "ill, economically speaking," and Roosevelt wished to draw up a large-scale development plan for Mexico, financed by the U.S. (Sarro, 1938a and b; Suárez, 1977: 188). Coming as it did

TABLE 7.2. Price Indexes: 1934-1940

Year	Wholesale	Cost of Food	Workers' Cost of Living
1934	17.6	11.4	
1935	17.6	11.6	14.6
1936	18.7	12.7	15.5
1937	22.2	16.3	18.3
1938	23.6	18.3	20.8
1939	23.3	19.5	21.1
1940	23.9	20.8	21.3

Source: Wholesale, cost of food, Banco de México, S.A. Workers' cost of living, Ministry of Industry and Commerce, General Bureau of Statistics (Nacional Financiera, 1977: 219)

in the middle of the confrontation between the Mexican government and the petroleum companies, this offer was presumably intended to shape Cárdenas' response to the crisis.[4]

INTERNAL CONFLICT AND INCREASING POLARIZATION

At the same time, price increases had begun to cut into the wage gains of the workers. (See Table 7.2.) To some extent, price increases reflected the fact that fewer agricultural products were reaching urban markets, in part due to reductions in agricultural production (resulting from climatic conditions as well as from problems resulting from transfers of ownership and production cutbacks by owners fearing expropriation), in part due to increased consumption in the rural sector. But price rises also occurred in the industrial sector, where industrial owners sought to maintain their profit levels by offsetting costs due to wage increases. Labor leaders attributed price increases to speculation and to manipulation by the capitalist class as a reprisal against labor and a means of embarrassing the Cárdenas government (Anguiano, 1975: 81-82; *Mexican Labor News*, 2 Feb. 1937, 7 April

[4] A harmonious solution to the petroleum conflict would certainly have been in the interests of the Roosevelt administration, which was being pressured by the press and Congress to take a hard line in defense of the companies' interests. And a substantial U.S. loan could have enabled the Cárdenas government to expand its reform programs, now heavily dependent upon deficit financing, assuming the Mexican government would have some control over the way such a loan would be spent.

1937). Already by the beginning of 1937 workers were staging strikes and demonstrations to protest the increased cost of living.

Government initiatives in other areas also provoked controversy. In June, the government nationalized the national railroads (already majority government-owned). And in the following month Cárdenas presented the civil service bill to Congress, which granted government workers the right to organize and even to strike under certain conditions. This bill became the occasion of an open confrontation between conservative groups and government supporters within Congress, and was passed only after lengthy debate.

Also during this period, the expropriation of commercial agricultural estates continued: during August and September 1937 the henequen plantations of Yucatán and in October the rice and wheat haciendas of Sonora were expropriated—the latter affecting U.S. as well as Mexican owners. Conflicts in the countryside continued as peasants, with the support of rural teachers and government agrarian officials, petitioned for land while the landowners and their hired guards attempted to block their efforts and harassed the new ejiditarios. In May 1937 the formation of the Unión Nacional Sinarquista—the Sinarquista movement—injected a new element of organization and militance into the attacks against the agrarian reform. A religious quasi-militaristic movement, the Sinarquistas rejected not only the Mexican revolution but also Mexico's post-independence history, promoting the values of colonial Mexico and "Hispanidad." It was formed by young professionals, including sons of hacendados of the Bajío region, but attracted the peasants of this area, especially in the states of Jalicso, Michoacán, Guanajuato, Querétaro, and Zacatecas, which had formed the core of the Cristero movement in the 1920's. Among the major targets of the Sinarquistas were the rural schoolteachers, who epitomized government opposition to the traditional values that the Sinarquistas stood for; it was estimated that in this region an average of three teachers a month were killed in the first six months of 1938.

The reaction of the private sector to government support of labor, the agrarian expropriations, and the petroleum conflict began to be manifested in a low level of investment (Confederación de Cámaras Nacionales de Comercio e Industria, 1940: 100-101). And by December 1937 the withdrawal of bank deposits and the export of capital had reached critical proportions; gold, silver, and foreign exchange reserves of the central bank dropped from 62 million dollars in March 1937 to 26 million the following December (Rippy, 1972: 244-245). Already in August 1937, the government had ordered strict economies by federal government agencies. Subsequently, government public works programs were restricted or temporarily suspended; payments to contractors working on irrigation and highway programs as well as to U.S. exporters for machinery, tractors, and trucks were postponed; and assistance to government banks was temporarily discontinued. On December 31, the government decreed tariffs on imports in an effort to improve the trade balance—a move which was strongly criticized by the U.S. State Department (Welles, 1938).[5]

THE PETROLEUM EXPROPRIATION

It was in this climate of increasing economic crisis and political polarization that the petroleum conflict reached its conclusion. On March 1, 1938 the Supreme Court came to a decision upholding the judgment of the Federal Labor Board, giving the companies until March 7 to put the terms of the decision into effect. The companies failed to meet this deadline, and on March 8 President Cárdenas asked the members of the cabinet for their opinions regarding measures to be taken against the companies.[6] Apparently there was a sharp split in the cabinet on the question. General Francisco Múgica, Secretary of Communications and Public Works,

[5] Welles recalls an earlier conversation with Suárez in which he had suggested that, instead of instituting tariffs, Mexico pursue a "sound economic policy"; that the present course was steering Mexican and non-resident capital out of Mexico; and that he feared a violent reaction from Congress due to the "unfair treatment given to U.S. citizens."

[6] While the Cárdenas government had evidently not developed a carefully planned nationalization program, there is evidence that expropriation was contemplated. On June 23, 1937, when the National Railroad was nationalized, Cárdenas noted in his diary that the petroleum industry should also be under state control. In another note at the beginning of 1938, Cárdenas referred to the nationwide anxiety resulting from the petroleum problem and the refusal of the companies, supported by their governments, to adhere to Mexican laws. He also referred to the need to regulate the mining industry, the nationalization of the electrical industry, and the socialization of banking (Cárdenas, 1972b: 371, 381). There can be little doubt that he had previously discussed the question of expropriation with close associates (e.g., Múgica and Lombardo Toledano) although the actual expropriation of the petroleum companies seems to have constituted a pragmatic response to an opportunity which presented itself.

Contribution of the People to the Petroleum Expropriation, March 18, 1938. By Elizabeth Catlett de Mora.

the most radical member of the cabinet and a strong opponent of the petroleum companies, urged expropriation. The Secretary of Finance, Eduardo Suárez, at the time deeply involved in very promising loan negotiations with the United States, opposed this measure in view of its obvious consequences with respect to Mexico-U.S. relations and to Mexico's economic and financial crisis (Mondragón, 1966: 111). The expropriation was also favored by the CTM, which had cooperated closely with the STPRM throughout the conflict and had mobilized national and eventually international support for the Mexican government. As early as February 22, Lombardo Toledano had indicated that the crisis might be resolved through the nationalization of the companies (Chassen, 1977: 107).

The Supreme Court rejected a pending appeal by the companies against the resolutions of the Federal Labor Board on March 12. A series of last-minute meetings, negotiations, and diplomatic notes failed to result in agreement. On March 16, at the request of the STPRM and the CTM, the Labor Board declared the existing contracts between the petroleum companies and the workers nonexistent and the petroleum companies "in rebellion." On March 17 at 4:00 p.m. the workers placed guards in the offices and fields of the petroleum companies, and on March 18 work was suspended (Chassen, 1977: 110). That evening at 10:00 p.m. President Cárdenas announced the expropriation of the sixteen British- and U.S.-owned companies, stating that all other constructive programs of the administration would be sacrificed if necessary to meet economic obligations resulting from the expropriation (Mexico, Cámara de Diputados, 1966, V: 773-778).

The petroleum expropriation was unquestionably the most popular act of the Cárdenas government and probably of any Mexican government since the revolution. On March 23 the CTM organized a demonstration in Mexico City in which not only workers but also peasants, teachers, bureaucrats, and professionals participated. The expropriation was supported by business groups linked to the government. Even the Church, traditional enemy of the revolution and of the government, urged parishioners to contribute to the government's efforts to collect funds to pay indemnification. For a brief but euphoric moment, the action of the government against the petroleum companies united broad sectors of the population in "a struggle of the nation, of all the people of Mexico, against imperialism" (cited in Anguiano, 1975: 63).

The company owners, who had believed until the last minute that the Mexican government would not dare to expropriate, exerted efforts with their respective governments to end diplomatic relations; some foreign interests in Mexico called for military intervention and even annexation of Mexico by the United States. The petroleum companies also gave moral and possibly monetary support to a rebellion led by General Saturnino Cedillo, former Minister of Agriculture under Cárdenas and caudillo of the state of San Luis Potosí, in April 1938. However, this rebellion was quickly crushed by government forces, which further strengthened the position of Cárdenas. The British government refused to concede Mexico's right to expropriate; it broke relations with Mexico in May 1938 and prevented would-be purchasers in England from buying Mexican petroleum. The Netherlands also took a hard line, but neither country was in a position to effectively pressure Mexico. This they entrusted to the U.S. State Department, which recognized the right to expropriate and directed its pressures toward an "immediate, effective, and just" compensation to the petroleum companies (L. Meyer, 1972b: 371-373, 472; 1968: 215). The Cárdenas government had announced its intention of compensating the companies within a ten-year period; an immediate payment was out of the question, and subsequent negotiation revealed considerable disagreement as to what would constitute a "just" compensation.

The State Department issued a sharp note of protest, attempted to withdraw Ambassador Daniels, and requested the cancellation of the silver purchase agreement. Although delaying tactics on the part of Daniels prevented the first two measures from taking effect, the U.S. Treasury Department ended its special purchase of Mexican silver, which resulted in a 50 percent reduction in exports of silver (which continued to be sold on the open market) between 1937 and 1938, in turn resulting in a further reduction in fiscal income from export taxes (Cronon, 1960: 192-197; L. Meyer, 1971: 2).[7]

The foreign corporations assumed that Mexico would not be able to manage the oil industry unaided, especially since foreign technicians in charge of key operations were removed. Depend-

---

[7] The cancellation of the silver purchase agreement was against the wishes of U.S. Treasury Secretary Morgenthau, who subsequently attempted to provide a loan to Mexico to aid in the settlement of the petroleum dispute; this move was blocked by the State Department (Bernstein, 1965: 186).

ence on the managerial and technical skills of the corporations would
have given them considerable leverage in demanding the return of
the companies to their control. Thus, from the perspective of the
Mexican government, maintaining the industry in production was
essential for the success of nationalization. The government received some technical assistance from abroad, but in effect depended upon the workers for operation of the industry, with the
31 sections of the Union of Petroleum Workers each given responsibility for production in their respective locations. The task
of the workers was compounded not only by the removal of foreign technicians but also by the poor condition of many of the
installations, the initial inability to obtain inputs and supplies, and
the fact that the companies had maintained secrecy regarding the
overall production processes. Members of the union held frequent
meetings to obtain an overview of industry operations through
exchanging information on specific processes. They agreed to reductions in the wage increases won in their conflict with the petroleum companies ranging from 8 to 15 percent (up to 25 percent
for confidential employees), and worked extra hours without pay.
They used considerable initiative in coping with shortages, in-
venting new techniques when former methods could not be used,
and restoring old and sometimes sabotaged equipment to operation. Despite inevitable problems and mistakes, the workers succeeded in restoring the industry to operation in the critical months
following the expropriation.

The petroleum companies instigated a campaign of economic
warfare in an attempt to further destabilize the Mexican economy
and to bring about the fall of the Cárdenas government. The major tactic was a systematic boycott of Mexican petroleum exports,
including pressures on important European markets to refuse
Mexican petroleum despite its competitive price. At this time, approximately half of the petroleum produced in Mexico was exported, and petroleum exports accounted for over 18 percent of
its total exports. The oil companies also persuaded U.S. manufacturers to refuse Mexico's prepaid cash orders for equipment needed
to run the oil industry. Total income from petroleum exports fell
from 153,460,426 pesos in 1936 to 79,378,642 pesos in 1938, increasing slightly to 82,605,560 pesos in 1939. The State Department banned U.S. government purchases of Mexican oil, intervened to prevent storage of Mexican petroleum in New York state
for re-export to Europe, and attempted to prevent export of Mex-

ican oil to Latin American countries. Although various Mexican spokesmen, including President Cárdenas, had initially declared that Mexico would sell only to the democratic nations, the economic boycott obliged the Mexican government to place the bulk of its petroleum in Germany, Italy, and Japan, until these three markets were also lost with the outbreak of war in 1939.[8]

One immediate effect of the reprisals by the petroleum companies and their governments was a reduction in the value of the peso. The decline in export earnings resulting from the cancellation of the silver purchase agreement and the petroleum boycott, added to continued capital exports, aggravated Mexico's foreign exchange problem. The strain on the peso became intolerable, and the government abandoned the existing rate of exchange. The peso, which had previously been fixed at 3.5 pesos to the dollar, fluctuated in the following months, finally settling at 5 pesos to the dollar.

The petroleum expropriation brought the loan negotiations with Washington to an abrupt halt and precluded the implementation of the paternalistic arrangement of U.S. assistance to Mexico described to Suárez by Morgenthau, although Mexican officials in Washington continued to hope that a "saving formula" could be found in the petroleum conflict which would permit continuation of the negotiations so favorably begun. Even at this critical moment, there were assurances by U.S. government officials to the effect that a prosperous Mexico was in the interest of the U.S. as well as of Mexico, and the Mexican officials tended to interpret the hard line taken by the State Department as due to pressures from the U.S. press and from Congress.[9]

[8] Initiatives of petroleum workers in maintaining the industry in production are discussed in *Mexican Labor News*, 28 July 1938; Benítez, 1978: 149-153; González, 1972: 147; Gilly, 1975: 357; Rippy, 1972: 264-265; Rodríguez, 1958: 125. On the reprisals by the petroleum companies, see L. Meyer, 1968: 227; 1972b: 352, 412-413, 474; 1971: 3; Rippy, 1972: 244-259; Cronon, 1960: 233-234. One concern of Daniels was that barter with German manufacturers would turn Mexican imports to German rather than American made goods. In the first year following the expropriation, imports from the U.S. declined while Mexican trade with Germany, Italy, and Japan increased sharply (Cronon, 1960: 235; Rippy, 1972: 255). Reports from the U.S. Embassy in Mexico noted that American exporters of heavy machinery and equipment and other articles were suffering from European competition, particularly from Germany, as a result of barter arrangements (Daniels, 1938e) (enclosure, p. 7), 1939b (enclosure, pp. 8-9), 1939c (enclosure, p. 2).

[9] In several letters to Montes de Oca (Sarro, 1938c and d), Enrique Sarro, a central bank official involved in the loan negotiations in Washington, expressed

But, for the present, considerations of mutual interest were definitely secondary to differences resulting from the petroleum controversy. The State Department tended to discourage loans even to the private sector. Thus, in July 1938, when the State Department was consulted regarding the advisability of a loan to the privately owned steel company, Fundidora Monterrey, the Advisor on International Economic Affairs, Herbert Feis, advised against it on the grounds of Mexico's unstable economic situation and the fact that the Mexican government had "made no satisfactory move toward settlements" of the questions in dispute between the U.S. and Mexico (Boal, 1939a). By the end of the decade, Mexican financial officials had become increasingly disturbed at the U.S. government's unfavorable treatment of Mexico in comparison with Brazil and other Latin American countries which were receiving Eximbank credits and other forms of economic assistance (Suárez, 1977: 231).

Negotiations between Mexico and the United States regarding compensation and the terms of indemnification were complicated by several basic disagreements. The decree of expropriation established that indemnification would be paid in cash within a 10-year period, with funds to be taken from petroleum profits (Mexico, Cámara de Diputados, 1966, V: 779). The oil companies and the State Department, however, insisted on immediate indemnification; the latter also insisted on a concrete plan of compensation to U.S. farmers affected by the agrarian reform. There were also differences regarding the amount of indemnification and whether it should include payment for petroleum reserves. The Mexican government estimated the value of the properties at $112 to $180 million, while the companies demanded payment for petroleum deposits as well as for facilities, estimating the total value at $500

---

the hope that the Mexican government would reconsider its attitude (of course in a form which "saved the national dignity") and noted that he had been assured of the good will of the State Department which had taken such action as suspension of the silver purchase agreement under considerable pressure from the U.S. press and Congress. Subsequently (1939e) he related a conversation with Treasury official White, who stated that he and higher officials in the Treasury wished to help Mexico: ". . . tanto por razones de amistad para México como por considerarlo conveniente para los mismos Estados Unidos, desean que México sea un país independiente y prospero, y que se siente optimista respecto al futuro inmediato y lejano." (Both for reasons of friendship with Mexico, and for the convenience of the United States itself, they want Mexico to be an independent and prosperous country, and feel optimistic regarding the immediate and long-term future.)

million to \$600 million. It was not until May 1940 that the boycott was ended through a separate negotiation with Sinclair,[10] and only in 1942 was agreement reached with the U.S. government and petroleum companies regarding compensation for the companies.[11] Difficulties in the sale of petroleum ended with the U.S. demand for Mexican petroleum during the war. By the end of the war, Mexico was consuming 90 percent of its petroleum production internally, and domestic markets had replaced external markets lost as a result of the boycott by the petroleum companies (L. Meyer, 1968: 20, 264; 1971: 4).

DEMOBILIZATION OF THE PROGRESSIVE COALITION

The immediate repercussions of the petroleum expropriation—specifically, the effects of retaliation by the petroleum companies and their respective governments—can be best understood in the context of the structural constraints resulting from Mexico's peripheral status and particularly its dependent relation with the United States. It is precisely because these structures had rendered the internal economy so vulnerable to external pressures that metropolitan reaction to the expropriation had such serious effects. The dominance of foreign companies in key sectors of the Mexican economy had important repercussions on Mexico's balance of pay-

[10] The united front of the companies as well as the oil boycott were broken when the Mexican government succeeded in negotiating a separate agreement with Sinclair (which had accounted for 25 percent of production and 40 percent of the refining and distribution of American companies in Mexico). Sinclair agreed to a payment of \$8.5 million in cash and the purchase of 20 million barrels of oil over the next four years at 25 to 30 cents below its market value, bringing the total compensation to \$13 or \$14 million (Cronon, 1930: 251-252).

[11] A study by the U.S. Department of the Interior to assess the value of the petroleum properties following the expropriation found the company claims highly exaggerated; even the State Department was shocked by the findings and the fact that it had been deceived by the petroleum companies regarding the value of their holdings. A subsequent study by two experts—one Mexican, one American—confirmed these findings, reporting obsolete equipment 25 years old and in need of repair, and miles of pipeline corroded beyond use (Cronon, 1960: 260-261, 264). Agreement was reached in 1942 whereby Mexico would pay \$23,995,991 to the U.S. companies, although this did not end their attempt to regain their hegemony over Mexican petroleum production (these efforts are analyzed in L. Meyer, 1974b). However, the petroleum industry remained under the control of the Mexican government.

ments since profit repatriation had become an important negative balance of payments item, which was further aggravated by a deliberate policy on the part of foreign interests in Mexico of capital export. Trade dependence on the U.S. made the Mexican economy vulnerable not only to deliberate actions by U.S. interests but also to unintended effects of changes in the U.S. economy, such as the 1937 recession, which shifted price relations between the two countries and led to increased imports and a decline in exports. Since taxes on mineral production and exports constituted an important source of government revenues, foreign control of that sector gave it a certain leverage over government expenditures.

An example of these constraints was the failure of Cárdenas to follow up the petroleum expropriation with nationalizations of other foreign industries, although the Mine and Metalworkers' Union pressured the government to expropriate the mining industry. As noted above, the mining sector accounted for approximately 60 percent of Mexico's exports, and was over 95 percent foreign-controlled. Also, in contrast to the petroleum industry, the major market for mineral exports was the U.S., a market which would have been effectively closed if the mining companies had been expropriated. Given the economic and political costs of such an act, Cárdenas gave public and private assurances to mineowners that their properties would not be affected (Bernstein, 1965: 184-185).

At the same time, the economic problems resulting from pressures exerted by the petroleum companies, the U.S. State Department, and other foreign governments aggravated and were reinforced by those resulting from internal pressures—production cutbacks in certain sectors, price increases, as well as constant and increasing attacks by the organizations and publications directly or indirectly representing the interests of private capital on government policies and labor "agitation." To this was added the increased level of conflict in the countryside resulting from the Sinarquista movement. Thus, direct economic intervention by foreign capital combined with both indirect and direct forms of intervention by Mexican capital to limit the options for state action. The aggravation of the economic crisis and economic and political pressures from foreign and national capital influenced a shift in internal policy and a de-emphasis on working-class and peasant mobilization for reform and structural change. On the one hand, the inadequacy of economic resources with which to finance the public works program and the agrarian reform, not to mention the new costs entailed in state control of the petroleum industry, was aggravated by the necessity to pay compensation to the expropriated companies and by the drain on fiscal resources resulting from the economic boycott and other measures of the petroleum companies and of the U.S. State Department. On the other hand, political pressures from the United States, added to increased trends to reaction among Mexican business groups and the growing conservatism on the part of some officials of the government itself, reinforced the existing conservative alliance between sectors of the state and private groups and helped to solidify the opposition to the Cárdenas government. The Mexican economy and government revenues did recover to some extent, beginning in the middle of 1938 with the government's success in finding markets for petroleum exports in Germany, Italy, and Japan and the institution of the new export tax, which resulted in a substantial increase in revenues from exports. But during the second half of 1939 the Mexican economy was again negatively affected by external events: a decline in the price paid for silver; the outbreak of war in Europe in September 1939, with the consequent cutoff of exports to Germany; the institution of U.S. tariffs which blocked mineral exports to the United States. Government revenues again declined, resulting in cutbacks in public works programs, and the mining industry continued in a state of depression throughout 1940 (BNM, 1934-1941: Jan. 1939: 16; May 1939: 7-8; Dec. 1939: 7; Sept. 1940: 15; May 1941: 12).

In the meantime, conservative forces within the government were among the first to take advantage of the situation to force concessions. In a meeting with the President at the end of March 1938, state governors promised their support for the expropriation, in return for which Cárdenas agreed to return to them jurisdiction over aspects of the agrarian reform which, following the implementation of the six-year plan, had been transferred to the Agrarian Department. He also promised protection to small property holders, and in the following month an office was established to deal with complaints by small holders allegedly affected unjustly by the land distribution program. Undoubtedly some of these complaints were legitimate, but small holders often acted as a "front" for large landowners and a defense of small holders generally constituted a justification for the protection of private agricultural property—including large-scale property. Also, while most gov-

TABLE 7.3. The Agrarian Reform Under Cárdenas: Land and Peasants
Affected by Presidential Resolutions, 1935-1940

Year	Amount of Land (Hectares)	Number of Beneficiaries
1935	1,923,457	110,286
1936	3,985,701	194,427
1937	5,811,893	199,347
1938	3,486,266	119,872
1939	2,223,733	96,480
1940	2,705,885	55,433

Source: Reyes Osorio, 1974: 50

ernors had ostensibly supported the government's agrarian policies
in the interests of political survival, several were known to be
linked with the landowners of their respective states, and others
had undoubtedly been affected by pressures from commercial
landowners and from their associates, as well as from small holders. These changes presaged a shift in the orientation of agrarian
reform from distribution to "consolidation" and from the ejidi-
tario to the "small property holder" (González Navarro, 1963: 145-
146; Shulgovski, 1971: 68-69).

Financial considerations also influenced the land distribution
program. Despite massive financial assistance from the government, the Ejidal Bank was able to provide credit for only a small
proportion of the new ejiditarios, and, as indicated above, the
government had come to rely increasingly on private financial
sources—including private banks and foreign merchandising companies—to supplement its contributions to the Ejidal Bank. As a
consequence of the political pressures as well as of the inability of
the Ejidal Bank to meet the credit needs of land reform beneficiaries, the amount of land and number of peasants affected by the
agrarian reform declined rapidly in the last years of the Cárdenas
administration, as indicated in Table 7.3.

At the same time, increased pressures on the Cárdenas government were translated into attempts to decrease the level of labor
mobilization. With the petroleum conflict and expropriation, the
growing influence of internal conservative and reactionary forces,
and subsequently the outbreak of war in Europe, the policy of
CTM leadership tended increasingly to unquestioned support of
the government, justified on the basis of national unity of all democratic forces against imperialism and internal reaction, and sup-

port for democratic countries in the war against fascism.[12] Already in 1937, Cárdenas had protested against several strikes, and in 1938 various strikes were called off or postponed at the request of the government or the CTM (*Mexican Labor News*, 21 April, 22 Sept., 11 Aug. 1937, 6 Oct. 1938). The number of strikes began to decline after 1936 and particularly after the petroleum expropriation in 1938:

Year	Strikes
1934	202
1935	642
1936	674
1937	576
1938	319
1939	303
1940	357

The fact that the government and CTM policy led to a partial abdication of the struggle for labor benefits was indicated in a joint statement issued by the CTM and the CNC, asking all workers to give broad and enthusiastic support to the Cárdenas government, to work to form a unanimous consciousness favoring the government program, and to postpone any conflicts which might be exploited to undermine efforts to resolve the petroleum question. According to the statement, authorities responsible for handling conflicts between workers and employers should intervene to solve them before they arise (*Mexican Labor News*, 11-18 Aug. 1938; *El Nacional*, 10 Aug. 1939). Another indication was an editorial of *El Popular*, the daily newspaper of the CTM, which stated that "workers understand that in difficult times their mission is to protect their conquests and not to attempt to precipitate progress. There are times . . . and the present is one . . . when forcing a too rapid progress would be a provocation and might quite likely produce a reaction" (*Mexican Labor News*, 15 Nov. 1940).

These changes by no means indicated a total abdication of the agrarian reform or the labor struggle. It was in the last years of the Cárdenas administration that the sugar estates were expropriated and turned over to the peasants, the lengthy textile strike in Orizaba was brought to a successful conclusion, mineworkers and

[12] The shift in CTM policy was first evident in a speech by Lombardo Toledano on November 20, 1937 in which he stated that the sharpening of the political struggle in Mexico was due not to the landowners or even imperialism: the dilemma was no longer communism or fascism, but democracy or fascism (Lombardo Toledano, 1937: 3-6).

other workers succeeded in increasing their wages to combat the growing cost of living, and legislation to permit unionization and strikes by state workers was passed. But, in general, the policy of the government and of labor officials shifted from support of class conflict to advocacy of class conciliation and national unity. For the workers "national unity" meant indefinite postponement of their redistributive efforts and a concentration on rising productivity, and identification of labor leaders with the government—an identification which would continue under subsequent conservative governments to the detriment of the Mexican working class.

SUMMARY AND CONCLUSIONS

Given the importance of structural constraints resulting from Mexico's position as a peripheral state within the world economy and its increasing dependence on the United States, the nationalization of the foreign-owned petroleum companies was the most significant indication of the relative autonomy of the Mexican state under Cárdenas. It ended a particularly abrasive relationship to foreign capital, constituted a first major step in the elimination of foreign control of the export sector, and placed a major resource under the control of the state, increasing the potential ability of the state to direct the process of capitalist industrialization. The expropriation was possible due in part to the "weakening" of international structural constraints through the depression, a shift in policy orientation by the U.S. government and its consequent promise of non-intervention in Latin American countries. But a further condition was the level of mobilization of the progressive coalition, which, having roots in the Mexican revolution, went beyond that of populist coalitions in other Latin American countries. A specific aspect of this alliance was the collaboration of the petroleum workers with the government, not only in events leading up to the expropriation but particularly in subsequently restoring the industry to operation, which in turn helped to insure that the industry remained under Mexican control.

Events leading to the petroleum expropriation can be understood only in terms of the climate of increasing conflict and polarization in Mexican society as a result of the offensive by the government and by urban and rural workers. Increasing opposition to labor mobilization through price increases and production cut-

backs, the growing level of violence in the countryside in response
to the agrarian reform, and the general climate of opposition fostered by statements of dominant groups, intellectuals, and the right-
wing press, were aggravated by export of capital and other forms
of pressure by the petroleum companies and their governments.
The economic relation of Mexico to the United States made it
vulnerable to these pressures and particularly to retaliation by these
powers once the expropriation was decreed. But, more important,
they reinforced the pressures exerted by national groups, including
factions within the state, which intervened to limit the offensive
of the progressive forces. The result was a demobilization of these
forces, manifested in the decline in the amount of land distributed,
in the number of peasants affected by the agrarian reform, and in
the number of strikes.

In short, the Cárdenas government had gone as far as it could
in radically restructuring Mexican society within the constraints of
the existing capitalist order. In collaboration with the working class
and peasantry it had promoted the organization of labor and state
support for labor rights, eliminated the traditional form of labor
exploitation in agriculture, distributed a substantial proportion of
the cultivable land of the country to peasants and to rural workers,
promoted cooperative ownership and labor control in agriculture
and industry, and nationalized the railroads and the petroleum industry. To a greater extent than any previous government, it had
realized the ideal of the "autonomous" state implicit in the Mexican constitution.

But the very success of the Cárdenas government in utilizing
the autonomy of the state, based on the progressive coalition, to
confront the dominant groups in Mexican society, including U.S.
investment interests, had strengthened the opposition and increased the cohesion of these groups. This opposition, which in
itself threatened to destabilize the existing system, was in turn a
factor in the efforts of Cárdenas to expand his base of support and
at the same time to increase his control of working class and peasant mobilization.

Eight ‖ The Limits of the Progressive Alliance

 The repercussions of the petroleum conflict and the expropriation of the petroleum companies demonstrated both the extent and the limits of state autonomy in relation to foreign capital in the specific historical and structural conditions of post-revolutionary Mexico. It also had the paradoxical effect of deepening the polarization between conservative and progressive forces, with economic reprisals by the companies and their governments further limiting the sphere of action of the state, while at the same time broadening internal support for the government around the specific issue of national sovereignty. Conservative groups within the state took advantage of the situation to force concessions from the Cárdenas government; the government took advantage of the momentary unity to expand its base of support, with the inclusion of "moderate elements" in the progressive coalition, and tightened its control over labor and the peasantry. In both cases, the result was to neutralize the effectiveness of the progressive alliance and ultimately the possibility of state autonomy based on such an alliance.

THE PARTY OF THE MEXICAN REVOLUTION (PRM)

One of the first measures taken to institutionalize a broader support base was the establishment of a new political party. The formation of a party which would unite all "revolutionary" sectors of the country had apparently been a goal of Cárdenas from an early stage of his administration. In effect, it would constitute an "institutionalization" of the progressive alliance in which the state would, of course, be dominant.

A first initiative in changing the party structure had been taken in September 1936 with a manifesto published by the PNR stating that all organized workers belonging to trade unions were eligible to join the party (*Mexican Labor News*, 18 Sept. 1936). Subsequently, accusations by peasants and workers of irregularities in the designation of the PNR candidates to the legislature and to municipal posts in the state of Mexico resulted in a change in the method of designating candidates. In the elections of the federal district and two states in 1937, the PNR delegates were selected by the agrarian leagues and by the labor unions (although apparently in reality they were appointed beforehand by the government or—in the case of labor delegates—by the CTM leadership) (Gómez Jara, 1970: 121; Anguiano, 1975: 69).

The organization of the new party—the Party of the Mexican Revolution (PRM)—was announced in December 1937, at the height of the petroleum controversy, and its constitutional congress was held on March 30, 1938, less than two weeks after the expropriation. The geographic representation of the PNR was replaced by a representation based on four sectors: labor, peasant, military, and popular. The labor sector would consist of the three major confederations (CTM, CGT, and the dissident anti-Morones faction of CROM, which included the majority of CROM members), plus independent national unions such as those of the electricians and miners.[1] The peasant sector would comprise the state agrarian leagues and the CCM (Mexican Peasant Confederation) initially, and subsequently the CNC (National Peasant Confederation) which was formed a few months later. The military sector would consist of elected representatives from each military zone in the country, headed by two trusted division generals, Juan José Ríos and Heriberto Jara, selected by Defense Secretary Manuel Avila Camacho.[2] The popular sector was composed of an amorphous mixture—federations of state employees and teachers, organizations of small landowners, students, professionals, and women's groups. This sector in fact included various middle-class elements, taking advantage of the expanded support for Cárdenas following the expropriation. At the time of its formation, the new

[1] Subsequently, the CGT labor groups withdrew from the party and the CGT was expelled officially at the end of 1938.

[2] Edwin Lieuwen suggests that the inclusion of the military in electoral politics was a means of controlling their existing political influence, since they participated as representatives, not of the armed forces, but of a political organization which was balanced through equal representation with three other sectors. At the same time, military participation in the PRM was limited by various restrictions and the President was able to control the selection of military generals through the Secretary of Defense (Lieuwen, 1948: 124-125). However, the source of political power of the military consisted, as always, in its control of arms, and the influence of military leaders continued to be exercised outside the party structure.

party—the party of the Mexican Revolution (PRM)—allegedly included more than four million Mexicans: 1,250,000 in the labor sector; 2,500,000 in the peasant sector; 500,000 in the popular sector, and 55,000 in the military sector (Furtak, 1974: 39-40).[3]

The initial declaration stated that the political activities of member organizations would be confined to the framework of the party, but these organizations would retain their autonomy and freedom of action in pursuing their own specific objectives. The corporate structure had the ostensible purpose of eliminating elitist control of politics—exercised through the manipulation and division of individual voters—by giving members of the constituent organizations weight as aggregate forces in the electoral process (Córdova, 1974: 147). But, given the authoritarian structure of the two major labor and peasant organizations—the CTM and the CNC—their incorporation in the government party in effect served to reinforce the control exercised by the hierarchy over the membership, placing the institutions themselves under the control of the state. The PRM was organized from above, and the majority of constituent organizations were led into the party by their directors (Anguiano, 1975: 136; Weyl and Weyl, 1939: 340). Since interaction between sectors was limited, the party structure also reinforced the segregation between the urban/industrial working class and the peasantry. In addition, the government had opposed the newly formed union of state workers joining the CTM, and its inclusion (and that of teachers) in the "popular" sector represented a further obstacle to labor unity. The absorption of radical and leftist forces into the ranks of the government party precluded effective leftist opposition outside the party; at the same time, leftist groups within the party were neutralized by the inclusion of moderate and right-wing elements in the popular and military sectors (Raby, 1972: 52, 57; Ashby, 1963: 90).

The implications of the party structure were soon revealed in a shift in the ideological orientation of the party and the forced resignation of its first president, Luis Rodríguez. At the constitutional

---

[3] Activities of the four sectors were to be coordinated by party committees organized at the local, state, and national levels. All four sectors would participate in the nomination of the presidential candidate; for senators and governors, the positions were divided among the various sectors (with the exception of the military sector). For a given position, the designated sector would select the candidate from its own ranks and he would be supported by the other sectors (González Navarro, 1963: 148-149).

congress of the party, Rodríguez stated that the party would strive for a workers' democracy in preparation for the eventual socialization of production. This orientation was also incorporated in the party's statutes, which called for the progressive nationalization of large industries. But it was soon replaced by an orientation stressing national unity, and Rodríguez was subsequently forced to resign as a result of pressures from right-wing groups within the government. Although the new PRM president, Heriberto Jara, had the support of labor, the Rodríguez resignation indicated the strength of more conservative elements within the party and the government, and the willingness of Cárdenas to conciliate these groups.

The creation of the PRM thus completed the process of state control of the working-class and peasant organizations, at the same time reinforcing the authoritarian control of members by the leadership within these organizations. In broadening the support base of the Cárdenas government to include "moderate" elements, it further limited the effectiveness of this support base in confronting capital and its allies within the state.

THE CONTRADICTIONS OF WORKER MANAGEMENT

As indicated above, by 1937 government policy began to be affected by economic factors beyond its immediate control, and this situation was aggravated following the petroleum expropriation. These factors affected the labor movement both directly, by cutting into wage gains, and indirectly, as a consequence of government efforts to respond to economic and political pressures by curbing labor demands. This policy shift was obviously facilitated through the increasing control of labor by government and by labor leaders.

The shift in emphasis had particular reverberations in the area of worker management. The policy to promote cooperatives, worker control, and labor management was in itself beset with contradictions and ambiguities. Cárdenas discussed the cooperative as a form of socialist production or as preparatory to a transition to socialist society or a workers' democracy (*Excelsior*, 14 April 1935). Certainly his injuction to those "tired of the labor struggle" to turn their factories over to the workers and to the state was widely interpreted as a direct assault on private capital.

The establishment of the collective ejidos and of forms of labor management in the railroads and in the petroleum industry indicated an openness to experimentation with quasi-socialist forms of production control in crucial industries.

But certain critics within the progressive faction of the government pointed out that, in the absence of a complete change in the mode of production, the cooperative movement would produce privileged groups within the working class or even situations in which one group of workers would exploit another (Shulgovski, 1968: 308 f). Lombardo Toledano claimed that production cooperatives outside agriculture constituted an attempt to counter the force of unions in the class struggle; therefore only consumer cooperatives, which contributed to the relative improvement of wages, should be supported (Lombardo Toledano, 1938: 16-24). Debate on the question of productive cooperatives continued throughout the Cárdenas administration, with actual experiments in this area tending to add to the confusion rather than clarifying the issue.

Cárdenas' suggestion that owners tired of the labor struggle turn their firms over to the state or to the workers was (not surprisingly) followed chiefly by those unable to remain in business on their own. This meant that firms turned over to the workers were among the most inefficient and least profitable; sometimes the workers received them burdened with heavy debts. Often lacking credit and market access (since the funds of the Banco Obrero were limited), several cooperatives fell prey to intermediaries who paid low prices for products which they sold at high prices to consumers. Some "cooperatives" were also characterized by exploitation of the workers by "administrators." Since cooperative workers were not covered by the Federal Labor Law, they were often forced to work longer hours at lower wages, particularly in mining cooperatives, where safety regulations were also often ignored. False cooperatives were sometimes created as a means of deliberately avoiding the Federal Labor Law (Shulgovski, 1968: 309-313; Bernstein, 1965: 205-209).

During 1938 and 1939 several mines were turned over to mineworkers on a temporary or a permanent basis, on the grounds that owners were unable to meet increased costs accruing from workers' demands (Mexico, Departamento de Trabajo, 1937: 23, 24; 30-32; 1939: 13). Often agreements were made whereby workers would pay previous owners a proportion of the profits as well as indemnification for the property in installments. When the coop-

erative failed, and market conditions became favorable, the previous owner would re-purchase the company. In other cases, the
mines were nearly depleted when they were given to the workers—e.g., the mines of Don Carlos and San Rafael in Pachuca, La
Nova and El Bote in Zacatecas, and Dos Estrellas in Michoacán
(Bernstein, 1965: 202-203). As a result, mineworkers were unable
to benefit from control of mining operations for more than a few
months.

The most important experiments in worker management occurred in the two crucial sectors nationalized under the Cárdenas
government: the National Railroad of Mexico, and the petroleum
industry. Already 51 percent government-owned, the National
Railroad was completely nationalized in June 1937, and subsequently, in 1938, at the request of the workers, the company was
turned over to the union to administer through the election of a
seven-member executive council, subject to recall. The government continued to exercise ultimate control, e.g., approval of freight
rates.

The railroad workers' union had the reputation of being one of
the best-organized and most class-conscious unions in Mexico and
had been instrumental in organizing workers in other sectors. As
the first large-scale attempt at labor management, the administration of the railroads by the workers was conceptualized by the
railroad workers as well as by other sectors of the working class
as a significant experiment toward future collectivization of the
means of production (De la Peña, 1937: 222). During its first year
the union administration succeeded in paying 20 million pesos of
the foreign railroad debt, repaired 300 freight cars, reduced operating costs, repaired tracks, and increased the percentage of loco-
motives in operation. The accomplishments of the workers'
administration during its first weeks of operation were recognized
in President Cárdenas' annual address to Congress (Mexico: Cámara de Diputados, IV: 88). Even the U.S. commercial attaché
expressed the belief that, despite complaints, the National Railroad
was being operated with much greater efficiency and honesty by
the railroad workers' union than in the years prior to its control
(Lockett, 1938b).

But the contradictions of worker management of a state-owned
railroad within the context of a capitalist system soon became apparent. With the increase in the cost of living, the workers began
to press for higher wages and suggested that freight rates be raised

to provide sufficient income. But, although certain rates were low, including those for the transfer of mineral products of the U.S.-owned mining companies and other exporters, the government refused to raise them and at the same time insisted that tax payments by the railroad company (amounting to ten percent of annual railroad receipts) be continued. The crisis in the mining industry—due to the cutback in U.S. silver purchases, the lower prices for industrial minerals in the U.S., and (by mid-1939) the decline in the price of silver—was undoubtedly a factor in the government's unwillingness to raise freight rates at this time, particularly since it had already imposed a twelve percent tax on exports which chiefly affected the mining industry. The mining industry was also an important source of government income: the government received approximately 28 percent of its revenues from various taxes on the mining industry and was dependent on advance tax payments from some of the larger mining companies to relieve its critical fiscal situation (Daniels, 1938a: enclosure; Blocker, 1939a). The refusal to increase freight rates and the continuation of tax payments, despite the critical conditions of the railroads, suggest an evident conflict of interests between the financial needs of the state and the economic needs of the workers and of the industry itself.

Difficulties also resulted from the dual role of the union leaders as managers of the industry and representatives of the workers; high-level union officials in the workers' administration identified with the state and the enterprise rather than with the workers, who thus found themselves deprived of effective union representation. The fact that large sums had to be directed to pay the existing debt meant that little or nothing could be spent for badly needed repairs or replacements or even for the rehabilitation of repair shops. Between 1911 and 1936, freight tonnage per kilometer had increased 90 percent, whereas the number of freight cars had declined from 20,389 to 14,621. Business groups and the conservative press, adamantly opposed to the administration of the railroads by the workers, lost no opportunity to criticize the union or the workers when problems arose.[4] Several accidents, some involving injuries and deaths, were blamed on worker negligence, although the state of disrepair of the equipment and apparently

[4] For example, a publication by the Cámaras Nacionales de Comercio y Industria blamed the union for high wages, excess personnel, and inability to finance capital replacement (BNM, 1934-1941: Oct. 1938).

deliberate sabotage were also factors. Since the government took the position that the state represented the interests of the nation within the nationalized industries, requests by workers for wage increases were labeled "unpatriotic," constituting a further element—in addition to the poor state of the railroads and their declining living standards—in the demoralization of the workers.

As a result of these problems, the union administration of the railroad was gradually divested of control. In April 1940, technical and economic administration was placed under the jurisdiction of the Secretaries of Finance and Public Works. In June, the President stated that if the situation of the lines did not improve, they would be returned to control by the government. The union management proposed to reduce its expenditures by one million pesos monthly through "readjustments" of wages and personnel—a proposition which was rejected by the workers and resulted in the resignation of the general manager. One of the first acts of the Avila Camacho government, which succeeded that of Cárdenas in November 1940, was the suppression of the labor administration.[5]

The second important case of labor management was the administration of the petroleum industry. In contrast to the nationalized railroads, administration was not controlled by the union, but by the government, with the union having minority representation. However, the union had responsibility for industry operations, and, as indicated in Chapter Seven, the ability of the workers to maintain the petroleum industry in operation in the initial months following the expropriation was important in the success of nationalization. But differences soon developed between the petroleum workers and the government officials within the administration, aggravated by problems within the union and by export difficulties, and in many cases directly promoted by agents of the expropriated companies.

The formation of the Union of Petroleum Workers (STPRM) in 1935 had brought new leaders to national-level positions who were subsequently active in promoting the collective contract and the strike. The rapidity of events and the technical nature of many of the questions under debate had resulted in decisions being taken at top levels without consulting rank-and-file union members—contrary to the democratic practices which had characterized local

[5] Sources on the union administration of the railroad include Anguiano 1975: 88 f, Ashby, 1963: 130-141; Shulgovski, 1968: 314-320; BFM, 1935-1941: 1 Jan. 1940, 23 Oct. 1939, 1 Jan. 1941; and Graf Campos, 1975.

petroleum unions in the past. The separation between union members and leadership was aggravated when many of the leaders took top administrative positions within the nationalized industry, some of them receiving salaries five times their previous wages; in many cases management positions were invented when there were not enough to reward union leadership. In addition, the introduction of friends and relatives of the administrators and workers into positions within the industry resulted in an expansion in employment, which increased from 15,895 in April 1938 to 19,316 in April 1939 (still below the 1937 level of 20,864); by October 1939 it had reached 23,073. Expenses for personnel increased by 81.82 percent between 1937 and 1939 (from 55 million pesos to over 100 million) (Silva Herzog, 1941: 229-242).[6]

Initially the government had hoped to meet the terms of the 1937 labor board decision; although deductions from wages continued, other benefits—including compensation for house rent, a savings fund, increased vacations and extensive medical services—were put into effect. In addition, the government undertook a vast capitalization program—in part required by shortages resulting from the expropriation (e.g., purchase of tank boats and supplies) and in part in an effort to expand production and to increase refinery capacity (Silva Herzog, 1941: 228, 244, 249).

Despite problems of external markets, increased expenditures were not seen as critical until the outbreak of war in Europe brought a closing of export markets (particularly that of Germany) and a drastic reduction in foreign sales, from approximately $2 million in July and August 1939 to $800,000 in September. At the same time, machinery and parts had to be purchased in the United States, at higher prices than in Germany. By the end of 1939, PEMEX had a deficit of 22 million pesos.

At the beginning of 1940, the presidents and general managers of the two state petroleum organizations, Petroleos Mexicanos (PEMEX, responsible for petroleum production), and Distribui-

---

[6] There were cases in which union leaders took high posts from a sense of responsibility without accepting the high salaries that went with them, but this was apparently the exception. According to one source, both union members and the government authorities recruited new employees (González, 1972: 210). One of the major sources on the administration of the petroleum industry is Jesús Silva Herzog (1941) who served as manager of PEMEX during much of this period. Other sources include Ashby, 1963: 245 f, Rippy, 1972: 263 f, and *Rumbo*, a publication of one of the sections of the Union of Petroleum Workers (especially June, July, August and September 1940).

dora de Petroleos Mexicanos (responsible for the sale of petroleum and its derivatives) presented a report to President Cárdenas on the situation of the industry and made a series of recommendations for its reorganization. The report accused the workers of a lack of discipline, inefficiency, arbitrary pay raises, and thefts of oil and gasoline for private sale. The petroleum workers' union responded that the report had been based on the previous situation of the oil industry and that the problems indicated had either been due to the confusion and disorganization of the industry following expropriation, conditions which no longer existed, or had subsequently been corrected—e.g., by dismissal and in some cases prosecution of workers guilty of theft.

The conflict continued throughout 1940, with the government, supported by the majority of the PEMEX administration, presenting various proposals for the reorganization of the industry which were rejected by union representatives on the board as well as by union leadership.[7] By June 1940, the severe financial straits of the industry (with a deficit of 67,909,544.35 pesos for the first five months of the year) resulted in a new directive from the government, calling for drastic improvment of the industry or the immediate implementation of cuts in wages and benefits. The general managers of PEMEX and Distribuidora placed a dispute of economic order before the Federal Labor Board, which appointed a committee of experts to study the industry, but, in the mean-

---

[7] On February 26, Cárdenas presented fourteen propositions for the reorganization of the industry, including the reduction of personnel and the elimination of unnecessary posts. While acknowledging the contributions of the workers, Cárdenas accused the STPRM of having an attitude toward PEMEX similar to its attitude toward the petroleum companies. He pointed out that profits did not go to shareholders but to the nation, and should be distributed, through the budget, to benefit the people of the country as a whole (Silva Herzog, 1941: 244-253; González, 1972: 208-209).

The union was unwilling to accept Cárdenas' proposals, and negotiations between the union, the PEMEX administration, and the government continued throughout the year. The union defended the increase in personnel as due in part to the deliberate understaffing of the industry prior to the expropriation (Rippy, 1972: 278). With respect to financial deficits, the union stated that these could be attributed to the low prices contracted for the export of oil by the Distribuidora management; these contracts were often secret, and not the responsibility of the union (*Rumbo*, 14 Aug. 1940: 16, 37; Rippy, 1972: 278). The union accused administrative officials of inefficiency, exorbitant salaries, and poor economic management in selling petroleum products at low prices while paying high prices for materials (Ashby, 1963: 262-263).

time, presented a temporary reorganization plan in July 1940. By this time, relations between the union and the government administrators had become bitter; various "accidents" and apparent acts of sabotage were attributed to the workers. Local unions in the federal district condemned the new plan as discriminating against workers in lower categories and proposed a strike, which was supported by the executive committee of the petroleum union but condemned by Cárdenas, the CTM, and the other major industrial unions.

The strike threat and acts of sabotage could be attributed at least in part to agitation by agents of the petroleum companies, who took advantage of the conflict and bribed union leaders to oppose the reorganization plan proposed by Cárdenas (Silva Herzog, 1941: 277-282). The conflict between the union and the government was also played up in the conservative press, with the periodical *El Economista* and the newspaper *El Hombre Libre* (both conservative, with fascist overtones) frequently publishing accusations by the Union of Petroleum Workers against the government.

Partly because of lack of support from other sectors of labor, the proposed strike was called off. However, a special commission was formed of representatives from the petroleum union, the CTM, and other unions, to make a study of PEMEX. It found that 53.4 percent of the gross receipts of PEMEX went to the government for taxes, capital works, and amortization of the petroleum debt. Finally, on October 31, 1940, the committee of experts appointed to study the economic situation of the industry made its report, which constituted the basis for the decision by the Federal Labor Board on November 28, two days before Cárdenas was to leave office. In general, the report and the subsequent decision by the board supported the requests of the PEMEX administration, but certain workers' benefits which had been threatened in the course of the conflict were left intact.

Throughout the dispute, relations between the government and the petroleum union were considerably complicated by division within the union itself, which may have been a factor in its failure to present its own plan of reorganization. Among rank-and-file workers as well as union section leaders, there were complaints of opportunism and corruption by union leadership and other union members, and of the presence of agents of the companies within the industry. Central to this confusion was the ambiguity regarding the role of the union—fundamentally an institution for the defense of the interests of its members in relation to capital—in state-controlled and worker-managed industries. Accustomed to the government's being a defender of their interests, the workers were not prepared to deal with it as a substitute employer.

To what extent, and why, did the experiments in worker administration fail? It was clearly not a question of the technical ability of the workers, who proved capable of managing the railroad and petroleum industries in difficult circumstances. Nor does it seem to have been a problem of economic inefficiency. The railroad workers succeeded in paying off part of the national debt, made repairs, cut costs; and many of the accusations against the petroleum union were considerably weakened by the discovery that over half of the gross revenues were going to the government and that the administration had exported petroleum at prices considerably below the pre-expropriation prices. Divisions within the unions, and the ambiguity of the position of union leaders as part of the administration and as representatives of the interests of the workers, were undoubtedly complications, although the effects were different in the two cases.[8]

As in the case of the collective ejido, worker administration in industry confronted the problem of operating within an environment which was hostile to the introduction of non-capitalist forms

[8] The Mexican Communist party criticized the system of union administration as endangering the principal function of the union as defender of the workers, since the administrator tended to defend the firm. Labor administration in the railroad industry was considered a failure, and Communist members of the petroleum union were asked to oppose worker administration (García Treviño, 1939: 38-39; see also Shulgovski, 1968: 454 for the Communist party viewpoint). Although the CTM initially supported the introduction of worker administration into the nationalized railroads and petroleum industry, it eventually took a line similar to that of the Communist party. In a speech to the CTM congress of 1941, Lombardo Toledano stated that worker administration resulted in a dispersion of the economic and social energies of the workers and placed them in the position of sacrificing social conquests in the economic interests of the firm (CTM, 1941: 1074-1075).

An intermediate position, suggested by García Treviño, noted the problems of labor administration within a capitalist economy and criticized the belief that worker administration constituted a step toward socialism. Nevertheless, labor administration was an authentic conquest of the workers and *could* constitute a progressive step in their historic struggle, particularly through organizational and technical training. Like participation in municipal government and parliament, labor administration could result in corruption and cooptation, or become a source of support for a progressive movement (García Treviño, 1939: 26-37, 40).

of production. In contrast to the ejiditarios, however, which at least during the Cárdenas administration received moral and financial support from the government, relations between the government and the railroad and petroleum workers became increasingly antagonistic. The major issue in fact seems to have been the relationship of the workers with a government which—while operating within a capitalist context—claimed to represent the interests of the nation and particularly of subordinate groups within that nation, a claim which was probably sincere and not unjustified, given the record of the Cárdenas administration. It was also true, as some government officials pointed out, that in terms of wages and benefits the railroad and petroleum workers constituted a relatively privileged sector of the working class.

But government opposition to the workers was based on the necessity to respond to increasing pressures from capitalist class interests at a time when intervention by these groups was growing in importance. In the case of the railroad workers, worker demands for higher wages financed through higher freight rates came into conflict with the demands of the foreign-owned mining industry, which had experienced a decline in prices for its products and was providing needed revenues to the government through advance tax payments. In this sense, it also conflicted with the interest of the government, which lacked sufficient revenues, and for which the tax income from the mining companies constituted a major source of funding. In the case of the petroleum industry, the workers were clearly being asked to make sacrifices in the interests of rapid debt amortization and in the development of the industry. Both could, of course, be construed as the national interest, but they undoubtedly responded in part to pressures by foreign companies (and the U.S. State Department)—apart from the question of how, and by whom, the national interest is interpreted.

Worker administration in the state-owned petroleum and railroad industries became another form of control of workers by the state, ultimately with the collaboration of corrupt or state-imposed union leadership. Thus the relationship between the loss of autonomy and the development of authoritarian control within the main labor and peasant confederations also characterized the unions of those industries which became part of the public sector, where incorporation of labor unions into state-controlled administration entailed both a loss of autonomy and an erosion of their previous democratic institutions.[9]

THE PRESIDENTIAL SUCCESSION

The conflict between the state and the workers in state-controlled industries was characteristic of a basic shift in coalitions and alignments which was occurring during the last two years of the Cárdenas administration. In expanding its social base—e.g., through the organization of the PRM—to include other groups in addition to the subordinate classes, the government limited its effectiveness in representing the latter. Certain sectors of the working class, including some of those in state-controlled industries, became alienated from the government. Thus superimposed on the class conflict between subordinate groups and progressive sectors of the government, on the one hand, and dominant classes and their allies within the state, on the other, was another set of cleavages between the state and broad sectors of society, including elements of the working class. This new polarization resulted in strange alliances, as indicated in the support by such quasi-fascist periodicals as *El Economista* and the newspaper *El Hombre Libre* for the petroleum workers' union in its accusations against the government. Its significance became evident in the struggle for presidential succession.

At the time of the petroleum expropriation, opposition had already developed in Congress to legislation proposed by the executive, notably the law project which would permit state employees to organize and strike, although eventually the law was passed as originally presented. In July 1938, the same deputies who had led the opposition to the state employees' law, Ramón Iturbe and Bolívar Sierra, formed the Frente Democrática Constitucional Mexicana as a national association against fascism and communism. The Frente was condemned by the CTM as a thinly veiled attack against communism and the left in general—an allegation which seems to have been reasonably accurate, since the Frente subsequently concentrated its attacks on Lombardo Toledano and Luis Rodríguez, left-wing director of the PRM (CTM, 1941: 592-

[9] Members of these unions have struggled against authoritarianism, corruption, and *charrismo* (the imposition of state-controlled leadership) within the unions throughout the post-Cárdenas period (Schaffer, 1974-75: 79).

593; Daniels, 1938f). The PRM condemned the two deputies as attempting to establish a rival party and dismissed them from the PRM (Daniels, 1938d, enclosure). It was also during the summer of 1938 that conflicts broke out between the governor of the states of Sonora and Nuevo León, both military, and the CTM organizations in those states (Medina, 1978: 23-24). Congressional opposition was also indicative of increasing opposition among certain factions within the military (Contreras, 1977: 16).

A significant change had taken place in the character of the military as a political force by the end of the Cárdenas administration. The defeat of Cedillo in 1938 eliminated the last military threat from a revolutionary caudillo who could mobilize his own army against the central government. In his efforts to control the military, Cárdenas had utilized many of the same tactics as his predecessors: generals were shifted to new command posts away from their armies; military opponents were forced into early retirement; and the general policy of encouraging generals to become capitalists was continued. Thus the military was to some extent dominated by officers who had benefited from entrepreneurial opportunities in post-revolutionary Mexico, who identified with dominant class interests, and who were therefore hostile to progressive sectors within the government which threatened the status quo and their vested interests. And in many cases military officers continued to dominate key political and government posts.

The Calles-Cárdenas confrontation of mid-1935 was in certain respects a turning point. Many generals formerly identified with Calles chose not to oppose Cárdenas in order not to risk losing their new economic positions. The change was evident in the opportunistic shift in allegiance of members of the legislature—where military representation was strong—from Calles to Cárdenas, when it was demonstrated that Cárdenas was in command. The military was apparently also capable of shifting again to oppose the Cárdenas government if it was perceived to threaten its interest.[10] The growing opposition to the Cárdenas labor and agrarian policies, and to the mobilization of the affected sectors, was a factor in the emergence of a number of opposition political organizations, many of them headed by former revolutionary generals, in 1938 and 1939.

[10] During this period reports from U.S. consuls in various parts of Mexico mentioned the possibility of military intervention by high level officials.

The strength of right-wing groups within the government became obvious with the conflict over the candidate of the new PRM to succeed Cárdenas as president. For those interested in a continuation of the progressive orientation of the Cárdenas administration, the logical successor to Cárdenas, believed to have been the choice of Cárdenas himself, was General Francisco Múgica, the Secretary of Communications and Public Works, who was proposed by the Secretary of Education, Vázquez Vela, in July 1938. Múgica had been the first of the constitutionalist generals to carry out an extensive land distribution in 1913 (on a large hacienda near Matamoras) and, as noted in Chapter Two, had played an important role as the leader of the radical sector of the constitutional congress of 1916-1917. As Secretary of Communications under Cárdenas, Múgica had worked to protect consumers and small producers (e.g., by cutting rebates given by railroads which favored large producers and by giving preferential rates to small mines, ejidos, small holders, and cooperatives). Múgica favored the unionization of state employees and, on the international front, supported Republican Spain in the civil war and was instrumental in persuading Cárdenas to grant asylum to Leon Trotsky. A close friend and advisor to Cárdenas, he had been in continuous consultation with the president in the crucial days prior to the petroleum expropriation, which he consistently promoted.

At roughly the same time that Múgica's candidacy was proposed, in summer 1938, a manifesto appeared in Guadalajara proposing General Manuel Avila Camacho, the Secretary of Defense, as a presidential candidate. Signed by officials of the Comité Central Pro Avila Camacho and of various political groups, as well as the Jalisco delegation of the National Peasant League Ursulo Galván, the manifesto praised President Cárdenas but at the same time condemned "pseudo revolutionary elements," including demagogic leaders who "misled" the laborers and peasants in "irresponsible strikes and attacks on small property," and called for the unity of all sectors of the population with workers and peasants, with a concentration on production rather than on political maneuvers. General Avila Camcho, Secretary of Defense and close collaborator of the Cárdenas government, was the appropriate choice to lead the nation along the path of well-being and prosperity (Daniels, 1938b: enclosure 2).

As Secretary of Defense under Cárdenas, Manuel Avila Camacho had been instrumental in the modernization of the Mexican army, particularly through securing new weapons from the U.S., and had completed a program to increase army salaries and social security benefits. The military was an important element in the promotion of his candidacy. His reputation as an amiable, mild-mannered individual who had loyally served the Cárdenas government facilitated his presentation as a candidate of conciliation and "national unity." But the nature of his support indicated conservative tendencies. His brother, Maximino Avila Camacho, as governor of Puebla had clashed with the labor and peasant movements on various occasions and was a close associate of William Jenkins, whose spectacular and not altogether legal acquisition of wealth he had consistently supported.[11] It was at a banquet given by Maximino Avila Camacho in December 1938, to which state governors and conservative elements among the national senators and the military had been invited, that the candidacy of Manuel Avila Camacho was officially proposed.

Both Múgica's radical perspective and his reputation for uncompromising honesty had won him many enemies within the ranks of the party and the government, including opportunists among the Cárdenas faction, who felt that as president Múgica would end their privileges and the use of the government for self-enrichment. Although Múgica's candidacy was supported by certain peasant groups as well as by sectors of the teachers and of the state bureaucracy, his support for Trotsky had alienated the CTM and the Communist party leadership, eliminating the possibility of a strong base of support among the organized left.

State governors and conservative groups within the PRM had already united against this candidacy several months prior to the official announcement for Avila Camacho. Among governors who collaborated in efforts to defeat Múgica and to promote the candidacy of Avila Camacho were Marte Gómez of Tamaulipas, Rojo

---

[11] Jenkins was the ex-consul of Puebla who took over the Atencingo sugar holdings as well as other sugar properties when their owners defaulted on loans he had made to them after the revolution. He was supported by Governor Avila Camacho in his efforts to have the workers on his estates receive the expropriated holdings rather than the villagers. He also became owner of two chains of movie houses which operated a total of 400 houses, and established a virtual monopoly over cinema, first in Puebla, and subsequently throughout the country. In this and other projects he was also assisted by Maximino Avila Camacho. He and another close associate of Avila Camacho, Espinosa Iglesias, later took over the Banco de Comercio, one of the most important banks in the country (Ronfeldt, 1973: 19; Archivo de Recortes: "Wm. O. Jenkins").

Gómez in Hidalgo, Wenieslao Labra of the state of Mexico, Miguel Alemán of Veracruz, and Alberto Salinas in Nuevo León. Most of these were friends of Portes Gil, who as head of the PNR had been opposed by Múgica in the early years of the Cárdenas government and who was apparently responsible for uniting state governors, senators and deputies, and agrarians within the PNR around the candidacy of Avila Camacho.[12] By November 1938, the majority of the senators were supporters of Avila Camacho, and declared themselves openly in favor on January 12, 1939. In the following months declarations in favor of Avila Camacho came from a group of high-ranking military officers and various state agrarian leagues, labor federations, and ejidal commissions.

Although the majority of senators, governors, and important sectors of the military were against him, Múgica thought he had the support of Cárdenas and of the CTM and CNC bureaucracies when he formally announced his candidacy on January 20, 1939. But Cárdenas had remained aloof from the pre-election maneuvers, his only intervention consisting of warnings against electoral "futurism"—warnings which were interpreted as implicit support for Múgica and which were generally unheeded. According to a subsequent interpretation of events by Múgica supporters, Cárdenas' refusal to designate his successor had led to panic among local government, union, and peasant bureaucracies, who quickly rallied to Avila Camacho. At the end of February, conventions of the CTM and the CNC endorsed Avila Camacho as presidential candidate. Although the official PRM nomination would not take place until the party congress nine months later, with support from

---

[12] On Portes Gil's support for Avila Camacho, see the interview with Marte Gómez in Wilkie and Wilkie, 1969: 120, 132. It will be remembered that Portes Gil had a similar role—with a similar coalition—in promoting the candidacy of Cárdenas in 1933. Many of the governors of this group were indebted to Portes Gil, who has been accused of using his former position as head of the PNR to push his favorites, such as Miguel Alemán, who allegedly "won" the election to become governor of Veracruz with 7,134 votes to 22,299 for his opponent (Weyl and Weyl, 1939: 344). Múgica apparently also felt that political activity by Portes Gil had been partly responsible for causing the early resignations of the candidates from their political posts and thus weakening his electoral chances (Daniels, 1939a).

Athough there were other candidates for the PRM nomination, Múgica and Avila Camacho were the most important. Detailed analyses of the 1940 elections can be found in Michaels 1971, Raby 1972, Contreras 1977, and Medina 1978.

On the Múgica candidacy, see De María y Campos, 1939: 351, 356-359. Ongoing coverage of events from the CTM perspective may be found in the issues of *Mexican Labor News*, especially January through March 1939.

the major confederations of the labor and peasant sectors, as well as the military, the majority of state governors, and a significant proportion of senators and deputies, Avila Camacho was candidate in all but name.

The action by the CTM and CNC conventions eliminated any illusions regarding the democratic functioning of the new revolutionary party, as the candidacy of Avila Camacho was virtually imposed by the CTM and CNC leadership on their respective members. In the case of the labor confederation, rank and file membership had been instructed not to discuss the pre-candidates—presumably following the line of Cárdenas against electoral "futurism" but at the same time foreclosing the possibility of membership involvement in the selection of the party candidate. But the imposition of the Avila Camacho candidacy by the CTM and the CNC leadership did not go unprotested by the rank and file. Two members of the executive committee, several state peasant leagues, and 3,500 agrarian communities refused to join the CNC endorsement, and several labor organizations, including those of electricians, railroad workers, and petroleum workers, had not sent delegates to the CTM congress. On March 27, dissident CTM unions published a manifesto which called for a repudiation of the CTM leadership which had imposed the candidacy of Avila Camacho behind the backs of the unions, and for a national congress to elect a new national executive committee. The CTM responded by declaring the dissident unions "non-existent." In its state congress, the Federation of Workers of the State of Michoacán voted to repudiate the national CTM leadership.[13] The Communist party also lost militants due to its tactics with respect to the presidential succession.

Múgica campaigned independently for the PRM nomination, not with the expectation of winning it but with the hope of maintaining a strong, influential minority within the party. However, his campaign was obstructed by local government, labor, and ejidal officials who were in a position to take reprisals against peasants and workers who failed to support Avila Camacho.[14] In July

[13] In the state of Campeche, where a strong organization for Múgica had been developed by rural teachers and union leaders, the decision of the CTM to support Avila Camacho brought numerous defections, which undoubtedly also occurred in other parts of the country (Raby, 1972: 50-51).

[14] Among the tactics to obstruct Múgica's candidacy were threats by local government officials against would-be Múgica supporters. In Cuernavaca, local offi-

1939 Múgica withdrew from the race, denouncing the obstructions to meaningful elections. Subsequently, in November 1939 Manuel Avila Camacho became the official candidate of the PRM.

Although Cárdenas did not have a direct role in the selection of Avila Camacho as PRM candidate, it constituted a natural continuation of efforts by Cárdenas and other progressives to conciliate conservative groups in a period of economic and political pressures. The opposition to Múgica by powerful factions within the government, especially the military (and even fear of a right-wing military coup if a candidate acceptable to the military were not nominated), and probably relief that such antagonistic factions within the state as the military and labor bureaucracy could unite around a single candidate, were undoubtedly overriding factors in Cárdenas' failure openly to support Múgica and his eventual endorsement of Avila Camacho as the candidate of "national unity."

Lombardo Toledano justified the selection of Avila Camacho (whom he dissociated with the openly anti-labor policies of his brother) on the grounds that the new six-year plan—which labor would help to draft—would set the direction of the new government; all that was needed was a "good administrator." The growth of fascism and the imminence of war in Europe had also resulted in an ideological shift on the part of the government and of labor leadership from anti-imperialism to the unity of democratic forces against fascism. Many undoubtedly saw the projected Avila Camacho administration as an "interim" government during the international crisis: Avila Camacho would probably not initiate new reforms but would "consolidate" existing ones or at least leave them intact, and the progressive work of the Cárdenas government could be resumed once the crisis was past.

The creation of the PRM had represented the expansion of the progressive alliance to include conservative groups and its institutionalization under the domination of the state. As the inclusion of organized sectors of labor and the peasantry in the party structure had eliminated the bases for effective leftist opposition outside this alliance, the nomination of Avila Camacho indicated the neutralization of progressive elements within it. In effect, its character had been changed to a vertical alliance in which the conservative faction was now dominant.

---

cials threatened ejiditarios with expulsion if they did not participate in the Avila Camacho campaign (North and Raby, 1977: 54).

THE RIGHT-WING OFFENSIVE: THE ALMAZÁN CANDIDACY

The selection of Avila Camacho as PRM candidate avoided the feared split of the military with the government and forced a unity of sorts on the various sectors of the party, but did not have the desired effect of unifying the nation. Opposition to the Cárdenas administration increased during its last two years, taking various forms, including the formation of anti-government groups by old revolutionary generals; the growth of the Sinarquista movement among the peasants of western Mexico; the establishment of the conservative, pro-Catholic Partido de Acción Nacional (PAN); and, finally, the emergence or re-emergence of fascist groups, aided and promoted by German agents and members of the Spanish Falange in Mexico, which added an international dimension to the right-wing offensive.

The National Action Party (PAN) was formed in 1939 at the instigation of Manuel Gómez Morín and attracted conservative professionals, intellectuals, merchants and industrialists (including the Garza Sada interests in Monterrey), as well as important elements of the Spanish colony in Mexico, chiefly professionals and businessmen. Its immediate cause was opposition to the policy of Cárdenas in general and the proposed reform of Article 3, for socialist education, in particular (Loaeza, 1974: 357, 365). Its program was pro-Church, pro-Hispanidad (rejecting the emphasis on Mexico's Indian heritage which had been part of the ideology of the Mexican revolution and which received particular emphasis during the Cárdenas administration), hierarchal, and authoritarian.

The resurgence of the fascist movements (such as the gold shirts) in the last two years of the Cárdenas administration was undoubtedly facilitated by German agents and by members of the Spanish Falange in Mexico. Fascist groups were able to take advantage of strong anti-U.S. and anti-British sentiment that had resulted from the boycott of Mexican petroleum, particularly since it had been the Axis countries, Germany, Italy, and Japan, which provided markets when the allied powers refused to purchase it. Several U.S. consulates reported strong pro-German sentiments among various groups and in periodicals in their regions (Eaton, 1940). When the German agents were expelled from Mexico, fascist movements continued to operate through the Falange, and when the Cárdenas government dissolved the Falange and expelled its leaders, they went underground and operated through Mexican front organizations. These groups were able to cause various disruptions, including anti-Jewish riots in Mexico City in 1939, and undoubtedly had a role in the virulent anti-Semitism which characterized certain elements of the right-wing press in those years (for example, several articles in *El Hombre Libre* in 1938 on "El Peligro Judio") (26 August 1938, 14 September 1938). But the full impact of their activities on the general population is not clear, nor is the nature of support by fascist organizations to the PAN and the Union Sinarquista apparent.[15]

For the government, the most immediate threat to national unity and stability was the appearance, in May 1939, of an opposition candidate, General Juan Andréu Almazán, who within six months attracted support from all sectors of the population. Almazán had a revolutionary career which was at best ambiguous, having at various times supported Madero, Zapata, and the counter-revolutionary government of Victoriano Huerta. Subsequently he had spent several years as a military chief in Nuevo León, where he became one of the "millionaires of the revolution," his wealth originating from control of railroad, mining, petroleum, and coal concessions in the zone and subsequently expanded through real estate operations and control of construction companies which received government contracts. He had also endeared himself to Monterrey businessmen by keeping the zone relatively free of strikes. Almazán supported the nomination of Cárdenas in 1933, partly due to existing ties of friendship and partly as a result of his opposition to Calles, and continued to support Cárdenas through the confrontation with Calles in 1935 and the Cedillo rebellion in 1938 (Michaels, 1971: 25-26; Medina, 1978: 98-100). During the pre-election campaign Almazán did not oppose Cárdenas directly and his proved loyalty to Cárdenas in the past undoubtedly drew adherents among those who supported Cárdenas personally but had

[15] Kirk claims that both were controlled by the Spanish Falange, and the Falange undoubtedly provided support to PAN (whether or not it controlled it), given the links of both with the Spanish colony in Mexico (Kirk, 1942: 235-236, 285-286). Mario Gill also suggests that the Sinarquista movement as well as the Partido Revolucionario de Unificación Nacional (which supported the Almazán candidacy) and other parties and organizations were linked with Japanese, Italian, Nazi, and Falangist agents (Raby, 1972: 57). See also Weyl and Weyl, 1939: 359-361, 369.

In any event, although in 1939 the Cárdenas government deported Falange leaders for conspiring against the government, it did not appear to be particularly concerned about the fascist movement, feeling that it was under control (Boal, 1939b).

been alienated by certain individuals and influences connected with this government (Kirk, 1942: 243).

As presidential candidate, Almazán received financial support from northern industrialists and businessmen, especially from Monterrey; he was also supported by Callistas, among them the former CROM leader Luis Morones and by former revolutionary generals, and was officially endorsed by the new National Action Party (PAN). But at the same time Almazán attracted former Múgica supporters, including the sons of Emiliano Zapata, and the muralist Diego Rivera, who shifted his support to Almazán after an unsuccessful attempt to persuade Múgica to form an opposition party. In addition, substantial sectors of the working class—particularly the industrial unions—fed up with the authoritarian and corrupt practices of the CTM bureaucracy and disillusioned with the conservative shift in government policy, joined the Almazán campaign. In many respects their allegiance to his campaign represented a continuation, however misguided, of the aborted struggle against the CTM leadership, and they hoped to utilize the Almazán movement to strengthen the democracy and the independence of the unions. An important group of railroad workers (although not a majority) formed a Partido Central Ferrocarrilero pro Almazán, in opposition to "demogogues who trafficked with the votes of men whose opinion they had not consulted." Almazán support committees were also formed among mine, electrical, and streetcar workers; groups within the union of state workers; a faction of the teachers' union (which split in 1939); even some peasants and ejiditarios supported Almazán.[16]

The approach of the two candidates to issues was remarkably similar, in part because Almazán had expanded his program to appeal to the working class and to the peasantry, whereas that of Avila Camacho was modified to attract members of the bourgeoisie. Both campaigns emphasized unity and order, and with respect to capital-labor relations, both campaigned in favor of class har-

[16] For example, the new ejiditarios of the Atencingo sugar estates, under the domination of the sugar refinery management, which was still controlled by Jenkins, were attracted to Almazán's advocacy of individual land holdings. The absence of an effective opposition to the left of the dominant labor federation had also led to workers joining right-wing organizations. Thus the Bloque Revolucionario Magisterial (the Bloc of Revolutionary Teachers) which broke with the CTM-dominated union, ended by joining a right-wing political group due to the absence of effective and independent leftist leadership (*Clave*, Feb. 1939: 46; April 1939: 59).

mony. On the issue of the ejido vs. the small property holding, both supported the latter, advocating that the ejiditarios be given individual titles to their plots. Both approved foreign capital investment, with protection for Mexican capital, and, with respect to the war in Europe, both promoted western hemispheric solidarity and support to the allies. Both were pro-Catholic (a departure from the strong anti-clerical position of previous presidential candidates), but Almazán was able to go further on this issue, condemning the new socialist education law. In fact, Almazán had the advantage of being able to attack the existing government, taking an anti-communist line and condemning the six-year plan as a copy of the Russian model (Michaels, 1971: 27-42). Above all, he was able to take advantage of the strong sense of malaise and antagonism caused by labor mobilization and the instability inherent in the Cárdenas reform program, as well as of the generalized disgust against government authoritarianism and corruption at various levels.[17]

Business groups, national and foreign, supported both candidates. According to William B. Richardson, manager of the National City Bank in Mexico, either candidate would be an improvement, and the majority of businessmen, industrialists, and well-informed people felt that a business revival could be expected with the new government (Bursley, 1940b, and enclosure). Luis Legorreta of the Banco Nacional assured U.S. government officials that whether Avila Camacho or Almazán was elected, conditions for foreign investors would improve—including probably change in the regulation of the labor law, with longer contract periods and the elimination of the exclusion clause. Legorreta himself indicated a preference for Avila Camacho, noting that in either case there would be a turn to the right, but with Almazán it would probably be too rapid and lead to internal instability (Bursley, 1940a). The U.S. government apparently also favored Avila Camacho, presumably for similar reasons: fear that the institutional stability which had been gradually restored following the revolution might be jeopardized by an Almazán victory.

Avila Camacho supporters succeeded in obtaining financial aid from U.S. companies in Mexico: the Hearst interests contributed

---

[17] Although Cárdenas had spoken strongly against corruption in government, apparently there was as much corruption during his administration as in those which preceded (and followed) it, in some cases involving his close associates (Michaels, 1970: 73-74).

an amount estimated at $10,000 in return for a promise not to apply the agrarian reform to the Hacienda Barbicora, part of the Hearst estates (Blocker, 1939b).[18] American companies also supported the Almazán campaign; a Pro-Almazán Organization of American Citizens and Companies was formed to elicit contributions (Boyle, 1940). Among Mexican businessmen, Almazán supporters included those most committed to non-intervention by the state, including the businessmen of Monterrey, those linked to PAN, and (within the government) Luis Montes de Oca, who had offered his resignation as director of the Banco de México in order to work in the Almazán campaign.[19]

With the selection of Avila Camacho and Almazán as candidates in the 1940 presidential election, the axis of conflict within Mexican society shifted from polarization based on class antagonisms to a struggle between two vertical coalitions, each dominated by conservative factions. The basic class cleavages were obscured, and the issues dividing the two groups were not ideological questions, but the nature of their relation to the Mexican state.

Almazán supporters were united by their opposition to the state, although for widely divergent reasons. Aside from landowners and foreign interests opposed to the agrarian and nationalist policies of the Cárdenas administration, conservative Mexican businessmen feared and distrusted state control over property and its intervention in the economy, and resented its support for labor and the peasantry during the Cárdenas administration. At the same time, as indicated above, Almazán drew support from a large number of industrial workers and peasants who opposed the anti-democratic practices which characterized the party, labor, and peasant bureaucracies and resented the imposition of the Avila Camacho candidacy. Working-class supporters of Almazán tended to be predominantly from the stronger industry unions, less dependent upon the government or upon the labor confederation for success in labor conflicts. At least part of Almazán's support came from gen-

[18] This was apparently maneuvered by Joe Navarro, a lobbyist for the Hearst interests in Mexico who was also close to the PRM and, according to the U.S. consul in Juarez, "entirely too sympathetic toward the Avila Camacho group to be a representative of an American company." Forty thousand hectares of the hacienda had already been provisionally granted; with the Hearst contribution, provisional grants were ordered cancelled (Blocker, 1939a).

[19] The resignation was not accepted until after the election; apparently Montes de Oca served as financial director of the Almazán campaign while still a member of the Cárdenas administration.

uinely progressive groups disoriented by Múgica's withdrawal from the race and seeing Almazán as the only viable alternative.

The Avila Camacho following among workers and peasants was to a large extent a controlled constituency under the domination of the party, labor, and peasant bureaucracy. But it also included peasants who had received land or hoped to receive land, and sectors of the working class—many of recent rural origins—whose gains in wages and other benefits were directly attributable to support from the CTM and to the government. Also aligned with Avila Camacho were business groups who benefited from government contracts or from their linkages with the state (which might account for the preference expressed by Luis Legorreta of the Banco Nacional) as well as those who had been recruited into the private sector from positions within the government and the military. The Avila Camacho constituency probably also included the new groups of industrialists who were not directly tied to the state but who had benefited from state promotion of industry.

Most important was the state-party-labor-peasant bureaucracy, which in a sense was fighting for its life. The Almazán candidacy constituted a direct attack on the corporate party structure; an Almazán victory would probably destroy it, since the hierarchy of domination and clientelism on which it was based depended on access to state power. An Almazán victory would also lead to a more or less thorough dismantling of the substantial reforms of the Cárdenas regime, particularly in the agrarian sector. Thus progressive as well as opportunistic elements within the state (and these were not always distinct individuals) had reason to oppose Almazán. For the progressive groups, the state represented the achievements of the revolution, however limited, as well as its future promise.

It is presumably for these reasons that the promises made by Cárdenas of a democratic election were not fulfilled. The campaign was bitterly contested, and on election day polling places became arenas for pitched battles between supporters of the two candidates, leaving several persons dead and many wounded. Where supporters of one candidate obtained control of the ballot box, supporters of the opposition candidate were not permitted to vote (Kirk, 1942: 240 f).[20] The official returns gave 2,476,641 to Avila

---

[20] Cárdenas himself was unable to vote for his successor because his polling place had been closed (Michaels, 1971: 43).

Camacho and 151,101 to Almazán—a result which was scarcely credible, given the enthusiastic crowds which had turned out spontaneously for Almazán during his election campaign. Many observers believed that Almazán would have won a fair election, and he and his supporters threatened armed struggle to defend his real victory at the polls. But Almazán was apparently discouraged by the refusal of the U.S. State Department to offer any support, and by the fact that he did, after all, have much to lose.[21]

THE END OF THE PROGRESSIVE ALLIANCE

With the Avila Camacho victory, the institutional continuity of the Mexican state and its subsequent central role in Mexico's economic development were assured. But it was also a victory for the conservative forces of Mexican society. In the last months before Avila Camacho took office, business groups who had supported Almazán were reassured that Avila Camacho's government would not constitute a continuation of the Cárdenas administration. Avila Camacho's inaugural address emphasized the necessity for national unity and for increased production. The ejidal sector, focus of the agrarian reform under Cárdenas, was not mentioned, and promises of guarantees to small holders, implemented in the first months of the government, indicated that the private agrarian sector would

[21] In July 1940, shortly after the elections, U.S. Embassy official Pierre Boals had lunch with Almazán supporters Manuel Gómez Mórin and Luis Montes de Oca. Montes de Oca raised the question as to whether the United States would provide arms to the Mexican government on credit. According to Boals, Montes de Oca stated: "Of course we realize that the United States cannot and should not take any part in Mexican politics. Nevertheless, it is of primary importance to the United States to have friendly and solid governments in the Latin American countries at a time like this. Will it be constructive to this purpose for the United States to have in Mexico a government which is imposed against the will of the great majority of the people? . . . Our problem is whether the United States will continue to support the Mexican government with arms and credit if a serious revolt occurs. If revolutionists should control Nuevo Laredo and Monterrey, would that be a basis for recognizing their belligerancy?" Boals's response was noncommittal, to the effect that Mexican politics was for Mexicans to decide (Bursley, 1940c). In effect, the Almazanistas received no assurance that the U.S. would not intervene on behalf of the Mexican government in the event of an armed uprising. Thus the U.S. government manifested its support for the continuity of the post-revolutionary Mexican state—which was again affirmed by the presence of Henry Wallace, U.S. Vice President, at the inauguration of Avila Camacho.

receive preferential treatment (Mexico, Cámara de Diputados, 1966, IV: 149-152).

In December, the executive power to expropriate private property in the national interest (according to the Expropriation Law of September 1936) was rescinded (BNM, 1934-41, Dec. 1940: 3-4). A Supreme Court decision in 1941 made it relatively easy for employers to dismiss workers after paying a stipulated amount (Wyeth, 1945: 287-288). The Avila Camacho government also marked the beginning of a steady decline in real wages, from 8.96 pesos daily in 1940 to 4.79 pesos in 1951 (urban wages at constant prices); it was 1962 before they again reached their 1940 level (King, 1970: 26).

Many of those conservative groups which had supported Almazán became reconciled to the Avila Camacho government as its first initiatives demonstrated its sympathy with private enterprise. In effect, those forces directly or indirectly aligned with dominant class interests again controlled the state, with the difference that the state itself had been strengthened through its control of the government party and thus of the working class and peasantry, and through the "revolutionary legitimacy" given the state by the Cárdenas government. At the same time, the incorporation of the peasantry and the working class into the authoritarian structures of the government party and its constituent organizations had deprived these sectors of a base from which effectively to pressure the government.

Under Avila Camacho, the collaboration of Mexican government and business with foreign capital was continued and expanded. In the last year of the Cárdenas administration, the U.S. State Department and the Mexican government reached agreement on a variety of projects for military cooperation during the war. Also during this period, Mexican financial groups approached U.S. government and business circles with projects for increased foreign investment in Mexico, either through joint private investment with Mexican business or through U.S. government loans. The settlement of payment of compensation to the petroleum companies in 1942 laid the basis for renewed U.S. investment in Mexico; during the war years the Mexican-American Economic Commission was formed and facilitated U.S. export of products needed by Mexican industry. Mexico began to receive loans from Eximbank for highway construction as well as foreign assistance for the construction of a new steel plant, Altos Hornos, which was financed partly by Nacional Financiera and subsequently came under government control. The Celanese Corporation of America collaborated with the Banco Nacional and Nacional Financiera in the establishment of two celanese plants in Mexico. These projects—and foreign capital assistance in general—were limited during this period, but they were indicative of the three-way collaboration between state financial institutions, Mexican private capitalists, and foreign capital, which has come to characterize the capital-intensive sector of the Mexican economy (Suárez, 1977: 126-131; Clash, 1972: 113-114, 122-123; *Journal of Commerce*, 1940: 26).

Contrary to the hopes of progressive elements in the Cárdenas government, Avila Camacho was succeeded not by a progressive regime but by the most conservative and openly pro-business administration that Mexico had known since the revolution. Headed by Miguel Alemán, who had been governor of the state of Veracruz during the Cárdenas administration, the new regime reversed certain of the more progressive reforms of the Cárdenas period and at the same time reinforced the authoritarian structures for state control of labor established at that time. The collective ejidos had suffered from neglect under Avila Camacho; with Alemán's policy of cutting off credit to ejidos which were not farmed individually, they all but disappeared. The practice of *charrismo*—the replacement of dissident, democratically elected union leaders by those imposed by the regime—became institutionalized. Assassination became an accepted method of eliminating independent peasant leaders. At the same time, the process of "recruitment" from the state to the private sector through legal and extra-legal means received new impetus (Hewitt de Alcántara, 1974: 172-176; Hansen, 1974: 115-118, 167).

CONCLUSIONS

The inclusion of conservative elements within the PRM and the selection of Avila Camacho as PRM candidate for the presidency in 1949 in effect ended the progressive alliance as the basis of the limited structural autonomy of the state in relation to dominant classes under Cárdenas. While factions within the state took the initiative in shifting the nature of the basic alliance supporting the government, these changes can largely be explained by pressures

from dominant class segments, external and internal, and their allies within the state, in the absence of sufficient countervailing
pressures from subordinate classes.

The state had been politically strengthened through the incorporation of the working class and peasantry within the government party and the legitimacy it received through the reforms and
structural changes under Cárdenas. In the coming decades its economic power would be strengthened through its increased control
over economic resources in such vital sectors as petroleum, mining, transportation, communications, steel, and other basic industries. Within the context of an economic structure in which it is
linked—through a variety of complex financial and organizational
arrangements—to foreign capital and the dominant segment of the
national bourgeoisie, the state exercises a certain degree of instrumental autonomy which has to some extent enabled it to direct
and channel private capital investment, dictate conditions to foreign capital, and even on occasion reinforce its legitimacy through
response to demands and needs of subordinate groups and classes.
But its linkages to capital and its cooptation and repression of subordinate classes preclude the possibility of structural autonomy based
on an "independent" state or a new "progressive" alliance with
urban and rural workers.

Nine ‖ State Autonomy: A Reconsideration

 What insight does the specific experience of Mexico under Cárdenas provide into the general theoretical issue of state autonomy within a peripheral capitalist country? Before we return to this question, it will be helpful to review and analyze the specific conditions favoring and limiting state autonomy in the Mexican case. What were the structural options and constraints (internal and external) which confronted the new Mexican state following the revolution? How did the interaction between the state, internal social classes, and foreign interests shape the new social order? What conditions account for the emergence of a relatively autonomous state, based on a coalition between progressive factions within the state and mobilized sectors of the peasantry and working class in the 1930's? What were the achievements of this alliance, and how were these limited by the class structure within which it operated? And why was the progressive thrust of this alliance arrested during the Cárdenas administration and reversed in subsequent regimes?

CÁRDENAS AND THE LIMITS TO STATE AUTONOMY IN MEXICO

Post-Revolutionary Mexico: Structural Constraints and Latent Alliances. By the end of the Mexican revolution, the previous Porfirian state bureaucracy had been destroyed and the Porfirian bourgeoisie considerably weakened, leaving a power vacuum to be filled by the new revolutionary leadership. The constitution drafted in 1917 established the basis for an interventionist and implicitly autonomous state, above classes, which would eliminate monopolies, establish Mexican sovereignty over its natural resources, provide the peasantry with access to land, and assure the rights of labor. But the new leadership acted within specific constraints—among them continued foreign control of substantial sectors of the economy; increasing U.S. hegemony in relation to other foreign powers in Mexico; the limited and uneven development of productive forces in Mexico, which limited the resources of the new state; demands by sectors of the population mobilized through the revolution; and factionalism and divisions within the revolutionary leadership itself.

Within the next fifteen years, a powerful governing group—the Sonoran dynasty—emerged and achieved the centralization of state power, eliminating regional military and political power bases; and established an institutional framework for state direction of the economy. By the end of the 1920's the group of revolutionary leaders who controlled the state apparatus achieved a new modus vivendi with foreign, especially U.S., capital, and remnants of the Porfirian bourgeoisie—its ranks replenished through recruitment of revolutionary generals and government officials. This new alliance also succeeded in deflecting the mobilization of rural and urban groups through partial reforms and through the cooptation or repression of alternative organizations to those controlled by the central government. At the local level, regional generals, state governors, and other local officials supported efforts of landowners, foreign companies, and Mexican businessmen to control the peasantry and the working class in their particular regions, in some cases involving the cooptation of certain peasant and labor leaders. Nevertheless, the failure to respond adequately to peasant demands for land postponed rather than solved the problem, and the continuing conflict between peasant and landlord was to some extent reproduced within the state, where the "agrarians" advocating a radical restructuring of rural Mexico confronted the "veterans," who defended the large landowners in the name of agricultural productivity and efficiency.

Also during the 1920's, alliances had been formed among sectors of the mobilized peasantry, groups within the working class, and progressive elements within the state, including certain state governors and groups within the official party and government bureaucracy. Working-class organizations, particularly those led by members of the Communist party, supported the formation of peasant leagues in some localities. Rural schoolteachers supported efforts of peasant villagers to have the agrarian reform implemented. In some states, progressive governors promoted labor and peasant organizations and carried out land-distribution programs. But these efforts were generally fragmented and limited, due in part to the isolation of the groups involved, in part to local opposition, and in part to deliberate efforts of the federal government to control peasant and working-class movements (e.g., through control of the major labor confederation and efforts of the government party, the PNR, to take over the peasant leagues).

The lines between "progressive" and "conservative" forces and alliances were also considerably obscured by such factors as the formation of cliques within the government, clientele relations, personal loyalties which crossed ideological lines, corruption and opportunism at various levels, and shifting orientations on the part of many initially progressive individuals whose incorporation into the economically privileged groups pushed them toward defense of the status quo.

Emergence of the Progressive Alliance. Several factors—the increased (though still fragmented) mobilization of peasants and workers due to frustration at the detention of agrarian reform and dislocations resulting from the depression, and a coalescence of groups within the state opposed to the dominant clique—enabled progressive state factions to take control of the government party and ultimately, through the promulgation of a six-year plan and the presidential candidacy of Lázaro Cárdenas, of the government. The new administration formed an alliance with the mobilized peasants and workers who would constitute a new basis for state autonomy and for a concerted attack on the remaining institutions of the old order.

With the election of Cárdenas in 1934 and the subsequent defeat of the formerly powerful Calles clique within the state in June 1935, elements of the progressive alliance, which had previously been isolated and fragmented, strengthened and consolidated their position. In coalition with the federal government, the labor movement was able to obtain immediate concessions from capital and organizational cohesion which, it was presumed, would strengthen it for future confrontations. With the moral and economic support of the federal government, the organized peasants could successfully pressure for the application of agrarian reform and its implementation against the obstacles created by landlords, local government officials, inept or corrupt officials of the state credit banks, and alliances among these groups. There was a reciprocal relationship between the mobilization of the workers and the peasants and the action of the state: the emergence of the Cárdenas government and its victory over the Calles forces were in part a consequence of mobilization which Cárdenas in turn encouraged to the point that the government (as Cárdenas himself

put it) would be *forced* to respond. Thus peasant and worker mobilization was both cause and justification of the radicalization of
the government program. It was also a means of controlling corruption and opportunism within the state bureaucracy itself.

In alliance with the peasants and the working class, the government was able to control capital by establishing limits within which
it could operate: constraining the exploitation of industrial labor
by achieving a "balance" between the "factors of production";
limiting the size of agrarian estates through the agrarian reform;
expropriating the properties of foreign-owned petroleum companies when these refused to abide by Mexican laws—an important
first step in the elimination of the export enclave; and establishing
state control over key sectors of the economy, thereby increasing
its ability to direct economic development. These achievements
constituted structural changes with long-term implications for
Mexico's social and economic development. (One indication of
their importance is the fact that export enclave dependence and
traditional forms of rural exploitation have endured until the 1960's
in countries like Chile and Peru.)

Contradictions of the "Autonomous" State. At the same time, state
support to the process of capital accumulation continued during
the Cárdenas administration, strengthening the dominant class.
Previous post-revolutionary governments, often with the collaboration of private sector interests, had been responsible for the
reconstruction of the Mexican financial system, including legislation regulating relations between the public and private financial
sectors, and particularly between the government, the central bank,
and the private banks; the establishment of the major official banks;
government support for the creation of private banks; efforts to
create a capital market; and the nationalization of banking institutions. Continuity during the Cárdenas administration was indicated in the special regulation for bank employees which in effect
removed them from the sphere of class conflict and "labor agitation"; the establishment of the Foreign Trade Bank and other official banks; investment by official banks in private investment banks
and provincial (agricultural) banks; the insurance law of 1935, which
freed insurance reserve funds for investment; and the purchase of
securities of private firms by the government development bank,
Nacional Financiera.

The Cárdenas government also continued support to the sugar

industry, initiated by previous administrations, including central bank support for financing and the re-establishment of the sugar cartel in a slightly different form; it supported the tourist industry, indicated by the completion of the Nuevo Laredo-Mexico City highway, the sale of road bonds, and the establishment of a mortgage bank to support hotel construction; and it introduced a series of tax measures generally oriented to the encouragement of industry.

Government policy with respect to private capital was apparently oriented by a belief that the state could control and direct capitalism so as to eliminate its worst abuses and to meet the needs of the whole society—an assumption which was not illogical, given the crisis of world capitalism and the incipient stage of capitalist development in Mexico. But the process of capitalist development strengthened the dominant class as well as the links of certain sectors within the state with that class. This is particularly notable in the financial agencies of the state which were most closely linked with private national and foreign capital. Thus government legislation and support for the private financial sector had facilitated the establishment of private banks and insurance companies, many of which were quite profitable, but during this period they failed to have the desired effect of channeling financial resources to productive investment. Certain private groups were able to establish their own financial networks, however, largely through the formation of more or less structured associations of shareholders of industrial, financial, and commercial firms. These informal capital markets constituted a factor in capital concentration to the extent that they excluded firms outside these networks.

There was also continuity between the earlier post-revolutionary governments and that of Cárdenas in their relations with dominant capitalist countries, notably the United States. While the depression had weakened the interventionist tendencies of these states, economic ties continued to be important, including foreign domination of Mexico's export sector and utilities and dependence on U.S. markets and exports. Partly as a consequence of Mexico's dependence on foreign and especially on U.S. capital, prior administrations had established or reinforced contacts with specific government officials and business sectors in the U.S. This was evident in the contacts between officials of the Mexican finance ministry such as Alberto Pani and Luis Montes de Oca, private banking interests in Mexico such as the Legorretas of the Banco

Nacional, financial groups from Morgan Guaranty Trust such as Thomas Lamont of the International Bankers Committee and Dwight Morrow, who became Ambassador to Mexico, and officials of the U.S. Department of the Treasury and Federal Reserve Board. These groups shared an interest in the capitalist development of Mexico and in U.S.-Mexican relations, although for somewhat different reasons: U.S. groups were interested in Mexico as a growing market for U.S. manufactured goods, and Mexican groups were interested in access to U.S. capital and technology, as well as continued access to its markets, particularly for mineral exports. Individuals such as Pani, Legorreta, and Morrow exerted considerable influence on the Calles government.

Both the structural constraints and the informal alliances linking groups in the U.S. and Mexico continued throughout the Cárdenas period. As noted in Chapter Seven, Mexico's economic dependence on mineral exports and the government's dependence on taxes from the U.S. mining companies constituted an obvious constraint on the Cárdenas nationalization program. The U.S. recession of 1937 and the decline in the price of silver had immediate repercussions on Mexico's exports and capacity to import. When structural constraints were insufficient to prevent the petroleum expropriation, the companies retaliated with a petroleum boycott, withdrawal of capital, and various other attempts to undermine the Mexican economy. At the same time, the continuity of informal alliances was indicated by the silver purchase agreement, loan negotiations with the U.S. government, encouragement of U.S. investment in Mexican industry on the part of the Mexican government, and support among the treasury officials of both countries for continued good relations between the U.S. and Mexico.

In short, although the progressive alliance was now dominant, the previously dominant coalition of foreign interests, domestic banking and industrial interests, and certain factions within the state did not disappear. Moreover, certain groups within this alliance, especially the more powerful members of the national bourgeoisie, continued to be strengthened during this period, in part through state initiatives favoring private accumulation. The contradictions inherent in the role of the state were further evident in the fact that certain officials, notably Cárdenas himself, were to some extent involved in both alliances.

At the same time, the alliance between progressive sectors of the government and the mobilized peasantry and working class involved a confrontation with capital—both national and foreign—and its allies at all levels of Mexican society. For these groups, such an alliance suggested that while the state continued to perform the functions of accumulation in the interests of the dominant class, it had abdicated its social control function and was in fact participating in the class struggle on behalf of the subordinate class. This confrontation clarified the underlying cleavages dividing Mexican society and resulted in an intensification of political and economic opposition to the government. Elements in this opposition included investment cutbacks and capital export, the petroleum boycott and an attempted credit and trade blockade, a military revolt (quickly crushed), the mobilization of right-wing and fascist groups such as the Sinarquistas and the Gold Shirts, the formation of opposition groups such as the National Action Party, and increasing political opposition within the government, particularly among those sectors allied with the capitalist class.

Increasing polarization revealed the contradictions of state autonomy based on a progressive alliance within a peripheral capitalist society: either the demands of subordinate groups must be controlled or the economic and ultimately the political base of the state would be undermined. Economic constraints—aside from continued dependence on trade with the U.S.—included government dependence on taxes, among them advance payments by foreign-owned mining companies, and its dependence on loans from private national and foreign sources for continuation of its agrarian program. The political mobilization and increasing cohesiveness of right-wing groups, both within and outside the government, constituted pressures for a discontinuation of reforms. The solution for the government was the incorporation of the labor and peasant organizations into the government-controlled political party—a solution which was also consistent with the concept of the Cárdenas government that the state should control both labor and capital. The working-class and peasant movements were unable to resist incorporation into the government party for the same reason that they were unable to exert pressures on the government to continue its reform program or to oblige it to take a more radical position in confrontation with increasing pressures from the right. As indicated above, the labor movement was small and heterogeneous and the peasantry fragmented; support by government officials, and particularly the Cárdenas government, had been an important factor in their ability to confront the forces and alliances of the opposition. These characteristics and experiences had in turn been factors in the establishment and consolidation of authoritarian institutions within the peasant and labor movements and their linkages with the state. Partly as a result of these conditions, the peasants, the working class, and their leadership were unable to provide an ideological justification for the independence of these movements, in opposition to the ideology of the revolution, claimed by the state, which rationalized their incorporation into the government party. Thus the peasant and labor organizations were led into the party by their leadership, which was also able to control or deflect demands for continued reform.

The government strategy was thus to avoid polarization into horizontal groups through the creation of a vertical alliance based on "national unity"—initially through the creation of the government party which would incorporate workers, peasants, "popular" sectors, and the military, and subsequently through the imposition of a "national unity" candidate for the presidency in 1940, General Manuel Avila Camacho, who would unite both conservative and progressive sectors within the state, their allies in the private sector, and the controlled workers and peasants. The defeat of a progressive government candidate, General Francisco Múgica, whose victory would presumably have meant an effort to continue the Cárdenas reforms and would have been a definite threat to opportunistic and conservative groups within the state, resulted in the disorientation and disillusion of leftist groups in the working class and the peasantry and within the state itself.

Thus the final confrontation was not a class confrontation resulting from polarization but a confrontation between two vertical groups, both dominated by conservative elements. On the one hand, the state, including the government and the military and civil bureaucracy, achieved a certain degree of cohesion around the candidacy of Avila Camacho, supported by business groups linked with the state, and groups controlled through the government party. On the other hand, the opposition candidate, General Juan Andréu Almazán, had attracted a heterogeneous assortment of groups estranged from the government for various reasons—ranging from fascist groups and conservative businessmen adamantly opposed to the Cárdenas administration to sectors of the working class disoriented by the opportunism and corruption of working-class leadership and the government's apparent desertion of its former progressive orientation.

Victory of the Conservative Alliance. Neither Cárdenas nor the progressive elements within the labor and peasant movements fully recognized the implications of the Avila Camacho candidacy and the incorporation of the labor and peasant movements into the government party. The imposition of the Avila Camacho candidacy did not mean simply the victory of a conservative faction within the state, any more than the Cárdenas administration had signified merely an internal victory of progressive groups. In both cases, implicit alliances of these respective factions with groups and classes in the larger society became explicit and consolidated. The progressive coalition of the Cárdenas government with the working class and peasantry was able successfully to confront obstacles to change in the agricultural sector and relations of dependence which none of the partners of this coalition could have done on its own. But other groups within the state, basically concerned with—and in some cases directly benefiting from—the process of capitalist accumulation, continued to be allied with various segments of the dominant class and foreign interests and, with the victory of Avila Camacho, this alliance again became dominant. In fact, it was the state, through the government of Avila Camacho, which actually forged this unity—the actions of the government in its first months reconciling many of the Almazanistas and clearly indicating that the orientation of the previous Cárdenas government had been reversed.

But in contrast to the Cárdenas victory, the victory of Avila Camacho marked not merely a defeat of the progressive alliance but its virtual elimination as an effective force for change. The possibility of an alliance between progressive groups within the state and the working class and the peasantry was foreclosed by the cooptation of the former into the dominant alliance and by the loss of autonomy of the latter. The control of the working-class and peasant movements by their leadership and their incorporation into the state-dominated political party was in fact decisive in enabling the state to control class conflict and thus contributed significantly to the strength of the dominant coalition.

Subsequent Mexican history and the existing structure of Mexican society indicate that the possibility that such an alliance will re-emerge has been precluded. In the 1930's, the state was still sufficiently dynamic for progressive groups within it to respond to peasant and worker mobilization. Since that time, conservative groups within the state have become consolidated, structures uniting the state and dominant class interests at various levels have been considerably strengthened, and progressive groups and individuals brought into positions within the state apparatus have been easily isolated. The state has been limited as an arena for class conflict; in general it functions to repress mobilized groups it cannot coopt. Even if a progressive coalition were possible, the experience of the Cárdenas government has demonstrated the limits of such an alliance as a basis for state autonomy. Any impetus for change must come from outside the state and must ultimately confront the state itself as an integral part of peripheral capitalism in Mexico.

THE LIMITS OF STATE AUTONOMY

What are the implications of the experience of Mexico under Cárdenas for the broader question of state autonomy? Given the limitations of a case-study approach, the findings are not necessarily conclusive. There are further limitations having to do with the nature of the case itself. Mexico in the 1930's was a dependent country with limited resources. While in Chapter One it was indicated that state control of substantial economic resources does not necessarily result in state autonomy, the lack or scarcity of resources obviously places constraints on what a reform-oriented government can do. At the same time, Mexico's economic position, including foreign control of the export sector and dependence on trade with the United States, was an additional constraint on state action, a fact which may limit the possibility of comparing it with states having a more secure or dominant position within the world market. Perhaps more important, the goals of the state were limited in that the Cárdenas government was not seeking to do away with capitalism but to "humanize" it, at the same time eliminating pre-capitalist or "feudal" structures and establishing national control of the economy. These efforts brought it into confrontation with important segments of the dominant class and foreign capital, and there *was* the possibility that the increasing level of polarization in Mexican society might have eventually resulted in a confrontation with the capitalist class as a whole. But such a confrontation was not intended by those who controlled the state apparatus. While socialism may have been considered a desirable long-term goal, neither Cárdenas nor his associates believed it was a realistic possibility for the immediate future.

Despite these limitations, the Mexican case does provide support for more general propositions regarding conditions favoring and limiting state autonomy. Three sets of conditions can be identified which facilitated state autonomy during the Cárdenas period. First, the Mexican experience lends support to the hypothesis suggested in Chapter One that relative state autonomy is facilitated in a situation in which the previous dominant class (including foreign capital) is weakened due to internal or external crisis. In Mexico, the national bourgeoisie had been weakened as a consequence of the Mexican revolution, and international capitalism as a consequence of the depression. The national bourgeoisie had to some extent recovered during the intervening period of the 1920's, but this recovery had been largely with the assistance and under the direction of the Mexican state. The bourgeoisie was still dependent upon state action to insure its position within the Mexican economy, which continued to be largely dominated by foreign capital.

The effect of the depression was temporarily to eliminate the likelihood of certain types of foreign intervention. Subsequently, Mexico and other Latin American countries were also able to take advantage of U.S. anxiety regarding the pending war in Europe to obtain assurances that the U.S. would not intervene militarily in Latin American countries. Thus, while Mexico continued to be economically dependent on the U.S., specific sanctions formerly attached to this dependence (though obviously not all) were removed. The statist solutions to the crisis in the advanced capitalist countries and the model of state-promoted industrialization of the Soviet Union also reinforced the ideological orientation of the Mexican constitution toward state intervention.

Second, state autonomy is facilitated by an alliance of the state with subordinate groups and classes as a means of confronting the dominant class. Elements of this alliance existed in Mexico even in the 1920's when the latent alliance between the state, the national bourgeoisie, and foreign capital was dominant. The "progressive" alliance became increasingly organized and cohesive and, with the victory of the Cárdenas faction and the organized working class over Calles in 1935, became dominant for the next three years. There is little doubt that the support and mobilization of the peasants and the working class were necessary for the reforms and structural changes instituted by the Cárdenas government. What is in question in such a case is whether the state controls these groups and classes or is controlled by them, in which case it ceases to be autonomous and becomes instead the instrument of new class forces. While the organized workers and peasants pushed the government to carry out reforms, these reforms did not go beyond those the more progressive elements within the government were willing to carry out. Within the progressive alliance, the state was dominant and ultimately brought these groups under its control.

A third condition affecting state autonomy is the degree of cohesion and unity within the state itself. While this unity did not exist, in the sense of ideological cohesion, within the Mexican state—as became increasingly apparent in the last years of the Cárdenas administration—the Cárdenas faction was able to obtain dominance within the state with the defeat of Calles and to maintain it for a three-year period. Certain reforms could be imposed against the will of state governors, local officials, and lower level bureaucrats. Failures of implementation at these levels could to some extent be countered through the mobilization of the population involved.

But while relative state autonomy is facilitated by certain conditions, the experience of the Cárdenas administration indicates that such autonomy is limited. What are some of the conditions limiting state autonomy?

First, actual or apparent efforts of those who control the state to challenge existing structures will confront increasing opposition in the form of intervention by the dominant class itself. It has been noted that the bourgeoisie was weakened but not eliminated by the revolution, and that foreign capital (through the U.S. state) abdicated certain forms of intervention, but not all. Thus, groups which felt threatened by the policies of the Cárdenas government could intervene directly or indirectly, individually or collectively, through economic or political forms, against these policies or to prevent them from taking effect. Obvious examples of collective direct intervention included the petroleum boycott as well as other measures taken by oil companies and their governments to sabotage the production and sale of Mexican-controlled petroleum; statements and declarations published by the major business groups;

the formation of rival political movements; and financial and moral support for the Almazán candidacy. These measures obviously varied in importance—the petroleum boycott and the Almazán candidacy being the most significant. Indirect intervention includes individual actions taken by members of the dominant class to protect their own self-interest which, if sufficiently widespread, could result in destabilizing the economy. In the case of Mexico, examples included investment cutbacks and capital exports, attributed to unstable business conditions, and price increases, rationalized on the basis of higher wages and production costs. It goes without saying that such methods could also be part of a deliberate, organized effort to undermine the government or to force it to change its policies.

Intervention is also the ultimate sanction of structural constraints to state autonomy. Such intervention is usually not necessary since the government, recognizing that a challenge to certain structures will evoke a response it cannot cope with, will hesitate to act. Following the petroleum expropriation, for example, mineworkers urged Cárdenas to expropriate the U.S. mining companies. But such a move would have led—even at a minimal level—to the closing of U.S. markets to Mexican minerals, at the time over half of Mexico's exports. Following the petroleum expropriation, expropriation of U.S. mineral properties would undoubtedly also have led to more severe sanctions by the U.S. government and possibly by other segments of U.S. capital (e.g., groups exporting to Mexico). Expropriation of the petroleum companies challenged a powerful but limited segment of foreign capital. Expropriation of the mining companies would have threatened the entire structure of U.S.-Mexican economic relations, and the repercussions would have followed accordingly. In any event, the projected costs to Mexico were too high, and the mining companies were not expropriated.

In short, structural constraints limiting state autonomy are based on direct or indirect power relations, i.e., control by the dominant class (or foreign interest) of the economic resources of the state and society. In the last instance, structural contraints are enforced by the actual or threatened intervention of the relevant interests or class.

Second, one of the most important constraints limiting the autonomy of the state is the relationship of certain state factions and institutions with dominant class interests. In general, the state is characterized by its interpenetration with the social order at various levels and in various forms. During the early post-revolutionary period (the 1920's) two latent alliances emerged: a "conservative" alliance linking groups at all levels of government and within the state apparatus with different segments of the dominant class, and a "progressive" alliance linking certain state officials, governors, and bureaucrats with segments of the working class and of the peasantry. During this period and the succeeding decade, the class conflict which characterized Mexican society was to some extent reproduced within the state. During most of the pre-Cárdenas period, the conservative faction was dominant, but the progressive faction became increasingly important in the early 1930's and achieved dominance with the defeat of Calles in 1935. But, even during the subsequent period, resistance to change occurred within the state itself—for example, resistance to concrete reforms (such as the agrarian reform) at the level of implementation, and the political organization of factions within the state to impose a conservative candidate in 1940. To some extent, class interests are internalized within the state through certain individuals, factions, or agencies. An obvious example is the role of Luis Montes de Oca, director of the Banco de México, in promoting legislation regulating the relations of banks to bank employees in a manner favorable to banking interests. Related to this is the contradiction within a state which of necessity supports the process of capital accumulation while confronting capital as part of a progressive coalition.

Finally, state autonomy based on an alliance with subordinate classes is limited by its internal contradictions. Essentially it involves a form of class conflict which, if not controlled, would mean an increasing polarization of society and ultimately threaten the stability of the state itself. Given this possibility, a crucial element limiting state autonomy is the level of consciousness and cohesion of the subordinate classes. The incorporation of these groups into the Mexican government party prevented the loss of state autonomy in relation to these groups, but it also weakened state autonomy in relation to dominant groups by weakening the progressive alliance on which it was based. The failure of the Mexican rural and urban workers and their leadership to recognize and to define their interests and their differences with the state was a crucial factor in their loss of independence and their inability to effectively counter pressures for containment of reform and structural change.

In short, state autonomy based on an alliance with subordinate classes and groups within a capitalist system is limited by three basic contradictions:

1. The contradiction between the goals of this alliance and the implicit or explicit strength and cohesion of the dominant class, which will intervene to prevent it from carrying out policies to meet these goals.

2. The contradictions within the state, which on the one hand establishes and maintains conditions for private capital accumulation but on the other appears to abdicate its function of social control and to side with subordinate groups and classes in the class struggle. This contradiction is reproduced in the personnel, factions, and institutions of the state which are aligned with different groups and classes of society.

3. The contradiction between the goals of the state, limited to possibilities within the existing socio-economic structure, and those of its allies among subordinate groups, which are, ultimately, not structurally limited. The implication of this contradiction is that it is in the interests of the state to control these groups, while it is in the interests of the latter to maintain their independence. These contradictions never became explicit in the Mexican case, and efforts of the government to incorporate these groups under its control met only limited resistance. The subsequent history of these groups in Mexico suggests that their loss of independence not only lessens their effectiveness in making new demands on the state but also weakens their capacity to defend existing gains.

In suggesting the limits to state autonomy based on an alliance with subordinate groups and classes, the Mexican case also indicates the limits of reformism and the fallacy of efforts to "humanize" capitalism. Given the context of a capitalist system, the state functions to aid the process of private accumulation which strengthens the capacity of the capitalist class to resist policies perceived to be a threat to its interests. Even on rare occasions when progressive state factions, linked to subordinate groups and classes, constitute the dominant group within the state, entrenched alliances between other state factions and dominant classes remain and set limits on what the progressive alliance can accomplish. And, given pressures from dominant groups and their allies within the state, progressive factions within the state will be unwilling to implement goals which will threaten their position or perhaps the state itself. Only an effective counter-pressure by the subordinate groups allied to these factions will enable and in fact force the state to maintain and perhaps expand its progressive orientation.

The above analysis suggests that alliances between progressive state factions and subordinate sectors of society may constitute the basis for reform, but the effectiveness of the state itself as a guarantor for reform is limited. The impetus for lasting structural change must come from outside the state. It is not through an "autonomous" state, but only through the autonomous organization of subordinate groups and classes that a social transformation benefiting these sectors can be brought about.

Appendix A ‖ **Private Banks and Financial Groups: 1932-1941**

 The formation of private banks and financial groups in post-revolutionary Mexico was an important element in the process of capitalist development. It was during the early post-revolutionary period that the major government banks and many of the most important private financial institutions—those which today constitute the nucleus of the major financial groups of Mexico—were formed. This process again reveals the importance of the relationship between the state and the private sector in shaping the development of the Mexican economy.

Of the 23 Mexican financial institutions (commercial, investment, and mortgage banks) which in 1969 had assets of one billion pesos or more, sixteen existed by 1941:

Commercial Banks (Date of Establishment)
Banco Nacional de México (1884)
Banco de Londres y México (1864)
Banco de Comercio (1932)
Banco Mexicano (1932)
Banco de Industria y Comercio, formerly Banco Azucarero (1932)
Banco Internacional (1941)
Banco Comercial Mexicano (1934)

Investment Banks (Financieras)
Crédito Minero y Mercantil (1934)
Financiera Internacional, formerly Cia. Central Financiera (1939)
Financiera Banamex, formerly Crédito Bursatil (1936)
Sociedad Mexicana de Crédito Industrial (SOMEX) (1941)
Financiera Aceptaciones (formerly Cia. General de Aceptaciones) (1936)
Financiera del Norte (1937)

Mortgage Banks
Asociación Hipotecaria Mexicana (1933)
Crédito Hipotecario (1936)
Banco de Cédulas Hipotecarias, formerly Cédulas Hipotecarias (1941)

As indicated above, today most of these institutions belong to major financial groups—generally consisting of one or more commercial, investment and mortgage banks, insurance companies, and in some cases real estate companies, controlled by a small number of investors. Often financial groups are in turn part of economic groups, a broader group including industrial and possibly commercial firms, agricultural and mining interests as well as financial institutions, also united through ownership by a small number of individuals or families, i.e., an investment group.

One factor in the formation of financial groups was the strict legal segregation of various financial activities (which in the United States, for example, may be carried out by a single institution) into separate institutions for commercial banking, investment loans, mortgage loans, etc. While the associations among these institutions have been recognized for some time, recent legislation legally permitted these connections, and many of the financial institutions openly took the names of their leading institutions. For example, institutions associated with the Banco Nacional de México were formally designated the Banamex group; the investment bank became Financiera Banamex; the insurance company, Seguros America Banamex, etc.

While the financial groups (as well as economic groups) are looked on as a relatively recent phenomenon, many of the institutions which today form part of these groups existed or were formed in the 1930's or early 1940's. And, while the development of the contemporary financial (and economic) groups can be explained in part by events and trends of the post-World War II period, their origins in the immediate post-revolutionary period suggest a continuity between dominant class interests of that period and those of contemporary Mexico. Of particular interest are the sources of capital, the role of the state, the role of foreign capital, and the relationship of these financial institutions and groups to firms of other sectors, especially to industry.[1]

Banamex Group

One of the two largest financial groups in the country, the Banamex group is centered in the Banco Nacional de México, one

---

[1] Data on financial institutions may be found in ABM, *Anuário Financiera*, 1975; information on industries is based on economic data contained in Mexico, SIC, "Los Empresas Industrialies del Pais—Datos Economicos." A listing of the contemporary economic groups may be found in Cordero and Santín, 1977. Information on shareholders of banks established between 1932 and 1941 is from the Registro Público de la Propiedad y del Comercio (RPPC) and the Archivo de las Notarias (AN), both in Mexico City. Contemporary data on ownership, unless otherwise noted, are taken from World Trade Directory Reports, U.S. Embassy, Mexico City. Lists of shareholders and subscriptions for some of the banks can be found in Hamilton, 1978.

of Mexico's oldest commercial banks, and the Financiera Banamex (established in 1936 as Crédito Bursatil), today the second largest investment bank in Mexico. Other institutions in the Banamex group include another investment bank (Financiera de Ventas Banamex), the fifth largest mortgage bank in the country, and Seguros América Banamex, founded in 1933. In turn, these institutions and/or individuals associated with them have significant investments in certain of the most important industries in the country—often in conjunction with Nafinsa (Nacional Financiera, the government development bank) and foreign interests—among them Celanese Mexicana (with the Celanese Corporation), the most important chemical firm in Mexico; Industrias IEM (with Westinghouse and Nafinsa); Fertilizantes Fosfantanos Mexicanos; Moto Equipos; and Indetel (with IT&T and SOMEX, a formerly private development bank, now government controlled). Largely due to its international connections, the Banco Nacional was one of the first and most aggressive financial interests to seek out joint investment projects in the World War II and postwar period.

Banco Nacional de México. The Banco Nacional de México was established in 1884 as a result of a fusion of two banks created with French and Spanish capital a couple of years earlier. It was given a special concession as banker of the government of Porfirio Díaz and acted as intermediary between the government and foreign sources of credit. It received a series of privileges: its notes were the only ones accepted by the government for the payment of taxes, and the Banco Nacional itself was virtually exempt from all existing or new taxes to capital shares, notes, and dividends. Initially, the government had agreed not to authorize any new issue banks and to restrict existing ones, but the latter protested against this prerogative and it was withdrawn (Rosenzweig, 1965c: 806-807, 817; BNM, 1934: 9, 16, 93). However, a new government contract with the Banco Nacional in 1896 enabled it to collect notes of other banks for the federal government—a privilege it apparently abused by accepting notes from other banks for federal offices, letting them accumulate, and then presenting them to the banks of issue for reimbursement, resulting in a decrease in the metallic reserve of these local banks and seriously compromising their liquidity (Lobato López, 1945: 216). In general, the position of the Banco Nacional was a privileged one throughout the Porfiriato.

Reconstruction of the bank following the revolution was the

work of its president, Agustín Legorreta, who had entered the bank in 1902 and who subsequently constituted an important link between the post-revolutionary government and international financial interests. The Legorreta family has continued to control the position of director from the 1920's; following the death of Agustín in 1937, his brother Luis succeeded him. Upon the retirement of Luis, the post passed on to his son Agustín, who continues as director. French capital was apparently still dominant until the 1930's and the bank had a Paris board (consisting of leading French bankers and financial representatives), as well as a Mexican one, until 1962. The Legorreta family continues to control an unspecified but significant number of shares, and the Banamex group is sometimes referred to as the Legorreta group.

Following the revolution, officials of the Banco Nacional attempted to re-establish the favored position it had enjoyed with the Díaz government with the new post-revolutionary governments, utilizing its international connections. In the early 1920's, the Banco Nacional was involved in negotiations of the Mexican government with the International Bankers Committee respecting the repayment of Mexico's foreign debt. During negotiations between the Committee and the Obregón government, it was decided to use the Banco Nacional de México as a medium for the deposit of funds of the Mexican government destined for the committee for debt repayment. Agustín Legorreta also participated with Mexican officials and U.S. banking officials in meetings with the U.S. government during the petroleum crisis of 1926-1927, negotiated with U.S. and European banking interests to obtain initial support for the establishment of a central bank, and was involved in subsequent negotiations for loans with U.S. government officials on behalf of the Mexican government during the 1930's (BNM, 1900-1975, *Informe 1923:* 14; Lockett, 13 Oct. 1936).

The close relation between the Banco Nacional and the Banco de México is indicated by two transactions during this period. First, when the Banco de México terminated its commercial bank operations following the 1932 banking legislation, the business of several of its branches was passed on to branches of the Banco Nacional. Second, the Banco Nacional sold its shares of the Pan American Trust Company in New York, which it had acquired in 1935, to the Banco de México.

The Banco Nacional also worked closely with U.S. government officials. According to one official in Mexico, the Banco Nacional gave instructions to its branch banks in Mexico to provide confidential information to U.S. government representatives in Mexico regarding Mexican firms, trade conditions, and the feasibility of investments (Hillyer, 1929). In addition to the Pan American Trust Company in New York, the bank opened an office in Los Angeles in 1940 to represent it in California, Arizona, and New Mexico (BNM, 1900-1973, *Informe 1940, 1941*).

While several new banks were established during the 1930's, the Banco Nacional continued to dominate the private financial sector of Mexico. In 1940, the total loan portfolio of all the banks in the country (excluding the Banco de México) was 250 million pesos, of which 150 million constituted the portfolio of the Banco Nacional (*Universal*, 21 June 1940). Of fifty bank branches in the country in 1937, 36 belonged to the Banco Nacional (Polit, 1957: 338). The bank participated in the establishment of several financial societies, including Crédito Bursatil, subsequently affiliated with the Banco Nacional; and the Legorretas and other interests connected with the Banco Nacional were also instrumental in the establishment of América Latina, a general insurance company, in 1933 (name changed to "América" Cia. General de Seguros in 1942), which also became part of the Banamex group. It was also linked to industries, including the Fundidora Monterrey, one of the most important industries of Monterrey and at that time the major steel foundry of the country.

With the elimination of European markets as a consequence of the Second World War, the bank advocated a policy orientation to a continental American economy, reflecting the trend to Pan Americanism which was being promoted by certain U.S. interests and Latin American governments and was manifested in mutual assistance pacts between the U.S. and various Latin American countries, including Mexico, during the war years. An example of the investment pattern which would characterize the bank's postwar activities was the establishment of Inversiones Latinas in 1944, constituted with 51 percent Mexican capital and 49 percent U.S. capital, to finance and promote industry in Mexico (BNM, 1900-1973, *Informe 1945:* 23). The principal North American interest was the Wall Street firm of Kuhn Loeb and Company, with which the Banco Nacional had had close contacts for several years; there were also investments by Chase Bank.

This pattern has continued to characterize the Banco Nacional, with the bank, its major stockholders, or another institution of the

Banamex financial group (usually Financiera Banamex, the former Crédito Bursatil) participating in joint investments with foreign corporations, in some cases with assistance from the government banks, usually Nafinsa. An early example was Celanese Mexicana, established in collaboration with Celanese Corporation; it benefited from contacts with the Mexican-American Commission for Economic Development in obtaining permits for the import of equipment from the U.S. during the war years. Today, Celanese Corporation has about forty percent of the total investment in Celanese Mexicana with important holdings by Banco Nacional stockholders Legorreta, Gastón Azacarraga, and Pablo Jean. Other joint investments during this period include Reynolds Internacional de México, in which Reynolds Metal Company owned 51 percent, with the remaining 49 percent controlled by Banco Nacional and Inversiones Latinas, and a joint investment by Westinghouse, Nacional Financiera, and the Banco Nacional. After the restoration of Mexico's international credit standing in 1960, the Banco Nacional acted as agent and advisor to the government for the issue and placement of bonds in foreign markets, especially the U.S., France, and Germany (BNM, 1900-1973: *Informe 1964:* 19; *1969:* 15).

Financiera Banamex. The major investment bank of the Banamex Group was established as Crédito Bursatil in 1936, with an authorized capital of one million pesos (10,000 shares) of which only 20,000 (2,000 shares) were subscribed. Several different financial institutions seem to have been represented in this initial subscription of shares and in the board of directors, including the Banco Mexicano, the Banco Nacional, and La Nacional, an insurance company. Shortly afterward, notary records indicate that an "important group" of businessmen had entered the firm, subscribing the remaining 8,000 shares. The names of these businessmen are not given, although the new board of directors appointed at that time includes Agustín Legorreta among others (RPPC L3-98-170-92; AN, Carlos Garciadiego, 41, #17,865, f. 126).

Serfín Group

The Grupo Serfín (Servicios Financieros) is one of the four largest financial groups in the country and is associated with the Cuauhtémoc (or brewery) and Alfa (steel) groups, controlled by the Garza Sada investment group (see Appendix B). Its major institutions are Financiera Aceptaciones, the third largest investment bank in the country (with assets of 12.7 billion pesos in 1974); the Banco de Londres y Mexico, the oldest and today third largest commercial bank in Mexico (1974 assets: 8 billion pesos); and Monterrey, Cia. de Seguros (the sixth largest insurance company).

Banco de Londres y Mexico. The Banco de Londres was one of several banks established in Latin America through the financial cooperation of London banks, English commercial firms in Latin America, and a small number of local politicians and businessmen, during the 1860's, a period when British trade relations with Latin America were expanding. Subsequently the bank established ties with French and Spanish investors as well as with Mexican industrialists. Its links with the Barcelonnette group (members of which came to Mexico in the nineteenth century and established several commercial firms and manufacturing establishments) were particularly important; the position of the family of Maximino Michel of the Puerto de Liverpool in the Banco de Londres is a contemporary indication of this connection. The Barcelonnette group joined with the Banque de Paris et des Pays Bas and a consortium of Swiss banks to form an investment society (Societé Financiere pour l'Industrie au Mexique) with the purpose of investing in real estate, commercial, and industrial activities in Mexico. By the end of the Porfiriato over 45 percent of the capital of the Banco de Londres was French, much of it controlled by the Banque de Paris (which also held controlling interest in the Banco Nacional de México).

As one of the major national issue banks of the Porfiriato, the Banco de Londres shared in the privileges of the Porfirian banks, and the relatively favored position of national banks over regional ones. Like the Banco Nacional, it was linked to the Porfirian government elite through stockholdings and interlocking directorates, although it did not enjoy the special prerogatives of the Banco Nacional as government treasurer and in fact successfully checked some of the exclusive privileges granted to the Banco Nacional (Lobato López, 1945). Like other banks which survived the revolution, it was considerably weakened and its assets reduced through successive reorganizations. In 1934 a group of major shareholders was formed, and within this group the Cia. General de Aceptaciones obtained the major block of shares (see Appendix C).

Financiera Aceptaciones. The establishment of the Cia. General de Aceptaciones in 1936 coincided with the reorganization of the Garza Sada interests of Monterrey into two distinct groups—the Cuauhtémoc (brewery) group and the Vidriera (glass) group. As indicated in Appendix B, the family and its associates continued to constitute the major shareholders in both groups, but management tended to be under different branches of the family. The Cia. General de Aceptaciones was established to facilitate financial transactions among different firms of the Cuauhtémoc group by enabling companies having surpluses to transfer balances to companies having deficits, and to facilitate or guarantee credit operations of the Cuauhtémoc firms. Subsequently, Aceptaciones expanded its activities to members of the Vidriera group, including the facilitation of credit among various member firms and the intervention in the issue of obligations to be placed through other financial institutions. In 1937 Financiera del Norte was established as a financial organization of the Vidriera group; today it is the leading organization of the financial group Banpaís, which also includes the Banco del País and the Banco de Nuevo León, and is part of the Vidriera Group (Cordero and Santín, 1977: 46).

Grupo Bancomer

The Grupo Bancomer includes the Banco de Comercio, the second largest commercial bank in the country (assets of over 11 billion pesos in 1974), the largest investment bank (Financiera Bancomer, with assets of 23.9 billion), the largest mortgage bank, and one of the major insurance companies. The Banco de Comercio also operates as a holding company for 34 affiliated banks (three of them with assets of over one billion pesos).

Banco de Comercio. The Banco de Comercio was established in 1932 by Salvador Ugarte, Raúl Bailleres, and Liberto Senderos, with a small social capital of 500,000 pesos (5,000 shares). According to the initial list of shareholders, Ugarte, a former subdirector of the Banco Nacional, was the major shareholder, with 3,350 shares; the other shareholders were Liberto Senderos (750 shares), Maximino Michel, Raúl Bailleres, and Antonio Signoret (each with 250 shares), Manuel Gómez Morín (100 shares), and Graciano Guichard, another former Banco Nacional employer (with 50 shares). However, it is possible that Ugarte was representing other persons—

possibly four others listed as shareholders who represented the wealth of the group; Michel and Signoret of the Barcelonnette group, Senderos, a Spanish businessman; and Bailleres, a Mexican banker of French descent, who had been formerly associated with Chase Manhattan and Equitable Trust in Mexico City.

From this modest beginning, the equity of the bank grew rapidly; by 1940 it had increased its capital to 10 million pesos. New individuals and institutions were represented in subsequent capital increases, including Agustín Legorreta of the Banco Nacional and Pablo Macedo of the Banco de Londres (although the use of *prestanombres*—name-lenders—makes it difficult to judge the importance of those listed as shareholders). The Banco de Comercio also began to expand its activities almost at once through the establishment and purchase of banks in various major cities outside the federal district, establishing a series of affiliate banks in which the Banco de Comercio has majority control (51 percent) while local capital controls 49 percent. Financial investments seemed a secure source of profits during this period; the Banco de Comercio paid dividends of 12 percent after one year of operation and 18-20 percent by its fourth year (Banco de Comercio, 1942).

In the years following its establishment, the Banco de Comercio formed, with Crédito Minero y Mercantil and other institutions— among them the Banco General de Capitalización, established in 1934 at the instigation of Ernesto Amescua of La Nacional (insurance company) and La Comercial, another insurance company established in 1936—the center of the so-called BUDA group, comprised of Bailleres, Ugarte, Mario Domínguez, and Amescua. This group invested in a broad range of financial institutions, including commercial banks, financieras (investment banks), capitalization banks, and insurance companies.

Subsequently the BUDA group apparently split into different groups, the most important being the CREMI group (Crédito Minero y Mercantil) of Bailleres, and the Banco de Comercio, which came under the control of William Jenkins and Manuel Espinosa Iglesias (although Ugarte remained president until his death in 1962). The wealth of Jenkins, a former U.S. consul in Puebla, was initially based on real estate and the sugar plantations and refinery of Atencingo, and was subsequently expanded into other areas. The Jenkins group included Manuel Espinosa Iglesias (through which it obtained control of the Banco de Comercio) and General Maximino Avila Camacho, governor of Puebla during the Cárdenas administration and brother of the subsequent president, General Manuel Avila Camacho.[2] Today, Espinosa Iglesias is president of the bank and controls over half of its shares.

Grupo CREMI

The CREMI group, named for its major financial institution, Crédito Minero y Mercantil, is also referred to as the Bailleres group, for the family which controls it. It also includes Crédito Hipotecario, one of the largest mortgage banks in the country, and approximately 30 other mining, industrial, commercial, and financial firms, among the Cervecería Moctezuma, the second largest brewery in the country, and Palacio de Hierro, one of the major commercial houses, both dating from the nineteenth century.

Crédito Minero y Mercantil. Crédito Minero was established in 1934 by the same group of Mexican businessmen who had founded the Banco de Comercio two years earlier, among them Raúl Bailleres, Salvador Ugarte, and Liberto Senderos, with added support from banks, insurance firms, and mining companies (RPPC: L 3-89-182-381). The shareholdings by financial institutions are indicative of two characteristics of investment banks established during this period: government support for private investment banks (indicated by the inclusion of the Banco de México and Nacional Financiera among the original stockholders) and the tendency of financial institutions to invest in other financial institutions, partly because their high profit levels made them an attractive investment and at the same time made funds available for such investment. In the case of Crédito Minero, private financial institutions subscribing to shares included the Banco Nacional, the Banco Mexicano, and the Banco de Comercio, as well as the insurance company La Nacional (represented by Amescua of the BUDA group).

Crédito Minero initially functioned as a financiera for mining companies—buying and selling metals and financing transport, export and machinery purchases (BFM, 18 March 1935: 2-3). As noted above, Bailleres' experience in banking and mining included previous employment with Equitable and Chase Manhattan Banks in Mexico, and fifteen years' experience in managing nearly all the

---

[2] Information on the Jenkins-Espinosa group is based on various interviews. According to one source, after Espinosa Iglesias entered the bank it was suddenly discovered that the majority of its shares were controlled by Jenkins.

business of buying and selling gold, silver, and mercury in the country ("Una nueva sociedad . . ."). Subsequently, Crédito Minero branched into industrial finance.

Crédito Hipotecario. Crédito Hipotecario, established in 1936, was one of several mortgage associations formed in the 1930's. Its shares were subscribed largely by insurance companies (La Nacional, La Latina Americana, La América Latina, La Comercial, and La Azteca) and by financial institutions associated with the BUDA group (Banco de Comercio, Banco General de Capitalización, and Crédito Minero y Mercantil) (Bailleres, 1936).

Banco de Industria y Comercio

Established in 1932 as the Banco Azucarero, the Banco de Industria y Comercio is today part of the Sáenz group. This group consists primarily of sugar refineries and manufacturers of sugar products, but the Sáenz holdings have also included, at various times, hotels, airlines, paper companies, and steel products. The Banco Azucarero was initially established to finance sugar production; it was formed at the same time as Azúcar, S.A., an association of sugar refinery owners having the purpose of rationalizing sugar production and marketing at a time when the industry was suffering from a crisis of overproduction in an effort to maintain a profitable price level (see Chapter Three). Those listed as major shareholders at the time the bank was established represented the most important sugar holdings of the country: Diego Redo, owner of the Haciendas de Redo y Cia. in Sinaloa; Roberto García, owner of the Ingenio San Cristóbal, Veracruz; Harry Shipsey, representing British sugar interests; and Aarón Sáenz, owner of the El Mante plantations and refinery and at that time Secretary of Commerce, Industry, and Labor. Others listed as shareholders apparently represented the sugar refinery owned by William Jenkins in Puebla (Tomás de Rueda) and probably the U.S.-owned United Sugar companies in Sinaloa. The inclusion of Alfonso Castillo, general manager of the Banco Nacional de Crédito Agrícola, as an important shareholder, indicates government support to the Banco Azucarero, in keeping with official promotion and support of the sugar industry which characterized post-revolutionary administrations.

Several of these sugar properties were expropriated during the last years of the Cárdenas administration, but the refineries were usually retained by the former owners. An exception was the expropriation of the El Mante refinery, but Sáenz continued to expand his holdings, in some cases with government assistance (for example, the organization of the Cia. Azucarera del Río Guayalyo, with the support of Nafinsa, in 1945) and headed the quasi-official National Union of Sugar Producers (UNPASA) for several years. Sáenz also invested in other areas, including the Del Prado hotel and a major airlines company. In 1941, the Banco Azucarero expanded its activities to include other areas as well as the sugar industry and changed its name accordingly to the Banco de Industria y Comercio.

Banco Comercial Mexicano

The Banco Comercial Mexicano, the fourth largest commercial bank in the country (with assets of 5.6 billion pesos in 1974), is the major institution of the financial Grupo Comermex, which in turn is part of the Vallina economic group. The Vallina group is centered in the northern state of Chihuahua and includes a number of important commercial and industrial firms, among them Celulosa de Chihuahua, Bosques de Chihuahua, Plywood Ponderosa, and Viscosa de Chihuahua. The Banco Comercial Mexicano was established in 1934 by Eloy Vallina, who had previously worked in several U.S. banks and subsequently as sub-manager in the Banco Mercantil de Chihuahua of his brother Rafael. Its capital was principally from the state of Chihuahua, and its projected purpose was to aid regional development. Later the Banco Comercial began to purchase banks in various parts of the country which were then fused with the Banco Comercial.

The first industrial firm of this group—Cementos de Chihuahua—was established in 1941. In many ventures, including the purchase of Teléfonos de Mexico and the establishment of Celulosa de Chihuahua, the Vallina group was associated with that of Carlos Trouyet. In the 1940's, Vallina and Trouyet received assistance from the Banco de México in acquiring preferential stock in the Ferrocarril del Noroeste de México. Several industries have technical and capital input by foreign firms, among the Celulosa de Chihuahua (Snia. Viscosa of Milan) and Viscosa de Chihuahua (Snia. Viscosa and the FMC Corporation, American Viscose Division) (Fuentes Mares, 1968: passim).

Grupo SOMEX

The SOMEX group is another major economic group in which financial firms constitute the leading institutions. The most important are the Sociedad Mexicana de Crédito Industrial (SOMEX), the fourth largest investment bank in the country, and the Banco Mexicano, the sixth largest commercial bank. The SOMEX group also includes a number of important industrial, commercial, and real-estate interests, among them several automobile parts firms, chemical companies, and metal products enterprises. In 1963 the SOMEX group was taken over by the government, on the grounds that several member firms were near bankruptcy.

Banco Mexicano. The Banco Mexicano was established in 1932 by a group of businessmen associated with Abelardo Rodríguez, who was at that time president of Mexico, and others within his government. Its management included several individuals who had been associated with the Banco de México (Banco Mexicano, 1957: 3-5; Cunningham, 1932).

SOMEX. SOMEX was established in 1941 by a group of financial and business interests, including the Banco de Londres y México, the Banco Nacional de México, and the Banco Mexicano, as well as by official institutions—the Banco de México and Nacional Financiera (Sociedad Mexicana de Crédito Industrial, 1944: 4). It apparently also included substantial equity from Spanish refugees who came to Mexico following the Spanish Civil War.

Grupo Internacional

The Grupo Internacional, like the Grupo SOMEX, came under state control when the commercial bank (Banco Internacional) was sold to the government in 1970. When the Banco Internacional was established in 1941, several of the sugar interests who had investments in the Banco Azucarero also invested in it; subsequently the bank came under the control of various sugar-mill owners of whom García Mora of the San Cristóbal mill in Veracruz was especially important. It thus became implicated in the problems of the sugar refineries during the 1960's. Government-controlled prices and antiquated facilities precluded efficient production and high profits; several refineries went bankrupt and were taken over by the government. Government loans to sugar-mill owners for the purpose of expanding production were used instead to invest in other areas. When the government called in these loans, the millowners were unable to repay them and sold the Banco Internacional.

Banco Internacional. The Banco Internacional was established in 1941 at the instigation of Luis Montes de Oca, former Secretary of Finance (1927-1932) and Director of the Banco de México during most of the Cárdenas administration (1935-1940). The social and subscribed capital were high (6 million and 2.8 million respectively) in comparison with earlier banks. According to the registered list of shareholders, the major shareholder was Alfonso Cerrillo, who was manager of the semi-official Mexican Mortgage Association and of its affiliate Crédito Hotelero, which had been established by Cerrillo and Montes de Oca in November 1937 expressly to finance private hotel construction (Cerrillo, 1937). Cerrillo subscribed 875 shares of the Banco Internacional (at 1,000 pesos each); other major shareholders included Aarón Sáenz (sugar industry), 250; Montes de Oca, 170; Roberto García (sugar industry, Ing. San Cristóbal), 150, and Cayetano Blanco Vigil (various industrial and financial interests), 140. Also among the initial shareholders were sixteen banks of various states throughout the country, including three provincial banks which had been established with the assistance of the Banco de México in the late 1930's (Banco Provincial de Sinaloa, Banco de Zamora, and the Banco Provincial de Jalisco) (RPPC L3-130-114-170). Financial interests are also important among the first directors; 16 of the 32 board members and commissioners were also board members, managers, and/or commissioners of at least one, and often several, commercial, mortgage, or investment banks or insurance companies. At the same time they represented a broad range of other interests, including mining, manufacturing, and especially the sugar industry.

Although various interests were represented by the stockholders and board members, which were recipients of loans in the succeeding years, the investment policy of the bank was apparently to concentrate on financial institutions at least initially, citing the "inconvenience" of participation in industrial and commercial firms. During its first year of operations, the Board of Directors approved investments in the Banco Industrial de Jalisco (50,000 pesos); the Banco Provincial del Valle de México—one of the provincial banks organized by the Banco de México under Montes de Oca (50,000); Financiera Minera (100,000); Crédito General de México (100,000); a new mortgage bank (200,000); the Banco Capitalizador de Ahorros (200,000 or 300,000); the Banco de Puebla (on the basis of an exchange of shares, 30,000). At the same time, shares of the Banco Internacional were purchased by the other financial institutions (Banco Internacional, 1941-1946: Actas #1-28, 19 Aug. 1941 to 5 Aug. 1942).[3]

Financiera Internacional

The Financiera Internacional was established in 1939 as the Cia. Central Financiera. Subsequently it became part of the Banco Internacional group, but, as in the case of Crédito Bursatil, this association is not evident from the initial list of shareholders. Also similar to other investment banks during this period, a number of its shareholders are representatives of financial institutions, both public and private.

In contrast to other entries in the Notary Archives, the registration of the establishment of the Cia. Central Financiera includes marginal notes indicating the sources of checks sent to cover initial stock subscriptions. In most cases, individuals listed as stockholders are representatives of banks or companies. Several government financial institutions are represented, including the Agricultural Credit Bank (Manuel Mesa), the Ejidal Bank (Candelario Reyes), and Nacional Financiera (Espinosa de los Monteros). Of greater interest is the fact that foreign companies are represented by Mexican names; thus one of the shareholders is Anderson Clayton Company, apparently represented on the list of stockholders by Alfonso Herrera Sepúlveda, a Mexican employee (AN: Notary 47, Vol. 284, No. 12,314). This provides a rather striking example of the use of *prestanombres* (stand-ins) for actual shareholders, and indicates that the foreign share of equity in private financial institu-

---

[3] The preference for investments in financial institutions did not extend to government banks. When the Banco de México invited the Banco Internacional to subscribe 3,500 pesos in the capital of the Banco de Pequeño Comercio del Distrito Federal, the board members expressed the opinion that government institutions constituted dangerous investments; while they would accept this invitation, they indicated that they would not contribute to the organization of other similar institutions (Banco Internacional, 1941-1946: Acta 30, 9 Sept. 1942).

TABLE A.1. Interlocking Directorates: Private and Public Financial Institutions, 1940

Institutions	1	2	3	4	5	6	7	8	9	10	11	12	13	14	15	T1	16	17	18	19	20	21	T2	GT
1. Banco Nacional de México	2								1	1	1					5	2	1	1		1	1	4	9
2. Crédito Bursátil	2								1	2	1	1				8	2	1	1				4	12
3. Banco de Comercio				3		1		3								11	2	1	1				5	16
4. Crédito Minero y Mercatil	1	1	3		5											11	2	1	1			1	5	16
5. Crédito Hipotecario	1		4	5											1	10	2	1		1			4	14
6. Banco de Londres y México			1					3						1		6	1	1					2	8
7. Cia. General de Aceptaciones																								
8. Banco Mexicano	1	1	3	1		3		1								5	2	2	4	3		1	3	8
9. Sociedad Mexicana de Crédito Industrial		2		1							1	1		3	1	15	3	1		1			13	28
10. Banco Azucarero																4	1		1	1			1	5
11. Banco Internacional	1					1			1	1	1			2		5	1	1	1				2	7
12. Cia. Central Financiera	1	1							1	1	1			2		7	1	2	3	2	1	1	10	17
13. Banco Comercial Mexicano																								
14. Asociación Hipotecaria Mexicana						1		1	3	1		1	2		1	10	3	2	7	2		1	15	25
15. Cédulas Hipotecarias								3	1					1		5								5
Total Links: Private Institutions (T1)	5	8	11	11	10	6		5	15	4	5	7		10	5	**102**	20	9	21	10	7	1	68	170
16. Banco de México	2	2	2	2	2	1		3	3	1	1	1		3		20		1	1	2	1	1	5	25
17. Nacional Financiera			1	1	1	1		2	1		1	2		2		9	1		1	4	1		7	16
18. Banco Nacional Hip. Urb. y de O.P.	1	1	1	1		1		4		1		3		7		21	1	1		1	3		6	27
19. Banco Nacional de Comercio Exterior			1		1			1	3	1		3		2		10	2	4	1		2	2	11	21
20. Banco Nacional de Crédito Agrícola	1	1	1					2	1			2				7	1	1	3	2		4	11	18
21. Banco Nacional de Crédito Ejidal												1				1	1			2	4		6	7
Total Links: Public Institutions (T2)	4	4	5	5	4	2		3	13	1	2	10		15		68	5	7	6	11	11	6	46	114
Total Links: Public & Private Inst. (GT)	9	12	16	16	14	8		8	28	5	7	17		25	5	170	25	16	27	21	18	7	114	284

Compiled on the bases of data in ABM, 1940–75: 1941

tions may have been considerably greater than the stockholder lists indicate. Among the initial directors of the bank are several who do not appear to have been stockholders, including William Richardson of the National City Bank and Diego Redo, one of the major sugar capitalists.

Mortgage Banks

Asociación Hipotecaria Mexicana (Mexican Mortgage Association). The association is actually a quasi-official institution, having been established by the government Public Works Bank, but it is operated as a private mortgage bank and its equity is held by both private and public institutions. Its purpose was to meet needs for credit for housing construction and debt payment. It was the first institution in post-revolutionary Mexico to experiment with mortgage certificates, guaranteed with real estate, which proved to be a highly successful mode of obtaining financial resources from a public wary of non-tangible assets. This may explain its popularity among private bankers, who were generally reluctant to subscribe to shares of government banks. During its first years of operation the majority of shares were held by the Public Works Bank and the central bank (Banco de México), but there are a number of private banks represented (Banco Nacional, Banco de Londres, Banco de Comercio, and the Banco Mexicano), as well as private industries, such as the Fundidora de Acero y Fierro of Monterrey.

Banco de Cédulas Hipotecarias. Established in 1941 as Cédulas Hipotecarias, the Banco de Cédulas Hipotecarias is part of a group headed by Elias Sourasky, a U.S. businessman resident in Mexico. Two of its initial shareholders were also shareholders of the Banco Mexicano.

Relations among Financial Institutions in the 1930's

The relationship among financial institutions in the post-revolutionary period are reflected in the interlocking directorates among private and official institutions. Table A.1, based on information on the Board of Directors of 15 private and 6 official institutions in 1940, indicates 51 interlocks among directors of the private institutions, 23 among official banks, and 68 between private institutions and official banks (ABM, 1940-1975: 1941 passim). (Each interlock appears twice; hence the total is divided by two.)

The large number of interlocks between the Banco de Comercio, Crédito Minero y Mercantil, and Crédito Hipotecario reflects the presence of members of the BUDA group. As indicated above, their interests also included other institutions, among them the insurance company La Comercial, the Banco General de Capitalización, and important holdings in La Nacional, Cia. de Seguros. With this exception, links among private financial institutions do not indicate the subsequent development of financial groups (Banco de Londres—Cia. General de Aceptaciones; Banco Nacional-Crédito Bursatil, Banco Mexicano-SOMEX, Banco Internacional-Cia. Central Financiera). The two regional banks (Cia. General de Aceptaciones and Comercial Mexicano) are not linked to the other financial institutions. Perhaps the most striking element in private bank relations is the large number of institutions associated with the investment banks (especially SOMEX and Crédito Minero) and mortgage banks (especially Crédito Hipotecaria and the Asociación Hipotecaria Mexicana). The investment banks were often formed by bankers of various institutions. The relatively large number of directors associated with the Asociación Hipotecaria presumably reflects its position as the country's most important mortgage institution (at a time when mortgage bonds and certificates constituted the most popular form of securities which did not carry real-estate guarantees).

Interlocks among government institutions obviously reflect the fact that investments in these institutions came largely from each other. What is of interest is the large number of interlocks between private and government institutions. While to some extent these reflected the investments (generally small) of private banks in public institutions, they also indicate government support for private banks—notably the investment banks (SOMEX, Cia. Central Financiera) and its role in the formation of the Asociación Hipotecaria Mexicana.

Conclusions

The patterns of stock ownership in private banks during the decade between 1932 and 1940 suggest the following generalizations:

1. The initial capital subscription of these banks was quite low (especially if compared to the assets of the Porfirian banks) but increased substantially during their first decade.

2. The initial capital appears to have been held by Mexicans or by foreigners resident in Mexico, or in some cases by foreign companies operating in Mexico. Although the use of *prestanombres* may disguise the importance of foreign capital, it apparently did not have the importance it had in the Porfirian banks.

3. The majority of shareholders appear to be bankers, lawyers, or businessmen, with relatively few industrialists or agricultural interests. Financial institutions become increasingly important in the last years of the decade, presumably reflecting the profitability of the banks and the insurance companies during much of this period, with the result that they had funds to invest and the banks constituted a preferred investment.

4. Government banks (or officials) contributed to the initial subscriptions of banks in several instances, reflecting government concern with financial institutions which would provide investment in productive activities.

In general, patterns of stock ownership within the banks indicate both continuity and change in the composition of the post-revolutionary bourgeoisie. The Banamex and Serfín groups clearly have their origins in pre-revolutionary Mexico. Although the major institution of the Serfín group, Financiera Aceptaciones, was established in 1936, it constituted from the beginning an institution of the Cuauhtémoc group of the Garza Sada interests, which began operations during the Porfiriato.

In contrast, most of the other financial groups seem to have originated in the post-revolutionary period, many of them in the decade following the banking legislation of 1932, although in certain cases the wealth of the original founders could be traced to the pre-revolutionary period. This was the case, for example, with the Banco de Comercio and CREMI groups, which were initially established in part by French and Spanish businessmen from the Porfiriato. Although the CREMI group has continued to be dominated by the Bailleres family, the Banco de Comercio subsequently came under the control of the Jenkins-Espinosa Iglesias group, whose wealth originates in post-revolutionary Mexico. This seems to have definitely been the case with the founders of the Banco Mexicano, established by Abelardo Rodríguez, one of the millionaires of the revolution; and with SOMEX, which apparently benefited from capital brought over from Spain by Spanish businessmen in the late 1930's following the civil war; as well as with the Banco Comercial Mexicano in the state of Chihuahua. The Banco Azucarero and the Banco Internacional are post-revolutionary banks although their initial shareholders included groups from the Porfiriato as well as capitalists of the revolution such as Sáenz.

As indicated in Chapter Three, the reconstruction of the banking system involved extensive collaboration between the state and private capital: here we see that this collaboration extended to the formation of private financial institutions. The process of bank formation also demonstrates the opportunities available to the new "capitalists of the revolution" as well as for certain Porfirian groups to accommodate themselves to conditions in post-revolutionary Mexico.

Appendix B ‖ The Garza Sada Investment Group: The Origins of the Cuauhtémoc and Vidriera Groups

 The Garza Sada family and its associates constitute one of the most dynamic and cohesive investment groups in Mexico. It is also one of the oldest: its first firm, the Cuauhtémoc brewery, was established in 1890 and it already displayed contemporary "group" characteristics by the mid-1930's (see Table B.1). The pattern of development of the Garza Sada group is somewhat atypical, given its relative independence of the state in comparison with other such groups. This pattern is of interest both in its distinctiveness and as an early example of the investment groups which today dominate the Mexican private sector.

Today the interests of the Garza Sada group include four major economic groups—each with some twenty or more industrial, financial, and commercial firms (in some cases also including mines, transportation lines, and agricultural holdings), as well as several minor groups. The four major groups are:

1. The Cuauhtémoc (or brewery) group, centered in the Cuauhtémoc brewery, the first industrial firm established by this group and today the largest brewery in Mexico.

2. The Vidriera (glass) group, consisting of several firms manufacturing different types of glass and crystal which dominate the Mexican glass industry, as well as firms producing its own machinery.

3. The Alfa or steel group (formerly known as the HyLSA group), which consists of a fully integrated steel complex ranging from iron ore mines to foundries to various processing firms.

4. The CyDSA, or chemical group, which produces a wide variety of chemical products ranging from industrial salts to fabrics and tire treads.

The smaller groups include firms controlled by certain branches of the family, such as the Garza Laguero, Sada Gómez, and Sada Rivero groups, founded by children and grandchildren of the original founders (the third and fourth generations in the geneology). (See Table B.1.)

TABLE B.1. Garza Sada Family: Genealogy

First *generation*	*Muguerza Crespo children* Carmen Muguerza, m. Lic. Francisco Sada, founder of Cuauhté- moc brewery Daughter, m. Calderón José A. Muguerza, m. Adelaida Lafón
Second *generation*	*Children of Lic. Francisco Sada and Carmen Muguerza* Francisco G. Sada, founder of Cuauhtémoc, m. Mercedes García Consuelo Sada Muguerza, m. Isaac Garza Garza, founder of Cuauhtémoc brewery Alberto M. Sada, m. Magdalena Gómez. (Started Sada Gómez group) Others: Ricardo, Concepción, María, Rosario, Enrique, Carlos, Jesús *Children of Calderón-Muguerza* José Calderón Muguerza, founder of Cuauhtémoc, m. Graciela Ayala *Children of José A. Muguerza and Adelaida Lafón* Ing. José Muguerza Lafón (1899), founder Productos de Cemen- tos, m. Virginia Pozos
Third *generation*	*Children of Francisco G. Sada and Mercedes García (Sada García)* Roberto G. (1887), Hon. Pres. Monterrey, Cia. de Seguros, m. Mercedes Treviño Diego G. (1900), m. María de los Angeles Zambrano Andrés G. (1902), founder of chemical group (CYDSA), Pres. Financiera del Norte, m. Beatriz Zambrano Luis G. Margarita, m. Roberto Garza Sada (son of Isaac Garza and Con- suelo Sada) *Children of Isaac Garza Garza and Consuelo Sada Muguerza (Garza* *Sada)* Isaac, m. M.A. Sepúlveda Eugenio (1891-1973), former head of Cuauhtémoc group, founder of Garza Laguera group, m. Consuelo Laguera Roberto (1895), honorary president of Serfín, m. Margarita Sada García (daughter of Francisco G. Sada and Mercedes García) Others: Dionisio, Díego *Children of Alberto Sada Muguerza and Magdalena Gómez (Sada* *Gómez)* Alberto (1897), m. Concepción González Hernán (1900), Hon. Pres. Financiera y Fiduciera de Monterrey, m. Consuelo Derby Jorge, m. María Rivero Salvador, President, Fin. y Fic. de Monterrey (Control Sada Gómez group. Began with Sada Gómez, S.A. im- porter, wholesaler and retailer of industrial agricultural and mining machinery.)

TABLE B.1. Garza Sada Family: Genealogy (*cont.*)

	Children of José Calderón Muguerza and Graciela Ayala (Calderón Ayala)
	José Calderón Ayala (1931), member of board VISA, Financiera Aceptaciones, m. María Teresa Rojas
	Nora, m. Javier Garza Sepúlveda (son of Isaac Garza Sada and M.A. Sepúlveda)
	Children of Ing. José Muguerza Lafón and Virginia Pozas
	Virginia María, m. César E. Gutierrez Lozano
	Graciela, m. Rodrigo Treviño M.
	Cristina, m. Joaquín Garza Lewis
	Miriam, m. Patricio Sada Sosa (great grandson of Lic. Francisco Sada)
Fourth generation	*Children of Roberto G. Sada and Mercedes Treviño (Sada Treviño)*
	Roberto G. Sada Treviño (1918-72), former director FIC (holding company Vidriera group) m. Irma Salinas
	Ing. Adrian Sada Treviño (1920), President FIC, m. María N. González
	Children of Diego G. Sada and María Zambrano (Sada Zambrano)
	Silvia, m. Armando Garza Sada, son of Roberto Garza Sada and Margarita Sada García
	Díego, m. María Eugenia Santos de Hoyos, daughter of Alberto Santos González and Francisca de Hoyos
	Children of Andrés G. Sada and Beatriz Zambrano (Sada Zambrano)
	Ing. Andrés Marcelo, Director CYDSA, m. Pilar Flores
	Rogelio (1935), Director FIC, m. Cecilia Pérez Madero
	Gerardo
	Gertrudes, m. Julio Erasmus
	Beatriz, m. José Antonio Maryl
	Lucie, m. Hernando Cortez García Marcelo
	Children of Isaac Garza Sada and M.A. Sepúlveda (Garza Sepúlveda)
	Javier Garza Sepúlveda (1926), founder Auto-Mercados, m. Nora Calderón Ayala, daughter of José Calderón Muguerza and Graciela Ayala
	Children of Eugenio Garza and Consuelo Laguera (Garza Laguera)
	Eugenio, President VISA, President Crédito de Monterrey, head of Garza Laguera group, m. Eva Gonda
	Alejandro (1926), Director General, Cerv. Cuauhtémoc, m. María del Consuelo Rangel
	David, Member Board, Banco Comercial Mexicano de Monterrey and Crédito de Monterrey, m. Yolanda Santos de Hoyos, daughter Alberto Santos González and Francisca de Hoyos
	Alicia
	Gabriel, m. María Elena Rangel
	Marcelo
	Consuelo
	Manuel (1939), Sales Manager, Cerv. Cuauhtémoc, m. Celina Rivero Santos

TABLE B.1. Garza Sada Family: Genealogy (*cont.*)

Children of Roberto Garza Sada and Margarita Sada García (Garza Sada)
Roberto Garza Sada, Jr. (Lic.), Director, Financiera Aceptaciones, m. Carmen Delgado
Margarita
Dionisio
Bernardo, Director General VISA, m. Sylvia de La Fuente
Ing. Armando, Director General, Financiera Aceptaciones, m. Silvia Sada Zambrano, daughter of Diego G. Sada and María Zambrano
Children of Hernán Sada Gómez and Consuelo Derby
Hernán, Jr.
10 others
Children of Jorge Sada Gómez and María Rivero
Manuel (1926), General Manager Fanal (Sada Rivero group), m. Graciela Alareis
Jorge, operates Fanal

As indicated in Appendix A, this family also controls its own financial groups, including Serfín, which includes the Banco de Londres and Financiera Aceptaciones, and constitutes the financial group for the Cuauhtémoc and Alfa groups; and the Grupo Banpaís, the financial group for the Vidriera group, which includes the Banco del País and Financiera del Norte.

The contemporary Garza Sada group had its origins in the industrial expansion of Monterrey at the turn of the century. During the nineteenth century the northern city of Monterrey had been an important commercial center; as its commercial importance declined, capital was diverted to other sectors, including industry, which was also promoted by the state government through tax exemptions and protectionist policies. Among the industries established during this period was the Cuauhtémoc brewery (Cervecería Cuauhtémoc), established in 1890, chiefly with capital from the commercial house Casa Calderón y Cia.; its founders included two generations of three interrelated Mexican families: Francisco G. Sada Muguerza of a landowning family in the state of Coahuila; his brother-in-law Isaac Garza Garza, a member of the Casa Calderón; an uncle José A. Muguerza; and a cousin José Calderón Muguerza; as well as a German technician, José M. Schneider (Vellinga, 1975: 149-150; Contreras Méndez, 1976: 20, 33). Subsequently, in 1901, Cervecería Central was established by the shareholders of Cuauhtémoc to supply Mexico City and the surrounding states, and in 1911 a separate glass factory, Vidriera Monterrey, began operations to provide glass bottles for the brewery.

Monterrey's industrial expansion—and that of the Garza Sada family interests—was temporarily halted during the revolution. But during the 1920's several departments were established within Cervecería Cuauhtémoc to manufacture inputs to the beer industry. A crown top was developed to replace the corks previously used for beer bottles; this function was subsequently given to an independent enterprise, Fábricas Monterrey (FAMOSA), established in 1939 by Francisco G. Sada, Isaac Garza, Roberto Garza Sada (his son) and related families—José Calderón, Ing. José F. Muguerza, and Antonio Muguerza. It subsequently diversified into other products, including metal containers (*Monterrey: una ciudad en marcha*, 8 July 1956). A department to produce cardboard boxes was also included in FAMOSA. Also in 1929, Malta, S.A. was established to produce malt for the Cuauhtémoc breweries, and during this period a branch of Vidriera Monterrey was established in Mexico City (Vidriera México).

The Garza and Sada families were also instrumental in the establishment of COPARMEX (Employers' Confederation of the Mexican Republic), an association specifically oriented to defense of the class interests of the bourgeoisie. In general, they were in the forefront of efforts by conservative businessmen of Monterrey to control the labor movement. In their own firms, they attempted to exercise this control through a repression of independent labor organization on the one hand and a paternalistic private welfare system on the other (Vellinga, 1979).

By 1936, the holdings of the Garza Sada families and their associates had been divided into two groups: the Cuauhtémoc (brewery) group and the Vidriera (glass) group. While both sides of the family (descendants of Isaac Garza and those of Francisco Sada) continued to hold shares within each group, management of the Cuauhtémoc enterprises was largely the responsibility of the Garza Sada family, particularly Eugenio Garza Sada and Roberto Garza Sada, sons of Isaac Garza, while their cousins, the Sada brothers—Roberto G. Sada and Andrés G. Sada (sons of Francisco Sada Muguerza)—were in charge of the Vidriera group (Arch. MGM, #105, Cuauhtémoc, Memo 21 Sept. 1959).

Until this time, the principal firms of both groups (Cervecería Cuauhtémoc, and Vidriera Monterrey) had also constituted hold-

ing companies for other firms of their groups, but this resulted in
certain problems. First, the extent and expansion of family control
was highly visible, exposing the firms to accusations of concentration and monopoly. Second, problems of the central firms in each
group tended to spread to other firms. In the case of the Cuauhtémoc group, the Garza Sada family had attempted, with little success, to form a cartel with the two other major breweries of the
country to maintain price levels; it was now involved in negotiations—also ultimately unsuccessful—to purchase the Moctezuma
brewery, the second largest in Mexico, which would have given
it control over 70 percent of the beer produced in the country.
There was concern that the problems of the brewery industry would
have repercussions on the other firms of the group. At the same
time, Vidriera Monterrey had been the nucleus of an intensive
labor conflict (which had resulted in a one-day lockout by Monterrey businessmen and a confrontation between these and President Cárdenas). Its owners were anxious to prevent labor militance from spreading to other firms of this group (Gómez Morín,
1935: 17 May; Good, 1972: 20-21). Tax incentives for new industries may have also played a role in the transformation of former
departments into "independent" firms.

With the Cuauhtémoc group reorganization, former departments of the brewery and of FAMOSA—including Empaques de
Cartón Titán, the former packaging department—became autonomous companies, and Valores Industriales S.A. (VISA) was created as a holding company which would hold the majority of shares
of the firms formerly held by Cuauhtémoc. VISA, in turn, would
be controlled by the group of Cuauhtémoc shareholders and would
have the function of maintaining unified direction of the "autonomous" firms. "External" elements not directly linked with the
group would not participate in VISA but would simply continue
to hold shares of the individual companies (Gómez Morín, 17 May
1935, 2 Jan. 1936). In 1938 after two years of reorganization, the
VISA group consisted of twelve companies, including VISA, the
holding company; FAMOSA; four breweries; a malt company; a
packaging company; a technical services firm; a distribution firm;
and two financial agencies (Cerv. Cuauhtémoc, 1938). (See Table
B.2.)

The plan for the reorganization of the Vidriera group called for
the existing Vidriera Monterrey to become a holding company—
Fomento de Industria y Comercio (FIC)—and its assets and name
to be taken over by a new organization. The holdings of FIC in-

TABLE B.2. Assets and Capital of Companies of Cuauhtémoc Group, 1938

	Assets	Capital
Cervecería Cuauhtémoc	18,343,378.66	6,000,000
Malta	2,068,010.09	1,000,000
Empaques—Cartón Titán	1,718,255.87	750,000
Fábricas Monterrey (FAMOSA)	2,078,176.07	1,250,000
Técnica Industrial	436,026.82	100,000
Cia. Cervecería Veracruz	832,409.46	250,000
Cia. Comercial Distribuidora	632,724.56	80,000
Cervecería Central	3,544,484.67	1,500,000
Cia. General de Aceptaciones	2,436,067.04	500,000
Inversiones Mercantiles	150,157.65	25,000
Cervecería de Oeste	435,198.77	200,000
Valores Industriales, S.A. (VISA)	5,069,935.49	3,000,000

Source: Cervecería Cuauhtémoc, 1938

cluded the new Vidriera Monterrey, Vidriera México, and Vidrio Plano, another new organization which began operations in May 1936 to manufacture plate glass, with Andrés G. Sada as general manager (Sada, 1935). In August of that year, Cristalería was established as part of the Vidriera group to manufacture crystal.

The Garza Sada groups also began to expand their financial network. In 1932, investors linked with the Cuauhtémoc brewery formed the Banco Industrial de Monterrey to finance their operations (Contreras Méndez, 1976: 26). The Cia. General de Aceptaciones was established in 1936 as part of the reorganization of the Cuauhtémoc group to facilitate financial transactions among its various firms by enabling companies having surpluses to transfer balances to companies having deficits, and to facilitate or guarantee credit operations of the Cuauhtémoc firms with other financial institutions or in the market. Subsequently Aceptaciones expanded its activities to members of the Vidriera group (Gómez Morín, 7 July 1936).

At the same time, these groups were linked with financial institutions in Mexico City—notably the Banco de Londres y México, and, through it, to other interest groups. In 1934 a group of shareholders was formed who jointly held a majority of shares in the Banco de Londres (Gómez Morín, 1933a & b). Within this majority bloc, the Cia. General de Aceptaciones held 28.09 percent and Enrique Sada Muguerza, of the Central brewery, held 1.87 percent, totalling just under 30 percent for the Cuauhtémoc group. Other major shareholders included Maximino Michel, of the Puerto de Liverpool (an important commercial house, established during the Porfiriato) and Angel Urraza of Hulera Euzkadi (a major tire company, in which B. F. Goodrich had substantial interest) (see Appendix C).

The interests associated with the Banco de Londres participated in efforts of the Garza Sada family and other Monterrey interests to broaden Monterrey's financial network. In 1939 they formed a holding company, Unión Financiera, through which they exercised control over four institutions established within the next two years: a life insurance company (Monterrey, Cia. de Seguros sobre la Vida), a capitalization bank (Banco Capitalizador de Monterrey), a mortgage bank (Crédito Provincial Hipotecario), and a construction company (Construcciones, S.A.); they also bought controlling interests in other financial institutions including the Banco de Nuevo León. Monterrey subscribers of the initial capital of Unión Financiera included some of the major business families of the city:

Members of the Garza Sada families, their associates and directors of firms of the group: Roberto Garza Sada, Luis G. Sada, Roberto G. Sada, Eugenio Garza Sada, Jaime Garza, Virgilio Garza Treviño, Jr., Antonio L. Rodríguez, Fernando A. González, and Juan A. Farias;

The Santos brothers (Ignacio, Alberto, Manuel), another economic group in Monterrey, whose interests included flour milling concerns and financial institutions;

Ricardo, Andrés, and José Chapa, of the Chapa commercial firm;

Jesús Llaguno of the Llaguno economic group, with interests particularly in textiles as well as various financial institutions, and

Benjamín Salinas and Joel Rocha, of the commercial firm Salinas y Rocha.

Individual subscribers from Mexico City were associated with the Garza Sada interests:

Manuel Gómez Morín, Banco de Londres, Sofimex;
Ignacio Hornik, Sofimex, América Cia. de Seguros;
Maximino Michel, Banco de Londres, Puerto de Liverpool;
Angel Urraza, Hulera Euzkadi.

These shareholders would subscribe an equal number of common and preferred shares, the former giving them collective control over the enterprise. In addition, 500,000 pesos in preferred shares would be subscribed by financial institutions in Monterrey—Banco Mercantil, Crédito Industrial, Sociedad General de Crédito, Cia. General de Aceptaciones, and Financiera del Norte—and by insti-

TABLE B.3. Subscription to Shares of Unión Financiera

Name	Common	Preferred	Total
Roberto G. Sada	25,000	25,000	50,000
Jaime Garza	25,000	25,000	50,000
Benjamín Salinas	25,000	25,000	50,000
Joel Rocha	25,000	25,000	50,000
Eugenio Garza Sada	25,000	25,000	50,000
Roberto Garza Sada	25,000	25,000	50,000
Luis G. Sada	25,000	25,000	50,000
Manuel Santos	25,000	25,000	50,000
Ignacio A. Santos	25,000	25,000	50,000
Alberto Santos	25,000	25,000	50,000
Virgilio Garza Jr.	25,000	25,000	50,000
Antonio L. Rodriguez	25,000	25,000	50,000
Jesús J. Llaguno	25,000	25,000	50,000
Ricardo Chapa	20,000	20,000	40,000
Andrés Chapa	15,000	15,000	30,000
José Chapa	15,000	15,000	30,000
Manuel Gómez Morín	25,000	25,000	50,000
I. Hornik	25,000	25,000	50,000
M. Michel	25,000	25,000	50,000
Angel Urraza	25,000	25,000	50,000
Fenanado A. González	12,500	12,500	25,000
Juan A. Farias	12,500	12,500	25,000
Banco Mercantil		70,000	70,000
Sociedad General de Crédito		40,000	40,000
Cia. General de Aceptaciones		40,000	40,000
Financiera del Norte		30,000	30,000
Instituciones de México (D.F.)		250,000	250,000
	500,000	1,000,000	1,500,000

Source: Memo to Sec. de Hacienda, 8 November 1939. Archivo MGM: I, 8, Cia. de Seguros

tutions in Mexico City (Archivo MGM, Cia. de Seguros: Memorandum 8 Nov. 1939). Although several groups of Monterrey businessmen held shares in Unión Financiera, the subscriptions by the members of the Garza Sada families and their associates, combined with those of the four Mexico City subscribers with whom they were associated through the Banco de Londres, gave them a total of 3,000 of the 5,000 common shares—more than sufficient for control. (See Table B.3.)

The Garza Sada family expanded into steel production and chemicals during the 1940's. Hojalata y Lámina was founded by the Cuauhtémoc group to produce steel sheet for metal bottletops during World War II, when former supplies from the U.S. were cut. Subsequently it has expanded into a fully integrated steel complex, its activities ranging from mining and ore processing to finished steel products. Today it consists of 26 companies controlled through a holding company, Grupo Industrial Alfa, S.A. In 1974 there was a split between the Garza Laguera and Garza Sada families which resulted in the former taking control of the Cuauhtémoc (VISA) group, whereas the latter controlled the steel group.

As the family diversified into steel production to meet the needs of the Cuauhtémoc group, CyDSA (Celulosa y Derivados, S.A.) was formed to meet the chemical needs of the Vidriera group. It has expanded to include nineteen companies producing fibers, films, packings, chemicals and plastics. More than other groups of the Garza Sada family, the CyDSA firms have drawn extensively on foreign capital and technology although maintaining group control over individual firms. It has several joint investments with U.S. and other foreign firms, and both the steel and chemical groups have been recipients of foreign loans. In all four groups, management has passed to the fourth generation, with the grandchildren and great-grandchildren of the original founders holding key positions within the industrial firms, banks and holdings companies.

The development of the Alfa and CyDSA groups, as well as much of the expansion of the Cuauhtémoc and Vidriera groups, took place after 1940, but by the mid-1930's the Garza Sada family constituted a self-conscious investment group and two of its four major economic groups existed as cohesive entities by that time. Although the Garza Sada family is in many respects unusual, it provides an example of a Porfirian business group which survived the revolution to become a major business group in post-revolutionary Mexico. It also demonstrates the importance of the immediate post-revolutionary period in the formation of a significant segment of the dominant class.

Appendix C ‖ **Banco de Londres-Sofimex Group**

 The association of individuals and families of the private sector in groups of various types for the purpose of combining sufficient capital for investment is a characteristic of many developing countries where capital and other resources are scarce (Leff, 1978: 662-668). In Mexico, such groups existed from the nineteenth century. An example was the Barcelonnette group, composed of immigrants from southern France who united to form several businesses, often through the Societé Financiere pour l'Industrie du Mexique, which also included capital of the Banque de Paris et des Pays Bas and of private Swiss banks.

In post-revolutionary Mexico, and especially by the 1930's, several types of groups began to take form—among them the BUDA group (at this time, chiefly a financial group), and the Cuauhtémoc and Vidriera groups of the Garza Sada family, early examples of the contemporary economic groups.

The Banco de Londres-Sofimex group constitutes another type of group formation which seems to have been of particular importance from the 1930's.

The Banco de Londres y México

At the beginning of the 1930's, the Banco de Londres was apparently still dominated by foreign capital, partly Spanish, partly French, with important holdings by the Banque de Paris et des Pays Bas as well as the Societé Financiere pour l'Industrie au Mexique, in which the Banque de Paris had interests. The Banque de Paris also represented the Banco de Londres before the French government for quotations of its shares in the Paris market, and an extended controversy with the Banque de Paris regarding taxes owed to the French treasury was probably a factor in the attempts of the Banco de Londres officials to secure a majority of shares in Mexican hands.[1]

---

[1] Association with the Banque de Paris dated from 1904 (if not before) when the Banque and the Societé Financiere signed for 40,000 shares of a capital increase of

Like other Porfirian banks, the Banco de Londres was forced to reduce its capital as a consequence of losses suffered during the revolution: by 1934, through a series of capital reductions and new share issues, capital had decreased from 21.5 million to 5 million pesos. In that year, the bank was the victim of a crisis which forced a further reduction of its capital. In an apparently deliberate act of sabotage, a shareholder delivered 6,000 shares to the stock market to be sold at less than one-third of their value—3.75 pesos per share rather than 12.00, which was the value at which they were quoted—leading to a panic among the bank's clients and a massive withdrawal of deposits. At the instigation of the Banco de México, a group of official and private banks subscribed shares of the Banco de Londres on a temporary basis, saving it from bankruptcy by enabling it to meet requests for deposit withdrawals (Banco de Londres, 1964: 109-110, 114-115; *El Nacional*, 10 March 1934).

---

the Banco de Londres totaling 65,000 shares and made arrangements to have them quoted in the Paris stock market. Subsequently, the number of shares quoted in Paris was increased to the total of 215,000 shares. In 1926 (at the time that the value of the stock was reduced to half to cover losses from the 1910-21 period), the Banco de Londres requested that its shares be withdrawn from quotation in the Paris market. The Banque de Paris responded that the nature of the commitment to the French treasury meant that such an action could result in an embargo on the bank's property in Paris by the tax administration and a legal basis for French shareholders to demand reparation for damages resulting from the fact that their shares could no longer be quoted in France. The Banco de Londres responded that few shareholders would be affected since the majority did not hold shares in France; in addition to Mexicans, there were a large number of shareholders in Spain, Switzerland, and other countries. It pleaded its difficulties following the revolution and pointed out that the entire essence of the bank had changed; while it had associated with the Paris market as an issue bank it was now a refractionary bank, and that the high cost of quotation in Paris prejudiced the majority of shareholders elsewhere for the benefit of a few in France. In its response, the Banque de Paris claimed that the number of French shares had increased; in the general assembly of 1926 they had constituted 62 percent of the total shares represented (67,520 of a total of 109,664). The Banco de Londres decided to maintain the agreement.

A further controversy arose in 1931, when the French government demanded back payment from 1924 for the stamp tax, from which the Banco de Londres (under advisement of the Banque de Paris) had believed itself exempt. A letter of the Banco de Londres to the Banque de Paris of May 1931 was not answered until January 1933, at which time the Banque de Paris noted that the tax had been suspended pending a court decision regarding an analogous case of another foreign bank. In its response, the Banco de Londres held the Banque de Paris responsible for its failure to keep it opportunely informed of French legal dispositions (*Extracto de Comunicaciones Cambiados*).

One of the results of the reorganization in response to the 1934 crisis was the formation of a group of Mexican businessmen who jointly held the majority of the bank's shares (Gómez Morín, 19 Sept. 1933a and b). This was apparently instigated by Gómez Morín with the purpose of securing Mexican control over the bank. Most of these businessmen were members of the Board of Directors in 1935: Maximino Michel, President; Alfonso Vega, Vice President; Enrique Sada Muguerza, Federico A. Williams, Angel Urraza, and Manuel Gómez Morín. By the early 1940's, shares of this majority block of shareholders were divided as follows:

Cia. General de Aceptaciones	28.09%
J. B. Ebrard/Maximino Michel	22.47
Angel Urraza/Cia. Hulera Euzkadi	14.98
Trapaga, Garcia y Cia.	11.24
Sres. C. Noriega y Cia.	8.03
Sociedad Financiera Mexicana	6.42
Lic. Manuel Gómez Morín	4.68
Enrique Sada Muguerza	1.87
Alfonso Vega	1.29
La Provincial	0.93
	100.00

This block united several important interests in Mexico, including the Cuauhtémoc group of the Garza Sada family (Cia. General de Aceptaciones and Enrique Sada Muguerza who was at that time a representative of Cervecería Central, a subsidiary of Cervecería Cuauhtémoc in Mexico City); Spanish businessmen connected with Hulera Euzkadi, a major tire company, and French businessmen connected with Maximino Michel and the Puerto de Liverpool. During the 1930's, individuals associated with these groups and with the Banco de Londres established an insurance company, La Provincial, in conjunction with a British insurance group; and an investment bank, Sociedad Financiera Mexicana (Sofimex) in collaboration with Ignacio Hornik, a Swiss businessman connected with European interests and the Banco Nacional de México. They also came into conflict with members of the BUDA group for control of the life insurance company La Nacional, and undertook joint investment projects. Although less tightly knit than the contemporary investment groups, there is substantial evidence that the Banco de Londres-Sofimex group constituted a stable, relatively long-term coalition linking different institutions and investment groups.

Hulera Euzkadi

Hulera Euzkadi, a tire company, was formed in 1935 through a fusion of the Cia. Manufacturera de Artefactos de Hule Euzkadi (Euzkadi Manufacturing Company of Rubber Products), established in 1925 by a group of Mexican and Spanish businessmen, and the B. F. Goodrich subsidiary in Mexico. In the new company preferred shares (representing 90 percent of the combined assets) were divided between the former shareholders according to the assets of the two companies; the Euzkadi group held a majority of common shares (65 percent) although B. F. Goodrich had the option to buy an additional 10 percent over a five-year period as well as the first option on shares sold by Euzkadi shareholders. Since preferred shares could vote only in "extraordinary circumstances," the former Euzkadi shareholders apparently had majority control. However, aside from the option of purchasing additional shares, Goodrich also had veto power on the Board of Directors (two out of five members, with four votes required for a decision) (Hulera Euzkadi, 1935 and 1936; Gómez Morín, 1937: 16 July).

In subsequent years, Hulera Euzkadi expanded and diversified its operations in Mexico and began to invest in foreign corporations in conjunction with B. F. Goodrich. As of 1955, the Euzkadi group (which included shareholders from the former Goodrich subsidiary) controlled twelve Mexican firms and, in conjunction with B. F. Goodrich, three foreign companies. (See Table C.1.) Euzkadi also had minority holdings in other firms, including CyDSA (controlled by the Garza Sada investment group), and continued to be linked to the Banco de Londres and other firms of this group.

Puerto de Liverpool

The Puerto de Liverpool, a commercial house, was established in 1888 by Juan Baptiste Ebrard, who had left his home in France Jausueres (Basses Alpes) in 1847 to go to the United States and from there came to Mexico. It constituted one of the most important commercial houses of the Barcelonnette group. In 1906, when Alfonse Michel was director of the Puerto de Liverpool, his nephew,

TABLE C.1. Holdings of the Euzkadi Group, 1955

Mexican firms	Canada Dry Bottling Company of Mexico, S.A.
	Canada Dry Bottling Company of Guadalajara, S.A.
	Canada Dry Bottling Company of Aguascalientes, S.A.
	Embotelladora Canada Dry del Sur, S.A.
	Predios Industriales, S.A.
	Motores Reconstruidos, S.A.
	Clima Control, S.A.
	Productos Kelite, S.A.
	Comercial Euzkadi, S.A.
	Geon de México, S.A.
	Inmobiliares Sta. Maria, S.A.
	Cri-Aves, S.A.
Foreign companies, established with	
B. F. Goodrich	Cia. Gomera Goodrich Cubana
	Industria Colombiana de Llantos (Incollantos)
	Lima Rubber Company

Source: Fournais, 1955

Maximino Michel, came to Mexico from Barcelonnette to work with him. Maximino Michel subsequently became a major shareholder and director of the Puerto de Liverpool as well as the Banco de Londres, of which he was president for a number of years. He participated with other major investors of the Banco de Londres in various projects, among them the establishment of Sofimex, an investment bank, and the insurance company La Provincial. The continued relationship with the Banco de Londres-Sofimex group (as well as the BUDA group) is indicated in the list of investments (of 500,000 pesos or more) of the Puerto de Liverpool as of 1952 (Table C.2).

La Provincial

La Provincial was one of several insurance companies established in Mexico in the wake of the insurance legislation of 1935. By insisting that insurance company reserves be invested in Mexican enterprises, the 1935 law had resulted in the exodus of most foreign insurance companies from the country, although their technical staff often remained and formed the nucleus of new Mexican companies. According to correspondence between Ma-

TABLE C.2. El Puerto de Liverpool: Investments (500,000 Pesos +) 1952

Bodegas, S.A. (estabished by J. B. Ebrard in 1941)	1,986,075.11
Common shares	
Termidor, S.A.	1,392,000.00
Banco de Juárez	819,050.00
Banco Agrícola y Comercial de Saltillo	902,880.00
Hilados del Norte (Llaguno group-Monterrey)	500,000.00
Preferred shares	
Malta, S.A. (Cuauhtémoc group)	792,647.06
Mortgage bonds	
Banco Nacional Hipotecario Urbano y de Obras	
Públicas (government)	522,000.00
Financial bonds	
Crédito Minero y Mercantil (BUDA)	101,490.00
Crédito Minero y Mercantil (BUDA)	226,547.50
Crédito Minero y Mercantil (BUDA)	572,150.00
Sociedad Financiera Mexicana (Sofimex)	273,720.00
Sociedad Financiera Mexicana (Sofimex)	994,680.00
Mortgage obligations	
Cervecería Cuauhtémoc (Cuauhtémoc group)	661,220.00
Empaques de Cartón Titán (Cuauhtémoc group)	1,960,800.00
Hojalata y Lámina (Cuauhtémoc group)	2,755,425.00
Maderera del Trópico (Sofimex)	682,500.00
Malta, S.A. (Cuauhtémoc group)	1,204,125.00
Planta de Fuerza Eléctrica en Monterrey	
(Monterrey, various groups)	2,336,400.00

Source: Archivo MGM: Puerto de Liverpool

nuel Gómez Morín and members of the Garza Sada family on setting up an insurance company, there was sufficient capital held by "interested groups" to establish two companies, taking advantage of the technical personnel, portfolios, and organization of two companies which had operated in Mexico for forty years, but the "interested groups" seem to have focused on La Provincial. (The second company was apparently La Territorial, organized by the Levy family.)

Among the interested groups were two British businessmen associated with existing Mexican companies: Arturo B. Woodrow, whose family was associated with Anglo Mexicano, Cia. General de Seguros, and Federico Williams, president of La Nacional (the oldest life insurance company in Mexico). The above-mentioned correspondence also indicated a French group (Maximino Michel), groups from Chihuahua, and the Banco de La Laguna, in addition to the Garza Sada group and, presumably, the Banco de Londres

(Woodrow, 1936). Various Monterrey businessmen subscribed to the new insurance company through the Sociedad General de Crédito; among the Monterrey firms providing capital support were Cervecería Cuauhtémoc (37,500 pesos), Vidriera Monterrey (35,000), Crédito Industrial de Monterrey (25,000), and Cementos Mexicanos (27,500) (Rodríguez, 1936).

The initial authorized capital of La Provincial was 2 million pesos, represented by 20,000 shares of 100 pesos each, of which 7,000 were immediately subscribed. The list of initial shareholders was as follows:

Federico A. Williams, British businessman	1,500
Maximino Michel, French businessman	500
Leonardo Crocchio, Italian businessman	300
Manuel Gómez Morín, Mexican lawyer	130
Pablo Salas y López, Mexican industrialist	2,000
Estéban S. Castoreña, Mexican industrialist	250
Daniel Maretulli, Spanish industrialist	50
Miguel R. Cárdenas, Mexican lawyer	100
Epigmenio Ibarra, Jr., Mexican banker	250
Mario Domínguez, Mexican insurance agent	50
Ernesto J. Amescua, Mexican manager, La Nacional	20
Romualdo Trapaga, Spanish businessman	50
Jesús Rivera Quijano, Spanish industrialist	100
Roberto Casas Alatriste, Mexican public accountant	50
Higinio Gómez, Mexican industrialist	250
Arthur B. Woodrow, British businessman	1,450
	7,000

Source: Registro Público de la Propiedad y del Comercio, III-99-74-147.

It is probable that the large blocks of shares listed for Woodrow, Williams, and Salas y López are in part due to their representation of shareholders outside Mexico City, in particular those of Monterrey. This list also includes representatives from La Commercial and/or the Banco General de Capitalización (Mario Domínguez), La Nacional (Ernesto Amescua), the Banco Mexicano (Epigmenio Ibarra), and Hulera Euzkadi (Miguel R. Cárdenas).

One of the purposes of La Provincial was to provide investment funds for associated firms. Its investment portfolio for 1948 includes shares of La Nacional and several Monterrey firms in which the Garza Sada investment group had substantial and in some cases controlling interest (Table C.3).

TABLE C.3. La Provincial, Cia. General de Seguros, S.A.: Investments, 1948

Investments 1948		
	Shares, bonds and obligations	7,617,147.06
	Mortgage loans	298,511.54
	Real estate	2,046,345.81
	TOTAL	9,962,004.41
Shares, Bonds, and Obligations		
Shares		
55	Alianza	96,250.00
409	Banco de Londres y México	61,759.00
150	Central Hipotecaria	22,500.00
99	Crédito Alfianzador	18,315.00
520	La Nacional	309,920.00
1,500	La Provisora, S.A.	198,750.00
875	Cervecería Cuauhtémoc (preferred)	83,125.00
250	Harinera Monterrey (preferred)	25,500.00
250	Harinera Torreón (preferred)	25,000.00
1,500	Malta (preferred)	142,500.00
		980,619.00
	Minus Reserve for Re-evaluation	151,939.00
		828,680.00
	Plus Reserve for Re-evaluation	129,097.95
	TOTAL	957,777.95
Bonds		
441	Road bonds, México	1,188,332.52
704	Convertible road bonds, México	1,484,675.37
2	Commercial bonds, General Motors	100,000.00
129	Bonds, national public debt	42,000.00
1,480	Bonds, Sociedad General de Crédito	148,000.00
3	Treasury bonds, U.S.A.	172,950.51
		3,135,958.40
	Plus Reserve for Re-evaluation	8,000.00
	TOTAL	3,143,958.40
Certificates and Securities		
52	Certificados de participación, Nafinsa	180,699.40
228	Financial securities (dollars), Nafinsa	784,017.91
	TOTAL	964,717.31
Mortgage Obligations		
61	Aceites Grasas y Derivados	61,000.00
14	Cementos Veracruz	59,000.00
17	Cia. Mex. Refractarios, A.P. Green	53,000.00
340	Gas Industrial de Monterrey	500,000.00
370	Empresa de Teléfonos Ericssón	239,773.30
80	Planta Eléctrica Monterrey	79,183.20
54	Textiles Monterrey	19,754.06

TABLE C.3. La Provincial, Cia. General de Seguros, S.A.: Investments, 1948 (*cont.*)

450	Troqueles y Esmaltes	45,000.00
1,290	Hilados del Norte	124,632.84
300	Empaques de Cartón Titán	286,500.00
100	Ladrillera Monterrey	94,500.00
250	Vidriera Monterrey	238,750.00
	TOTAL	1,801,093.40
Mortgage Certificates		
	Central Hipotecaria	36,200.00
	Asociación Hipotecaria Mexicana	148,700.00
	Crédito Hipotecario	58,700.00
	Crédito Provincial Hipotecario	394,500.00
	General Hipotecaria	111,500.00
	TOTAL	749,600.00
	GRAND TOTAL	7,617,147.06

Source: Informe de la Dirección sobre el Ejercicio Social de 1948, Archivo MGM: IV, 40, La Provincial

Sociedad Financiera Mexicana (Sofimex)

Sofimex was established in 1937 to assist in obtaining capital and technology, within Mexico and through contacts abroad, for the organization of firms in Mexico. The founders seem to have envisioned an investment society similar to the Societé Financiere of the Porfiriato but one which would be controlled by Mexicans and would invest in enterprises needed in Mexico (Gómez Morín, 11 May 1935; 14 June 1937). (Inversiones Latinas, established by the Banco Nacional, was based on a similar idea.)

Among the founders of Sofimex were Maximino Michel, Enrique Sada Muguerza, Angel Urraza, and Manuel Gómez Morín, all associated with the Banco de Londres; Federico A. Williams (of La Nacional and La Provincial insurance companies), and Ignacio Hornik, who was vice-president of the New York office of the General Insurance Company, Ltd. of Trieste and Venice. Hornik also had holdings in La América (formerly América Latina), the insurance company associated with the Banco Nacional-Legorreta interests, which subsequently invested in Sofimex, and was also a liaison for contacts in New York and Europe. Sofimex was also associated with La Provincial and La Nacional through mutual shareholdings. The major shareholders were Williams (with 2,900 shares) and Hornik (2,700); the others had 400 or less. Some concern was initially expressed by Roberto Garza Sada about the fact that the Gómez Morín group would have minority participation. Gómez Morín responded that their representation could be increased to 300,000 (3,000 shares), but the other two groups (presumably Williams and Hornik) would still have the majority, as would either of the other two groups and his. On the Board, directors were Pablo Macedo, Enrique Sada Muguerza, and Gómez Morín (3), Federico Williams (1), and I. Hornik (1). In any case, he concluded, Sofimex consisted of a "club of gentlemen" more than anything else (Gómez Morín, 25 May 1937).

Sofimex apparently developed a dual role as an investment bank (financiera) and holding company, and by the mid-1940's had holdings in an assortment of firms and financial institutions, several of them part of the Banco de Londres group. (See Table C.4.) In a letter to I. Hornik of August 1947, Gómez Morín described the different categories of Sofimex investments and the reasons for each:

1. Firms which Sofimex helped to organize or reorganize through placing shares and obligations or through direct investments. These included vegetable oils (Aceites, Grasas y Derivados; Aceitura Nueva Galicia), wood products (Maderos de Yucatán, Maderera del Trópico, Caobas Mexicanas), publishing houses (La Enseñanza Objetiva, Propaganda y Anuncias), textiles (Atoyac Textil, Almacenes Textiles), and Berel.

2. Insurance companies—La Nacional, La Provincial, La América—due to the value of investment and relations of friendship.

3. Financial institutions (Banco de Comercio, Financiera Industrial de Jalisco, Banco de Nuevo León, Banco de Londres y México). The investment in the Banco de Comercio (dating from the establishment of Sofimex) was being reduced in view of the limited benefit Sofimex could obtain from the bank; the investment in the Financiera Industrial de Jalisco had been circumstantial and was also being reduced; that in the Banco de Nuevo León was due to excellent relations with the Monterrey group, and in the Banco de Londres as in the case of insurance companies, due to relations of friendship and the value of the investment itself.

4. Investments in Nuevo Chapultepec, Técnica Constructora, and Layne Hispanoamericana were considered excellent from the perspective of yield and useful in terms of contact with a very interesting group of persons associated with these companies.

5. Incidental investments in preferred shares and obligations: Cuauhtémoc, Malta, Hojalata, Titán (Cuauhtémoc group), Aceites

TABLE C.4. Sociedad Financiera Mexicana, S.A.: Investments, 1947

Investments 1947 (Summary) *(Common shares unless otherwise noted)*	*Total amount (book value)*
Shares, etc. quoted	
Atoyac Textil, S.A.	40,500.00
Cerv. Cuauhtémoc (preferred shares)	9,100.00
La Nacional, Cia. de Seguros s/la Vida	100,500.00
La Provincial, Cia. Gral. de Seguros	298,720.00
Malta, S.A. (Cuauhtémoc group) (pref.)	17,500.00
Hojalata y Lámina (Cuauhtémoc group) (pref.)	47,500.00
Empaques de Cartón Titán (Cuauhtémoc group) (pref.)	10,000.00
	533,820.00
Shares of Credit Institutions, etc.	
Banco de Nuevo León	12,700.00
Financiera Industrial de Jalisco	70,000.00
Banco de Comercio	70.00
Banco de Londres y México	271,049.25
	353,819.25
Other Securities Issued by Societies	
Aceites, Grasas y Derivados	268,040.35
Aceites, Grasas y Derivados (preferred)	39,162.50
Berel, S.A.	50,000.00
Cia. Lit. La Enseñanza Objetiva	185,252.99
Cia. Lit. La Enseñanza Objetiva (pref.)	23,735.14
Editorial Jus (preferred)	12,000.00
Layne Hispanoamericana	50,000.00
Maderas de Yucatán	80,000.00
Maderera del Trópico	160,000.00
Propaganda y Anuncios	85,252.96
Cementos Guadalajara (mortgage obligations)	510.00
Maderera del Trópico (mortgage obligations)	20,625.00
Hojalata y Lámina (Cuauht. group) (pref.)	4,800.00
Nueva Chapultepec Heights	65,500.00
Técnica Urb. y Const. América	6,550.00
Aceitura Nueva Galicia	268,040.35
Caobas Mexicanas	66,667.20
Gas Industrial de Monterrey	204,750.00
	1,590,886.49
Securities, Stocks, etc. Given in Guarantee	
Banco de Comercio	35,840.00
La Nacional, Cia. de Seguros	2,615,250.00
La Provincial	48,000.00
Banco de Londres y México	89,000.00
	2,788,090.00
Minus reserves of La Provincial	13,720.00
	2,774,370.00
Reportos—Titulos a Recibir	
Almacenes Textiles	78,750.00

TABLE C.4. Sociedad Financiera Mexicana, S.A.: Investments, 1947 (*cont.*)

Investments 1947 (Summary) (Common shares unless otherwise noted)	Total amount (book value)
América, Cia. Gen. de Seguros	187,500.00
Atoyac Textil	162,000.00
La Provincial, Cia. Gral. de Seguros	147,000.00
Banco de Comercio	412,160.00
	987,410.00

Source: Sociedad Financiera Mexicana, 1947

Grasas y Derivados, Cementos Guadalajara, and Maderera del Trópico.

As an investment bank, it became a central institution for placing securities and carrying out other financial transactions for firms within the Banco de Londres group.

A comparison of lists of major shareholders of Sofimex in the years 1937, 1944, 1954, and 1959 (Table C.5) indicates the continuity of ownership uniting the above-noted interests. For 1937, listed are those with 100 shares or more; in subsequent years, the top ten shareholders are listed with those beyond this number in parentheses. The asterisks denote the fact that the shares of Federico Williams passed to his family at his death and those of Angel Urraza to a family trust, Cia. Administrador de Valores. It also seems probable that part of the shares belonging to La América, Cia. General de Seguros may have passed to the Banco Nacional de México. Valores Industriales was the holding company of the Cuauhtémoc group, and Enrique Sada Muguerza was the manager of Cervecería Central, a subsidiary of the Cuauhtémoc brewery.

Of seven shareholders having 100 shares or more in 1937, five continued to be among the top ten shareholders: Federico A. Williams/Williams family; Angel Urraza/Cia. Administrador de Valores; Ignacio Hornik; Maximino Michel (in some cases indicated by the Puerto de Liverpool or Ebrard), and Manuel Gómez Morín. Three additional shareholders which appear among the top ten in 1944, 1954, and 1959 are associated with the Banco de Londres group: VISA (Valores Industriales), La Nacional, and Roberto D. Hutchinson (Sofimex).

Thus, by the mid-1930's, through mutual shareholdings and investments and other links, relations were established between a

TABLE C.5. Major Shareholders of Sofimex: 1937-1959

Name	Number of Shares (Rank among shareholders)			
	1937	1944	1954	1959
Federico A. Williams★	2,900			
Ignacio Hornik	2,700	4,400 (1)	6,000 (1)	8,000 (1)
Enrique Sada Muguerza	400	(500)	(750)	
M. Michel/Ebrard/Pto. de Liverpool	400	2,260 (3)	3,160 (3)	4,214 (3)
Angel Urraza★	300	700 (10)		
Julio Freyssinier Morín	200			
Manuel Gómez Morín	100	920 (7)	1,880 (5)	2,140 (5)
América, Cia. General de Seguros		2,000 (4)		
Williams Family★		1,390 (5)	2,085 (4)	2,780 (4)
Nacional, Cia. de Seguros sobre la Vida		2,530 (2)	5,498 (2)	7,330 (2)
Roberto D. Hutchinson		1,000 (6)	1,500 (6)	2,000 (6)
Valores Industriales, S.A. (VISA)		752 (8)	1,485 (7)	1,982 (7)
C. Heynen		746 (9)		
Banco Nacional de México			1,345 (8)	1,726 (8)
Cia. Administrador de Valores★			1,100 (9)	1,467 (9)
S. Robert y Cia.			890 (10)	1,187 (10)
Banco de Londres y México			(750)	(1,000)
Cia. General de Aceptaciones		(470)	(700)	(931)
Sr. Gabriel M. Coronea				(1,000)

Source: Sofimex, 1937, 1954, 1959; Fernández Cueta, n.d. Rankings added

major national bank (Londres y México) and its associated financiera (Sofimex), two of the most dynamic industrial groups in Monterrey (the Cuauhtémoc and Vidriera groups, both controlled by the Garza Sada family or investment group), a major commercial house (Puerto de Liverpool), a major tire-producing company (Hulera Euzkadi), and two insurance companies (La Provincial and La Nacional); in addition, there were less direct links with other banks, industries, and insurance companies. Through Maximino Michel (of the Barcelonnette group) and Angel Urraza, there were ties with French and Spanish businessmen resident in Mexico; the latter also had interests in cotton production in La Laguna. Through Michel and Gómez Morín, there were also links with the Banco de Comercio, and through Hornik with the Banco Nacional-Legorreta group as well as European investors.

La Nacional: The Struggle for Control

Although members of the Sofimex group cooperated with those of the BUDA group in various projects, they eventually came into conflict, presumably as their respective "groups" became more clearly defined. In the case of La Nacional, the oldest life insurance company in the country, in which both groups had substantial holdings, this led to a protracted struggle for control.

As noted above, Sofimex had been established as a holding company; its securities had included shares of La Nacional as well as other insurance companies. Upon the death of Federico Williams, president of La Nacional, he was succeeded by Ernesto Amescua of the BUDA group, who also continued in the position of manager. Another BUDA member, Mario Domínguez, was consulting actuary.

In 1938, neither the BUDA nor the Sofimex group had a majority of shares in La Nacional. The largest single block of shares was that of the Moss Estate (5,040 of a total 18,720); holdings of individuals associated with the Banco de México-Sofimex groups (A. B. Woodrow, Mrs. Jessie Williams, the Williams family, Sociedad Financiera Mexicana, R. D. Hutchinson, M. Gómez Morín) totaled 6,429; and members of the BUDA group (Raúl Bailleres, Ernesto J. Amescua, and the Banco General de Capitalización) held at least 979. (Other holdings may have represented these groups as well.) Hubert E. Rogers of the New York firm Rogers and Condon, although not listed as a shareholder, was clearly (judging from correspondence) one of the most important if not *the* major shareholder of the company. It is possible that he was represented by the holdings of the Moss Estate or by a combination of holdings listed for a large number of small shareholders.

In any event, in May 1938 Amescua and Domínguez approached Hutchinson and Gómez Morín to inform them that they had formed a group with sufficient capital to buy Rogers' shares in La Nacional, and asked for a promise that Sofimex would refrain from buying these shares as well as others that might be offered for sale. They spoke of the unsuitability of one group's controlling a society (a reference to the Sofimex group) and the importance of a balance between two groups; there were also references to a possible conflict between the administration (Amescua as manager, Domínguez as consulting actuary) and the shareholders regarding the company's investment program, should the latter be dominated by Sofimex. Gómez Morín responded that Sofimex did not control La Nacional nor desire to, but that Sofimex could not make such a promise and must be free to buy shares if they were offered. In fact, Gómez Morín wrote to Ignacio Hornik at once, noting that to his knowledge Rogers was not interested in selling his shares, but, if so, Sofimex and its group of shareholders were prepared to buy them (Gómez Morín, 13 and 14 May 1938). In subsequent years various other differences arose between the Sofimex and BUDA groups within La Nacional, with frequent appeals to Rogers to act as arbiter (I. Hornik, 1940a, b, and c; Woodrow, 1942). In a letter to Rogers regarding a very involved arrangement between Sofimex and BUDA groups concerning (among other things) the composition of the board in 1950, Hutchinson noted: "I would venture to add that our inner group of the 'old' Nacional shareholders is quite a little perturbed by the expressed desires of some others to buy up the control of the destinies of the company for—frankly—we do not feel at all sure that such control might not be exercised in some way not mainly for the good of the company. It is of great reassurance for us to feel that the weight of your interest lies in the same scale as ours" (Hutchinson, 1949).

The listing of shares, bonds, and secured loans of La Nacional in 1962 indicates continued financial support of both groups (Table C.6). At the same time, these and similar instances suggest that self-conscious groups did indeed exist by the 1930's, and that they manifested a definite concern with obtaining and maintaining control over institutions within their particular spheres.

Joint Investments

The collaboration of individuals and institutions associated through the Banco de Londres in the establishment of La Provincial and Sofimex was described above. Of equal interest is a project which failed—the attempted purchase of the Cervecería Moctezuma, the second largest brewery in the country.

In 1935 there were 19 breweries in Mexico which sold approximately 70 million litres; of this amount, nearly 60 million were sold by 3 companies having a combined capital of 21 million pesos: Cuauhtémoc (10 million), Moctezuma (7 million), and Modelo (4 million). The Moctezuma brewery, like that of Cuauhtémoc, had been established in the nineteenth century. The majority

TABLE C.6. La Nacional, Cia. de Seguros Sobre La Vida: Investments, 1962

Investments, 1962 (Selected categories)	
Total Investments	363,801,420.01
Selected categories (10 million pesos or more)	
Goverment securities	86,374,120.05
Bonds and obligations	15,626,625.68
Stock	43,422,629.00
Secured loans	13,465,130.88
Ordinary and policy loans	62,952,996.50
Mortgage loans	50,497,941.04
Property	65,541,883.58
Government securities (most important)	
Nacional Financiera, certificates of participation	61,960,500.00
Banco Nacional Hipotecario Urbano y de Obras Públicas	6,112,124.90
Housing bonds	16,333,000.00
Bonds and other obligations (1 million pesos or more)	
Cerv. Cuauhtémoc★	1,900,000.00
Fierro Esponja★	1,191,474.00
Hilados del Norte	1,119,665.00
Stock (1 million pesos or more)	
Altos Hornos de México	2,165,971.00
Banco de Londres y México★	12,225,745.00
Cemento de Mixcoac	1,260,000.00
Cerv. Moctezuma★★	1,699,500.00
Cia. Fundidora Monterrey	2,317,840.00
Cia. Mexicana de Guarantia	1,155,180.00
Crédito Minero y Mercantil★★	2,003,500.00
Crédito Hipotecario★★	3,017,040.00
Fábrica de Papel Loreto y Peña Pobre	1,200,000.00
La Provincial, Cia. Gral. de Seguros★	2,000,000.00
La Nacional, Cia. de Terrenos y Fincas	2,000,000.00
Sociedad Financiera Mexicana★	3,000,000.00
Tubos de Acero de México	1,844,690.00
Secured loans (1 million pesos or more)	
Jesús Llaguno (3 loans)	1,562,000.00
Carlos Trouyet	21,000,000.00
Agustín B. Carrasca	1,000,000.00
Intercontinental	1,000,000.00
Cia. General de Aceptaciones★ (9 loans)	4,284,000.00
Sociedad Financiera Mexicana★ (4 loans)	1,000,000.00

★ Banco de Londres/Garza Sada Group
★★ Bailleres Group (BUDA)
Source: Archivo MGM: La Nacional, 1948-1960

of its shares had been taken over by the Societé Financiere pour l'Industrie au Mexique, the investment society formed in 1900 by a group of private banks in Geneva, the Banque de Paris et des

Pays Bas, and the Barcelonnette group (Gómez Morín, 31 May 1935; 2 Sept. 1936).

In 1924, the third company, Cervecería Modelo, entered the market. While the Cuauhtémoc brewery (combined with its subsidiary Central in Mexico City) maintained its share of the market, with 40 to 49 percent of the sales of the 3 companies between 1924 and 1934, those of Modelo increased from 3 percent in 1924 to 24 percent in 1934, whereas those of Moctezuma decreased from 52 to 31 percent. Competition between the breweries resulted in drastic price reductions and subsequent efforts to reduce competition and "rationalize" the industry. The failure of this effort was, in turn, blamed on the managers of the Moctezuma brewery in Mexico (Gómez Morín, 21 May 1935a). One may surmise that the Moctezuma brewery was attempting to recover its former proportion of the market through price reductions, at the same time taking advantage of the increased market resulting from wage increases under the Cárdenas government. In any event, a group of Mexicans—among them members of the Cuauhtémoc group in Monterrey—began negotiations with the Societé Financiere to purchase controlling interest in Moctezuma, which would have given Cuauhtémoc a clear monopoly in the brewery industry, although this fact was kept in the background throughout the negotiations (Garza Sada, 1937a). Gómez Morín wished to deal with the top levels of the Societé or the Banque de Paris, bypassing representatives in Mexico allegedly responsible for the problem, and there were extended negotiations between Ignacio Hornik, representing the Mexican group (which also included Maximino Michel, Angel Urraza, and Estéban Castoreña—another Spanish businessman—until the last two were obliged to withdraw due to problems with agricultural holdings and the match industry, respectively) and Gastón Descombes, in France, a former director of the Banco Nacional (Gómez Morín, 21 May 1935b, enclosed memo; Gómez Morín, 25 May 1937). Although negotiations continued for nearly a year, and the parties seemed close to an agreement at one point, the negotiations were finally broken off, apparently due to disagreement regarding the price. The Cervecería Moctezuma was subsequently purchased by Raúl Bailleres of the BUDA group in 1941.[2]

[2] Also during this period, members of the same group were involved in a project to purchase La Consolidada, an iron and steel foundry controlled by the Harry Wright family. At one point, there was consideration of a combination similar to

Subsequent investment projects of these groups were more successful. In 1945, the Vidriera group (Garza Sada) branched into chemicals with the establishment of Celulosa y Derivados, S.A., initiating what would become the nucleus of a separate (chemical) group within the Garza Sada complex. In 1952, it signed a contract with Hulera Euzkadi by which the latter would provide technical and capital support to expand Celulosa y Derivados operations into the production of rayon tire cord, subscribing 88,000 of 200,000 shares of Celulosa y Derivados (48,000 of the 160,000 common shares and the total of 40,000 preferred shares) (Celulosa y Derivados, 1950-58).[3] In the early 1950's, Sofimex formed a group of Mexican shareholders—among them members of the Garza Sada families, shareholders of the Banco de Londres, and Maximino Michel of the Puerto de Liverpool—to collaborate with Alcoa in the establishment of Alcomex in 1952 (Gómez Morín, 6 Dec. 1950; 16 Oct. 1952).

Conclusion

In December 1958, 4 of the 1942 group of major shareholders of the Banco de Londres y México were among its top 14 shareholders (those with stocks of 1,000 shares or more). The four stockholders (★)—Cia. General de Aceptaciones, Puerto de Liverpool, Cia. Administrador de Valores (Urraza), and Sofimex—account for 18,148 of the 36,397 shares of major shareholders. To these can be added three other firms belonging to the group (★★), Banco Industrial de Monterrey, Banco Capitalizador de Monterrey, and Monterrey, Cia. de Seguros, bringing this total to 22,058

the above, with Monterrey businessmen, members of the Urraza and Castoreña group, and members of the Michel group each purchasing 25 percent; the last 25 percent would be purchased by William Jenkins (the Puebla ex-consul who controlled the Atencingo sugar properties and subsequently obtained controlling interest in the Banco de Comercio). There was some concern expressed about inclusion of Jenkins, who had indicated interest in purchasing half of the company and was a friend of the Wrights (Palacios Macedo, 1938). In the end, this venture also failed to materialize.

[3] In a memo to R. F. Moody of Hulera Euzkadi, Gómez Morín pointed out that the Hulera Euzkadi minority could be sufficient to guarantee satisfactory intervention in view of the distribution of the remaining shares among a large group of persons (Gómez Morín, 28 March 1952). Since this large group of persons presumably consisted of members of the Garza and Sada families and their close associates, however, it is not clear in this case that such dispersion of stock guaranteed foreign control.

TABLE C.7. Major Shareholders of the Banco de Londres y México: 1958

La Nacional, Cia. de Seguros	3,809
*Cia. Administrador de Valores (Urraza)	4,758
*Banco Industrial de Monterrey	1,268
Gregorio Gutierrez	2,083
*Puerto de Liverpool	4,040
Banco de Comercio	1,791
*Sofimex	2,214
**Banco Capitalizador de Monterrey	1,322
*Cia. General de Aceptaciones	7,136
**Monterrey Cia. de Seguros	1,320
Banco Nacional de México	2,221
Arq. Juan Cortina Portilla	2,053
Moises Cassio	1,835
Financiera México	1,097
TOTAL	36,947

Source: Archivo MGM, Banco de Londres

(see Table C.7). In addition are the 3,809 shares of La Nacional, in which members of the Banco de Londres group held substantial interests.

Thus the association among institutions linked to the Banco de Londres was an enduring one. Elements of this association include:

1. Stock holdings by individuals and institutions of the group in member banks or firms—as indicated by the lists of major stockholders of the Banco de Londres in 1934 and 1958; the initial shareholders of the insurance company La Provincial, and the major shareholders in Sofimex in 1937, 1944, 1954, and 1959.

2. Holdings by banks and other institutions of stocks and securities of firms of the group, as indicated by the investment portfolio of Sofimex for 1947, the Puerto de Liverpool in 1952, La Provincial in 1948, and to a lesser degree La Nacional in 1962.

3. Joint investment projects, including the unsuccessful attempts to purchase the Moctezuma brewery in the 1930's and the more successful joint ventures in the late forties and early fifties—i.e., of Hulera Euzkadi with Celulosa y Derivados, and of various members of the group with Alcoa in the establishment of Alcomex.

The pattern of relationships among shareholders in the various firms and institutions holding majority control in the Banco de Londres suggests not so much an investment group as a coalition of different investment groups with some interlocking interests. At this point no one group had controlling interest in the others,

although they were all related to each other through stockholdings, joint investments, and various financial transactions.

Subsequently, however, the Garza Sada interests have become
dominant within this group. Today the Banco de Londres y México is part of the Serfín financial group which is dominated by
Financiera Aceptaciones (the former Cia. General de Aceptaciones
of the Cuauhtémoc group). Serfín is, in turn, the financial group
of the Cuauhtémoc and Alfa (steel) groups of the Garza Sada investment group.

The looser association of the Banco de Londres-Sofimex group
thus seems to have constituted a temporary phase before the more
cohesive economic groups became dominant among the Mexican
private sector. As such, it may have constituted one of the more
dynamic forms of cooperation during the immediate post-revolutionary period when capital sources were limited, permitting a relatively stable association of groups and interests over a period of
time and at the same time drawing capital for new investments
from different groups and institutions.

Bibliography

Aguilar M., Alonso, 1972. "La oligarquía," in Jorge Carrión and Alonso Aguilar M., *La burquesía, la oligarquía y el Estado*. Mexico: Editorial Nuestro Tiempo.

Aguilar M., Alonso, and Fernando Carmona, 1967. *México: riqueza y miseria*, Mexico: Editorial Nuestro Tiempo. S.A.

Albornoz, Alvaro de, 1966. *Trayectoría y ritmo de crédito agrícola en México*, Mexico: Instituto Mexicano de Investigaciones Económicas.

Alejo, Francisco Javier, 1974. "La política fiscal en el desarrollo económico de México," in Miguel S. Wionczek (ed.) *La sociedad mexicana: Presente y futuro*. Mexico: Fondo de Cultura Económica (2nd edition).

Alvarez, Alejandro, and Elena Sandoval, 1975. "Desarrollo industrial y clase obrera en México," *Cuadernos Politicos*, 4 (April-June), 6-24.

Amin, Samir, 1976-1977. "Social Characteristics of Peripheral Formations: An Outline for an Historical Sociology," *Berkeley Journal of Sociology*, XXI, 27-50.

Anderson, Bo, and James D. Cockcroft, 1972. "Control and Cooptation in Mexican Politics," in Cockcroft, Andre Gunder Frank and Dale Johnson, *Dependence and Underdevelopment: Latin America's Political Economy*. Garden City, N.Y.: Doubleday & Co. (Anchor Books).

Anderson, Gosta, Roger Friedland, and Erik Olin Wright, 1976. "Modes of Class Struggle and the Capitalist State," *Kapitalistate, Working Papers on the Capitalist State*, No. 4-5 (Summer), 186-220.

Anderson, Perry, 1976-1977. "The Antinomies of Antonio Gramsci," *New Left Review* (Winter).

Anderson, Rodney D., 1976. *Outcasts in Their Own Land: Mexican Industrial Workers 1906-1911*. DeKalb: Northern Illinois University Press.

Anguiano, Arturo, 1975. *El Estado y la política obrera del cardenismo*. Mexico: Ediciones Era.

Anguiano, Arturo, et al., 1975. *Mexico y la izquierda mexicana: Ensayo, testimonias, documentos*, Mexico: Juan Pablos Editor.

Archivo de las Notarías (AN), Mexico, D.F.

Archivo de Recortes, Biblioteca Nacional, Mexico, D.F.

Archivo Luis Montes de Oca (LMO), Mexico, D.F.

Archivo Manuel Gómez Morín (MGM), Mexico, D.F.

Archivos Económicos, Biblioteca Miguel Lerda de Tejada: Secretaría de Hacienda y Crédito Público, Mexico, D.F.

Ashby, Joe C., 1963. *Organized Labor and the Mexican Revolution under Lázaro Cárdenas*. Chapel Hill: University of North Carolina Press.

Asociación de Banqueros de México (ABM), 1937-1941. *Circulares* (Jan. 1937-Nov. 1941), Mexico: ABM.

Asociación de Banqueros de México (ABM), 1938. *Informes*, Convención de ABM, Mexico, D.F.: ABM.

———, 1940-1975. Anuario Financiera, Mexico, D.F.: ABM.

Ayala, José, 1977. "La devaluación: Antecedentes económicos y políticos," *Cuadernos Políticos* (Mexico), 11 (Jan.-March), 35-45.

Bailey, David C., 1978. "Revisionism and the Recent Historiography of the Mexican Revolution," *Hispanic American Historical Review*, 58, 1 (February).

Bailleres, Raúl, 1936. Letter to Antonio Rodríguez (22 May). Archivo MGM: Antonio Rodríguez.

Baird, Peter, and Ed McCaughan, 1979. *Beyond the Border: Mexico and the U.S. Today.* New York: North American Congress on Latin America.

"Balanza de pagos del comercio exterior de México y aumento de la tarifa de importación," 1937. Archivo Luis Montes de Oca: Banco de México, 8 Dec.

Banco de Comercio, 1942. *Diez años de servicio 1932-1942*, Mexico, D.F.

Banco de Londres y México, 1964. *Cien años de banca en México: 1864-1964*. Mexico: Cia. Impresora y Litográfica "Juventud" S.A.

Banco de México, 1935-1940. Actas del Consejo de Administración. Archivo Luis Montes de Oca: Banco de México.

———, 1937. Estudio del Consejo de Administración del Banco de México (1 Sept.). Archivo LMO: Banco de México.

———, 1938. *Informe 1937*. Mexico, D.F.

———, 1939. *Informe 1938*. Mexico, D.F.

———, 1940. Memorandum de la Dirección General (28 Feb.). Archivo LMO: Banco de México.

———, 1941. *Informe 1940*. Mexico, D.F.

Banco Internacional, 1941-1946 Actas del Consejo. Archivo Luis Montes de Oca, Banco Internacional: Actas del Consejo.

Banco Mexicano, S.A., 1957. *Commemoración de su XXV aniversario: 1932-1957*. Mexico, D.F.

Banco Nacional de Crédito Agrícola y Ganadero. n.d. *Veinticinco años del Banco Nacional de Crédito Agrícola y Ganadero, S.A., 1926-1951*. Mexico: Oficina de Biblioteca y Publicaciones del Banco Nacional de Crédito Agrícola y Ganadero, S.A.

Banco Nacional de Crédito Ejidal, S.A. (Banco Ejidal), 1936-1943. *Informes Anuales, 1935-1942*. Mexico, D.F.

Banco Nacional de México (BNM), 1900-1975. *Informes*. Mexico, D.F.

———, 1934. *Quincuagésimo Aniversario de su Fundación*. Mexico: Editorial "Cultura."

———, 1934-1941. *Examen de la Situacion Económica de México*. Mexico, D.F.

"Los bancos y el sindicalismo," 1937. *Boletín Financiera y Minera* (editorial) (18 May).

Baran, Paul A., 1957. *The Political Economy of Growth*, New York: Monthly Review Press.

Barbosa, A. Rene, and Sergio Maturana, 1972. *El arrendamiento de tierras ejidales: Un estudio en Tierra Caliente, Michoacán*. Mexico: Centro de Investigaciones Agrarias.

Barchfield, John W. (n.d.). *Peasants, Politics and Development in Mexico*. Manuscript.

Barkin, David, 1975. "Mexico's Albatross: The U.S. Economy," *Latin America Perspectives*, II, 2 (Summer), 64-80.

Bartra, Roger, 1974. *Estructura agraria y clases sociales en México*, Mexico: Ediciones Era, Serie Popular Era.

———, 1975. "La revolución domesticada: Del bonapartismo pequeño-burgués a la institucionalización de la burguesía," *Historia y Sociedad.* (segunda epoca), 6 (Summer), 13-30.

Basurto, Jorge, 1975. *El proletariado industrial en México (1850-1930)*. Mexico: Instituto de Investigaciones Sociales, Universidad Nacional Autónoma de México.

Bazant, Jan, 1971. *Alienation of Church Wealth in Mexico: Social and Economic Aspects of the Liberal Revolution. 1856-1875.* Cambridge: University Press.

Benítez, Fernando, 1956. *El drama de un pueblo y de una planta*. Mexico: Fondo de Cultura Económica.

———, 1978. *Lázaro Cárdenas y la Revolución Mexicana. v. III, El cardenismo.* Mexico: Fondo de Cultura Económica.

Bennctt, Douglas C., and Kenneth E. Sharpe, 1979. "Agenda Setting and Bargaining Power: The Mexican State versus Transnational Automobile Corporations," *World Politics*, XXXII, 1 (October).

———, 1980. "The State as Banker and Entrepreneur: The Last Resort Character of the Mexican State's Intervention, 1917-1976," Comparative Politics, 12, 2 (January), 165-189.

Bennett, Robert L., 1965. *The Financial Sector and Economic Development: The Mexican Case*. Baltimore: Johns Hopkins Press.

Bernstein, Marvin D., 1965. *The Mexican Mining Industry, 1880-1905: A Study of the Interaction of Politics, Economics, and Technology*, Albany, N.Y.: State University of N.Y.

Beteta, Ramón (ed.), 1935. *Programa económica y social de México (una controversía)*. Mexico: n.p. (November).

Bett, Virgil, 1957. *Central Banking in Mexico: Monetary Policies and Financial Crisis, 1864-1940.* Ann Arbor: Bureau of Business Research, School of Business Administration, University of Michigan.

Blackburn, Robin, ed., 1973. *Ideology in Social Science*. New York: Vintage Books.

Blair, Calvin P., 1964. "Nacional Financiera: Entrepreneurship in a Mixed Economy," *Public Policy and Private Enterprise in Mexico*, ed. Raymond Vernon. Cambridge: Harvard University Press.

Block, Fred, 1977. "The Ruling Class Does Not Rule: Notes on the Marxist Theory of the State," *Socialist Revolution*, 33 (May-June), 6-28.

Blocker, William A., 1938. NAW 812.00/30550 (5 April).

———, 1939a. Letter to Lawrence Duggan (7 August), NAW 812.00/3088½.

———, 1939b. Confidential letter to Herbert Bursley (13 Sept.), NAW 812.00-Camacho, Manuel A./5½.

Boal, Pierre, 1938. Letter to Secretary of State (21 June), NAW 812.001-Cárdenas, Lázaro/132.

———, 1939a. Letter to Secretary of State (1 Sept.), NAW 812.6511/7.

———, 1939b. Note to Lawrence Duggan (25 Nov.), NAW 812.00/30879½.

Bodenheimer, Suzanne, 1970. "Dependency and Imperialism: The Roots of Latin American Underdevelopment," *Politics and Society* (May).

Boletín Financiera y Mineral de México (BFM), 1934. III Convención Bancaria, celebrado en la ciudad de Guadalajara, Jalisco, April.

———, 1935-1941 (Mexico), Jan. 1935 to Jan. 1941.

———, 1937. *Revista del Año 1937.*

———, 1939. *Revista Financiera del Año de 1938.* (Mexico, D.F.) (1 Jan.).

Bosques, Gilberto, 1937. *The National Revolutionary Party of Mexico and the Six-Year Plan.* Mexico: National Revolutionary Party, Bureau of Foreign Information.

Bossert, Thomas John, 1977. "Dependency and the Disintegration of the State: Lessons from Allende's Chile." Paper presented at Annual Meeting of the American Political Science Association, Washington, D.C. (September).

Boyle, Lewis V., 1940. (2 April), NAW 812.000/30997.

Brandenberg, Frank, 1964. *The Making of Modern Mexico.* Englewood Cliffs, N.J.: Prentice-Hall.

Braunmuhl, Claudia von, 1978. "On the Analysis of the Bourgeois Nation State within the World Market Context," in *State and Capital: A Marxist Debate*, ed. Holloway and Picciotto. London: Edward Arnold.

Brenner, Robert, 1977. "The Origins of Capitalist Development: A Critique of Neo-Smithian Marxism," *New Left Review*, 104 (July-August).

Brown, Lyle C., 1971. "Los Comunistas y el Régimen de Cárdenas," *Revista de la Universidad de México*, XXV (May).

Bukharin, Nikolai, 1973. *Imperialism and the World Economy.* New York: Monthly Review Press.

Bursley, Herbert S., 1940a. Note to Lawrence Duggan (7 March), NAW 812.00/30968.

———, 1940b. Memo to Duggan and Welles (18 May). Enclosure: Letter from William B. Richardson to W. W. Lancaster, NAW 812.00/31005.

———, 1940c. Letter to Sumner Welles (25 July), NAW 812.00/31229½.

Calderón Rodríguez, Miguel Angel, 1976. "El impacto de la crisis de 1929 en México," Tesis, Escuela Nacional de Economía, Universidad Nacional Autónoma de México, Mexico.

Camp, Roderic Ai, 1976. *Mexican Political Biographies: 1935-1975*, Tucson: University of Arizona Press.

Campbell, Hugh G., 1976. *La derecha radical en México, 1929-1949*. Mexico: Sep Setentas 276.

Cárdenas, Lázaro, 1972a. *Ideario político*. Mexico: Ediciones Era, Serie Popular Era.

———, 1972b. *Obras: 1-Apuntes 1913-1940*. Mexico: Universidad Nacional Autónomo de México.

Cardero, Maria Elena, 1979. "Estructura monetaria y financiera de México: 1932-1940," *Revista Mexicana de Sociología* XLI, 3 (July-Sept.), 729-768.

Cardoso, Fernando Henrique, 1973. "Associated-Dependent Development: Theoretical and Practical Implications," in *Authoritarian Brazil*, ed. Alfred Stepan. New Haven: Yale University Press.

———, 1975. "Notos sobre el estado actual de los estudios de dependencia," in Sergio Bagu et al. *Problemas de desarrollo latinoamericano*. Mexico: Editorial Nuestro Tiempo.

Cardoso, Fernando Henrique, and Enzo Faletto, 1969. *Dependencia y desarrollo en América Latina*. Mexico: Siglo Veintiuno Editores.

———, 1978. *Dependency and Development in Latin America*. Berkeley: University of California Press.

Carr, Barry, 1976. *El movimiento obrero y la política en México, 1910-1929*. (2 vols.). Mexico: Sep-Setentas, 256, 257.

———, 1980. "Recent Regional Studies of the Mexican Revolution," *Latin American Research Review*, XV, 1.

Casas Alatriste, Roberto, 1937. Letter to Eduardo Suárez, 5 July. Archivo Luis Montes de Oca, Corespondencia Secretaría de Hacienda.

Casteñeda, Roberto, 1976. "Los límites del capitalismo en México: Las finanzas del régimen," *Cuadernos Políticos*, 8 (April-June), 53-74.

Celulosa y Derivados, 1950-1958. Varias memoranda. Archivo MGM.

Cerrillo, Alfonso, 1937. Memo (June). Archivo Luis Montes de Oca: Crédito Hotelero.

Cervecería Central, 1937. Memorandum, 22 April. Archivo MGM: Cervecería Central.

Cervecería Cuauhtémoc, 1938. Estados financieros del mes de julio. Archivo MGM, Cervecería Cuauhtémoc General, 1937.

Chase-Dunn, Christopher, and Richard Rubinson, 1977. "Toward a Structural Perspective on the World System," *Politics and Society*, 7, 4.

Chassen, Francine R., 1977. "La CTM y la expropriación petrolera" Memoria del Primer Coloquio Regional de Historia Obrera. Mexico: Centro de Estudios Históricos del Movimiento Obrero Mexicano.

Chevalier, François, 1963. *Land and Society in Colonial Mexico: The Great Hacienda*. Berkeley: University of California Press.

———, 1967. "The Ejido and Political Stability in Mexico," in *The Politics of Conformity in Latin America*, ed. Claudio Veliz. London: Oxford University Press.

Chilcote, Ronald H., and Joel C. Edelstein, ed., 1974. *Latin America: The Struggle with Dependency and Beyond*. New York: John Wiley & Sons.

Cinta G., Ricardo, 1972. "Bourgeoisie nacional y desarrollo," *El Perfil de Mexico en 1980*, III. Mexico, D.F.: Siglo Veintiuno.

Clark, Marjorie Ruth, 1934. *Organized Labor in Mexico*. Chapel Hill: University of North Carolina Press.

Clash, Thomas Wood, 1972. *United States-Mexican Relations, 1940-1946: A Study of U.S. Interests and Politics*, Thesis (Ph.D.), State University of New York at Buffalo.

Clave: Tribuna Marxista, 1939-1940. (Mexico, D.F.).

Coatsworth, John H., 1975. "Los orígenes del autoritarismo moderno en México," *Foro Internacional*, XVI, 2 (62) (Oct.-Dec.), 205-232.

Cockcroft, James D., 1968. *Intellectual Precursors of the Mexican Revolution, 1900-1913*. Austin: University of Texas Press.

———, 1972. "Social and Economic Structure of the Porfiriato: Mexico 1877-1911," in Cockcroft, Andre Gunder Frank, and Dale Johnson, *Dependence and Underdevelopment: Latin America's Political Economy*. Garden City, N.Y.: Doubleday & Co. (Anchor Books).

———, 1979. *El imperialismo, la lucha de clases y el Estado en México*. Mexico: Editorial Nuestro Tiempo.

Cockcroft, James D., Andre Gunder Frank, and Dale L. Johnson, 1972. *Dependence and Underdevelopment: Latin America's Political Economy*. Garden City, New York: Doubleday & Co. (Anchor Books).

Coello Salazar, Emilio, 1965. "El comercio interior," in *Historia moderno de México: El porfiriato* v. 7, Book 2, *La vida económica*, ed. Daniel Cosio Villegas. Mexico: Editorial Hermes.

Collier, David, ed., 1979. *The New Authoritarianism in Latin America*. Princeton: Princeton University Press.

Confederación de Cámaras Nacionales de Comercio e Industria, 1940 *Análisis económico nacional 1934-1940* (Nov.).

Confederación de Trabajadores de Mexico (CTM), 1941. *CTM, 1936-1941*. Mexico: Talleres Tipográficos Modelo.

Contreras, Ariel José, 1977. *México 1940: industrialización y crisis política: Estado y Sociedad civil en las elecciones presidenciales*. Mexico: Siglo Veintiuno.

Contreras Méndez, Enrique Arturo, 1976. *El grupo industrial Monterrey*. Tesis profesional, Escuela Nacional de Economía, Universidad Nacional Autónoma de México, Mexico, D.F.

Cordero, Salvador, and Rafael Santín, 1977. "Los grupos industriales: una nueva organización económica en México." Mexico: Colegio de Mexico (Cuadernos del CES 23).

Córdova, Arnaldo, 1972. "Las reformas sociales y la technocratización del Estado mexicano," *Revista Mexicana de Ciencia Política*, 70 (Oct.-Dec.), 61-92.

———, 1973. *La ideología de la revolución mexicana: La formación del nuevo régimen*. Mexico: Ediciones Era.

———, 1974. *La política de masas del cardenismo*. Mexico: Ediciones Era, S.A., Serie Popular Era.

Cornelius, Wayne A., Jr., 1971. "Nation-Building, Participation, and Distribution: The Politics of Social Reform under Cárdenas," in *Developmental Episodes in Comparative Politics: Crisis, Choice and Change*, ed. G. A. Almond and Scott C. Flanagan. Boston: Little, Brown and Company.

Council on Foreign Relations, 1931. *Survey of American Foreign Relations*. New Haven: Yale University Press.

Cronon, E. David, 1960. *Josephus Daniels in Mexico*. Madison: University of Wisconsin Press.

Cumberland, Charles C., 1968. *Mexico: The Struggle for Modernity*. London: Oxford University Press.

———, 1972. *Mexican Revolution. The Constitutionalist Years*. Austin: University of Texas Press.

Cunningham, Charles H., 1932. Memo of 10 Dec. NAW RG 151 (128.2).

Daniels, Josephus, 1934. Letter to Secretary of State (17 April). NAW 812.00/30041.

———, 1935. Letter to Secretary of State (25 June). NAW 812.00/30228.

———, 1938a. Letter to Secretary of State (15 April), Enclosure. NAW 812.00/30559.

———, 1938b. Letter to Secretary of State (7 July), Enclosure. NAW 812.00/30589.

———, 1938c. Letter to Secretary of State (12 July). NAW 812.52/2927.

———, 1938d. Letter to Secretary of State (13 Aug.), Enclosure. NAW 812.00/30610.

———, 1938e. Letter to Secretary of State (14 Oct.). NAW 812.00/50633.

———, 1938f. Letter to Secretary of State (10 Dec.). NAW 812.00/30662.

———, 1939a. Letter to Secretary of State (23 Jan.). NAW 812.00/30682.

———, 1939b. Letter to Secretary of State (17 Feb.). NAW 812.00/30697.

———, 1939c. Letter to Secretary of State (15 Mar.). NAW 812.00/30707.

DeJanvry, Alain, and Lynn Ground, 1978. "Types and Consequences of Land Reform in Latin America," *Latin American Perspectives*, V, 4 (Fall).

de la Cueva, Mario, 1967. *Derecho mexicano del trabajo*. Mexico: Editorial Porrua.

de la Peña, Moises T., 1937. "La expropriación de los ferrocarriles de México. *Trimestre Económico*, 15.

de Maria y Campos, Armando, 1939. *Múgica: Crónica biográfica.* Mexico: Cia. de Ediciones Popular, S.A.

Delli Sante, Angela M., 1979. "The Private Sector, Business Organizations, and International Influence: A Case Study of Mexico," in *Capitalism and the State in U.S.-Latin American Relations,* ed. Richard Fagan. Stanford: Stanford University Press.

Diario de los Negocios, 1935-1941. Jan. 1935-Jan. 1941, Mexico, D.F.

Diccionario Biográfica de México, 1968. Monterrey, Mexico: Editorial Revisa.

Diccionario Porrúa Historia, Biografía y Geografía de México, 1970. (3rd edition). Mexico: Editorial Porrua S.A.

Diez Artículos Publicados en *Informador Económica,* Organo Mensual del Banco Internacional, S.A. n.d. Mexico: Banco Internacional.

D'Olwer, Luis Nicolau, 1965. "Las inversiones extranjeras," in *Historia moderna de México, El porfiriato.* (vol. 8). Vida Económica, ed. Daniel Cosio Villages. Mexico: Editorial Hermes.

Domhoff, G. William, 1967. *Who Rules America?* Englewood Cliffs, N.J.:Prentice-Hall.

———, 1970. *The Higher Circles.* New York: Vintage Books.

Dos Santos, Theotonio, 1970. "The Structure of Dependence," *American Economic Review,* LX, 2 (Papers and Proceedings of the 82nd Annual Meeting of the American Economic Association, New York City, December 28-30, 1969) (May).

Draper, Hal, 1977. *Karl Marx's Theory of Revolution.* 1 *State and Bureaucracy,* Book I. New York: Monthly Review Press.

Duggan, Lawrence, 1937. Letter of 13 December, to Sumner Welles. NAW 812.52/2529.

Dunn, John, 1972. *Modern Revolution: An Introduction to the Analysis of a Political Phenomenon.* Cambridge: University Press.

Eaton, 1940. (2 February). NAW 812.00/30928.

Eckstein, Salomón, 1966. *El ejido colectivo en México.* Mexico: Fondo de Cultura Económica.

Eckstein, Susan, 1977. *The Poverty of Revolution.* Princeton: Princeton University Press.

———, 1982. "The Impact of Revolution on Social Welfare in Latin America," *Theory and Society,* forthcoming.

El Economista, 1939-1940. Organ of the Instituto de Estudios Económicos y Sociales. Mexico, D.F.

Engels, Frederick, 1959. *Anti-Duhring: Herr Eugen Duhring's Revolution in Science.* Moscow: Foreign Languages Publishing House.

———, 1972. *The Origin of the Family, Private Property and the State.* New York: International Publishers.

Espinosa Porset, Ernesto, 1958. "54 años de vida bancaria." Mexico: Banxico (special edition).

Evans, Peter, 1976. "Continuities and Contradictions in the Evolution of Brazilian Dependence," *Latin American Perspectives*, III, 2 (Spring).

————, 1979. *Dependent Development: The Alliance of Multinational, State and Local Capital in Brazil*. Princeton: Princeton University Press.

Excelsior, 1932-1960 (Mexico, D.F.).

Extracto de las Comunicaciones Cambiados entre el Banco de Londres y el Banco de Paris (n.d.). Archivo MGM: Banco de Londres y México, Reorganizacion 1933.

Fagen, Richard R., and William S. Tuohy, 1972. "Aspects of the Mexican Political System," *Studies in Comparative International Development*, VII, 3 (Fall).

Fajnzylber, Fernando, and Trinidad Martínez Tarragó, 1976. *Las empresas transnacionales: expansión a nivel mundial y proyección en la industria mexicana*. Mexico: Fondo de Cultura Económica.

Falcón, Ramona, 1978. "El surgimiento del agrarismo cardenista—Una revisión de las tesis populistas." *Historia Mexicana* (Mexico), XXVII, 3 (Jan.-March), 333-386.

Fernández Cueta, Francisco, n.d. Archivo MGM: Sofimex 1941-1947.

Fernández del Campo, Luis, 1937. "El movimiento obrero mexicano," *Futuro* (May).

Fitzgerald, E.V.K., 1979. "A Note on State Capital and Industrialization in Mexico," in *Industrialization and the State in Latin America*, ed. Jean Carriere. Amsterdam: Center for Latin American Research and Documentation.

Frank, Andre Gunder, 1967. *Capitalism and Underdevelopment in Latin America: Historical Studies of Chile and Brazil*. New York: Monthly Review Press.

Fournais, Knud, 1955. Memo (1 March). Archivo MGM (Nuevo) 117: Cia. Hulera Euzkadi Goodrich, Dirs.

Fuentes Díaz, Vicente, 1959. "Desarrollo y evolución del movimiento obrero a partir de 1929," *Ciencias Políticas y Sociales*, V, 17 (July-Sept.), 325-348.

Fuentes Mares, José, 1968. *Don Eloy S. Vallina*. Mexico: Editorial Jus.

Furtado, Celso, 1976. *Economic Development of Latin America* (2nd edition). Cambridge: Cambridge University Press.

Furtak, Robert K., 1974. *El partido de la revolución y la estabilidad en México*. Mexico: Universidad Nacional Autónoma de México, Facultad de Ciencias Políticas y Sociales (Serie Estudios 35).

Futuro, 1936-1940. Mexico, D.F.

Ganem, Narse M., 1967. *Evolución histórica de la industria azucarera mexicana*. Mexico.

García, Rafael, 1901. "El presente y el porvenir económico de la república": colección de artículos económico-políticos escritos y publicados en *El Universal* y *la Gaceta Comercial*. Mexico: Eusebio Sánchez, Editor.

García Cantú, Gastón, 1965. *El pensamiento de la reacción mexicana. Historia documental, 1810-1962.* Mexico: Empresas Editoriales.

García Díaz, Maria, 1953. "La intervención del Estado en la economía mexicana: Bases constitucionales y su evolución desde 1925," Tesis, Licenciado en Economía, Mexico, UNAM, Escuela Nacional de Economía.

García Treviño, Rodrigo, 1939. "Las administraciones obreras," *Clave*, Tribuna Marxista, 9 (1 July).

Garza Sada, Roberto, 1937a. Letter to Gómez Morín (28 March). Archivo MGM: Cervecería Cuauhtémoc, Asuntos Financieros.

———, 1937b. Letter to Gómez Morín (9 July). Archivo MGM: Cervecería Cuauhtémoc General.

Gerschenkron, Alexander, 1962. *Economic Backwardness in Historical Perspective.* Cambridge: The Belknap Press of Harvard University Press.

Gill, Mario, 1955. "Veracruz: Revolución y extremismo," *Historia Mexicana*, Vol. 2, 4 (8) (April-June), 618-636.

———, 1957. *La conquista del Valle del Fuerte.* Mexico: n.p.

———, 1962. *El sinarquismo: Su origin, su esencia, su misión.* (3rd edition). Mexico: Editorial Olin.

———, 1971. *Los ferrocarrileros.* Mexico: Editorial Extemporaneas.

Gilly, Adolfo, 1975. *La revolución interrumpida: México, 1910-1920, una guerra campesina por la tierra y el poder.* Mexico: Ediciones "El Caballito." (5th edition).

———, 1978. "Curva de salarios y conciencia obrera," *Coyoacán*: Revista marxista latinoamericana, I, 2 (Jan.-March), 95-113.

Glade, William P., Jr., and Charles W. Anderson, 1963. *The Political Economy of Mexico.* Madison: University of Wisconsin Press.

Gold, David, Clarence Y. H. Lo, and Erik Olin Wright, 1975. "Recent Developments in Marxist Theory of the Capitalist State," *Monthly Review* (October and November).

Goldfrank, Walter, 1979. "Theories of Revolution and Revolution without Theory: The Case of Mexico," *Theory and Society*, 7.

Gómez Arreola, Salvador, 1967. "Los seguros privados en México." Mexico, D.F.: (Mimeo).

Gómez Jara, Francisco A., 1970. *El movimiento campesino en México.* Mexico: Ed. Campesina.

Gómez Morín, Manuel, 1933a. (19 Sept.) Letter to Mario M. Blasquez. Archivo MGM: Banco Algondonera Refaccionario.

———, 1933b. (19 Sept.) Letter to Lic. Virgilio Garza. Archivo MGM: Lic. Virgilio Garza, Jr.

———, 1935. (11 May) Memo. Archivo MGM: Cervecería Cuauhtémoc (Asuntos Financieros).

———, 1935. (17 May) Letter to Francisco G. Sada. Archivo MGM: Francisco G. Sada.

———, 1935a (21 May) Letter to Ignacio Hornik. Archivo MGM: Cervecería Cuauhtémoc (Asuntos Financieros).

———, 1935b. (21 May) Memo. Archivo MGM: Estudios Diversos.

———, 1935. (31 May) Letter to I. Hornik. Archivo MGM: Cervecería Cuauhtémoc (Asuntos Financieros).

———, 1936. (2 Jan.) Letter to Francisco G. Sada. Archivo MGM: Estudios diversos, Estatutos.

———, 1936. (7 July) Letter to Francisco G. Sada. Archivo MGM: Cervecería Cuauhtémoc General 1937.

———, 1936. (2 Sept.) Memorandum. Archivo MGM: Estudios Diversos.

———, 1936. (21 Oct.) Letter to Descombes. Archivo MGM: Cervecería Cuauhtémoc (Asuntos Financieros).

———, 1937. (25 May) Letter to Roberto Garza Sada. Archivo MGM: Cervecería Cuauhtémoc, Nueva Emisión.

———, 1937. (14 June) Letter to I. Hornik. Archivo MGM: Cervecería Cuauhtémoc (Asuntos Financieros).

———, 1937. (17 June) Letter to Roberto Garza Sada. Archivo MGM: Cervecería Cuauhtémoc, Nueva Emisión.

———, 1938. (13 and 14 May) Letters to Ignacio Hornik. Archivo MGM: Dr. Ignacio Hornik.

———, 1947. (4 August) Letter to I. Hornik. Archivo MGM: Sofimex 1941-1947.

———, 1950. (6 Dec.) Letter to Roberto Garza Sada. Archivo MGM: Roberto Garza Sada, 1942-52.

———, 1952. (28 March) Memo to R. F. Moody. Archivo MGM: Celulosa y Derivados, 1950-58.

———, 1952. (16 Oct.) Letter to Eugenio Garza Sada. Archivo MGM: Roberto Garza Sada, 1942-52.

González, Francisco Alonso, 1972. *Historia y petroleo: México en su lucha por la independencia económica. El problema petroleo.* Mexico: Ediciones "El Caballito."

González, Luis, 1979. *Los Artifices del Cardenismo. Historia de la Revolución Mexicana*, v. 14. Mexico: Colegio de Mexico.

González Aparicio, Enrique, 1937. *El problema agrario y el crédito rural.* Mexico: Imprenta Mundial.

González Casanova, Pablo, 1970. *Democracy in Mexico.* New York: Oxford University Press.

González Navarro, Moisés, 1963. *La Confederación Nacional Campesina (Un grupo de presión en la reforma agraria mexicana).* Mexico: B. Costa-Amic, ed.

Good, Loretta Louise, 1972. *United States Joint Ventures and National Manufacturing Firms in Monterrey, Mexico: Comparative Styles of Management.* Ithaca: Cornell University.

Goodspeed, Stephen Spencer, 1955. "El papel del jefe del ejecutivo en México," *Problemas Agrícolas e Industriales de México*, VII, 1.

Gracey, Wilbur T., 1918. Letter to Henry P. Fletcher, U.S. Ambassador to Mexico (27 Nov.). NAW, RG 84. 1918, Part IV, Class 6.

Graf Campos, María del Carmen, 1975. Las empresas estatales en el desarrollo económico de México: Ferrocarriles Nacionales de México. Tesis, Escuela Nacional de Economía, Universidad Nacional Autónoma de México, Mexico, D.F.

Gramsci, Antonio, 1971. *Selections from the Prison Notebooks*. New York: International Publishers.

———, 1974. *Partido y revolución*. Mexico, D.F.: Ediciones de Cultura Popular, S.A.

Greuning, Ernest, 1928. *Mexico and Its Heritage*. New York: The Century Company.

Grieb, Kenneth J., 1971. "Standard Oil and the Financing of the Mexican Revolution," *California Historical Society Quarterly*, XLX, 1 (March).

Guerrero, Francisco Javier, 1975. "La colectivización capitalista del campo," *Cuadernos Políticos* 3 (Jan.-March), 70-81.

Gutelman, Michel, *Capitalismo y reforma agraria en México*. Mexico: Ediciones Era (Colección Problemas de México).

Hamilton, Nora Louise, 1978. Mexico: The Limits of State Autonomy. Ph.D. Thesis, Department of Sociology, University of Wisconsin, Madison.

Hammond, John Hays, 1919. "Wanted: A Foreign Trade Policy," *The Annals* (American Academy of Political and Social Sciences).

Hansen, Roger, 1974. *The Politics of Mexican Development*. Baltimore: Johns Hopkins University Press.

Harding, Timothy F., 1976. "Dependency, Nationalism and the State in Latin America," *Latin American Perspectives*, III, 4 (Fall), 3-11.

Harris, Richard, 1978. "Marxism and the Agrarian Question in Latin America" *Latin American Perspectives*, V, 4 (Fall).

Haynes, Keith Allen, 1981. " 'Orden y Progreso': The Revolutionary Ideology of Alberto J. Pani." Paper presented at the VI Conference of Mexican and United States Historians, Chicago, Illinois (September 8-12).

Hefley, James C., 1970. *Aarón Sáenz: Mexico's Revolutionary Capitalist*. Waco, Texas: World Books.

Hellman, Judith Adler, 1978. *Mexico in Crisis*. New York: Holmes & Meier Publishers, Inc.

Hernández Chavez, Alicia, 1979. *La Mecánica Cardenista. Historia de la Revolución Mexicana*, v. 16. Mexico: El Colegio de México.

Hewitt de Alcántara, Cynthia, 1974. *The Social and Economic Implications of Large-Scale Introduction of New Varieties of Food Grains: Country Report-*

Mexico. Geneva: United Nations Research Institute for Social Development, November.

————, 1978. *La modernizacion de la agricultura mexicana: 1940-1970.* Mexico: Siglo XXI.

Hillyer, A. S. (Chief, Commercial Intelligence Division, U.S. Bureau of Foreign and Domestic Commerce), 1929. Memo to Mexico City Office (27 Sept.). NAW, RG 151, 611 (Foreign Banks-Mexico 1925-1929).

Hodges, Donald, and Ross Gandy, 1979. *Mexico 1910-1976: Reform or Revolution?* London: Zed Press.

Holloway, John, and Sol Picciotto, ed. 1978. *State and Capital: A Marxist Debate.* London: Edward Arnold.

Hombre Libre (Mexico) 1938, 1940 (July-Oct. 1938) (Jan.-Oct. 1940).

Hornik, Ignacio, 1940a. Letter to Gómez Morín (26 July). Archivo MGM: Dr. Ignacio Hornik.

————, 1940b. Letter to Gómez Morín (20 Sept.). Archivo MGM: Dr. Ignacio Hornik.

————, 1940c. Letter to Gómez Morín (25 Sept.). Archivo MGM: Dr. Ignacio Hornik.

Huizer, Gerrit, 1970. *La lucha campesina en México.* Mexico: Centro de Investigaciones Agrarias.

Hulera Euzkadi, 1935. Convenio (29 Oct.). Archivo MGM: Cia. Manufacturera de Artefactos de Hule.

————, 1936. Agreement Goodrich, Euzkadi, and the International B. F. Goodrich Company (22 Jan.). Archivo MGM: Cia. Manufacturera de Artefactos de Hule.

Hutchinson, Robert, 1949. Letter to H. Rogers (22 November). Archivo MGM: La Nacional/Hutchinson.

Ianni, Octavio, 1975. *La formación del Estado populista en América Latina.* Mexico: Ediciones Era.

Iglesias, Severo, 1970. *Sindicalismo y socialismo en México.* Mexico: Ed. Grijalbo, Colección Nuestras Cosas.

Jiménez Ricárdez, Ruben, 1978. "Mariátequi y el marxismo en América Latina," *Cuadernos Políticos* (Mexico), 17 (July-September).

Jones, Grosvenor N., 1925. Letter to Lewis L. Strauss, Kuhn Loeb & Co. (27 May). NAW, RG 151, 611 (Foreign Banks-Mexico, 1925-1929).

Joseph, Gilbert M., 1979. "Mexico's 'Popular Revolution': Mobilization and Myth in Yucatán, 1910-1940," *Latin American Perspectives*, VI, 3 (Summer).

Journal of Commerce 1940. "Mexico and Her Relations to American Defense." 185, 14 (August), 2nd section.

Kaplan, Marcos, 1969. *Formación del Estado nacional en América Latiná.* Santiago, Chile: Editorial Universitaria.

Katz, Friedrich, 1974. "Labor Conditions on Haciendas in Porfirian Mexico: Some Trends and Tendencies," *Hispanic American Historical Review*, 54, 1 (February), 1-47.

Kaufman, Robert R., 1977. "Mexico and Latin American Authoritarianism," in *Authoritarianism in Mexico*, ed. José Luis Reyna and Richard S. Weinert. Philadelphia: Institute for the Study of Human Issues.

Kay, Geoffrey, 1975. *Development and Underdevelopment: A Marxist Analysis*. London: St. Martin's Press.

Keremitsis, Dawn, 1973. *La industria textil mexicana en el siglo XIX*. Mexico: Sep Setentas (67).

Kies, William S., 1920. "Latin American Securities," *The Annals* (American Academy of Political and Social Sciences).

King, Timothy, 1970. *Mexico: Industrialization and Trade Policies since 1940*. London: Oxford University Press.

Kirk, Betty, 1942. *Covering the Mexican Front: The Battle of Europe vs. America*. Norman, Okla.: University of Oklahoma Press.

Knight, Alan, 1981. "Intellectuals in the Mexican Revolution." Paper presented at the VI Conference of Mexican and United States Historians, Chicago, Illinois (September 8-12).

Kock, M. H. de., 1941. *La banca central*. Mexico: Fondo de Cultura Económica (2nd edition).

Kolko, Gabriel, 1963. *The Triumph of Conservatism*. Chicago: Quadrangle Books.

Krauze, Enrique, 1976. *Caudillos culturales en la revolución mexicana*. Mexico: Siglo Veintiuno.

————, 1977. *La reconstrucción económica. Historia de la revolución mexicana*, v. 10. Mexico: Colegio de México.

Labastida Martín del Campo, Julio, 1972. "Los grupos dominantes frente a las alternativas del cambio," *Perfil de Mexico en 1980*. Mexico: Siglo Veintiuno.

Lamont, Thomas, 1926. Letter to Kellogg (29 December). NAW 812.51/1315.

Landsberger, Henry A., and Cynthia Hewitt de Alcántara, 1970. *Peasant Organizations in La Laguna, Mexico: History, Structure, Member Participation and Effectiveness*. Inter-American Committee for Agricultural Development (CIDA), Research Papers on Land Tenure and Agrarian Reform. Research Paper 17, Washington, D.C. (November).

Latin American Economic Report (LAER), 1978-1979. London: Latin American Newsletters Ltd.

Latin American Perspectives, 1981. VII, 2-3 (Summer-Fall).

Lavín Isla, Gonzalo, 1939. Letter of 30 Nov. to Manuel Gómez Morín, Archivo MGM: Estudios Diversos—Seguros.

Leal, Juan Felipe, 1974. *La burguesía y el Estado mexicano*. Mexico: Ediciones "El Caballito" (second edition).

————, 1975a. "The Mexican State: 1915-1973. A Historical Interpretation," *Latin American Perspectives*, II, 2 (Summer), 48-63.

————, 1975b. *Mexico: Estado, burocracia y sindicatos*. Mexico: Ediciones "El Caballito."

Leal, Juan Felipe, and Mario Huacuja Rountree, 1977. "San Antonio Xala: Una hacienda mexicana en el cambio (1861-1925). Planteamiento y estado actual de la investigación." Mexico: Centro de Estudios Latino-americanos (Serie: Avances de Investigación 20), Facultad de Ciencias Políticas y Sociales, Universidad Nacional Autónoma de México.

Leff, Nathaniel H., 1978. "Industrial Organization and Entrepreneurship in the Developing Countries: The Economic Groups." *Economic Development and Cultural Change*, 26 (July).

Lenin, Vladimir Ilich, 1964. *Collected Works*. v. 22: December 1915-January 1916. Moscow: Progress Publishers.

León, Samuel, 1975. "Notas sobre la burocracia sindical mexicana," *Revista Mexicana de Ciencias Políticas y Sociales*, 82 (Oct.-Dec.).

————, n.d. "Clase obrera y cardenismo." Mexico: Centro de Estudios Latinoamericanos, Facultad de Ciencias Políticas y Sociales, Universidad Nacional Autónoma de México (CELA, Serie: Documentos 1).

————, 1977. "El Comité Nacional de Defensa Proletaria" *Memoria del Primer Coloquio Regional de Historia Obrera*. Mexico, D.F.: Centro de Estudios Históricos del Movimiento Obrero Mexicano.

Lerner, Victoria, 1979. *La Educación Socialista. Historia de la Revolución Mexicana*. v. 17. Mexico: El Colegio de México.

Levenstein, Harvey A., 1971. *Labor Organizations in the United States and Mexico: A History of Their Relations*. Westport: Greenwood Press.

Lewis, Cleona, and Karl T. Schlotterbeck, 1938. *America's Stake in International Investments*. Washington, D.C.: The Brookings Institution.

Lieuwen, Edwin, 1968. *Mexican Militarism: The Political Rise and Fall of the Revolutionary Army*. New Mexico: University of New Mexico Press.

Loaeza, Soledad, 1974. "El Partido Acción Nacional: La oposición leal en México," *Foro International*, XIV, 3 (Jan.-March).

Lobato López, Ernesto, 1945. *El crédito en México. Esbozo histórico hasta 1925*. Mexico: Fondo de Cultura Económica.

Lockett, Thomas, 1934. Financial report of 25 September. NAW, RG 151, 600: Mexico: Finance and Investments.

————, 1935a. Report of 12 February, NAW, RG 151/128.1.

————, 1935b. Financial Report of 17 July, NAW, RG 151, file 600 (Mexico).

————, 1936a. Financial Report of 20 April, NAW, RG 151/600.

————, 1936b. Financial Report 69, 5 June, NAW, RG 151/600.

————, 1936c. Financial Report 72, 20 June, NAW, RG 151/600.

————, 1936d. Financial Report of 13 October, NAW, RG 151/600.

————, 1936e. Financial Report 89, 23 October, NAW, RG 151/600.

Lockett, Thomas, 1936f. Financial Report 78, 2 November, NAW, RG 151/600.

———, 1937a. Financial Report of 8 January, NAW, RG 151/600.

———, 1937b. Financial Report 177, 29 March, NAW, RG 151/600.

———, 1937c. Financial Report 69 of 23 September, NAW, RG 151/600.

———, 1937d. Financial Report of 29 October, NAW, RG 151/600.

———, 1937e. Financial Report 168, 28 December, NAW, RG 151/600.

———, 1938a. Financial Report 291, 23 May, NAW, RG 151/600.

———, 1938b. Financial Report 154, 19 December, RG 151/600.

Lombardo Toledano, Vicente, 1937. "El veinte de diciembre," *Futuro*, 22 (Dec.).

———, 1938. "El cooperativismo y los trabajadores," *Futuro*, 23 (Jan.).

López Aparicio, Alonso, 1958. *El movimiento obrero en México: Antecedentes, desarrollo y tendencias.* Mexico: Editorial Jus (2nd edition).

López Zamora, Emilio, 1946. "Problema agrario de la region lagunera-análisis, *Problemas Agrícolas e Industriales de México*, I, 1 (July-Sept.) 123-154.

MacEwan, Arthur, 1972. "Capitalist Expansion, Ideology and Intervention," *Review of Radical Political Economics*, IV (Spring), 36-58.

El Machete 1937-1938. Organo Central del Partido Comunista de México.

Malloy, James, 1977. "Authoritarianism and Corporatism in Latin America: The Modal Pattern," in *Authoritarianism and Corporatism in Latin America*, ed. James M. Malloy. Pittsburgh: Pittsburgh University Press.

Mandel, Ernest, 1970. *Marxist Economic Theory*, Vols. I and II. New York: Monthly Review Press.

Manero, Antonio, 1957. La revolución bancaria en México. *Una contribución a la historia de las instituciones de crédito en México.* Mexico: Talleres Gráficas de la Nación.

Márquez Fuentes, Manuel, and Octavio Rodríguez Araujo, 1973. *El Partido Comunista Mexicana.* Mexico: Ediciones "El Caballito."

Marx, Karl, 1963. *The Eighteenth Brumaire of Louis Bonaparte.* New York: International Publishers.

———, 1967. *Capital*, Vol. III. New York: International Publishers.

Marx, Karl, and Friedrich Engels, 1955. *The Communist Manifesto.* New York: Appleton-Century-Crofts.

———, 1970. *The German Ideology* (C. J. Arthur, ed.). New York: International Publishers.

Maturana Medina, Sergio and Iván Restrepo Fernández, 1970. *El azúcar: Problema de México. Un estudio regional en Michoacán.* Mexico: Centro de Investigaciones Agrarias.

Mayer, Robert, 1973. "The Origins of the American Banking Empire in Latin America: Frank A. Vanderlip and the National City Bank," *Journal of Inter-American Studies*, 15, 1 (February), 60-76.

McDaniel, Tim, 1976-1977. "Class Dependency in Latin America," *Berkeley Journal of Sociology*, XXI, 51-88.

Medin, Tzvi, 1971. "Cárdenas. Del maximato al presidencialismo," *Revista de la Universidad de México*, XXV (May), 13-17.

——, 1972. *Ideología y praxis política de Lázaro Cárdenas*. Mexico: Siglo Veintiuno.

Mendieta y Nuñez, Lucio, 1942. *La administración pública en México*. Mexico: Imprenta Universitaria.

Medina, Luis, 1978. *Del cardenismo al avilacamachismo. Historia de la Revolución Mexicana*, v. 18. Mexico: El Colegio de México.

Mesa Andraca, Manuel, 1955. "La situación henequeneria en Yucatán," *Problemas Agrícolas e Industriales de México*, VII, 2 (April-June), 281-306.

Mexican Labor News, 1936-1940. Mexico: Workers' University of Mexico.

Mexico: Cámara de Diputados, 1966. *Los presidentes de México antes la nación: Informes, manifestas y documentos de 1821-1966* (Vols. IV and V).

Mexico: Departamento de Trabajo.

——, 1936. *Memoria*: Mexico: Talleres Gráficos de la Nación.

——, 1937. *Memoria: 1936-1937*. Mexico: D.A.P.P.

——, 1938. *Memoria: September 1937-August 1938*. Mexico: D.A.P.P.

——, 1939. *Memoria: 1938-1939*. Mexico: D.A.P.P.

——, 1940. *Memoria: September 1939-August 1940*. Mexico: D.A.P.P.

Mexico Industrial (Mexico) 1922-1923. December 1922-August 1923.

Mexico: Secretaría de Comunicaciones y Obras Públicas (SCOP) 1936a. *Memoria de los trabajos ejecutados durante el periodo de 1934-1935*. Mexico: Talleres Gráficas de la Nación.

——, 1936b. *Memoria: Septiembre. 1935-Agosto 1936*. September.

——, 1937. *Memoria: Septiembre 1936-Agosto 1937*.

——, 1941. *Memoria: Septiembre 1940-Agosto 1941*.

Mexico: Secretaría de la Economía Nacional (SEN). 1937. *Memoria de la Secretaría de la Economía Nacional de Septiembre de 1936 a agosto de 1937*. Mexico: D.A.P.P.

——, 1938. *Memoria de la Secretaría de la Economía Nacional, 1937-1938*. Mexico: D.A.P.P.

——, 1939. *Memoria de la Secretaría de la Economía Nacional, Septiembre 1938 a agosto 1939*. Mexico: D.A.P.P.

Mexico: Secretaría de Hacienda y Crédito Público (SHCP), 1951. *La Hacienda pública de México a través de los informes presidenciales a partir de la independencia hasta 1950*. Mexico: SHCP, Publicaciones Históricos.

——, 1957. *Legislación bancaria*, III. Mexico: SHCP, Dirección General de Crédito.

——, 1963. *Memoria de la Secretaría de Hacienda y Crédito Público*, 10 Dec. 1934-30 Nov. 1940 (6 Vols.). Mexico.

——, 1964. *Discursos* pronunciados por los cc. Secretarios de Hacienda y Crédito en las Convenciones Bancarias celebrados del Año 1934 a

1964. Mexico: Dirección General de Prensa, Memoria, Biblioteca y Publicaciones.

Mexico: Secretaría de Industria y Comercio (SIC), n.d. "Las empresas industriales del país—Datos económicos," Mexico: SIC, Subsecretaría de Industrias.

Meyer, Jean, 1973. *Problemas campesinas y revueltas agrarias (1821-1910)*. Mexico: Sep Setentas, 80.

———, 1973-1974. *La Cristiada*. Mexico: Siglo Veintiuno.

———, 1976. *The Cristero Rebellion: The Mexican People between Church and State, 1926-1929*. London: Cambridge University Press.

———, 1977. *Estado y Sociedad con Calles. Historia de la Revolución Mexicana*, v. 11. Mexico: Colegio de México.

Meyer, Lorenzo, 1968. *México y los Estados Unidos en el conflicto petrolero (1917-1942)*. Mexico: El Colegio de México.

———, 1971. "Los límites de la política cardenista: La presión externa," *Revista de la Universidad de México*, XXV, 9 (May).

———, 1972a. "Cambio político y dependencia. México en el siglo XX," *Foro Internacional*, 50, XIII, 2 (Oct.-Dec.).

———, 1972b. *México y los Estados Unidos en el conflicto petrolero*. Mexico: El Colegio de México (2nd edition).

———, 1973. *Los grupos de presión extranjeros en el México revolucionario, 1910-1940*. Mexico: Secretaría de Relaciones Exteriores, Colección del Archivo Histórico Diplomático Mexicano.

———, 1974a. "El Estado mexicano contemporaneo," *Historia Mexicana*, XXIII, 4, 722-752.

———, 1974b. "La resistencia al capital privado extranjero: El caso del petroleo, 1938-1950," in Bernardo Sepúlveda et al., *Las Empresas transnacionales en México*. Mexico: El Colegio de México.

———, 1977. "Historical Roots of the Authoritarian State in Mexico," in *Authoritarianism in Mexico*, ed. Reyna and Weinert. Philadelphia: Institute for the Study of Human Issues.

———, 1978a. *El conflicto social y los gobiernos del maximato. Historia de la revolución mexicana*. v. 13. Mexico: El Colegio de México.

———, 1978b. *Los inicios de la institucionalización, La política del maximato. Historia de la revolución mexicana*. v. 12. Mexico: El Colegio de México.

Michaels, Albert L., 1970. "The Crisis of Cardenismo," *Journal of Latin American Studies*, II (May), 51-79.

———, 1971. "The Mexican Election of 1940," Council on International Studies, State University of New York at Buffalo (September).

Middlebrook, Kevin, 1977. "State Structure and Labor Participation in Mexico." Paper presented at 7th National Meeting of the Latin American Studies Association, Houston, Nov. 2-5.

Miliband, Ralph, 1969. *The State in Capitalist Society*. New York: Basic Books.

———, 1977. *Marxism and Politics*. Oxford: Oxford University Press.

Mondragón, Magdalena, 1966. *Cuando la revolución se cortó las alas*. Mexico: B. Costa-Amic, ed.

Monterrey, una ciudad en marcha, 1956-1957. Monterrey, Mexico: Cia. General de Aceptaciones.

Montes de Oca, Luis, 1937a. Letter to President Cárdenas (17 July). Archivo LMO, Correspondencia Presidente de la República.

———, 1937b. Telegram to President Cárdenas (7 August). Archivo LMO: Correspondencia Presidente de la República.

———, 1937c. Telegram to Rafael C. Torres (11 Aug.). Archivo LMO: Correspondencia Secretaría de Hacienda.

———, 1938. Note to Eduardo Suárez (1 July). Archivo LMO: Correspondencia Secretaría de Hacienda.

Montes de Oca, Rosa Elena, 1977. "The State and the Peasants" in *Authoritarianism in Mexico*, ed. José Luis Reyna and Richard S. Weinert. Philadelphia: Institute for the Study of Human Issues.

Moore, Barrington, Jr., 1966. *Social Origins of Dictatorship and Democracy: Lord and Peasant in the Making of the Modern World*. Boston: Beacon Press.

Moore, O. Ernesto, 1963. *Evolución de las instituciones financieras en México*. Mexico: Centro de Estudios Monetarios Latinoamericanos.

Moore, Stanley W., 1957. *The Critique of Capitalist Democracy: An Introduction to the Theory of the State in Marx, Engels and Lenin*. New York: Paine Whitman.

Mosk, Sanford A., 1954. *Industrial Revolution in Mexico*. Berkeley: University of California Press.

Muñoz, Hilda, 1976. *Lázaro Cárdenas: Síntesis ideológica de su campaña presidencial*. Mexico: Fondo de Cultura Económica.

Murray, Robin, 1971. "The Internationalization of Capital and the Nation State," *New Left Review*, 67 (May-June), 84-100.

Myers, Willys A., 1938. Letter to Secretary of State (11 June). NAW 813.52/2820.

El Nacional, 1932-1960. (Mexico, D.F.).

Nacional Financiera (Nafinsa) 1949. *Quince años de vida: 1934-1949*. Mexico: Nacional Financiera, S.A.

———, 1977. *Statistics on the Mexican Economy*. Mexico, D.F.

Nacional Financiera, S.A., and Comisión Económica para la América Latina (Nafinsa/CEPAL), 1971. *La política industrial en el desarrollo económico de México*. Mexico: Nafinsa.

Naranjo, Francisco, 1948. "Los millonarios de la revolución," *Diario de Yucatán* (July-Sept.).

National Archives and Records Service, Washington (NAW). Record Group 59, General Records of the Department of State. Diplomatic Branch, Civil Archives Division.

National Archives and Records Service, Washington (NAW). Record Group 84, Records of the Foreign Service Posts of the Department of State. Diplomatic Branch, Civil Archives Division.

——. Record Group 151, Records of the Bureau of Foreign and Domestic Commerce. Industrial and Social Branch, Civil Archives Division.

National Chamber Foundation and Council of the Americas, n.d. *Impact of Foreign Investment in Mexico.*

Newfarmer, Richard S., and Willard F. Mueller, 1975. *Multinational Corporations in Brazil and Mexico: Structural Sources of Economic and Noneconomic Power.* Report to the Sub-committee on Multinational Corporations of the Committee on Foreign Relations, U.S. Senate. Washington: U.S. Government Printing Office.

Niemeyer, E. V., Jr., 1974. *Revolution at Querétaro: The Mexican Constitutional Convention of 1916-1917.* Austin: University of Texas Press.

North, Liisa and David Raby, 1977. "The Dynamics of Revolution and Counter-revolution: Mexico under Cárdenas, 1934-1940," *LARU Studies,* II, 1 (October), Toronto, Ontario, Canada.

Norweb, 1935. Letter to Secretary of State (14 June). NAW 812.00/30220.

Novoa, Carlos, 1937a. "Impuesto sobre exportación de capitales," in *Boletín Financiera y Mineral de México,* IV Convención Bancaria, 22-24 May, Mexico, D.F.

——, 1937b. Letter to Luis Montes de Oca (20 Nov.). Archivo LMO: Correspondencia.

O'Brien, Philip, 1973. "Dependency: The New Nationalism?" *Latin American Review of Books,* 1 (Spring).

O'Connor, James, 1973. *Fiscal Crisis of the State.* New York: St. Martin's Press.

O'Donnell, Guillermo, 1973. *Modernization and Bureaucratic-Authoritarianism: Studies in South American Politics.* Berkeley: Institute of International Studies, University of California.

——, 1975. "Reflexiones sobre las tendencias generales de cambio en el Estado burocrático-autoritario." Documento CEDES/G.E. CLASCO/ no. 1. Buenos Aires (agosto).

——, 1977. "Corporatism and the Question of the State," in *Authoritarianism and Corporatism in Latin America,* ed. James M. Malloy, Pittsburgh: Pittsburgh University Press.

——, 1979. "Tensions in the Bureaucratic Authoritarian State and the Question of Democracy," in *The New Authoritarianism in Latin America,* ed. David Collier. Princeton: Princeton University Press.

Offe, Claus, 1974. "The Theory of the Capitalist State and the Problem of Policy Formation." Mimeo (May).

Organization of American States, 1972. Constitution of Mexico, 1917 (as amended). Washington: General Secretariat, OAS.

Ortoll, Servando, 1981. "Los Orígenes Sociales del Sinarquismo en Jalisco, 1929-1939." Paper presented at the VI Conference of Mexican and United States Historians, Chicago, Illinois (September 8-12).

Oszlak, Oscar, and Guillermo O'Donnell, 1976. "Estado y políticas estatales en América Latina: Hacia una estrategía de investigación." Documento CEDES/G.E. CLASCO/ No. 4. Buenos Aires (Mar.).

PNR, 1934. *Plan sexenal del PNR.* Mexico: Partido Nacional Revolucionario.

PRM, 1940. *Cárdenas Habla.* Mexico: Partido Revolucionario Mexicano (1 Sept.).

Palacios Macedo, Miguel, 1938. Letter to Gómez Morín (13 August.). Archivo MGM: La Consolidada.

Palma, Gabriel, 1978. "Dependency: A Formal Theory of Underdevelopment or a Methodology for the Analysis of Concrete Situations of Underdevelopment?" *World Development*, VI, 7-8 (July-August).

Pani, Alberto J., 1926. *La política hacendaria y la revolución.* Mexico: Editorial Cultura.

Paoli, Francisco J., and Enrique Montalva, 1977. *El socialismo olvidado de Yucatán.* Mexico: Siglo Veintiuno.

Paré, Luisa, 1977. *El proletariado agrícola en México: campesinos sin tierra o proletarios agrícolas?* Mexico: Siglo XXI.

Pellicer, Olga, 1977. "La crisis mexicana: hacia una nueva dependencia," *Cuadernos Politicos* 14 (Oct.-Dec.), 45-55.

Peralta Zamora, Gloria, 1965. "La hacienda pública," in *Historia moderna de México: El porfiriato* (Vol. 8, *La vida económica*), ed. Daniel Cosio Villegas. Mexico: Editorial Hermes.

Petras, James, 1978. *Critical Perspectives on Imperialism and Social Class in the Third World.* New York: Monthly Review Press.

Polit, Gustavo, 1957. "El crecimiento de la banca de depósito en México," *Comercio Exterior*, VII, 5-8 (May-August).

Pompermayer, Malori J., and William C. Smith, Jr., 1973. "The State in Dependent Societies: Preliminary Notes," in *Structures of Dependency*, ed. Frank Bonilla and Robert Girling, Stanford: Stanford University Press.

El Popular, 1938. (Mexico, D.F.) Año 1, 1938.

Portes Gil, Emilio, 1954. *Quince años de política mexicana* (3rd edition). Mexico: Ediciones Batas.

Poulantzas, Nicos, 1969. *Poder político y clases sociales en el Estado capitalista.* Mexico: Siglo Veintiuno.

———, 1976. "The Capitalist State: A Reply to Miliband and Laclau," *New Left Review*, 95 (January-February).

Puga Espinosa, Maria Cristina, 1975. "Las industriales y la revolución mexicana (1917-1924)." Tesis profesional, Facultad de Ciencias Políticas y Sociales, Universidad Nacional Autónoma de México, Mexico, D.F.

Purcell, John F. H., and Susan Kaufman Purcell, 1977. "Mexican Business and Public Policy," in *Authoritarianism and Corporatism in Latin America*, ed. James M. Malloy. Pittsburgh: University of Pittsburgh Press.

Purcell, Susan Kaufman, 1977. "The Future of the Mexican System," in *Authoritarianism in Mexico*, ed. José Luis Reyna and Richard S. Weinert. Philadelphia: Institute for the Study of Human Issues.

Purcell, Susan Kaufman, and John Purcell, 1976. "El Estado y la empresa privada," *Nueva Política*, I, 2 (April-June).

Raby, David L., 1972. "La contribución de cardenismo al desarrollo de México en la época actual," *Aportes*, 26 (Oct.), 32-65.

———, 1974. *Educación y revolución social en México: 1921-1940*. Mexico: Sep Setentas, 141.

Redo, Diego, 1931. Memo (26 Oct.). Archivo MGM: Cia. Almacenadora de Azúcar, S.A.

Registro Público de la Propiedad y del Comercio. Mexico, D.F. (RPPC).

Rello, Fernando, and Rosa Elena Montes de Oca, 1974. "Acumulación de capital en el campo mexicano," *Cuadernos Políticos* (Mexico), 2 (October-December), 61-76.

Restrepo, Iván, and Salomón Eckstein, 1975. *La agricultura colectiva de La Laguna*. Mexico: Siglo Veintiuno.

Revista de Economía y Estadística, 1935. Mexico, D.F. (Organ of the Secretaría de la Economía Nacional).

Reyes Osorio, Sergio et al., 1974. *Estructura agraria y desarrollo en México: estudio sobre las relaciones entre la tenencia y uso de la tierra y el desarrollo agrícola de México*. Mexico: Fondo de Cultura Económica.

Reyna, José Luis, 1974. "Control político, estabilidad y desarrollo en México," Mexico: Colegio de México (Cuadernos de CES 3).

———, 1977. "Redefining the Authoritarian Regime, in *Authoritarianism in Mexico*, ed. José Luis Reyna and Richard S. Weinert. Philadelphia: Institute for the Study of Human Issues.

Reynolds, Clark W., 1970. *The Mexican Economy: Twentieth Century Structure and Growth*. New Haven: Yale University Press.

———, 1978. "Why Mexico's Stabilizing Development Was Actually Destabilizing (With Some Implications for the Future)," *World Development*, VI, 7-8 (July-August).

Rippy, J. Fred, 1944. *Latin America and the Industrial Age*. New York: G.P. Putnam's Sons.

Rippy, Merrill, 1972. *Oil and the Mexican Revolution*. Luden, Netherlands: E.J. Brill.

Rivera Marín, Guadalupe, 1961. "El movimiento obrero," in *México: Cincuenta años de revolución*. Mexico, D.F.: Fondo de Cultura Económica.

Robles, Gonzalo, 1960. "El desarrollo industrial," in *Mexico: Cincuenta años de revolución*. Mexico: Fondo de Cultura Económica.

Rodríguez, Antonio, 1935. Letter to Manuel Gómez Morín (10 May): enclosures. Archivo MGM: A. Rodríguez.

———, 1936. Letter and enclosed memo to Gómez Morín (22 April). Archivo MGM: Antonio Rodríguez.

———, 1940. Letter to Gómez Morín (22 June). Archivo MGM: A. Rodríguez.

Rodríguez, Antonio, 1958. *El rescate del petroleo: Epopeya de un pueblo*. Mexico: Ediciones de la Revista *Siempre*.

Ronfeldt, David, 1973. *Atencingo: The Politics of Agrarian Struggle in a Mexican Ejido*. Stanford: Stanford University Press.

Rosenzweig, Fernando, 1965a. "El Comercio Exterior," in *Historia moderna de México: El porfiriato* (Vol. 7, *La vida económica*), ed. Daniel Cosio Villegas. Mexico: Editorial Hermes.

———, 1965b. "La industria," in *Historia moderna de México: El porfiriato* (Vol. 7, *La vida económica*), ed. Daniel Cosio Villegas, Mexico: Editorial Hermes.

———, 1965c. "Moneda y bancos," in *Historia moderna de México: El porfiriato* (Vol. 8, *La vida económica*), ed. Daniel Cosio Villegas. Mexico: Editorial Hermes.

Ruíz, Ramón Eduardo, 1976. "Madero's Administration and Mexican Labor," in *Contemporary Mexico*. Papers of the IV International Congress of Mexican History, ed. James W. Wilkie et al. Berkeley: University of California Press, 187-203.

Rumbo, 1940-1941. (Mexico, D.F.) (Organo de la sección 5 de STPRM), Jan. 1940-Jan. 1941.

Sada, Roberto G., 1935. Letter to Manuel Gómez Morín (26 Sept.). Archivo MGM: Cerv. Cuauhtémoc General 1937.

Sáenz, Aarón, 1932. Letter to Luis Montes de Oca (16 May). Archivo Luis Montes de Oca: Correspondencia 1930-34.

Salamini, Heather Fowler, 1976. "Adalberto Tejeda and the Veracruz Peasant Movement," in *Contemporary Mexico*, ed. James W. Wilkie et al. Berkeley: University of California Press.

Salazar, Rosendo, 1956a. *La CTM: Su historia-Su significado*. Mexico: Ediciones T. C. Modelo, S.C.L.

———, 1956b. *Historia de las luchas proletarias en México: 1923-1946*. Mexico: Ed. Avante.

Salazar G., Roberto, 1971. *El empresario industrial: Patrones tradicionales de constitución y sucesión empresarial* (preliminary version). Mexico: El Colegio de México, Centro de Estudios Económicos y Demográficos (May).

Sarro, Enrique, 1938a. Memorándum confidencial a Dr. Francisco Castillo Najero (15 March). Archivo LMO: Correspondencia.

Sarro, Enrique, 1938b. Letter to Luis Montes de Oca (16 March). Archivo LMO: Correspondencia.

———, 1938c. Letter to Luis Montes de Oca (22 March). Archivo Luis Montes de Oca: Correspondencia.

———, 1938d. Letter to Luis Montes de Oca (25 March). Archivo Luis Montes de Oca: Correspondencia.

———, 1938e. Letter to Luis Montes de Oca (12 April). Archivo Luis Montes de Oca: Correspondencia.

Schaffer, Carlos, 1974-1975. "El capitalismo monopolista de Estado y los sindicatos en México," *Problemas del Desarrollo*, V, 20 (Nov.-Jan.), 63-90.

Schmitter, Philippe, 1972. "Paths to Political Development in Latin America," in *Changing Latin America: New Interpretations of its Politics and Society*, ed. Douglas A. Chalmers. New York: The Academy of Political Science, Columbia University.

Scott, Robert E., 1959. *Mexican Government in Transition*. Urbana: University of Illinois Press.

Seis años de gobierno al servicio de México: 1934-1940. 1940. Mexico, D.F.: Talleres Linotipográficos La Nacional Impresera (Nov.).

Semo, Enrique, 1975. "Las revoluciones en la historia de México," *Historia y Sociedad* (2a época), 8, 49-61.

Senior, Clarence, 1940. "Democracy Comes to a Cotton Kingdom: The Story of Mexico's La Laguna." Mexico: Centro de Estudios Pedagogicos e Hispanoamericanos.

———, 1958. *Land Reform and Democracy*. Gainesville: University of Florida Press.

Sepúlveda, Bernardo, and Antonio Chumacero, 1973. *La inversión extranjera en México*. Mexico: Fondo de Cultura Económica.

Sepúlveda, Bernardo, Olga Pellicer de Brody, and Lorenzo Meyer, 1974. *Las empresas transnacionales en México*. Mexico: El Colegio de México.

Shafer, Robert Jones, 1973. *Mexican Business Organizations: History and Analysis*. Syracuse, N.Y.: Syracuse University Press.

Shulgovski, Anatol, 1968. *México en la encrucijada de su historia*. Mexico: Fondo de Cultura Popular.

———, 1971. "Los ejidos y el desarrollo del capitalismo en el campo mexicano," *Revista de México Agraria*, IV, 3 (May-June), 49-72.

Silva Herzog, Jesús, 1964. *El agrarismo mexicano y la reforma agraria: Exposición y crítica*. Mexico: Fondo de Cultura Económica, 2nd edition.

———, 1967. *El pensamiento económico, social y político de México, 1810-1964*. Mexico: Inst. Mexicano de Investigaciones Económicas.

———, 1941. *Petroleo mexicano: Historia de un problema*. Mexico: Fondo de Cultura Económica.

———, 1975. Lázaro Cárdenas: Su pensamiento económico, social y político. Mexico: Editorial Nuestro Tiempo.

Simpson, Eyler N., 1937. *The Ejido: Mexico's Way Out*. Chapel Hill: University of North Carolina Press.

Skocpol, Theda, 1979. *States and Social Revolutions: A Comparative Analysis of France, Russia and China*. Cambridge: Cambridge University Press.

Skocpol, Theda, and Ellen Kay Trimberger, 1978. "Revolutions and the World-Historical Development of Capitalism," in *Social Change in the Capitalist World Economy*, ed. Barbara Hockey Kaplan. Beverly Hills: Sage Publications, Inc.

Smith, Peter H., 1977. "Does Mexico Have a Power Elite?" in *Authoritarianism in Mexico*, eds. José Luis Reyna and Richard S. Weinert. Philadelphia: Institute for the Study of Human Issues.

———, 1979. *Labyrinths of Power: Political Recruitment in Twentieth Century Mexico*. Princeton: Princeton University Press.

Smith, Robert Freeman, 1963. "The Formation and the Development of the International Bankers Committee in Mexico," *Journal of Economic History*, XXIII, 4 (December), 574-586.

———, 1973. *The United States and Revolutionary Nationalism in Mexico*. Chicago: University of Chicago Press.

Snyder, Carl, 1937a. Letter to Luis Montes de Oca. Archivo LMO: Correspondencia.

———, 1937b. Letter to Luis Montes de Oca (12 November). Archivo LMO: Correspondencia.

Sociedad Financiera Mexicana (Sofimex), 1937. Escritura (12 May). Archivo MGM: Sofimex, 1941-1947.

———, 1947. Relaciones de Inversiones al 21 de marzo de 1947. Archivo MGM: Sofimex, 1941-1947.

———, 1954. Accionistas (21 March). Archivo MGM: Sofimex, 1954-1956.

———, 1959. Aumento de Capital (Jan.) Archivo MGM: Sofimex, 1957-1960.

Sociedad Mexicana de Crédito Industrial, S.A., 1944. *Tres años de funcionamiento, 26 marzo de 1941-26 de marzo de 1944*. Mexico: SOMEX.

Solis, Leopoldo, 1940. *La realidad económica mexicana: Retrovisión y perspectivas*. Mexico: Siglo Veintiuno.

Soto Angli, Francisco, n.d. *El papel de los grupos financieros en el desarrollo de capitalismo en México*. Mimeo. Mexico: Escuela de Economía, Universidad Nacional Autónoma de México.

Spalding, Hobart, 1977. *Organized Labor in Latin America*. New York: New York University Press.

Stavenhagen, Rodolfo, 1975. "Collective Agriculture and Capitalism in Mexico: A Way Out or a Dead End?" *Latin American Perspectives*, II, 2 (Summer), 146-163.

———, 1976. "Reflexiones sobre el proceso político," *Nueva Política*, 1, 2 (April-June), 15-22.

Stein, Stanley J., and Barbara H. Stein, 1970. *The Colonial Heritage of Latin America: Essays on Economic Dependence in Perspective.* New York: Oxford University Press.

Stepan, Alfred, 1978. *The State and Society: Peru in Comparative Perspective.* Princeton: Princeton University Press.

Stuart, Graham H., 1938. *Latin America and the United States* (3rd ed.). New York: D. Appleton-Century Company.

Suárez, Eduardo, 1976. Interview of March 12, 1976.

———, 1977. *Comentarios y Recuerdos* (1926-1946). Mexico: Editorial Porrua.

Sunkel, Osvaldo, 1972. "Big Business and 'Dependencia'—A Latin American View," *Foreign Affairs* (April).

Szentis, Tamás, 1971. *The Political Economy of Underdevelopment.* Budapest: Akademiai Kiado.

Szymanski, Albert, 1978. *The Capitalist State and the Politics of Class.* Cambridge, Mass.: Winthrop Publishers.

Talavera Aldana, Luis Fernando, 1976. "Organizaciones sindicales obreras de la rama textil: 1935-1970," *Revista Mexicana de Ciencias Políticas y Sociales, XXI* (Nueva Epoca) (Jan.-March).

Tamagna, Frank, 1965. *Central Banking in Latin America.* Mexico: CEMLA.

Tannenbaum, Frank, 1950. *Mexico: The Struggle for Peace and Bread.* New York: Alfred A. Knopf.

Tardanico, Richard, 1978. "A Structural Perspective on State Power in the Capitalist World System." Paper presented at the meetings of the American Sociological Association, San Francisco (September).

———, 1979. "Revolutionary Nationalism and State Building in Mexico, 1917-1924." Paper presented at Annual Meeting of American Sociological Association, Boston (September).

Theisen, Gerald, 1972. "La mexicanización de la industria en la época de Porfirio Díaz," *Foro Internacional* (Mexico), XII, 4 (April-June), 497-506.

Tilly, Charles, ed., 1975. *The Formation of National States in Western Europe.* Princeton: Princeton University Press.

Torres, Rafael, 1937. Letter to Luis Montes de Oca (14 Aug.). Archivo LMO: Correspondencia.

Torres Mejía, David, 1975. "La política bancaria de la revolución." Tesis, Facultad de Ciencias Políticas y Sociales, Universidad Nacional Autónoma de México, Mexico.

Treviño Sillar, José G., 1944. *El Mante: Resultados económicos y sociales de las dotaciones agrarias.* Facultad de Derecho y Ciencias Sociales, Universidad Nacional Autónoma de México, Mexico.

Trimberger, Ellen Kay, 1977. "State Power and Modes of Production: Implications of the Japanese Transition to Capitalism," *The Insurgent Sociologist,* VII, 2 (Spring).

————, 1978. *Revolution from Above: Military Bureaucrats and Development in Japan, Turkey, Egypt and Peru.* New Brunswick, N.J.: Transaction Books.

El Trimestre Económica, 1934-1940. Mexico, D.F.

"Una nueva sociedad de crédito se inaugura en esta capital" 1934. *Excelsior* (2 Aug.).

U.S. Department of State, 1952-1969. *Papers Relating to Foreign Relations of the United States.* Volumes on the American Republics.

El Universal (Mexico, D.F.) 1932-1960. Selecciones.

Vaughan, Mary Kay, 1981. "Ideological Change in Mexican Educational Policy, Programs, and Texts, 1920-1940." Paper presented at the VI Conference of Mexican and United States Historians, Chicago, Illinois (September 8-12).

Velasco, Miguel, n.d. "El partido comunista durante el periodo de Cárdenas." Mexico: Facultad de Ciencias Políticas y Sociales, Centro de Estudios Latinoamericanos, Universidad Nacional Autónoma de México. (Serie: Documentos 2.)

Vellinga, Menno, 1975. "Economic Development and the Dynamics of Class: Industrialization, Power and Control in Monterrey, Mexico." Center for Comparative Sociology, University of Utrecht.

————, 1979. "Working Class, Bourgeoisie and State in Mexico," in *Industrialization and the State in Latin America,* ed. Jean Carriere. Amsterdam: Center for Latin American Research and Documentation.

Vernon, Raymond, 1963. *The Dilemma of Mexico's Development: The Roles of the Private and Public Sectors.* Cambridge: Harvard University Press.

————, 1964. *Public Policy and Private Enterprise in Mexico.* Cambridge: Harvard University Press.

Villa A., Manuel, 1972. "Las bases del Estado mexicano y su problemática actual," *Perfil de México en 1980.* Mexico: Siglo Veintiuno, Vol. III.

Villaseñor, Eduardo, 1974. *Memorias-Testimonio.* Mexico: Fondo de Cultura Económica.

Vizcaya Canales, Isidro, 1969. *Los orígenes de la industrialización de Monterrey (1867-1920).* Monterrey, Mexico: Publicaciones del Instituto Technológico y de Estudios Superiores de Monterrey. (Serie: Historia.)

Wallerstein, Immanuel, 1974a. *The Modern World-System. Capitalist Agriculture and the Origins of the European World-Economy in the Sixteenth Century.* New York: Academic Press.

————, 1974b. "The Rise and Future Demise of the Capitalist World System: Concepts for Comparative Analysis," *Comparative Studies in Society and History,* XVI (September), 187-415.

————, 1976. "Peripheral Countries and the Contemporary World Crisis," *Theory and Society,* 3, 4 (Winter).

Warren, Bill, 1973. "Imperialism and Capitalist Industrialization," *New Left Review,* 81 (September-October).

Wasserman, Mark, 1980. "The Social Origins of the 1910 Revolution in Chihuahua," *Latin American Research Review*, XV, 1.

Weaver, Frederick Stirton, 1976. "Capitalist Development, Empire, and Latin American Underdevelopment: An Interpretive Essay on Historical Change," *Latin American Perspectives*, III, 4 (Fall).

Weber, Max, 1958. "Politics as a Vocation," in *From Max Weber*, eds. Hans Gerth and C. Wright Mills. New York: Oxford University Press.

————, 1968. *Economy and Society*. 3 vols. New York: Bedminster Press, Inc.

Weinert, Richard S., 1977. "The State and Foreign Capital," in *Authoritarianism in Mexico*, ed. José Luis Reyna and Richard S. Weinert. Philadelphia: Institute for the Study of Human Issues.

Weinstein, James, 1968. *The Corporate Ideal in the Liberal State: 1910-1918*. Boston: Beacon Press.

Welles, Sumner, 1938. Memo re conversation with Ambassador Daniels (22 January). U.S. Department of State, *Papers Relating to the Foreign Relations of the United States*, Volumes on the American Republics, 1934–1944.

Weyl, Nathaniel, and Sylvia Weyl, 1939. *The Reconquest of Mexico: The Years of Lázaro Cárdenas*. London: Oxford University Press.

Whetten, Nathan L., 1948. *Rural Mexico*. Chicago: University of Chicago Press.

Whiting, Van R., Jr., 1977. "The Collective Ejido and the State in Mexico," Paper presented at Seventh National Meeting of the Latin American Studies Association, Houston, Texas, November 2-5.

Wilkie, James, 1970. *The Mexican Revolution: Federal Expenditure and Social Change since 1910*. Revised edition. Berkeley: University of California Press.

Wilkie, James W., and Albert L. Michaels, eds. 1969. *Revolution in Mexico: Years of Upheaval, 1910-1940*. New York: Alfred A. Knopf, Borzoi Books on Latin America.

Wilkie, James W., and Edna Monzón de Wilkie, 1969. *México visto en el siglo XX: Entrevistas de Historia Oral*. Mexico: Instituto Mexicano de Investigaciones Económicas.

Wilson, G.R., 1938. Letter of 5 March, NAW 812.52/2613.

Wionczek, Miguel S., 1964. "Electric Power: The Uneasy Partnership," in *Public Power and Private Enterprise in Mexico*, cd. Raymond Vernon. Cambridge: Harvard University Press.

Wolf, Eric R., 1959. *Sons of the Shaking Earth*. Chicago: The University of Chicago Press.

————, 1973. *Peasant Wars of the Twentieth Century*. New York: Torchbooks (Harper & Row, Publishers).

Wolfe, Alan, 1974. "New Directions in the Marxist Theory of Politics," *Politics and Society*, IV, 2 (Winter).

Womack, John, Jr., 1968. *Zapata and the Mexican Revolution*. New York: Vintage Books.

Wood, Bryce, 1961. *The Making of the Good Neighbor Policy*. New York: Columbia University Press.

Woodrow, Arthur B., 1936. Letter to Gómez Morín (2 June). Archivo MGM: Cerv. Cuauhtémoc General.

———, 1942. Letter to H. Rogers (17 Feb.). Archivo MGM: Sr. Roberto Hutchinson.

World Trade Directory Reports. U.S. Embassy, Mexico City.

Wright, Erik Olin, 1978. *Class, Crisis and the State*. London: New Left Books.

Wright, Harry K., 1971. *Foreign Enterprise in Mexico: Laws and Politics*. Chapel Hill: University of North Carolina Press.

Wyeth, George, 1925. Annual Report, Office of the Commercial Attache, Mexico City, for the year ending 30 June 1925. (2 July). NAW, RG 151. 128.2 Annual Reports, Mexico.

———, 1945. *Industry in Latin America*. New York: Columbia University Press.

Zeitlin, Maurice, ed. 1980. *Classes, Class Conflict, and the State*. Cambridge, Mass.: Winthrop Publishers.

Zeitlin, Maurice, W. Laurence Neuman, and Richard Earl Ratcliff, 1976. "Class Segments: Agrarian Property and Political Leadership in the Capitalist Class of Chile," *American Sociological Review*, 41, 6 (December), 1006-1029.

Index

382 Index

Library of Congress Cataloging in Publication Data

Hamilton, Nora, 1935–
Mexico : the limits of state autonomy.

Bibliography: p.
Includes index.
1. Mexico—Economic policy. 2. Mexico—Social policy.
3. Mexico—Foreign economic relations. 4. Investments, Foreign—
Mexico. 5. Elite (Social sciences)—Mexico. I. Title.
HC135.H27   338.972   82-47596
ISBN 0-691-07641-3   AACR2
ISBN 0-691-02211-9 (pbk.)